P9-DNF-813

# New Mexico

3-20-14

# New Mexico

Sharon Niederman

*with photographs by the author*

The Countryman Press ✳ Woodstock, Vermont

Also by Sharon Niederman

*Santa Fe & Taos, A Great Destination*

*Return to Abo: A Novel of the Southwest*

*A Quilt of Words: Women's Diaries, Letters & Original Accounts of Life in the Southwest 1860–1960*

*New Mexico's Tasty Traditions: Recollections, Recipes and Photos*

*Signs & Shrines: Spiritual Journeys Across New Mexico*

We welcome your comments and suggestions. Please contact Explorer's Guide Editor, The Countryman Press, P.O. Box 748, Woodstock, Vermont 05091, or e-mail countrymanpress@wwnorton.com.

Explorer's Guide New Mexico
ISBN 978-1-58157-169-1

Maps by Mapping Specialists, © 2013 The Countryman Press
Book design by Bodenweber Design
Text composition by PerfecType, Nashville, TN
Interior photographs by the author unless otherwise indicated

Published by The Countryman Press, P.O. Box 748, Woodstock, Vermont 05091

Distributed by W. W. Norton & Company, Inc., 500 Fifth Avenue, New York, NY 10110

Printed in the United States of America

10 9 8 7 6 5 4 3 2 1

## The Truth We Prefer

The young woman who opened a gift shop
Selling glass bead earrings, Mexican imports, replica flour sack aprons
Offering Dia de los Muertos workshops
Tells me this place was a stagecoach stop
No ghosts she knows of
But her aunt remembers stories
That doorway is narrow, watch your head
The real estate office across the street was a coffin factory, you know
The church was complete, except for the bell
So the women gave their silver
Scant history, legend perhaps, the truth we prefer
But it is true, isn't it
A hundred years ago, longer
The farmers from Alameda
And those from Los Griegos
Processed after Mass on San Lorenzo Day
And wherever they met held a fiesta, right here in this street?

Sharon Niederman

# EXPLORE WITH US!

*New Mexico: An Explorer's Guide* is broken down into sections representing different areas of the state. Because of the state's size, most of these geographic sections are subdivided into "mini-chapters" for easy navigation. Each chapter opens with a general introduction touching on the history and highlights of the area, and then continues with information on destinations, accommodations, and restaurants that guide you to the best of New Mexico.

I focus on independent venues for two reasons. Most readers are familiar with franchise food and lodgings and they are easy to find. More important, independent businesses, such as mom-and-pop cafés and vintage motels, are often less discovered and more likely to deliver an authentic New Mexican experience. I have done my best to share my knowledge of the state based on more than two decades of traveling and writing about its cuisine, history, culture and customs, architecture, and natural beauty. I want to show you my favorite places and give you the honest appraisals I appreciate when navigating a new place.

## GUIDANCE

**Guidance** lists such entities as chambers of commerce, visitors centers, and public land managers that you can refer to for information on the area.

## GETTING THERE

**Getting There** tells you the best routes to take and what means of transportation are available to get you there.

## GETTING AROUND

**Getting Around** lists means of public transportation or shuttles, where they are available.

## MEDICAL EMERGENCY

**Medical Emergency** lists hospitals and/or clinics. Dialing 911 is also an option at all times.

## TO SEE

**To See** lists attractions and points of interest you may want to visit, including museums, historic sites, scenic drives, and more.

## TO DO

**To Do** features key activities available in each area.

## LODGING

**Lodging** will give you ideas of where to find unique and consistently good places to stay, even in more remote areas.

# WHERE TO EAT

**Where to Eat** lists venues that serve dependably good food. There are two categories here: "Dining Out," the better restaurants, and "Eating Out," the more casual options. Please let us know if the food or service is up to the standard we expect—places do change hands and have off nights.

# ENTERTAINMENT

**Entertainment** gives suggestions on theater, music, and relaxing in the evening.

# SELECTIVE SHOPPING

**Selective Shopping** points you in the right direction for shopping, particularly for wares that are characteristic of a place.

# SPECIAL EVENTS

**Special Events** is a month-by-month compendium of the most important annual events and festivals in each community.

# KEY TO SYMBOLS

- ⚭ The wedding rings symbol appears beside facilities that frequently serve as venues for weddings and civil unions.
- ❧ The special-value symbol appears next to lodgings and restaurants that combine high quality and moderate prices.
- ✎ The kids-alert symbol appears next to lodgings, restaurants, activities, and shops of special appeal to youngsters.
- 🐾 The dog-paw symbol appears next to lodgings that accept pets (usually with a reservation and deposit) as of press time.
- ♿ The wheelchair symbol appears next to lodgings, restaurants, and attractions that are partially or fully handicapped accessible.

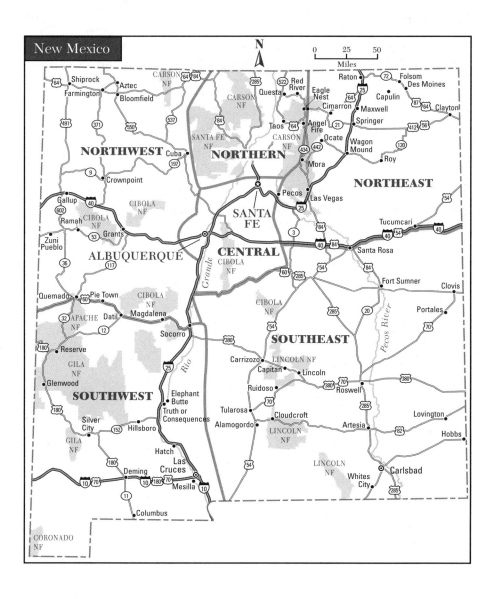

# CONTENTS

# MAPS

# HOW TO USE THIS GUIDE

## WHAT YOU REALLY NEED TO KNOW ABOUT EXPLORING NEW MEXICO

The first time I saw New Mexico was on a road trip with a school buddy many years ago. We drove down I-25 from Boulder, where I was attending graduate school at the University of Colorado. It was nighttime when we crossed Raton Pass into northern New Mexico. I had never seen so much empty space, and the expanse made me nervous.

"Why are there no people or lights out there? What's wrong?" I asked my friend.

A Colorado native, she laughed.

A few years back, I was showing my cousin around northern New Mexico. We drove from Albuquerque to Ojo Caliente Hot Springs.

She was visiting from New Jersey, the most densely populous state. As we turned out of Española onto the road north, she looked at me and asked, "Where are you taking me? This is the middle of nowhere!"

Now it was my turn to laugh. "No," I replied. "The middle of nowhere is the gas station in Vaughn where the wind is always blowing." As an interesting footnote, this cousin subsequently moved west, not to New Mexico, but to Arizona.

To paraphrase Governor Lew Wallace, who presided over the state during the tumultuous Lincoln County War era, "Calculations based on experience elsewhere do not work in New Mexico." Governor Wallace, who hailed from Indiana, made that observation from his vantage point in the Palace of the Governors in Santa Fe, while writing his classic novel, *Ben Hur,* and attempting to bring Billy the Kid to justice.

Governor Wallace may have been moved to make his observation because New Mexico operates in its own sort of time zone. While not exactly the land of mañana, it remains the land of *poco tiempe,* or "pretty soon," just as originally characterized by writer Charles L. Lummis in 1893.

New Mexico remains one place, perhaps the only place, in the United States where its oldest cultures remain alive. They have cohabited and adapted to the impacts of outsiders—including 21st-century urbanization—for centuries, and they continue to practice their languages, religions, and life ways. The 19 Indian pueblos (each a sovereign nation), the Navajo and Apache nations, Hispanic villages, and ranching towns with homesteader legacies persist. Indian ruins and mission churches, the graveyards and wealth of vernacular architecture, are no more than a short trip down the road from virtually anyplace in the state.

Speaking of roads, despite the fact that New Mexico was, and is, crisscrossed by many of the great trails across the continent—the north–south Camino Real de Tierra Adentro from Mexico City to the farthest reach of New Spain, Santa Fe; the east–west Santa Fe Trail trade route from Independence, Missouri, to Santa Fe; Route 66 from Chicago to Los Angeles; and the first paved intercontinental highway, the Ocean to Ocean Highway, US 60 (each bringing goods, ideas, visitors, colonizers, and eventual residents)—somehow the state remains remote. Today, even if traveling on the north–south I-25, or the east–west I-40, or any of the state roads that meander through the quadrants between, traces of the old roads remain, if one's imagination is open to a bit of a reconstruction process. Many of the sites named in this book will assist that process of assembling the fragments of history.

New Mexico's cuisine, festivals, arts, ancient customs, and history remain accessible, constant, and exciting. Consequently, the exotic, what one hungers for in planning a trip to a foreign land, may be experienced here by the explorer without so much as a visa.

While authenticity is available, New Mexico remains in its own time frame, with one foot planted in yesterday and the other in no hurry to get to tomorrow. Roads may not be marked well. You may receive such instructions as, "Turn left at the dip, then right at the big cottonwood," so detailed maps are necessary. Anyone can get lost, so bring water and don't let your gas tank go below half-full. The altitude really can cause discomfort, so be sure to adjust before hiking Wheeler Peak or the Aspen Vista Trail.

WEATHERED ADVERTISEMENTS SPEAK OF BYGONE DAYS ALONG ROUTE 66.

Outsiders may not find the efficiency, public transportation, speed of service, and promptly returned messages they are accustomed to. Hours posted do not always align with hours kept. New Mexico was the 47th state admitted to the Union, in 1912. Awareness that everything takes longer than expected is probably a good idea to adopt to avoid elevated blood pressure. In Santa Fe, the rapid turnover of employees means a likeliness of encountering inexperienced service people. If you are prone to frustration

on such matters, it is probably best to book a lodging that provides experienced concierge service.

Therefore, it is smart to call a planned destination ahead of time. Do not assume that it will be open or that it even still exists. Every effort has been made to ensure the reliability of establishments, but there is no guarantee that it has not gone out of business or moved.

If you love the outdoors, it is all here: hiking, fishing, skiing, river rafting, and birding. The beauty of the night skies; the fun of discovery in ghost towns; the power inherent in the great ruins of Chaco Canyon or the Gila Cliff Dwellings; the back road adventure of a finding a café serving real home cooking; the free-dom of driving an open two-lane without billboards under a huge wide-open sky make this journey memorable and worthwhile.


## GETTING AROUND

If you want to see New Mexico, you are best off driving. Otherwise, you will be at the mercy of slow and sporadic to nonexistent public transportation. For the greatest freedom and safety, bring or rent a car.

Amtrak runs one train each day from Raton to Albuquerque and back again, with stops in Las Vegas and Lamy. The train heads west to Gallup after Albuquer-que. The Rail Runner train runs from Belen all the way to Santa Fe and back.

Bus service in Albuquerque, Santa Fe, and Taos is better all the time.

Shuttles from the Sunport in Albuquerque run to Santa Fe and Taos. See those cities for specific information.

Some smaller towns have cab service, but not all. It's best to call the numbers in the "Guidance" section to check before you go.

# WHEN TO COME

There really is no bad time to come to New Mexico, no real "off-season." It is up to you to plan your visit to coincide with your interests, which may be skiing Taos in winter or attending the Santa Fe Indian Market in summer or the Albuquerque Balloon Fiesta in fall. You can be sure that if you are planning to come during a highly popular event, however, that lodging rates will be higher, and advance reservation times will be longer. The advantage to a perceived "off-season" time, say, October–November in northern New Mexico, or January–February in southern New Mexico, is, of course, less competition for rooms and tables. You will have the place more to yourself. The beauty of the place is always present, and there are always plenty of sights to see and events to attend.

# A FEW INTERESTING FACTS

New Mexico remains the fifth-largest state in land area, boasting a population of 2,085,538. Most of that is centered in the biggest cities: Albuquerque, Rio Rancho, Santa Fe, and Las Cruces.

The State Plant is the yucca; the State Tree is the piñon; the State Gem is the turquoise; the State Tie is the bolo; the State Motto is "Crescit eundo" (It grows as it goes); the state fish is the Rio Grande cutthroat trout; the State Bird is the roadrunner; and the State Animal is the black bear. The State Song, "Oh Fair New Mexico," was written by Sheriff Pat Garrett's daughter, Elizabeth.

The State Cookie is the *biscochito*, an anise-flavored shortbread. The State Pastry ought to be the sopaipilla, an adaptation of Indian fry bread—a crispy, chewy, and light doughnutlike pillow that is eaten with honey and doubles as dessert and bread.

The State Question is: "Red or Green?" The visitor's most frequently asked question might be, "Which is hotter, red or green?," but there is no way to generalize that. It is amazing how different establishments can take the same basic ingredients—chile, garlic, salt—and vary their flavors. When in doubt, ask for a small taste before you order, or ask for your chile on the side.

New Mexican food is quite different from Mexican food, but you may find some culinary terms used interchangeably as names of foods and in conversation. However, in this book, unless specified otherwise, eating establishments are serving the distinct New Mexican cuisine.

The holiday season brings displays of lights that are actually candles in paper bags full of sand. In the northern part of the state they are called *farolitos*, and in Albuquerque and south, they are called *luminarias*.

# A FEW KEY DATES IN NEW MEXICO HISTORY

1540–Francisco Coronado searches for the Seven Cities of Cibola through New Mexico.

1598–Juan de Oñate establishes the first permanent settlement at San Juan Pueblo.

1680–Pueblo Revolt drives Spanish governors and Franciscan fathers out of New Mexico.

1692–Diego de Vargas's Reconquest of New Mexico

1821–Mexico gains control of New Mexico and Santa Fe Trail opens.

1846–Stephen Kearney's "Army of the West" gains peaceful occupation of New Mexico for the United States.

1879–The railroad arrives.

1912–New Mexico becomes the 47th state.

1926–US Route 66 goes through New Mexico.

1945–The atom bomb is tested successfully at Trinity Site.

## IMPORTANT PHONE NUMBERS AND WEBSITES

Emergency: 911

To report drunk or dangerous driving (on your mobile phone): #DWI

Indian Pueblo Cultural Center: 866-855-7902; www.indianpueblo.org

Information on accessibility: www.newmexico.gov/accessibility.aspx

B&Bs: www.nmbba.org/index.php

Information about New Mexico: www.newmexico.org

Information about Santa Fe: www.santafe.com

To purchase a $25 bargain pass to museums and state monuments: www.new mexicoculture.org

Fairgrounds: www.countyfairgrounds.net/newmexico

YOU CAN STILL GET A HORSE-DRAWN RIDE IN SOUTHWEST NEW MEXICO.

Fishing: www.wildlife.state.nm.us/recreation/fishing
Motels: www.motelguide.com
Parks: www.nmparks.com
Road conditions: 800-432-4269; www.nmroads.com
New Mexico RV campgrounds: www.rv-clubs.us/newmexico_rv_campgrounds.html
Scenic byways: www.newmexicoscenicbyways.org
Skiing: www.skinewmexico.com
State parks: 888-NMPARKS or 888-667-2757; www.nmparks.com
Wine: www.winecountrynm.com

## PUEBLO ETIQUETTE

- When visiting a pueblo, think of your visit as if you were an invited guest in someone's home.
- Inquire ahead of time about visitor's hours. Remember that some pueblos are closed to outsiders on certain days for religious activities.
- Drive slowly.
- Never bring drugs or alcoholic beverages to a pueblo.
- For your comfort, bring along folding chairs to watch the dances from.
- Do not walk into or onto a kiva (a ceremonial structure sometimes, but not always, circular).

TRADITIONAL SPANISH DANCES.

- Follow the tour leader and remember that homes, kivas, and ceremonies typically are not open to visitors. However, if you are invited into someone's home to eat, it is considered impolite to refuse. (It is also considered polite to eat and leave promptly so others can enter and eat.)
- Do not step on or cross the plaza or area where dances are being performed—instead, walk on the perimeter.
- Applause is not appropriate at dances.
- No photography, recordings, or sketching is permitted, in general, at events open to the public. Observe each pueblo's regulations on use of cameras, tape recorders, and drawing. If you want to photograph a pueblo resident, ask permission first and give a donation to the family. In some cases, such as at Taos Pueblo, it is possible to purchase a photography permit.
- Any publication or public use of information about pueblo activities must receive prior approval from the tribal government.
- No pets are allowed.
- Questions about ceremonies, dances, and rituals are considered rude.
- When entering a structure, such as a church, observe the same protocols as you would in any sacred building.

## OTHER MATTERS—AND A FEW CAUTIONS

Rapid temperature changes are the norm. The thermometer may vary by 40 degrees or more from day to night. Therefore, always dress in layers, and be prepared for sudden weather changes. Weather warnings should always be heeded. In summer, dry arroyos (ditches) and roads can flood very rapidly from an afternoon thunderstorm. Every year, it seems, hikers set out to climb La Luz Trail in summer and end up with hypothermia. The sun here really is stronger.

Always wear sunscreen, hat, sunglasses, and take more water than you think you will need, as well as a few energy bars, just in case. Be alert for weather changes. A snowstorm may come up suddenly just while you are planning to drive over Glorieta Pass. It's better to wait it out, even if you have to adjust your plans.

You may have heard about cases of bubonic plague and hantavirus, but unless you are handling rodent feces or have contact with infected rodents, there is no need to worry.

## SMOKING

New Mexico is a smoke-free state.

## CELL PHONES

Only hands-free devices are permitted while driving in Santa Fe, Albuquerque, and Taos. You will be ticketed for talking or texting on a mobile device while driving.

## PRICE CODES

Dining costs are estimated per single entrée, tax, and gratuity.

| | |
|---|---|
| **Inexpensive** | Up to $15 |
| **Moderate** | $15–40 |
| **Expensive** | $40–65 |
| **Very Expensive** | Over $65 |

## CONTACT ME

I would like to hear from you. If you liked a place you found in this book, or if you found it did not work out for you as you had hoped, I want to know. If you have suggestions you would like to see included in future editions, I would like to hear them. Please contact me directly or through the publisher.

My website is www.sharonniederman.com. Please visit for travel information and articles.

## MY THANKS

I want to thank my publisher, The Countryman Press, and the staff, including editorial director Kermit Hummel, managing editor Lisa Sacks, copyeditor Iris Bass, and publicist Tom Haushalter. I am proud of my long relationship with Countryman. Thanks especially to friends around the state who generously provide homes-away-from home when I am on the road: Eleanor Bravo, Karen Schmidt, Kathy Matthews, Mike Taylor and Joan Clark, Carl and Becky Calvert, and Lynn Hamrick. Thanks to many other trusted friends, including Demetria Martinez, Cynthia Prelo, and Emily Drabanski, for their ongoing enthusiasm and suggestions, as well as the many coffees, glasses of wine, and inspired ideas we've shared along this long and winding road. Thanks to my husband, Charles Henry, for tending the hearth when I am away and supplying afternoon popcorn and fires in the fireplace in winter and ice cream on the front porch in warm weather. I also thank New Mexico's tourism professionals for being so good at their jobs and fun to work with.

Sharon Niederman
Raton, New Mexico

# WHAT'S WHERE IN NEW MEXICO

**ACCESSIBILITY** Please contact the
**Center for Development & Disability Information in New Mexico**
(800-552-8195) concerning accessibility at restaurants and lodgings, and
wheelchair rentals.

**ADMISSION FEES** If an admission
fee is $7 or less, it's simply listed as
"fee." Fees greater than $7 are spelled
out. Although fees were accurate
when this book went to press, keep in
mind that yearly increases are likely,
especially for the larger attractions
and theme parks.

**AIR SERVICE** Most people flying
into New Mexico arrive at the **Albuquerque International Sunport**
(505-244-7700; www.cabq.gov/airport).
**Santa Fe Municipal Airport** (505-955-2900; www.santafenm.gov)
receives nonstop flights daily from
Dallas and Los Angeles on American
Eagle; Great Lakes Airlines offers
daily flights to and from Denver.
Southern New Mexico travelers fly
into **El Paso International Airport**
in nearby Texas (915 780-4749; www.
elpasointernationalairport.com). Jet-Blue now offers a daily nonstop flight
between the New York area and
Albuquerque.

**AMTRAK** (see "Trains," page 34).

**ARCHAEOLOGY** Several of the
great ruins on the continent are
located in New Mexico: cliff dwellings
at Bandelier National Monument,
Chaco Culture National Historical
Park, Gila Cliff Dwellings National
Monument, Salmon Ruins, and Aztec
Ruins National Monument. Other
outstanding examples of New Mexico's built cultural history are Salinas
Pueblo Missions National Monument
and Jemez State Monument, as well
as petroglyph sites at Three Rivers
Petroglyph Site, Petroglyph National
Monument, and many others that
provide insight into the ancient past.
Going even further back in time, evidence of earliest North American
habitation may be found at the Folsom Man and Clovis Man sites at
Blackwater Draw.

**AREA CODES** New Mexico has two
area codes. Area code 505 works for
Albuquerque, Santa Fe, Espanola,
Gallup, and Los Alamos; 575 is for

the rest of the state. You may encounter some irregularities in coverage, so if one does not work, try the other.

**ARROYOS** Arroyos are wide ditches found throughout New Mexico that have gotten that way through repeated runoff. They can fill up astoundingly fast during a thunderstorm, when the runoff can be surprisingly powerful. Beware of them and stay out of them during and after rainfall.

**ART GALLERIES AND STUDIOS** Certain towns are known for their concentration of galleries, such as Canyon Road in Santa Fe, Sudderth Drive in Ruidoso, Old Town and Nob Hill neighborhoods in Albuquerque, and Yankie Street in Silver City. In addition to galleries, however, several towns, including Albuquerque, Las Cruces, and Truth or Consequences, offer monthly gallery tours. During the fall and spring, artists open their studios for tours along the High Road,

in Dixon, Abiquiu, Pilar, El Rito, Corrales, and Placitas, and many other places. For information the arts, please go to www.newmexico.org /art-and-culture.

**ARTIST STUDIO TOURS** For a list of open studio tours by date, go to www.collectorsguide.com/fa/fa103 .html.

**BALLOONING Albuquerque International Balloon Fiesta**, attracting over 500 hot-air balloons from around the world, held annually the first two weeks of October, is the state's premier event (888-422-7277 or 505-821-1000; www.balloonfiesta .com). Many other towns, including Chama, Taos, and Gallup, host balloon rallies throughout the year.

**BASEBALL** Albuquerque's Triple-A baseball team, the **Isotopes** (505-924-BALL or 505-924-2255; www.abq isotopes.com), a Pacific Coast minor

league, play April–September baseball in the beautiful stadium is a big-time event.

**BED & BREAKFASTS** From rustic to regal, there's a B&B for every taste and occasion in New Mexico. Taos and Santa Fe have a surfeit of these lodgings, while you may need to hunt a little harder while on the road or in more remote locations. **New Mexico Bed and Breakfast Association** (505-766-5380; www.nmbba.org) is a good way to find approved and inspected lodgings throughout the state.

**BICYCLING** For events, clubs, links, roads, and more, please go to www .nmcycling.org.

**BIRDING** With over 500 birds on New Mexico's list, the state, with its mountain to desert to wetlands ecosystems offers one of the largest counts in the United States. Especially fruitful are the Orilla Verde Trail on the Rio Grande, Bosque del Apache National Monument, Sandia Crest, and Randall Davey Audubon Center & Sanctuary, Santa Fe. Please visit www.wildlife.state .nm.us/recreation/birding/index.htm or http://nm.audubon.org/birding -trails-new-mexico for more information.

**BOATING AND WATER SPORTS** Visit Elephant Butte Lake, Heron Lake, Conchas Dam, Chama River, Navajo Lake, San Juan River, Cochti Dam, rafting the Taos Box on the Rio Grande or floating the Chama.

**BUREAU OF LAND MANAGEMENT** With an astounding wealth of recreational and outdoors opportunities, including the Continental Divide Trail, the El Camino Real Trail, and wilderness experiences galore, contact the (BLM) **Lands Public Information Access Office** in New Mexico (505-954 2000). Please see www.blm .gov/nm/st/en/info/directory.html for guidelines and information.

**BUS SERVICE Greyhound Bus Lines** (800-231-2222; www.grey hound.com) delivers travelers to New Mexico. To travel between Albuquerque Airport and Santa Fe, contact **Sandia Shuttle Express** (505-474-5696; www.sandiashuttlecom).

**CAMPGROUNDS** To make camping reservations at any of the state parks, please contact http://newmexicostate parks.reserveamerica.com/ to purchase a New Mexico Annual Camping or Day Use Pass.

**CHILE** The main item on the menu is chile—never chili. Starting in late July and through September, the fragrance of the roasting green chile, the fundamental ingredient in New Mexico cuisine, the fiery, spicy flavor that so many find addictive, may be enjoyed everywhere in the state, in stews, over enchiladas, and topping off cheeseburgers. Later on, when it ripens into its red stage, it is harvested and dried. Hatch calls itself the "Chile Capital of the World," and is famous for green chiles. The best of the old landrace red chile comes from Chimayo, but it is becoming harder to find.

**CITIES** The state's largest cities are Albuquerque, Las Cruces, Rio Rancho, and Santa Fe. For information on cultural and outdoor activities in Albuquerque, dial 311 or go to www .itsatrip.org/everyday. For activities in Santa Fe, go to www.santafe.com.

**CLIMATE** Sunshine, sunshine, and more sunshine is what you'll find in New Mexico, with an average of 256 days of sunshine a year. Even most rainy days have at least some sunshine; plus, after it snows, the sun usually melts it off pretty quickly. That said, "If you don't like the weather, just wait a half-hour and it will change," is the standard wisdom. Whether driving or in the outdoors, be sure to be prepared for unexpected temperature drops and precipitation by dressing in layers according to the season. A perfectly sunny summer morning will likely bring an afternoon thunderstorm. Expect temperatures to vacillate by 40 degrees during the day. The state is arid to semiarid, with about 9 inches of rain per year.

**COUNTIES** New Mexico has 33 counties and 102 towns.

**CRYPTO-JEWS** Jews who fled the Spanish Inquisition in 1492 looked for safety around the world. It is said that many of New Mexico's founding families, some of whom entered the region in 1598 with conquistador Juan de Oñate, and those who returned during the Reconquista of 1692, were actually Spaniards of the Jewish faith who practiced Catholicism in public and Judaism privately. Many of these families have been practicing Catholics for generations; a recent generation has discovered Jewish roots.

**CUISINE** A fusion of Native American, Mexican, and Spanish cuisine, using such local ingredients as beans, chiles, and corn, produces an amazing variety of flavors. Such aromatics, spices, and herbs as garlic, cumin, and oregano add to the mix. In addition, waves of immigrants and pioneers have tossed their cooking heritage into the stewpot: Albuquerque abounds with Vietnamese and Thai restaurants and cafés, fine Italian and

French dining is available, and you will find plenty of western-style barbecue and Route 66–style home cooking. Santa Fe chefs produce dishes fit for the world stage, and the farm-to-table movement has everyone excited.

**CULINARY EVENTS** Hatch Chile Festival, Wagon Mound Bean Day, Pie Town Pie Festival, Santa Fe Wine & Chile Fiesta, Roswell's Chile & Cheese Festival, Las Cruces' Whole Enchilada Festival, Silver City's New Mexico Tamal Festival, Rio Rancho's Pork & Brew State BBQ Championship, Southwest Chocolate and Coffee Festival, and National Fiery Foods & BBQ Show are some of the better-known feasts open to the public. During New Mexico Restaurant Week, held three weeks in late February–March, restaurants in major cities offer special bargains well worth taking advantage of.

**CULTURE PASS** The **New Mexico CulturePass** is one of the great deals for visitors: For $25, it allows admission to 14 museums and monuments. Visit www.newmexicoculture.org.

**DINOSAURS** The best places to encounter the remains of or learn about dinosaurs are the Museum of Natural History and Science in Albuquerque; Mesalands Dinosaur Museum in Tucumcari; and Florence Hawley Ellis Museum of Anthropology at Ghost Ranch, where the state fossil, the Coelophysis, the "littlest dinosaur," was found. The Dinosaur Trackway at Clayton Lake State Park is the Western Hemisphere's second-richest site of prints, and the Las Cruces Museum of Nature & Science showcases recent finds from the southern part of the state.

**EMERGENCIES** Call 911 for immediate help, or contact the **New Mexico State Police** (505-827-9300; 505-827-3476) or **Search and Rescue Resource Officer**, 4491 Cerrillos Road, Santa Fe (505-827-9228; Robert.Rodgers@state.nm.us). **Drunk Busters DWI Hotline** (877-DWI-HALT or 877-394-4258) is a toll-free hotline; #394 (or keypad letters DWI) is the convenience key for cell phones.

**FARMERS' MARKETS** Please visit www.farmersmarketsnm.org for information on dozens of farmers' markets throughout the state, CSAs, agritourism, and farm-to-table programs. New Mexico loves and celebrates its farmers' markets. Outstanding are the Las Cruces Farmers' and Crafts Market, the Santa Fe Area Farmers' Market, and, in Albuquerque, the Downtown Farmers' Market at Robinson Park and the Los Ranchos Farmers' Market.

**FIBER ARTS** The **New Mexico Fiber Arts Trail** (www.nmfiberarts .org or the-trails.html nmfiberartisans .org) will lead you to shops and galleries where you can purchase fiber, see the work of locals, and learn the arts of weaving, felting and more. Notable fiber arts resources in New Mexico include the Wool Festival at Taos, Victory Alpaca Ranch, and fiber arts galleries galore in Taos and Arroyo Seco.

**FISHING** New Mexico boasts an abundance of lake, stream, and river fishing. Holy grails of fly-fishing are the Quality Waters of the San Juan River near Farmington and the San Antonio River in the Valles Caldera National Preserve. Cimarron Canyon, the Rio Grande Gorge near Taos, and Elephant Butte Lake also offer fishing opportunities. Please visit www.wildlife.state.nm.us/ for fishing reports and license requirements.

**GAMING** Numerous Las Vegas–style casinos, operated primarily by Native American tribes, exist throughout the state. Some of the better-known gaming resorts include Inn of the Mountain Gods near Ruidoso and Buffalo Thunder north of Santa Fe. While casinos are clustered around Albuquerque and Santa Fe, you can find them also along I-40, such as Route 66 Casino and Sky City Casino, as well as in Dulce. Taos Mountain Casino is the only smoke-free casino in the state. Horse racing takes place at Ruidoso Downs, which hosts the All-American Futurity, the richest quarter horse event in the country, run on Labor Day and during State Fair, held in early September. **Sunland Park** (http://newmexico .casinocity.com) also has a well-known racetrack and casino, The Downs at Albuquerque, which features a casino and horse racing, is centrally located at Expo NM, a.k.a. the State Fairgrounds.

**GENEALOGY** is a popular activity in New Mexico. The Garrey Carruthers State Library and Archives in Santa Fe is a center of genealogical research. The Main Library in Albuquerque, downtown at Fifth and Copper, also has a fine special collections genealogy center. Get started at www .genealogybranches.com/newmexico .html.

**GOLF COURSES** Year-round opportunities for golfing exist here, in desert and high-altitude conditions.

Please see the individual chapters for specific courses, or visit www.golf newmexico.com.

**GUIDES AND OUTFITTERS** To discover outdoor adventures in New Mexico, visit www.newmexico.org /outdoor. Reliable and experienced guides also advertise in *New Mexico Magazine*'s annual *Vacation Guide*.

**HIKING** For information about hiking, go to www.explorenm.com/hikes/.

**HISTORIC MARKERS** For a region-by-region guide to New Mexico's historic markers, including the program for Women's Historic Markers, please visit www.nmhistoric markers.org/historicmarkers.php.

**HOT SPRINGS** Aaah. Mineral hot springs in New Mexico include Ojo Caliente Mineral Springs Resort & Spa, Ten Thousand Waves Japanese-style baths, Faywood Hot Springs, Gila Hot Springs, Jemez Springs, and, of course, Truth or Consequences. Undeveloped hot springs may be found in the Jemez National Forest and the Taos area. Contact the visitors centers listed in this guide for specific information.

**HUNTING** An abundance of big game—elk, mule deer, pronghorn, moose, and more—as well as smaller game, such as sage grouse, wild turkey, rabbit, and others, draw hunters to New Mexico. Once-in-a-lifetime nonnative ibex permits are granted by lottery. Nonresident big game hunting licenses are issued by a lottery system; hunters must apply far in advance of the season. Please visit the hunting section of the **New Mexico Game and Fish Department** website, www.wildlife.state.nm.us/, for license requirements.

**LODGING** Lodgings described in this book are focused away from national-brand hotels and motels and more on each region's unique offerings, whether the area in question has bed & breakfasts, lodges, family-owned and -operated budget motels, or some other sort of distinctive facilities. Try www.nmbba.org/nmvg, **New Mexico Bed and Breakfast Association**'s website, for distinctive lodgings.

**LUMINARIAS** Christmastime in New Mexico is made special by candles in paper bags, also known as farolitos. Christmas Eve luminaria walks in Albuquerque and Santa Fe are notable, as are luminaria events in Sugarite Canyon State Park and at Jemez State Monument and Coronado State Monument.

**MAPS** The *New Mexico Atlas & Gazetteer* (DeLorme, $19.95, available at www.delorme.com) will guide you to public and private lands, back roads and byways, and even ski areas and fishing spots—and much, much more. The *New Mexico Road & Recreation Atlas* (Benchmark Maps, $22.95) may be ordered at new mexico.mybigcommerce.com.

**MICROBREWERIES** Contact the **New Mexico Brewers Guild** (http://nmbeer.com) for information on the state's two dozen independent microbreweries and taprooms. Here you can find such distinctive brews as green chile beer and Pancho Villa Stout.

**MUSIC** With a sound for every taste, music festivals include the Clovis Music Festival in early September, celebrating rock and roll; Taos Solar Music Festival; Santa Fe Chamber Music Festival; Silver City Blues Festival; Santa Fe Bluegrass and Old Time Music Festival; and Albuquerque Folk Festival. In addition, the Santa Fe Opera; Cimarron's Shortgrass Music Festival; Music from Angel Fire; Taos School of Music's Summer Festival; Mariachi Spectacular; Festival Flamenco; Thirsty Ear Festival, KlezmerQuerque, and the Globalquerque! world music festival, held at the National Hispanic Cultural Center in Albuquerque, are glorious.

**NATIVE AMERICANS** Each of New Mexico's 19 Indian Pueblos is a sovereign nation. The Navajo and the Apache also have their own reservation lands, where their legal systems and police preside. The main contact for Indian feast days and celebrations open the public is the **Indian Pueblo**

**Cultural Center in Albuquerque** (www.indianpueblo.org/19pueblos/). Three special events showcasing Native dancing, arts, foods, and culture are the Gallup Inter-Tribal Indian Ceremonial, Taos Pueblo Pow Wow, and Gathering of Nations Pow Wow in Albuquerque.

**PENITENTES** Organized in the early 1800s as a lay religious order and prevalent mainly in outlying small towns along the High Road between Santa Fe and Taos, in small communities and other remote locations where a priest could seldom visit, the Penitente Brotherhood assisted the community with life events, burials, special blessings of land and water, and other observations. They gathered—and still do—in windowless *moradas*, and they traditionally maintain secrecy. Penitentes are historically known for rigorous "penance" rituals, such as flagellation, and are especially active during Holy Week and on Good Friday. You may observe their large white crosses on hillsides as you drive through New Mexico.

**PUBLIC LANDS** New Mexico contains more than 77,766,400 acres of national lands, including 13 national parks, two national monuments, numerous national forests, and about 18 million acres of land administered by the BLM; as well as state-owned lands, including a dozen state parks, a state recreation area, and numerous state historic sites.

**RESTAURANTS** This state is memorable for its cuisine. From four-star restaurants in Santa Fe to mom-and-pop cafés on back roads, to Route 66 nostalgic dining, New Mexico has a

venue for every taste. Each chapter is loaded with interesting dining opportunities that have been tested by the author for value, service, and culinary skill. You won't find chain restaurants listed here. To trace the New Mexico Green Chile Cheeseburger Trail and map your adventures, go to www .newmexico.org/culinary.

**REST AREAS** To download a map of New Mexico rest areas, go to http:// dot.state.nm.us/content/dam/nmdot /travel.../maps/Rest_area05.pdf or www.interstaterestareas.com/new -mexico/. Rest areas are maintained along I-40 and I-25, as well as US 285.

**RETREAT CENTERS** New Mexico has many centers for retreat, contemplation, and education. Among the better-known such places are the Benedictine Monastery of Christ in the Desert; Ghost Ranch near Abiquiu; the Mandala Center in Des Moines; the Center for Action and

Contemplation in Albuquerque; the Lama Foundation north of Taos, which hosts high-mountain hermitage retreats; and Roshi Joan Halifax's Upaya Zen Center in Santa Fe. It is possible to arrange stays to accommodate your situation, from a couple of days to weeks.

**ROAD REPORTS** Go to http:// nmroads.com for the most current weather and road condition reports throughout the state.

**ROCK CLIMBING** For rock-climbing opportunities by region, visit www. rockclimbing.com/routes/North_ America/United_States/New_Mexico/.

**ROCKHOUNDING** Deming is as good a place to give the honorary title of "Rockhounding Capital." At Rockhound State Park there, it is possible to haul 25 pounds of rocks, and Rockhound Roundup is held in Deming every mid-March.

**RODEOS** New Mexico State Fair, the county fairs, Colfax County Fair, Gallup Inter-Tribal Indian Ceremonial, and Maverick Rodeo on the Fourth of July in Cimarron are but a few of the events at which to enjoy a real rodeo. For a complete calendar, go to www .coyotesgame.com/rodeo.html.

**RV PARKS** Visit www.rv-clubs.us /newmexico_rv_campgrounds.html for a directory, by region, of New Mexico's RV parks and campgrounds.

**SCENIC BYWAYS** The state's 25 designated scenic byways, including eight of America's 126 scenic byways within the state, celebrating its diverse beauty and rich history, can be traced at www. newmexico.org /parks-and-byways. Among the most celebrated is the **Route 66 National Scenic Byway** (www.rt66nm.org).

**SHOPPING** Perfectly normal citizens have been known to lose their wits—and the contents of their wallets—when shopping in Santa Fe. Save your allowance! There are too many things on Canyon Road you "must have." The portal of the Palace of the Governors in Santa Fe, and the flea markets, will make you a shopper even if you are not. Also, the southern edge of Santa Fe boasts an outlet mall. Other top shopping destinations are Nob Hill and Old Town in Albuquerque, Sudderth Drive in Ruidoso, Bent Street in Taos, and arts-and-crafts festivals throughout the year.

**SNOW SPORTS** With eight alpine ski areas and four Nordic parks, New Mexico offers plenty of ski adventure and family fun. Visit www.skinew mexico.com and www.newmexico .org/ski for more information. *Cross-*

*Country Skiing in Northern New Mexico*, by Kay Matthews, is still the best guide to forest and park trails.

**SPACE HISTORY** Astronomical destinations include the Very Large Array, featured in the movie, *Contact*; the National Solar Observatory at Sacramento Peak; the New Mexico Museum of Space History; and White Sands Missile Range Museum, also in Alamogordo. A reconstruction of Robert Goddard's rocket workshop is found at the Roswell Museum and Art Center. **Follow the Sun, Inc.** (505-897-2886; http://ftstours.com) offers tours of the Spaceport facility outside Truth or Consequences. The **New Mexico Space Trail** (www .nmspacemuseum.org/documents /SpaceTrails_map.pdf) charts 52 historic sites across the state UFOs are celebrated annually at the **Roswell UFO Festival** (575-624-7704; www.ufofestivalroswell.com) held during the Fourth of July weekend.

**SPEED LIMITS AND SEAT BELTS** Seat belts are mandatory. If you are stopped and not wearing a seat belt, expect a minimum $40 fine. The speed limit on the interstates is 75 mph and lower within city limits. The speed limit on state roads is 55–60 mph. Be wary of driving through small towns, such as Cimarron and Eagle Nest, which have posted speed limits of 35 mph. Exceed posted limits and you will be ticketed.

**STATE CAPITAL** The state capital, the oldest government seat in the United States, is Santa Fe.

**STATE PARKS AND MONUMENTS** New Mexico has 35 state parks. See www.emnrd.state.nm.us/prd/parktours.htm or www.stateparks.com/nm.html for more information. For a great deal, go to www.nmstatemonuments.org/ to buy an annual pass for $40 that provides a year's worth of unlimited admission to all state parks and seven historic sites.

**STATISTICS** With a land area of 121,599 square miles, including 234 square miles of inland water, New Mexico is the fifth-largest state. The highest point is Wheeler Peak, at 13,161 feet. Lowest point is Red Bluff Reservoir, southeast of Carlsbad, at 2,842 feet. The population of New Mexico is 2,085,538: approximately 47 percent Hispanic and 10 percent Native American.

**TRAINS** New Mexico Rail Runner Express (866-795-7245; www.nmrail runner.com) commuter trains run daily between Belen and Santa Fe, stopping in downtown Albuquerque and elsewhere; and Amtrak's *Southwest Chief* makes one stop each day, both ways, between Chicago and Los Angeles, in Raton, Las Vegas, Lamy (Santa Fe), Albuquerque, and Gallup. The narrow-gauge train ride on the **Cumbres Toltec Scenic Railroad** (888-286-2737; www.cumbrestoltec .com) between Chama and Antonito, Colorado is one of the best ways to experience the beauty and history of the land.

**TRAVEL INFORMATION** The New Mexico Department of Tourism operates eight strategically located visitors centers around the state. Here you can pick up free brochures, maps, and travel advice. They usually offer coffee, restrooms, picnic areas, and

WiFi. They can be found in Anthony, Chama, Gallup, Glenrio, La Bajada (near Santa Fe, just off I-25), Raton, Santa Fe, and Texico. Be sure to pick up the very handy free New Mexico Vacation Guide, also available online.

**WILDERNESS AREAS** To find your wilderness escape in New Mexico's 166,658 acres of wilderness, go to www.nmwild.org/2011/maps/map -of-new-mexicos-wilderness-areas/ or www.blm.gov/nm/st/en/prog /wilderness.html.

**WILDFLOWERS** With New Mexico's varied ecology, from mountain to desert, wildflowers are profuse. Starting up north, in Sugarite Canyon State Park, the wildflower season progresses from wild iris to columbine, wild rose, and geranium, lupine, marsh marigold, and sunflower. The desert blooms from the Rio Grande south with the yucca blossom, cholla, prickly pear. The Organ Mountains, Bosque del Apache, Cloudcroft area, Gila and Pecos Wilderness are good places to hunt beautiful blooms. In general, the wildflower season in New Mexico runs from February to April as the early autumn, depending on altitude. A photographic field guide of New Mexico mountain wildflowers and desert wildflowers will help you identify the flowers you see in New Mexico. *Wild Plants of the Pueblo Province,* by William Dunmire and Gail Tierney, is a book that goes beyond plant identification.

**WILDLIFE** Pronghorn, elk, mule deer, coyote, and wild turkey are commonly sighted on roadways in northern New Mexico. Big horn sheep, fox, and raccoon may also be seen. Yes, this is the land where the antelope roam.

**WILDLIFE REFUGES** Bosque del Apache National Wildlife Refuge south of Socorro is probably the best-known wildlife refuge in the state, primarily for bird-watching; however, the Maxwell National Wildlife Refuge; the Las Vegas National Wildlife Refuge; and the Bitter Lake National Wildlife Refuge, a riparian habitat in Roswell, are also prime viewing areas.

**WINERIES AND WINE FESTIVALS** As the oldest wine-producing state, New Mexico has experienced a renaissance of wine-making and now produces excellent bottles. More than 40 wineries may be found, scattered in just about every part of the state. Most offer tastings at selected times. Special events featuring wine include Memorial Day weekend's Southern

New Mexico Wine Festival, Fourth of July weekend's Santa Fe Wine Festival at Ranchos de las Golondrinas, Labor Day weekend's New Mexico Wine Festival at Bernalillo, and the Las Cruces Harvest Festival. Contact www.winecountrynm.com for a complete, free map, including drive times, of New Mexico wineries.

ZOOS The state's premier zoo is located at the **Albuquerque BioPark** (505-768-2000; www.cabq .gov/culturalservices/biopark). Alamogordo is home to **Alameda Park Zoo** (575-439-4290), the Southwest's oldest zoo; and Carlsbad, to **Living Desert Zoo and Gardens State Park** (575-887-5516; www .nmparks.com).

# Central New Mexico: Rio Grande Country

## 1

**WEST OF ALBUQUERQUE**
Rio Rancho, Bernalillo, Placitas,
Corrales, Jemez Springs

**EAST OF ALBUQUERQUE**
Belen, Moriarty, Mountainair, Madrid,
Cerrillos

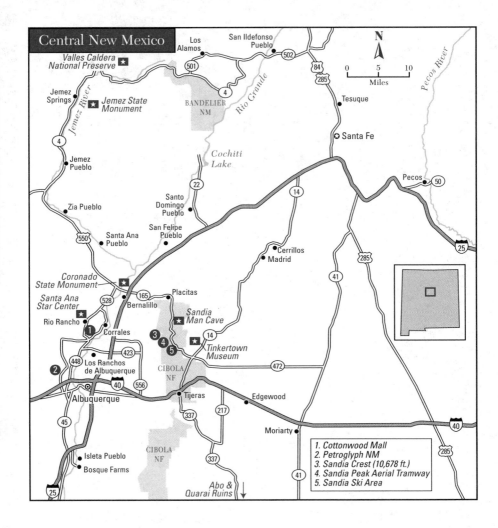

# WEST AND EAST OF ALBUQUERQUE

The Rio Grande Valley surrounding Albuquerque is rich with overlays of Spanish and Native American history. Here markers of the earliest Spanish settlements in New Mexico coexist with Native American arts and ceremonies. Here, too, are communities of the Manzano Mountains, characterized by homesteading roots that extend into today's multigenerational ranching families. Winemaking, dating in Sandoval County to the 1620s, is continued in several local wineries and celebrated each Labor Day weekend at the Bernalillo Wine Festival. Small farming still thrives in much of the region, and farmers' markets bursting with fresh local produce are crowded each summer, with growers selling their vegetables, jams, cheese, and garlic.

This is a region fascinating for the multiple layers of history generated at trail convergences. The Camino Real—the north–south colonial Royal Road between Mexico City and Santa Fe, which followed the Rio Grande—and the original 1926 Route 66 alignment that ran more or less north to south, as well as the post-1937 Route 66 east–west alignment—tell several stories simultaneously.

This is the land of the Turquoise Trail National Scenic Byway, a colorful back road to Santa Fe that links the East Mountains to mining towns of Golden, Madrid, and Cerrillos. To the west is the Jemez Mountain National Scenic Byway that courses through the glorious red rock country of Jemez Pueblo.

Although the Rio Grande Valley area has grown and urbanized during recent decades, values that characterize small-town life and independence, religious faith, and practices endure—sustained by generations that continue to live in the same place and in much the same ways as did their ancestors.

The traveler will find an abundance of recreational opportunities in easy reach: snow sports, camping, golfing, hiking, fishing, and enjoyment of nature are accessible and part of the way of life here.

The presence of a half-dozen Indian pueblos makes Bernalillo and Sandoval Counties unique. Here, ancient cultures continue to live and practice traditional ways. Many of these Indian tribes have opened splendid resorts offering luxurious dining, accommodations, entertainment, and gaming.

The spirit of the place is as strong as an enormous cottonwood tree in the bosque that has watched change come and go yet remains deeply rooted in the *acequia* that nourishes its thick bark, profuse leaves, and multistoried branches.

Enjoy your stay, and may the place nourish you and yours as well.

## WEST OF ALBUQUERQUE

**GUIDANCE Corrales Visitor Center** (505-897-0502, www.visitcorrales.com), 4324 Corrales Rd., Corrales. Open Mon.–Fri. 8–5.

**Rio Rancho Chamber of Commerce and Visitor Center** (505-892-1533; www.rrchamber.org), 4001 Southern Blvd. SE, Rio Rancho. Open Mon.–Fri. 8–5.

**Rio Rancho Convention and Visitors Bureau** (888-746-7262 or 505-891-7258; www.rioranchonm.org), 3001 Civic Center Circle, Rio Rancho. Open Mon.–Fri. 8–5.

**Sandoval County Visitor Center** (800-252-0191 or 505-867-8687; www.sandovalcounty.org), 264 Camino del Pueblo, Bernalillo.

**Walatowa Visitor Center** (575-834-7235), 7413 NM 4, Jemez Pueblo. Fifty-five miles northwest of Albuquerque on US 550, north on NM 4. Open daily 9–5.

**GETTING THERE** Please see "Getting There" in chapter 2.

**MEDICAL EMERGENCY Lovelace Westside Hospital** (505-727-2000), 10501 Golf Course Rd. NW, Rio Rancho.

**McLeod Medical Center** (505-832-4434; 505-286-2396), 1108 US Rt. 66 W, Moriarty.

**Presbyterian Family Healthcare** (505-864-5454), 609 Christopher Dr., Belen.

**UNM Sandoval Regional Medical Center** (505-994-7000), 3001 Broadmoor Blvd. NE, Rio Rancho.

**University of New Mexico Hospital** (505-272-2411), 2211 Lomas Blvd. NE, Albuquerque.

## ✳ To See

**TOWNS Bernalillo.** One of the first areas settled by the Spanish, this ancient pueblo site is where Coronado is said to have spent the winter of 1540/41. Distinctly Catholic, it is inhabited by many descendants of old Spanish families. Traditions, such as the mid-August Matachines dances performed annually in the streets in honor of the patron saint, San Lorenzo, involve much of the village. Because of its proximity to Albuquerque, but well on the way to Santa Fe, Bernalillo is sprucing itself up bit by bit, refurbishing its buildings even as new condos and homes appear on the edges of town. Yoga studios, cafés, galleries, and boutiques now grace the main street, whose character remains steadfastly small town and working class. Just beyond that main street, snug little houses with carefully tended rosebushes remain enclaves of privacy.

THE MYSTERIOUS MATACHINES DANCES HAVE BEEN PERFORMED EVERY AUGUST ON SAN LORENZO DAY FOR MORE THAN 350 YEARS IN BERNALILLO.

**Corrales.** An agricultural community settled by Hispanic, French, Basque, and Italian farmers through the 19th and 20th centuries, Corrales is an exclusive village of pricey homes and beautiful horses, shaded by gracious old cottonwoods. Interesting galleries and boutiques, a winery, and a microbrewery, make this pretty town worth a prowl.

**Jemez Springs.** A tiny, picturesque community due north of Jemez Pueblo, this village is primarily dedicated to the service of tourists, with bed & breakfasts, hot springs, and a few galleries, a café, and a notable bar.

**Placitas.** A bedroom community of both Albuquerque and Santa Fe, this town is populated mainly by those who prefer to stay off the beaten track, enjoy their 360-degree views and their privacy, and can afford to do just that.

**Rio Rancho.** In the 1960s, Rio Rancho was inhabited largely by coyotes and rattlesnakes, with retirement acreage staked out and a small population of brave retirees from the East Coast hanging in there. Growth accelerated with the arrival of Intel, and Rio Rancho has for years remained New Mexico's fastest-growing city, sparking Albuquerque's boom. It now boasts Cottonwood Shopping Mall and nearly every chain store and restaurant found across America. There's really no longer any need to cross the river for shopping or entertainment unless you absolutely want to.

**HISTORIC LANDMARKS, PLACES, AND SITES** Coronado State Monument (505-867-5351), I-25 exit 242, US 550 west 1.7 miles. Wed.–Mon. 8:30–5. Closed Tues. The 81-year-old visitors center and small museum, designed by Santa Fe–style architect John Gaw Meem, houses the restored kiva paintings of Kuaua, which exude a kind of sacredness and grant insight into the roots of Native American art. Walk the grounds of pueblo ruins on the 0.2-mile self-guided trail. Take in the panoramic view overlooking the Rio Grande and Sandias, especially impressive at sunset when the mountains turn watermelon red, and imagine yourself one of the first conquistadors, said to have spent the winter of 1540/41 on this spot. The ramada-covered tables are perfect for a picnic anytime. $3; Sun. $1 day pass for NM residents; Wed. free for seniors 65 and older. Call for RV and camping availability.

**Jemez State Monument** (575-829-3530), 43 miles north of Bernalillo, NM 4, 1 mile north of Jemez Springs. Open daily Wed.–Mon. 8:30–5. Closed Tues. Dramatic ruins of 14th-century Towa pueblo and Spanish mission ruins of the church of San José de los Jémez dates to the 17th century. $3, age 16 and under free.

**Petroglyph National Monument** (505-899-0205), 4735 Unser Blvd., Rio Rancho. West from Albuquerque on I-40 to exit 154, north 3 miles to Western Trail, go left and follow the signs. Open daily 8–5. Closed Thanksgiving, Christmas, and New Year's Day. From the Unser Blvd. Visitor Center, get maps to the prehistoric rock art trails on West Mesa volcanic escarpment. The monument has over 20,000 examples of indigenous rock art, including animals, birds, insects, and geometric designs, such as the spiral. This is a sacred landscape to Native Americans. All trails are a short drive from the visitors center. Boca Negra Canyon is 2 miles north of the visitors center and has three self-guided trails. All are easy walks. Bring water, stay on trails, keep pets leashed, and beware of rattlesnakes. $1 weekdays, $2 weekends.

**San Ysidro Church** (505-898-1779), 5015 Corrales Rd., Corrales. Call for hours. This lovingly restored 1875 village church with twin bell towers and pitched tin roof serves as a venue for community events, acoustic and chamber music concerts, lectures, and festivals. The Corrales Historic Society cares for this treasure.

**Soda Dam** (no phone). Two miles north of Jemez Springs on NM 4 is a 300-foot natural dam made of mineral deposits.

**MUSEUMS** Casa San Ysidro (505-898-3915), 973 Old Church Rd., Corrales. Open Wed.–Fri., tours at 9:30 and 3, Sun. at 3. Reservations required. As a branch of the Albuquerque Museum, the Gutiérrez/Minge Casa houses rare and exquisite New Mexican rugs, textiles, furniture, and art. The Ward Alan Minge family painstakingly and authentically restored this 18th- to 19th-century rancho, down to matching the original wall colors, as a labor of love. $4 adults, $3 seniors, $2 children.

**DeLavy House** (505-867-2755), 151 Edmond Rd., Bernalillo, west of Coronado State Monument and east of Santa Ana Star Casino. Watch closely the north side of US 550 for the Sandoval County Historical Society sign. The former home of local artist Edmond DeLavy, now the home of the historical society and its archives and photo collection, this is often the site of lectures and community meetings, including the Sandoval County Historical Society. Monthly programs second Sunday of the month. Open Thurs. 9:30–11 AM.

**J & R Vintage Auto Museum and Bookstore** (505-867-2881), 3650 NM 528, a half-mile south of US 550, Rio Rancho. Open Mon.–Sat. 1–5, Sun. 10–5. Nov.–Apr. closed Sun. Founder Gab Joiner is a vintage car collector and restorer whose collection just got too big to store at home. The more than 60 restored classic cars and trucks on display, including Packards, Buick Roadsters, and so many more, are all for sale. There's a huge gift shop with die-cast toys, books, and memorabilia. If you don't have an auto nut in your clan, you may have to become one yourself when you see this. $6 adults, $5 seniors, $3 children ages 6–12, under age 6 free.

## EAST OF ALBUQUERQUE

**GUIDANCE Belen Chamber of Commerce/Visitor Center** (505-864-8091; www.belenchamber.org), 712 Dalies Ave., Belen.

**East Mountain Chamber of Commerce** (505-281-1999; www.eastmountain chamber.com) 481 Hwy. 66 E., Tijeras.

**Mountainair Chamber of Commerce** (505-847-2795; www.discovermountain airnm.com), Mountainair.

**Turquoise Trail Association** (505-281-5233; www.turquoisetrail.org), 121 Sandia Crest Rd., Sandia Park.

**Valencia County Chamber of Commerce** (505-352-3596; www.newmexico .org/valencia-county-chamber-of-commerce), 3447 Lambros Loop, Los Lunas. Open Mon.–Fri. 8–5.

## ✳ To See

**TOWNS Belen** is a town that grew up with the railroad, and it still serves as a switching station for as many as 300 Burlington Northern Santa Fe trains every day. The main attraction here is the Belen Harvey House Museum beside the railroad tracks.

**Cerrillos.** Mining town, abandoned western film set, ghost town—Cerrillos melds these identities into a place so quiet it is almost spooky, yet it has its own irresistible allure for artists, photographers, and wanderers. The streets, where the only being you are likely to see is a lazy dog parked in the road, seem about to reveal their secrets any moment. For conversation, walk into Mary's Bar, where you are likely to find the locals and old-timers.

**Madrid.** Through its incarnations as a 20th-century coal mining town, an abandoned ghost town that was once entirely for sale, and, from the 1970s onward, a magnet for hippies and artists who moved into the abandoned miners' homes and subsequently turned them into pricey real estate, galleries, and cafés, Madrid makes an enjoyable and worthwhile stop along the Turquoise Trail. The more than 30 galleries are lively and varied. It has always been known for its especially lovely Christmas lights.

**Moriarty.** Contrary to popular legend, there is no relationship between the name of this town and a character created by Arthur Conan Doyle, though the Sherlock Holmes Society did gather here annually. This crossroads town, once the supply center for Estancia Valley dryland farmers, still retains its Route 66 character in its main street architecture. It was named for Michael Moriarty, a young health-seeker from Iowa who arrived in 1887 and found relief for his rheumatism under the sunny skies. Corn, alfalfa, pinto beans, and pumpkins are grown nearby.

**Mountainair,** formerly "the pinto bean capital of the world," located along US 60, the "slow road" or two-lane across New Mexico, is the geographic center of the state. As the headquarters of the Salinas Pueblos National Monument and the site of the Pueblo Deco Shaffer Hotel, with some of New Mexico's most interesting folk art created by jack-of-all-trades Pop Shaffer in the early 20th century, Mountainair harkens back to its homesteading and ranching roots. New waves of artists and retirees continue to move here and call it home.

**HISTORIC LANDMARKS, PLACES, AND SITES J. W. Eaves Movie Ranch** (505-474-3045; www.eavesmovieranch.com), 14 miles from Santa Fe via NM 14, west on NM 45, 75 Rancho Alegre Rd., Santa Fe. Call for hours. If this movie set looks familiar, don't be surprised. Many gunfights have been staged here, so you've likely seen the place in a western or two. Daily tours, parties, and events are offered, and large groups may book staged gunfights.

MADRID IS LOADED WITH COLORFUL GALLERIES.

KASHA-KATUWE TENT ROCKS NATIONAL MONUMENT.

**Kasha-Katuwe Tent Rocks National Monument** (505-761-8700), I-25 north, exit 259, follow signs to Forest Rd. 266. Open daily Mar 11–Oct. 31, 7–7; Nov. 1–Mar. 10, 8–5. Gates close one hour earlier. Comanaged by BLM and Cochiti Pueblo. Hike the hoodoos, the conelike structures unique in New Mexico. These magical-looking rock formations, the result of volcanic activity, resemble gigantic sand castles from a fantasy story. The 2-mile Cave Loop Trail is easy, while the steep 1.5-mile Slot Canyon Trail is rated difficult. $5.

**Mystery Rock**, west of Los Lunas on NM 6 about 15 miles at the base of Mystery Mountain. One of the area's most curious "unsolved mysteries," this rock with the Ten Commandments carved into it has long been a source of intrigue. Who put it here? No one knows for sure. Stout shoes and good knees are required for the short scramble to view the rock close up.

**Salinas Pueblo Missions National Monument** (505-847-2290). Closed Thanksgiving, Christmas, and New Year's Day. This monument comprises three separate pueblo ruins located within a 50-mile radius, with impressive ruins of Spanish mission churches built on these sites. Call each site for specific hours: Abo (505-847-2400), Gran Quivira (505-847-2770), and Quarai (505-847-2290). As of this writing, much of Gran Quivira is being backfilled to protect the site. Free.

**Sandia Peak Tramway** (505-856-7325; www.sandiapeak.com), 30 Tramway Rd. NE, Albuquerque. From I-25, exit 234 at Tramway Rd., follow it east 6 miles to Sandia Peak Tramway. Open Memorial Day–Labor Day 9–9, Labor Day– Memorial Day 9–8, Tues. 5 PM–9 PM, Balloon Fiesta first two weeks in Oct., 9–9. Billed as "the world's longest aerial tramway," a ride, or flight as it is called, carries visitors in a dramatic ride from the desert to the crest of the mountain for

2.7 miles through four of the earth's six biozones and astounding views of the rugged mountainside, its rocky outcroppings, and canyons. Atop the crest is the Four Seasons Visitor Center, open May–Nov., as well as restaurants and a gift shop. $20 adults, $17 seniors, teens ages 13–20, and military; $12 children ages 5–12, under age 5 free.

**Tome Hill** (no phone). From Albuquerque, go south on NM 47; pass Peralta and Los Lunas, then left on Tome Hill Rd. to Tome Hill. This landform is a Camino Real landmark and Good Friday pilgrimage site. Witness New Mexico's Calvario, as marked by crosses on top of the hill. The main path to the top, the South Trail, begins at Tome Hill Park at the intersection of La Entrada—the sculpture designating the three cultures, Native, Spanish, and homesteader, who have resided here—and the Rio del Oro Loop Roads. The climb is steep and strenuous.

**MUSEUMS Belen Harvey House Museum** (505-861-0581), 104 N. First St., Belen. Open Tues.–Sat. 12:30–3:30. Closed Sun.–Mon., major holidays. Sitting beside the railroad tracks, this museum was originally a Fred Harvey Co. dining room, from 1908 to 1939. The collections relate to the history of the area and primarily to Santa Fe railroad history. Free.

**Los Lunas Museum of Heritage & Arts** (505-352-7720), 251 Main St. SE, Los Lunas. Open Tues.–Sat. 10–5. Closed Sun.–Mon. This recently opened museum concentrates on the heritage and families of the region, with exhibits on founding families, the Civil War in New Mexico, educational exhibits for teachers, and a Genealogy Resource Center. Free.

**Old Coal Mine Museum** (505-438-3780), 2846 NM 14, Madrid. Open daily, weather permitting. Located on 3 acres filled with vintage vehicles and other

WHEN IN MADRID, MAKE A STOP AT THE OLD COAL MINE MUSEUM TO FIND OUT ABOUT LIFE IN BYGONE DAYS.

remnants of the days when this was a working coal mining town, the museum itself houses Engine 767, the most complete nonoperating steam locomotive in the United States. During summer, it serves as a theater for weekend melodramas. Also on view are the coal mineshaft and original mining headquarters. Refurbished in 2012. $5 adults, $3 seniors and children.

⚓ **Tinkertown Museum** (505-281-5233; www.tinkertown.com), 121 Sandia Crest Rd., Sandia Park. I-40 east, exit north at exit 175, NM 14 north 6 miles, left on NM 536. Tinkertown is 1.5 miles on your left. Open daily Apr. 1–Oct. 31, 9–6. There's no other museum like this. "I did all this while you were watching TV," folk artist

BIKE RIDING IN THE SHADOW OF THE SANDIAS AT HYATT TAMAYA ON SANTA ANA PUEB-
LO LAND.

Ross Ward said of his carving, which amounts to a 22-room collection of miniature animated scenes of Americana. Prediction: In years to come, this environmental folk artist and his work will be discovered and acclaimed as simply
amazing. $3.50 adults, $3 seniors, $1 children ages 4–16, under age 4 free.

**U.S. Southwest Soaring Museum** (505-832-0755; www.swsoaringmuseum
.org), 918 E. Old Hwy. 66, Moriarty. Exit 197 from I-40, 30 miles east of Albuquerque. Open daily 9–4. Antique sailplanes, hang gliders, and a history of soaring from the 1920s to the present make this an interesting stop. The collection of
96 model gliders in miniature is most appealing. Call for admission prices.

## ✳ To Do

**BICYCLING Manzano Meander** (no phone) is a 55-mile round-trip from
Four Hills Shopping Center in Albuquerque over NM 333 (Old Route 66), 7
miles to Tijeras. At the intersection of NM 337 go right up to Cedro Canyon, the
roughest part of the trip, then coast down to Chilili, an old Spanish land grant
village. Be careful, though, because there isn't much in the way of shoulder
along NM 337.

**Straight and Easy** (no phone) is a perfectly good workout on a perfectly flat
road from Moriarty south on NM 41 to Estancia 17 miles, or if you are feeling
strong, you can pedal all the way to Willard for another 13 miles. You'll find lots
of big skies, fields, and farms along the way.

**BIRDING** See **Manzano Mountains State Park**, under *Green Space*.

## NATIVE AMERICAN PUEBLOS

For the most up-to-date information on pueblo dances and feast days, contact the **Indian Pueblo Cultural Center** (505-843-7270; www.indianpueblo .org). Christmas Eve Midnight Mass, Christmas Day, New Year's Day, King's Day (January 6), Easter, and Thanksgiving are customary times for dances to be performed, and the public is welcome.

**Cochiti Pueblo** (505-465-2244), population about 800, is due south of Santa Fe off I-25 and overlooks the Rio Grande. Storyteller pottery figures originated here with Cochiti potter Helen Cordero, and drums are another specialty of the pueblo. Feast day: July 14.

**Isleta Pueblo** (505-869-3111). From Albuquerque, I-25 south to exit 215 or take NM 47 to intersection with NM 147, go left, cross the river to the pueblo. While you can drive through the pueblo and visit the historic Church of San Augustine and buy oven bread, roasted blue cornmeal, and chile from various homes with signs offering them for sale, Isleta (which means "little island") also offers the sophisticated side of golfing, gaming, nightlife, and dining. Feast days: January 6, August 28, September 4.

**Jemez Pueblo** (505-834-7235), 7413 NM 4, Pueblo of Jemez. Go fifty-five miles northwest of Albuquerque, north to US 550 then to San Ysidro, north on NM 4. Feast days: November 12, December 12, Christmas Day, New Year's Day, January 6, Easter. See Walatowa Visitor Center, under "Guidance." For authentic dances, the opportunity to purchase fine pottery from the makers, and a warm welcome, Jemez Pueblo makes a wonderful introduction to the Indian way of life.

**Sandia Pueblo** (505-867-3317), 12 miles north of Albuquerque off I-25. Perhaps best known for its business enterprises, this pueblo of approximately 4,000 people has entered the 21st century with panache and now operates the grand new Sandia Resort & Casino (open 24 hours) with several fine restaurants, a high-end spa, the Bien Mur Indian Market Center (where pottery and fine hand-crafted jewelry are sold), and Sandia Lakes Recreation Area. Feast days: January 6, June 13.

**San Felipe Pueblo** (505-867-3381) is known for its annual Corn Dance on May 1, a celebration that includes the sale of food, pottery, and jewelry, but perhaps better known for its Casino Hollywood, only 32 miles north of Albuquerque at exit 252 off I-25. Feast day: May 1.

**Santa Ana Pueblo** (505-771-6700). The ancient site of this Keresan village along the Jemez River is reserved for ceremonial functions and open to visitors only during certain annual celebrations. Today, the pueblo is known for its various enterprises, including the magnificent Hyatt Tamaya Resort & Spa and the Santa Ana Star Casino west of Bernalillo on US 550. Feast days: June 29, July 26.

**Santo Domingo Pueblo** (505-465-2214) holds a complex and moving Corn Dance each year on August 4. Artist Georgia O'Keeffe is quoted as saying that witnessing the Corn Dance was one of the great experiences of her life. Several hundred dancers moving rhythmically on the plaza, the sounds of their shells and bells, and the drums and singing, make this an unforgettable event. A big carnival of wares from all over (but be sure what you are buying is authentic and handmade—if the price is too good to be true, it probably isn't) and native foods makes this a fine day to be here. Feast day: August 4.

**Zia Pueblo** (505-867-3304), a village of about 700 off US 550 about 15 miles west of Bernalillo, gave New Mexico its symbol, the Zia sun sign. The village was abandoned and then repopulated after the 19th century. Many of those who live here are superb potters and painters. Feast day: August 15.

*HORNO* BREAD BAKING IS DEMONSTRATED AT JEMEZ PUEBLO'S WALATOWA CENTER.

**Corrales Bosque Preserve** (505-350-3955). Birding, hiking, horseback riding, and walking along a quiet and unspoiled stretch of dirt trails shaded by giant cottonwoods along the Rio Grande. Free.

**BOATING Cochiti Lake.** See "Wind Surfing."

**CAMPING** See "Camping and Cabins," under *Lodging*.

**FARMERS' MARKETS Bernalillo Farmers' Market** (505-264-3013), 282 Camino del Pueblo, Bernalillo. Open July 6–Oct. 26, Fri. 4–7. It's likely you will encounter growers from San Felipe Pueblo at this market.

**Cedar Crest Farmers & Arts Market** (505-514-6981), 12127 N. NM 14, Cedar Crest. Open June 27–Oct. 15, Wed. 3–6. Get there early for the best selection.

**Corrales Growers' Market** (505-898-6336), next to the post office on Corrales Rd., Corrales. Open Apr. 22–Oct. 28, Sun. 9–noon, Wed. 4–7. A bustling lively market with the highest quality, and priciest, produce. Neighbors meet up here over coffee and breakfast burritos.

**FISHING Isleta Lakes & RV Park** (505-244-8102), 13 miles south of Albuquerque on I-25, exit 215, 4051 NM 47. Fish peacefully from the shores of two beautiful lakes. Open daily 6 AM–8 PM. Lakes stocked with channel catfish in warm weather and rainbow trout in fall and winter. There are also 50 full-service RV hookups. New Mexico fishing license is not required. Limit five fish per adult. $16 age 12 and above, $9 under age 12.

**Sandia Lakes Recreation Area** (505-771-5190), 100 NM 313, Sandia Pueblo, 100 NM 313. Three lakes here are stocked with rainbow trout during the cooler months and channel catfish during the summer. One lake is strictly catch-and-release. Twenty acres of water on 56 acres of bosque forest. New Mexico fishing license is not required. 7 AM–7 PM; Oct. 1–Mar. 31, 7 AM–5 PM. $20, $12 children, $3 visitors, $1child visitors.

**Shady Lakes** (505-898-2568), 11033 Fourth St. NW., Albuquerque. Take I-25, exit Tramway Blvd. to NM 313 for 2 miles. The place known as Shady Lakes is a pleasant area with small lakes that in summer are covered with water lilies and can, for a small fee, provide every child with the opportunity to catch a fish. New Mexico fishing license is not required. Mid-April–mid-Aug., 8 AM–6 PM; Feb. weekends only; Mar.–mid-April, 10 AM–5 PM. $7.95, children $5.95, visitors $3.95. Trout charge per inch $7 average cost per fish.

**Zia Lake** (505-867-3304), Zia Pueblo, south of San Ysidro on US 550. A tribal permit is required to fish here for bass, catfish, and trout. Gas motors are not allowed.

**GOLF Chamisa Hills Country Club** (505-896-5000), 500 Country Club Dr. SE, Rio Rancho. Rio Rancho 1 and Rio Rancho 2 courses, designed by Lee Trevino, provide a total of 27 holes for all skill levels. $20–28.

**Isleta Eagle Golf Club** (505-848-1900), 13 miles south of Albuquerque, exit 215. Open daily. This 27-hole native desert–style course offers play around three scenic lakes and the Rio Grande. Fees for 18 holes, including cart, $50–65.

**Santa Ana Golf Course** (505-867-9464), S. 288 Prairie Star Rd., Santa Ana Pueblo, is the naturally landscaped sister course of Twin Warriors. Golf around eight crystal-blue lakes, framed by three mountain ranges. $37–59.

**Twin Warriors Golf Course** (505-771-6155), Hyatt Tamaya Resort, 1300 Tuyuna Trail, Santa Ana Pueblo. This is the ultimate, an 18-hole high desert championship Guy Panks–designed course where play takes place around 20 ancient cultural sites. The setting provides a truly magical experience. $60–145, depending on time of year; $55–79 New Mexico residents.

**HIKING Battleship Rock**, along the Jemez Mountain Trail, is an easy 2-mile, extremely popular hike to the river, accessed at Battleship Rock turnout on NM 4, 5 miles north of Jemez Springs.

**Las Conchas Trail** provides moderate forested hiking along the East Fork of the Jemez River.

**Red Canyon/Ox Canyon Trail**, Manzano Mountains. This moderate 5.5-mile trail through Red Canyon is easily accessed. Go left in the town of Manzano along NM 337. The shady trail, good for mountain biking, too, is populated with alligator junipers and New Mexico swallowtail butterflies in summer. This is another favorite area hikes.

**Sandia Crest Trail**, Sandia Mountains. This 27-mile trail along the top, with panoramic views, is easy to moderate. Sandia Peak provides a convenient access point.

**10K Trail**, Cedar Crest. Take NM 536, the Crest Road, to the trailhead, to access this moderate 7-mile hike along a 10,000-foot contour.

**Tree Springs Trail**, I-40 to NM 14 (exit 175), go north, take NM 536, the Crest Rd., is one of the prettiest hikes on the east side of the Sandias, with wild primroses blooming May–June and a green, wildflower-filled landscape completely different from the desert vegetation of the west side of the mountain. It's a moderate 3-mile climb to the top, where you can connect with the Sandia Crest Trail. $3.

**HORSEBACK RIDING The Stables at Tamaya** (505-771-6037), Hyatt Regency Tamaya Resort & Spa, 1300 Tuyuna Tr., Santa Ana. A unique way to experience Pueblo backcountry is with experienced native instructors and trail guides. Journey peacefully on horseback through cottonwoods along the Rio Grande and Jemez rivers on twice-daily trail rides. Carriage rides, pony rides, and riding lessons are also available. Non–resort guests are welcome. $80 individual; $60 each in a group.

**HOT SPRINGS Giggling Springs Hot Springs** (575-829-9175), 40 Abousleman Loop, Jemez Springs. Open Wed.–Sun. 11–7. This lovely spot across the road from the Laughing Lizard is a hot spring pool next to the Jemez River. An

A GLORIOUS AUTUMN AFTERNOON RIDE THROUGH THE BOSQUE NEAR CORRALES.

intimate location with poolside beverage service. $18 per hour per person; $60 day pass; $30 two hours. Call for hours, which change seasonally.

**Jemez Springs Bath House** (575-829-3303 or 866-204-8303), 062 Jemez Springs Plaza, Jemez Springs. 10–7 daily. Owned and operated by the village of Jemez Springs. Built from 1870 to 1878, this bathhouse and gift shop is fed by a rich mineralized spring and retains its Victorian feeling. Individual private soaking tubs, massage and spa treatments available. $12 for 25-minute soak.

**MOUNTAIN BIKING** See **Las Huertas Canyon**, under *Green Space*, for a creekside moderate to difficult ride toward the Sandias, and **Red Canyon**, under "Hiking," in the Manzano Mountains is a favorite moderate 5.5-mile trail ride.

Also see **Turquoise Trail**, under "Scenic Drives," and East Fork of the Jemez, under "Snow Sports—Cross-Country Skiing," plus **Petroglyph National Monument** (see "Historic Landmarks, Places, and Sites") offers easy packed dirt cruises.

See **Sandia Peak Ski Area**, under "Snow Sports—Downhill Skiing." Lift open June 2–Labor Day. In the summer, you can bring your bike up the mountain on the tram and find 30 miles of easy, moderate, and difficult trails graded like ski runs. You can ride the chairlift at the ski area to King of the Mountain, a black diamond (or difficult) trail, to Golden Eagle, marked green (or moderate), and descend King of the Mountain for a trail marked blue (or easy). Rentals are available at the top and bottom of the lift.

**Corrales Rio Grande Bosque** makes a delightful, easy, mostly level ride, or walk, for 12 miles. Follow NM 425 (Corrales Rd.) through Corrales; at Mockingbird Ln. go left until you reach the bosque.

**SCENIC DRIVES**  For more information on NM Scenic Byways, call 800-733-6396, ext. 24371.

**Abo Pass Trail** connects the Salt Missions Trail and the Camino Real for 31 miles along NM 47 and US 60. It is a journey through big open skies and the empty loneliness of the Old—and older—West, and a time to speculate how life used to be. You can imagine riding it on horseback or by wagon and appreciate the modern comforts of air-conditioning and motorized vehicles.

**Corrales Road.** The pretty two-lane, 6.7-mile road that winds along NM 448 through the Village of Corrales shows off the beauty of this rural community squeezed between busy Rio Rancho and Albuquerque (be sure to drive slowly, to savor the view and to avoid a ticket). Fruit orchards, horses grazing beside adobe homes, and expansive views of the Sandia Mountains speak of a less-harried time and insist you slow down, if only just to get a good look.

**Jemez Mountain Trail National Scenic Byway.** From Albuquerque, the length of this trail runs 163 miles. Take I-25 north to US 550, go northwest on 550 to San Ysidro, then right on NM 4. Along the way take in the Walatowa Visitor Center—where across the road and beneath the red rocks, ladies may be selling bowls of chile, Indian tacos, and oven pies—Pueblo of Jemez; Jemez Springs; Jemez State Monument; past Battleship Rock, Soda Dam, and La Cueva; past the Valle Caldera, Bandelier National Monument, and on into Los Alamos. This is a great way to see a huge amount in one day. You can loop back around to Albuquerque via Santa Fe on I-25 for a quicker return trip. Note: Fill up before you leave. There is no reliable gas station on NM 4 until you get to White Rock.

**Salt Missions Trail.** From Albuquerque, take I-40 east to Moriarty, south on NM 333 at Moriarty, follow NM 41, US 60, NM 513, 55, 337, and 131 for a total of 140 miles to travel the entire length of the trail and see all three ruins: Abo, Quarai, and Gran Quivira, with their Indian pueblos and 17th-century Franciscan mission churches, through the Manzano and Cibola National Forests en route. Abo is 9 miles west of Mountainair on US 60, and Quarai is 8 miles north of Mountainair on NM 55. Gran Quivira is a longer drive, 39 miles south of Mountainair on NM 55. Note: Gran Quivira ruins are being backfilled for their preservation.

**Sandia Crest Scenic Byway.** Take I-40 east to Tijeras exit, north on NM 14, then to Sandia Crest on NM 536 for 13.6 miles. The drive up is beautiful and green, with many hiking trails along the way, but once at the top of the crest, you can see 100 miles in all directions. This is a favorite destination of first-time visitors, where friends and relatives introduce them to Albuquerque. Over a half-million people drive to the 10,687-foot crest annually, and another quarter-million ride the Sandia Tramway.

**Turquoise Trail National Scenic Byway** is the back road between Albuquerque and Santa Fe. Take I-25 to the Cedar Crest exit, go north on NM 536, then follow NM 14 for 48 miles through mining ghost towns of Golden and Madrid, now a lively, much-gentrified arts town rather than a ghost town or hippie hangout, and Cerrillos, then on into Santa Fe. The route gets its name from local turquoise mines. The serpentine, up-and-down two-lane carries you past the Ortiz Mountains to the right, with views of the Sangre de Cristos up ahead and the Jemez Mountains to the left. Allow a good day to take your time and explore and shoot photos, perhaps have dinner in Santa Fe, then loop back down I-25 to Albuquerque.

**SNOW SPORTS—CROSS-COUNTRY SKIING** La Cueva (800-252-0191). Take NM 4 east for Redondo Campground, Los Griegos area, and west of La Cueva on NM 126 and Valle San Antonio Rd. to Upper San Antonio Canyon.

**East Fork of the Jemez River** is mostly level through the Santa Fe National Forest, with plenty of ponderosa pine and the glorious silence of a landscape in deep winter. You'll find the trailhead 10 miles north of La Cueva. This trail also works for mountain biking.

**SNOW SPORTS—DOWNHILL SKIING** Sandia Peak Ski Area (505-242-9052). Take I-40 east to Cedar Crest exit 175, north on NM 14, left on NM 536 for 6 miles to ski area. Or take the Sandia Peak Ariel Tram at 30 Tramway Loop NE, Albuquerque. Open daily Dec. 19–Jan. 6, 9–4; Wed.–Sun. and holidays Jan. 10–Mar. 11, 9–4. Thirty trails are serviced by four chairlifts. The area has a children's lift, some of the longest cruising terrain in the state, snow sports school, ski rental shop, and café. Skiers and snowboarders need to rent equipment at the base if taking the tram, or drive up. There are no rentals at the lift. $50 all-day lift; $62 tram and lift.

**SPAS** Green Reed Spa (505-796-7500), Sandia Resort & Casino, 30 Rainbow Rd., Albuquerque. Total pampering waits in this full-service spa amid the soothing sounds of waterfalls, with body treatments that incorporate indigenous healing plants, such as the green reed found in the bosque for the Green Reed Polish and clay from the desert for the Clay Body Wrap.

**Tamaya Mist Spa & Salon** (505-867-1234), Hyatt Regency Tamaya, 1300 Tuyuna Trail. Inspired by the prehistoric journey of their people, the spa offers various pathways to rejuvenation and healing through salt scrubs, herbal wraps, expert massage, and facials. Pricey and worth the price.

**WIND SURFING** Cochiti Lake (505-465-0307). Sixty miles north of Albuquerque, west of I-25 at Santo Domingo exit. Wind surfing on this no-wake lake with paved boat ramp and campground is popular Apr.–Oct.

**WINERIES** Anasazi Fields Winery (505-867-3062), Camino de Pueblitos Rd. at the western edge of Placitas. Open Wed.–Sun. noon–5 summer months; winter weekends only, or by appointment. This winery has made a name for itself by featuring dry, not sweet, fruit wines of apricot, peach, plum, wild cherry, and New Mexico raspberry.

**Corrales Winery** (505-898-1819), 6275 Corrales Rd., Corrales. Tasting room open Wed.–Sun. noon–5. Specializing in producing unique flavors of small-batch New Mexico wines grown from New Mexico grapes, this winery is set beside its own vineyard. Especially recommended is its Muscat Canelli dessert wine.

**Milagro Vineyards** (505-898-3998), 985 W. Ella, Corrales. Tours of vineyards and winery, as well as tasting room hours by appointment only. "Handcrafted Vine to Wine" is the slogan of this boutique winery, dedicated to making wine from grapes grown in New Mexico. Small quantities of Merlot, Zinfandel, and Chardonnay are aged in French oak.

**Ponderosa Valley Vineyard and Winery** (575-834-7487), 3171 NM 290, Ponderosa. Tasting room open Tues.–Sat. 10–5, Sun. noon–5. With grapes planted in 1976 in the Ponderosa Valley of the Jemez Mountains, proprietors Henry and Mary Street produce award-winning Riesling, as well as pinot noir, Viognier, and more.

## ✷ Green Space

**Cibola National Forest and Grasslands** (505-346-2650). Six developed campgrounds and 100 miles of hiking and horse trails are found, mainly in the Manzano Mountains, within an hour to a two-and-a-half-hour drive from Albuquerque, east on I-40, and south at Tijeras exit. Two of the most popular camping areas are at Tajique, and Fourth of July Canyon is famous for its flaming red fall color. Roads and campgrounds are frequently closed during winter months, so be sure to call the above number before venturing out. Free.

**Fenton Lake State Park** (888-667-2757), 33 miles northwest of San Ysidro via NM 4, then left at La Cueva on NM 126. Open summer 6 AM–9 PM, winter 7–7. Ponderosa pines sweep down to the shore of this picture-pretty small 28-acre lake stocked with rainbow trout. Only small rowboats and canoes are allowed. There are 40 developed campsites, some with hookups. One trail that converts to an easy 2-mile cross-country ski loop in winter. Love this place! $5; $8 camping.

**Manzano Mountains State Park** (888-667-2757). Go northwest of Mountainair on NM 55 or about an hour south of Albuquerque on I-40 east, then south at Tijeras exit. Open Apr. 1–Oct. 31, 7:30–sunset. Birds love this place. Take the opportunity to spot 200 species, including mountain bluebirds, hummingbirds, jays, and hawks. There is also trout fishing in Manzano Lake. Campsites. $5 per vehicle; $10–18 camping. When fire danger is high, the park is closed.

**Ortiz Mountain Educational Preserve** (505-471-9103), A 1,350-acre Santa Fe County Preserve managed by the Santa Fe Botanic Garden. Reaches through the Ortiz peaks outside Madrid allowing for a moderate hike to 9,000-foot Placer Peak. Open Mar.–Nov. Available by tour only. Call for schedules. Under the management of the Santa Fe Botanical Garden (www.santafebotanicalgarden.org), which also includes the Botanic Garden on Museum Hill in Santa Fe and the Leonora Curtin Wetland Preserve near Galisteo.

**Sandia Ranger District** (505-281-3304), visitors center at Sandia Crest. Open 8–4:30. Closed Sat. and Sun. and during winter. Hiking, mountain biking, cross-country skiing best accessed by driving the Crest Road, NM 536 to Sandia Crest, or taking the Sandia Peak Aerial Tram. Day use only. $3.

**WILDLIFE REFUGES AND AREAS Ladd S. Gordon Waterfowl Complex** (505-864-9187), 4 miles north of Bernardo on NM 116. Over 5,000 acres along the Rio Grande are divided into several different units where wildlife viewing, fishing, and hunting in season take place at this state managed waterfowl area.

**Las Huertas Canyon** (no phone). Continue on NM 165 through Placitas and up the mountain 7 miles. This narrow scenic drive up through the rugged Sandia foothills often offers the running water of Las Huertas Creek, and there are several nice places to camp and fish. In the evening, you have a good possibility of sighting bear. I have seen them here, so keep alert and keep food locked up unless you plan on sharing your picnic with them. Las Huertas Canyon makes a moderate-to-difficult 15-mile mountain bike trail. Free.

**Sevilleta National Wildlife Refuge** (505-864-4021), 20 miles north of Socorro off I-25 at exit 169. Headquarters is located on the west side of I-25. This Chihuahuan desert ecosystem research center refuge hosts an annual open house with guided tours in October. Special educational tours may be arranged. Mon.–Fri. 7:30–4, Sat. 9–4. Closed Sun. Tour wetlands by foot or car; hike San Lorenzo Mountain; walk desert trails. Free.

✪ **Wildlife West Nature Park** (505-281-7655), I-40 east, exit 187, 87 N. Frontage Rd., Edgewood. Open daily summer 10–6, winter noon–4 or by appointment. This is an interactive 122-acre wildlife park where rescued critters, such as coyotes, cougars, bobcats, mountain lions, and wolves, may be observed in their natural habitats. An easy walk. Camping, plus music festivals, and other scheduled events, including chuckwagon suppers, makes this a good place to take the family. $5, $4 children over age 5, under age 5 free.

## ✳ Lodging

**BED & BREAKFASTS Blue Horse B&B** (877-258-4677; www .bluehorsebandb.com), 300 Camino de Las Huertas, Placitas. Utterly adobe, utterly Southwest, utterly situated to maximize the glorious sunsets, stars, and mesas up in Placitas, the Blue Horse promises privacy and the deep quiet that promotes deep rest in any of its three rooms. Gather around the kiva fireplace to unwind and enjoy breakfasts of Swedish pancakes,

crêpes, waffles, and omelets. You deserve this! $115.

**Casa Blanca Guest House and Garden Cottage** (575-829-3579), 17521 NM 4, Jemez Springs. Known for exquisite gardens, with a riverfront terrace and grandmother cottonwoods on the premises, this lodging is classically New Mexico, with thick vigas (ceiling beams) and a kiva fireplace in the guest house, which sleeps four and has a kitchenette. The cottage, where you can hear the Jemez River lull you to sleep, rents for $115 a night and sleeps two. The advantage here is that you can walk to town. $160–170.

**Casa de Koshare** (505-898-4500; www.casadekoshare.com), 122 Ashley Ln. NW, Corrales. The *koshares* are the sacred clowns of the Indian dances, and this delightful B&B goes all the way with the Native American–Southwestern theme, with a Storyteller Suite and a Warrior Room among its four accommodations. It's a little piece of heaven here, with breakfast catered to your needs and appetite and panoramic views of the Sandia Mountains and city lights from the garden patio. Discounts are offered for extended stays. $139–199.

**Chocolate Turtle B&B** (505-898-1800; www.chocolateturtlebb.com), 1098 W. Meadowlark Ln., Corrales. Four charming and colorful Southwest-style rooms, big picture views of the Sandias, free WiFi and 24-hour complimentary snacks, plus a huge delicious breakfast served on the covered portal in season make this an appealing alternative for the business traveler who is simply tired of hotel living. $129–159.

**Elaine's, A Bed & Breakfast** (800-821-3092 or 505-281-2467; www.elainesbnb.com), 72 Snowline Road, Cedar Crest. Elaine O'Neal has been providing hospitality in the East Mountains for so long, she must be doing something right. You can be sure you will be well taken care of here in this five-room rural setting, with hot tub and handicapped access. Elaine's also offers golf packages. $99–149.

♂ **Hacienda Vargas B&B Inn** (800-261-0006 or 505-867-9115; www.haciendavargas.com), 1431 NM 313, Algodones. Saturated with history, the seven rooms here, part of a 17th-century hacienda, each with private entrance, compose the only bed & breakfast actually located on the Camino Real in New Mexico. Sweet dreams will be yours within the serenity of thick adobe walls, and you will be greeted in the morning with the house special, pumpkin pancakes with roasted piñon nuts. You'll be ready for a day of exploring in either Albuquerque or Santa Fe. $89–149.

**HOTELS, RESORTS, AND LODGES** ☘ **Elk Mountain Lodge** (575-829-3159; www.elkmountainlodge.com), 37485 NM 126, La Cueva, just west of junction of NM 4 and NM 126. If you are seeking a romantic getaway that offers convenience to hiking, cross-country skiing, and fishing in the heart of the Jemez Mountains, this four-room, comfy rustic log lodge is the place. Reviews are uniformly positive. A candlelit in-room whirlpool spa helps soothe exercised muscles, and a simple continental breakfast is included. A café and general store are just across the way. Pet-friendly. $99–179.

& **Hyatt Regency Tamaya Resort & Spa** (505-867-1234; www.tamaya.hyatt.com), 1300 Tuyuna Trail, Santa Ana. Convenient to Santa Fe as well as Albuquerque, the Hyatt Tamaya works just as well as a secluded self-contained resort with the Sandias as backdrop. It has 350 rooms, many with private balconies; a fabulous spa; Twin Warriors Golf; the Rio Grande Lounge, with live entertainment; two restaurants; a knockout art collection; demonstrations of bread baking and other arts—all in an exquisite pueblo-style setting that qualifies it as a "cultural resort." You might find it worth the big bucks for the best money can buy. In the works are "Dude Ranch" packages, which include horseback riding in Santa Ana lands. Golf and spa specials and packages are available. Hypoallergenic rooms are available. A top choice! Visit the website for really good deals. $159–299.

& **Isleta Resort & Casino** (505-724-3800), 11000 Broadway SE, Albuquerque; 13 miles south of Albuquerque, exit 215 to NM 47. Known for its gaming, golf, fishing, camping, dining, and entertainment, this is a great place just to come and play. There's even the Isleta Fun Connection, which has you covered on bowling, billiards, laser tag, and arcade games. The big names headline here. Country stars who have appeared on this stage include Willie Nelson, Alan Jackson, and Randy Travis. Whatever your taste buds are craving, you can find it here in one of the seven restaurants. There's always something happening here. $159.

& **Sandia Resort & Casino** (505-796-7500), 30 Rainbow Rd. NE, Albuquerque. Following a recent multimillion-dollar expansion, Sandia Resort has emerged as a posh new seven-story hotel. It has 228 Southwest-style spacious rooms with Ernest Thompson–designed furnishings. The four restaurants are the Council Room Steakhouse; the rooftop Bien Shur, featuring New American cuisine (overseen by well-known chef Jim White); a deli; and a buffet. The resort also boasts a fitness center, salon, upscale spa, the Green Reed, plus a championship golf course. The likes of Trisha Yearwood, the Gipsy Kings, Lyle Lovett, and Harry Connick Jr. appeared recently in the

THE FIREPLACE AT HYATT TAMAYA IS A COZY PLACE TO RELAX.

HOMESTEADER AND JACK-OF-ALL-TRADES POP SHAFFER DESIGNED HIS OWN BRAND OF PUEBLO DECO ART FOR THE DINING ROOM CEILING OF HIS MOUNTAINAIR HOTEL.

Sandia Amphitheater, and the lounge has live entertainment nightly until midnight. $169–299.

**Shaffer Hotel** (505-847-2888; www .shafferhotel.com), 103 E. Main St., Mountainair. This art deco vintage hotel, a New Mexico treasure built by blacksmith, jack-of-all-trades, and folk artist Clem "Pop" Shaffer in 1923, has been remodeled, offering five rooms with shared bath, three suites and double suites for families, and 10 rooms with private baths, all done in period furniture. The rooms are not large, but they are adequate. The café on the premises has been up and down, much like the ownership of this hotel. All in all, this is probably your best base site for exploring the nearby ruins. Rates from $30 with shared bath, all the way up to $138.

**CABINS AND CAMPING** See "State Parks" under *Green Space*, for camping.

**Coronado Campground** (505-980-8256), 106 Monument Rd., Bernalillo,

US 550 next to Coronado State Monument. Open year-round. Tenting Mar. 1–Oct. 1 only. No discounts for tents. Reservations advised for this serene 27-hookup RV park, popular due to its views overlooking the bosque and the splendid northwest view of the Sandias. $22.

♦ **Trails End RV Park** (575-829-4072), 37695 NM 126, Jemez Springs. Open May 15–Oct. 30. Weekly and monthly only, age 20 and older only, preapproved pets okay, advanced reservations only for these 10 full hookup sites (WiFi included) located in old growth ponderosa pine close to all the outdoor recreational opportunities of the Santa Fe National Forest along the Jemez. $35. Prices reduced based on length of stay.

## ✳ Where to Eat

**DINING OUT Corn Maiden** (505-771-6060), Hyatt Tamaya Resort, 1300 Tuyana Tr., Santa Ana Pueblo. I-25 exit 242, US 550 to Tamaya Blvd., 1.5 miles to the resort. Dinner

ALTHOUGH HE NEVER CALLED HIMSELF AN ARTIST, POP SHAFFER'S GATE IN MOUNTAINAIR IS REGARDED AS ONE OF NEW MEXICO'S FOLK ART TREASURES.

only, Wed.–Sun. 5:30–9. This, the Tamaya's upscale restaurant, presents the signature rotisserie, more than you can possibly eat, of an assortment of gigantic skewers of meat, fish, sausage, and chicken, each flavored with its own delectable marinade, including signature salad and green chile potatoes. Also serves NM Heritage locally ranched beef, tableside clay pot chicken, and tapas. Thurs. night is a three-course rotisserie $45 prix fixe menu with complimentary valet. Very Expensive.

♂ **Luna Mansion** (505-865-7333), 110 W. Main St., Los Lunas. Open for dinner Tues.–Sun. 5–9, brunch Sun. 11–2. This grand 1821 historic mansion, an architectural anomaly of Southern plantation–style adobe architecture, with Ionic white columns spanning two stories, is a local institution that holds much of the area's history, with its vintage family photos of Luna and Otero families. It is a favorite of ghost hunters—many report seeing a ghostly figure of a woman in the rocking chair on the landing. The second-story Spirit Lounge has happy hour and wine specials, open daily 3:30. Serves aged prime steaks. Note: The posted menu says "prices subject to change any time." Moderate–Expensive.

**Prairie Star** (505-867-3327), 288 Prairie Star Rd., Santa Ana. Dinner only. Open Sun.–Thurs. 5–9, Fri.–Sat. 5–10. A special-occasion restaurant with everything you could want in the way of atmosphere and service, Prairie Star is located in an elegant 1920s adobe home. Chef Darren McHale combines imaginative flavors in ways that allow the ingredients to chime together without confusion. The second-floor lounge shows off the Sandias, and the soft lighting and New Mexico art on the walls sets the stage for a special evening. Under management of the Santa Ana Pueblo, the Prairie Star's menu features upscale Southwest-based (not dominated) cuisine, including the very best game, fresh fish, bison, and Niman Ranch sirloin. Bring someone you want to impress here. Start with the avocado caprese and go for the piñon-smoked beef tenderloin. Expensive–Very Expensive.

**EATING OUT Banana Leaf Asian Grill** (505-892-6119), 355 NM 528 SE, Rio Rancho. Open daily. Lunch and dinner. Serving what many believe is some of the Asian cuisine in the area, this small family-run café has been a hit ever since it opened not five years ago with its Thai, Vietnamese, and Chinese food, which are all delicious and well spiced. Go for the Thai. Curries and wraps are fresh and flavorful. And it has a surprisingly cool interior, considering the strip mall location. Inexpensive.

**Corrales Bistro Brewery** (505-897-1036), 4908 Corrales Rd., Corrales. Open daily. Brunch Wed.–Sun., lunch, dinner, entertainment nightly. Serving fare that is several cuts above standard brewpub food, with generous portions and reasonable prices, this place is always hopping. My friends and I love it. Put together in a darn friendly atmosphere, with homemade soup of the day; fresh salads; wraps and sandwiches, such as the embellished pastrami Pancho de la Plancha Greenblat; and the Tower of Power fries and burger, plus over a dozen New Mexico microbrews, and you've got a big winner. Kids welcome. Inexpensive.

**El Comedor de Anayas** (505-832-4442), 1009 W. Hwy. 66, Moriarty. Open daily 6:30 AM–9 PM. Breakfast, lunch, dinner. You can tell this place is a Route 66 icon by the twirling, multicolored neon "rotosphere," restored in 2003 as part of the Route 66 neon restoration project. From the old-timer ranchers and farmers who meet here for their morning coffee klatch to the families who stop in for dinner, all enjoy the homey atmosphere and home-cooked Mexican food served up in healthy portions. Chiles rellenos and sopaipillas rate highly, and the green chile is not to be scoffed at. Sunday buffet will fill you up for $8 per person. When in Moriarty, you won't find a better place to dine. Inexpensive.

**Flying Star Café** (505-938-4717), 10700 Corrales Rd., Corrales. Open daily 6 AM–11 PM, Fri.–Sat. 6 AM–11:30 PM. Located just north of Alameda Blvd. in front of the Bosque Trail, this is the perfect place to meet friends. Drop in for a late-night snack of Key lime pie, a morning latte and blueberry scone, or just a bowl of soup and a sandwich, anytime. Homemade egg salad and chicken salad, and the grilled beef and chile sandwich are favorites. Known for burgers and fries, milk shakes, vegetarian fare. But the tab can add up quickly. Moderate.

**Hannah & Nate's Market Cafe** (505-898-2370), 4512 Corrales Rd., Corrales. Breakfast, Lunch daily. The place for Sunday brunch, this is a cozy spot where neighbors and family meet up. It serves excellent coffee. I love the spinach and mushroom omelet and the huevos rancheros, and the heavenly hash, a pile of home fries topped with eggs and chile. Many

dishes, such as the NM Eggs Benedict, feature the café's tender *carne adovada*. A wonderfully relaxing way to begin a Sunday. Inexpensive.

**Joe's Pasta House** (505-892-3333), 3201 Southern Blvd. SE, Rio Rancho. Lunch, dinner Mon.–Sat. Baked cannelloni with homemade pasta, delicious pesto, saltimbocca, and a $15 early-bird dinner catering to seniors make Joe's a comfortable hangout for locals. The menu is extensive. Inexpensive–Moderate.

**Los Ojos Restaurant & Saloon** (505-829-3547), NM 4, Jemez Springs. Despite the relatively new addition of an outdoor patio, nothing could be better than the dark, woody interior of this classic western bar. Go for the "Famous Jemez Burger" or, on weekend nights, the prime rib special. There are always folks shooting pool. Count on waitresses with attitude and characters with plenty of tales at the bar. This is the place to warm up with a hot bowl of green chile stew or a plate of red chile enchiladas in front

TRY THE FAMOUS JEMEZ BURGER AT LOS OJOS RESTAURANT & SALOON IN JEMEZ SPRINGS.

YOU MAY RUN INTO A MOVIE STAR OR A SALTY OLD MINER AT MARY'S BAR IN CERRILLOS.

of the massive rock fireplace after a day's cross-country skiing. Inexpensive.

**Mama Lisa's Ghost Town Kitchen– No Pity Café** (505-471-5769), 2859 NM 14, Madrid. Mama Lisa's is the kind of roadside stop you dream about. Offering "good food that's good for you," Mama bakes everything, including her breads, rolls, red chile chocolate cake, and apple walnut strudel, fresh, by hand, daily. The barbecue brisket sandwich with chipotle sauce is a marvel worth the drive on its own. Absolutely so casual and laidback, you might think you've timetraveled back to 1968. Call for days and hours. "Probably" open every day but Monday, from, "like," 10–3. The availability of items and service may be inconsistent. Inexpensive.

**Mary's Bar**, Main St., Cerrillos. It may look closed on the outside, but this bar is inside the 120-year-old building built by Mary Mora's father. Bartender and befriender of movie stars (here on shooting schedules), 90-something Mary holds forth, pours forth, and remains the town historian and storyteller. Inexpensive. Warning to the allergic: Cats abound.

**The Merc at Placitas** (505-867-8661), 221 NM 165, Homestead Village, Placitas. A well-stocked grocery store and take-out deli with homemade soups, and a local hangout selling beer, wine, and spirits. The high point of the week is the 4–6:30 PM Friday wine tasting. Mon.–Sat. 9–8, Sun. 9–6.

**Mine Shaft Tavern** (505-473-0743), 2846 NM 14, Madrid. Open daily. Lunch, dinner. Sun.–Thurs. 11:30–7:30; Fri.–Sat. 11:30–9; bar open "late." "New Mexico roadhouse cuisine" is the specialty, as are the locally sourced green chile burgers with hand-cut fries, homemade guac, salsa, and green chile stew. Long a big-time biker hangout, the Mine Shaft was constructed in 1946 as a coal company town saloon with a 40-foot-long lodgepole pine bar. Fifteen beers are on tap. If you haven't been to the Mine Shaft, you haven't been to Madrid. Live entertainment on weekends. Moderate.

**Perea's Restaurant & Tijuana Bar** (505-898-2442), 4590 Corrales Rd., Corrales. Open Mon.–Sat. 11:30–2. Lunch only. This 300-year-old building was constructed of terrones, blocks of mud cut from the river. The original construction is displayed inside. You can't eat the history; however, you certainly can eat the classic green chile enchiladas, *carne adovada*, and the chicken enchilada casserole. Inexpensive.

**Range Café** (505-867-1700), 925 Camino del Pueblo, Bernalillo. Open daily 7:30 AM–9:30 PM. With live music on weekends; casual, consistent home cooking served in huge portions (e.g., meat loaf and mashed potatoes and chicken-fried steak); plus excellent pancakes, huevos rancheros, and divine desserts, with its trademark "Death by Lemon," no wonder this is a great gathering spot. Expect to wait in line for Sunday breakfast. Moderate.

**Santa Ana Café** (505-771-6060), Hyatt Tamaya Resort, 1300 Tuyuna Tr., Santa Ana. Open daily 6:30 AM–10 PM. Breakfast, lunch, dinner. A fine place to enjoy a Sunday brunch or Friday evening prime rib buffet, and a place to try interesting lighter fare, such as fish and salads, with a native twist the rest of the time. Moderate–Expensive.

**Teofilo's** (505-865-5511), 144 Main St., Los Lunas, across from the Luna Mansion. Lunch, dinner. Closed Mon. This simple, welcoming 1912 adobe

AT THE MINE SHAFT TAVERN IN MADRID, NOTHING GETS BETWEEN A MAN AND HIS DOG.

THE RANGE CAFÉ IN BERNALILLO IS THE PLACE TO HEAR LIVE MUSIC ON WEEKENDS, WATCH THE GAME, OR JUST HANG OUT.

home serves some of the best, most consistent New Mexican food anywhere. The yeasted hot sopaipillas are little pillows of heaven when slathered with honey, and the red chile is superb. There's no better place for Sunday lunch, and the patio is lovely in warm weather. Who needs Santa Fe? This is the real deal. Hours change seasonally. Inexpensive.

## ✻ Entertainment

**Old West Saloon & Engine House Theater** (505-438-3780), 2846 NM 14, Madrid. Full bar and menu on weekends; special events and concerts held in the historic theater. Open daily during summer (starting Apr.); winter Sat. and Sun. only.

**Sandia and Isleta Pueblos** offer big-name entertainment; popular comedians, musicians, and performers; as well as those who were big "back in the day." See listings under "Hotels, Resorts, and Lodges."

**Santa Ana Star Center** (505-891-7300), 3001 Civic Center, Rio Rancho. Find a busy schedule of sports events, car shows, concerts, ice shows, and much more at this spiffy facility.

✐ **Wildlife West Nature Park** (505-281-87655), 87 N. Frontage Rd., Edgewood. Sat. 6–10, June 30–Sept. 1, chuckwagon BBQ feast followed by vintage western swing music.

## ✻ Selective Shopping

**Bien Mur Indian Market Center** (505-821-5400), 100 Bien Mur Dr. NE. I-25 exit 234 east on Tramway Rd. Open Mon.–Sat. 9:30–5:30, Sun. 11–5:30. For high-quality, guaranteed-authentic Indian jewelry, rugs, pottery, baskets, and turquoise and silver jewelry, this is an excellent place to shop. You are sure to find something you simply must have at a fair price.

**Cowgirl Red** (505-474-0344), 2865 NM 14, Madrid. Everything cool for the cowgirl or wannabe, especially those prize vintage boots—500 pairs to tempt you, plus vintage and contemporary Native American jewelry and art. If you have time for only one shopping stop in Madrid, that's sad, but this here's the place.

**Just Imagine Gallery & Coffee House** (505-281-9611), 488 E. NM 66, Tijeras. Some of the prettiest dresses may be found at Just Imagine—dresses in a feminine, Victorian-Gypsy style that may have been popular in the 1960s do not look at all dated here. The shop also has beautiful jewelry and well-selected home and garden pieces. This is also the site of the **Tijeras Open-Air Arts Market**, weekends May–mid-Oct., 10–5, a delightful way to spend a summer afternoon, with live music and dance. Farmers' Market on Wed. afternoon.

**Johnsons of Madrid** (505-438-3780), 2846 NM 14, Madrid. In a town with 30 galleries, Johnsons remains the first and oldest, featuring regional textiles, fiber arts, photography, and fine art.

**Walatowa Visitor Center** (575-834-7235). See "Guidance."

## ✳ Special Events

*March and April:* Join **Hawk Watch** (505-255-7622; www.hawkwatch.org) for raptor counts in March and April in the Sandias—assist with the raptor count and learn about the migrating birds of prey from interpretive rangers on-site (see also September).

*May:* Memorial Day weekend, **Jemez Pueblo Red Rocks Arts & Crafts Festival** (575-834-7235).

*June–July:* **Music at the Ballpark** (505-471-1054), Madrid. Music festivals of all kinds held here. **Wildlife**

**West** (505-281-7655), Edgewood. Third weekend in June, **Bluegrass Weekend**, with bands, vendors, workshops, zoo tours, chuckwagon BBQ and western swing music. **Annual Pork and State BBQ Championship** (888-746-7262), early July, Rio Rancho.

*August:* **Las Fiestas de San Lorenzo** (505-867-5252), Bernalillo. Traditionally held August 9–10 to honor the town's patron saint, the fiesta features the ancient Matachines dances, performed in the streets.

*September:* Labor Day weekend, **Bernalillo Wine Festival**. Also in September, visit the **Manzano Hawk Watch Migration Site** (505-255-7622; www.hawkwatch.org), 1420 Carlisle Blvd. SE, Ste. 206, Albuquerque. Join Hawk Watch for raptor counts in September and October in the Manzanos, at Capilla Peak, off FR 245, near Manzano, in Cibola National Forest.

*October:* **Corrales Harvest Festival** (505-350-3955), Corrales: music, hayrides, produce, and storytelling. Also **National Pinto Bean Festival** (505-832-4087), Moriarty.

*December:* **Christmas in Madrid** (505-471-1054): an annual community open house and parade. **Christmas at Kuaua** (505-867-5351), Coronado State Monument, December 20, 5:30–8:30 PM, with luminarias and Pueblo and Spanish dancing. Free. **Farolito Tour** (505-829-3530), Jemez State Monument, 5–8 PM: Pueblo dances and music, plus 1,500 farolitos light up ancient Giusewa Pueblo ruins. Free.

# Albuquerque and Beyond

## 2

## ALBUQUERQUE: THE DUKE CITY

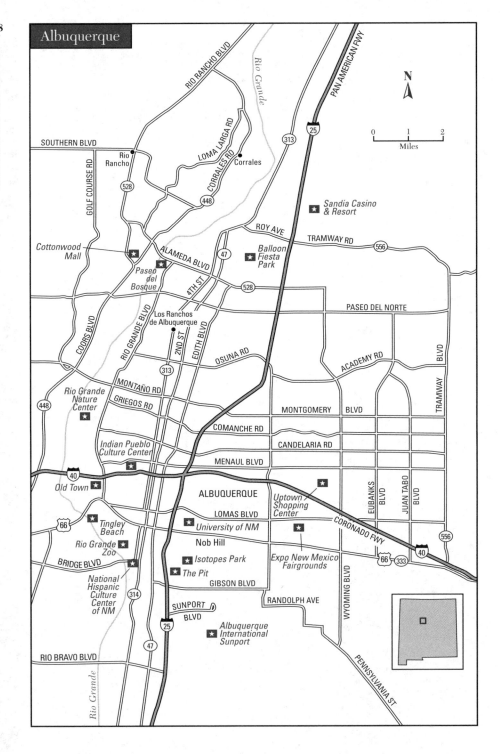

**Albuquerque**

# ALBUQUERQUE: THE DUKE CITY

Severeral years ago, a movement emerged to change the spelling of "Albuquerque." Some wanted to restore the missing r, so the city's name would be
spelled "Alburquerque," like its Spanish forebear, the original Duke of Alburquerque. Although that idea never took hold, there is no arguing that Albuquerque,
New Mexico, takes great pride in its Spanish heritage.

There were as many as 40 Indian pueblos in the province of Tiguex (t-gway)
existing in the Rio Grande Valley at the time of the Spanish conquest. The city
was founded by a determined band of families through a land grant from the
Spanish crown. They settled in the Old Town area and left a legacy of a Spanish identity that has endured, through subsequent waves of immigration, to the
present.

Today's Albuquerque, with a population of approximately 546,000 and a
growth rate of over 21 percent between 2000 and 2010, boasts a rainbow of Italian, Chinese, Indian, Japanese, Mexican, African American, Thai, Vietnamese,
and Native American communities, families, and neighborhoods. Ethnic identities continue to find expression in festivals, places of worship, restaurants, and
shops that give the city much of its vitality.

Centrally located within New Mexico at the crossroads of east–west I-40
and north–south I-25, Albuquerque is fairly easy to navigate as it is divided into
quadrants, with Central Ave., or Old Route 66, dividing the city into its north
and south sides. Route 66 neon lights up the night along Central, the boule-
vard that extends through the core of the city and where the University of New
Mexico, Nob Hill, Presbyterian Hospital, Downtown, and Old Town may be
found. Broadway is the street that divides the city into its east and west sides.
(One helpful navigational tool: The Sandia Mountains are to the east, while the
volcanoes and the river are to the west.) The Rio Grande meanders through
the length of the city north to south, providing a 15-mile greenbelt and a much-
loved running, walking, and bike path that serves as an urban park.

Albuquerque has gone through various transformations over the past 150
years. The arrival of the railroad in the 1880s brought a "new town" commercial and population expansion to merge with the historic Old Town area settled
originally in 1706. The town developed east of Carlisle Blvd. with World War
II and the Atomic Era as Sandia Laboratory and Kirtland Air Force Base again

expanded the numbers and diversity of the population. Then, in the 1970s, Intel Corp. arrived on the West Side, and with it a critical mass of newcomers that expanded the life of a small-town mom-and-pop business base into a magnetic relocation site for people and business. Mesa del Sol, a live-work "smart" community on the south end of town is heralded as a new growth center. Downtown, EDO (East of Downtown), Nob Hill and the International District, all along the Central Ave. corridor, are neighborhoods that continue to evolve and reimagine themselves. They are served increasingly well by public transportation and renovation.

The city has become something of a mecca for young creatives, web- and arts-savvy, educated, and energetic young folks who bring rich "cultural capital" that is finally being appreciated. Many are entrepreneurial and enterprising, and they find the diversity and openness, as well as the cultural richness of the town, to their liking. After all, Albuquerque has a tradition of small entrepreneurs. Religious and lifestyle freedom and toleration are givens, and alternative, artistic, and unconventional lifestyles coexist comfortably beside cowboy and blue-collar values. It is as if the positive side of the code of the West, particularly respect for individuality, as well as an appreciation for community, has taken hold here.

In the arts, theater, spoken word, and filmmaking have found a home. There's a lively visual arts community and a variety of music scenes, too, from folk to salsa to jazz. The presence of the University of New Mexico nourishes the arts here, and the push to bring filmmaking to New Mexico initiated during the Gov. Bill Richardson era drew the talent to create a superb theater scene.

Distinct neighborhoods well worth exploring include Nob Hill, a walking district packed with small shops and cafés east of the university; Downtown, with its movie theater and bars, generally considered the "entertainment district"; the University of New Mexico, with its prototypical southwest architecture; Huning Highlands, a stronghold of Victorian homes, overlapping with EDO; and Old Town. The North and South Valleys, each with their agrarian traditions, maintain their particular flavors and compounds of history, architecture, commerce, and cuisine. What we think of as the North Valley actually was a group of independent farming villages until after WW II.

The Sawmill neighborhood, in the area of 12th St. NW and Mountain Rd., and in walking distance of Old Town museums and the Harwood Arts Center, continues to gain popularity and interest. Cafés, bakeries, and galleries keep popping up along the convenient stretch of Mountain Rd. between Rio Grande and Fourth St. NW.

A walk or bicycle ride through these neighborhoods yields a feeling for the city that is impossible to obtain while driving through along the freeway, with its deceptive view of a city blockaded by mundane urban sprawl.

Route 66, the Mother Road, winds east to west through the city like a ribbon of neon, granting Central Avenue a nostalgic heart. From original Route 66 motels to restored historic gas stations now adapted as popular watering holes, it retains its sense as a destination for travelers and explorers, even as they mingle with the descendants of eight and twelve generations of families who have lived in the same community.

The city continues to interpret itself and its culture in a wider way, with the National Hispanic Cultural Center of New Mexico, the Museum of Art and History, and the Museum of Natural History and Science; intelligent and emerging galleries of significance; and a growing diversity of shopping, dining, learning, and entertainment venues. Annual festivals, such as Globalquerque, Folk Arts, Arts and Crafts, Balloon Fiesta, Weems Arts, State Fair, and many more, keep folks out and about and enjoying life.

A selection of gaming resorts nearby at Isleta, San Felipe, Santa Ana, Sandia, and Laguna Pueblo's Route 66 Casino are venues that attract top entertainment. The popularity of the Uptown outdoor shopping mall is triggering adjacent development. With 360 days of sunshine, as well as four distinct seasons, Albuquerque also appeals to those who appreciate easy access to outdoor activities.

Albuquerque has traded much of its old New Mexico edge for the influx of new people, money, ideas, shopping, and access to medicine and technology. While it continuously becomes more like everyplace else, there is something within it, perhaps the centuries of indigenous, then Spanish colonial, pioneer spirit, that refuse to be deleted from the city's cultural memory. It is not, nor will it ever be, completely prettied up or smoothed out. It continues to be a magnet for entrepreneurs, immigrants, artists, retirees, and especially for those with hopes of making it in the West.

To find out what is happening, check out www.dukecityfix.com, www.kunm .org, or look at calendars in the *Weekly Alibi* and *Venue* or the Friday entertainment section of the *Albuquerque Journal*.

**GUIDANCE Albuquerque Convention & Visitors Bureau** (505-842-9918), 201 First St. NW, Ste. 601, Albuquerque.

**Albuquerque Hispano Chamber of Commerce** (505-842-9003), 1309 Fourth St. SW, Albuquerque.

**Greater Albuquerque Chamber of Commerce** (505-764-3700), 115 Gold Ave. SW, Ste. 201, Albuquerque.

**Key Numbers:** Dialing 311 in town brings listings of cultural happenings; alternatively, phone 505-768-3556.

**GETTING THERE** *By car:* Albuquerque lies at the crossroads of I-25 and I-40.

*By bus:* **Greyhound Bus** (505-243-7922), 320 First St. SW.

**Grey Line and TNM&O Coaches** (505-242-4998), 420 First St. SW.

*By air:* Many major airlines, including United, Southwest, Continental, and Delta, fly to the **Albuquerque International Sunport** (505-244-7700), 2200 Sunport Blvd. SE.

*By train:* **Amtrak** (800-872-7245 or 505-842-9650) brings passengers to Albuquerque daily from Chicago and Los Angeles. The **Alvarado Transportation Center** (505-852-9650), First and Central, or 320 First St. SW, downtown is the terminal for both bus and train passengers.

**GETTING AROUND** **ABQ Ride** (505-243-7433; www.cabq.gov/transit) includes a public bus system known as Rapid Ride that extends through an 11-mile corridor along Central Ave. and promises to deliver you 11 minutes between each stop. Fare is $1, and it can get you most places you want to go. Rapid Ride operates 6 AM–9 PM daily, and 6 AM–3 AM during the summer. Pick up schedules at the Alvarado Transportation Center, 100 First St. SW. The **New Mexico Rail Runner Express** (505-245-RAIL or 505-245-7245; www.nmrail runner.com), which stops here also, goes south to Belen and north to Bernalillo and Santa Fe. Rates are determined by zones. Schedules vary with seasons and special events. **Albuquerque Cab** (505-883-4888) and **Yellow Cab Co.** (505-243-7777) operate 24-hour service.

**WHEN TO COME** The **Albuquerque International Balloon Fiesta**, held the first two weeks of October, is the city's premier event.

**MEDICAL EMERGENCY** **Heart Hospital of New Mexico at Lovelace Medical Center** (505-724-2000), 504 Elm St. NE, Albuquerque.

**Presbyterian Hospital** (505-841-1819), 1100 Central Ave. SE, Albuquerque.

**University of New Mexico Hospital** (505-272-2111), 2211 Lomas Blvd. NE, Albuquerque.

## ✳ To See

**HISTORIC LANDMARKS, PLACES, AND SITES** **Ernie Pyle Memorial Branch Library** (505-256-2065), 900 Girard SE. Open Tues.–Sat. 10–6, Wed. 11–7. Closed Sun.–Mon. This modest little house in southeast Albuquerque, once the home of WW II correspondent and pioneer American journalist Ernie Pyle, who was killed in action, is a cozy, beloved neighborhood library with Pyle memorabilia.

**Harwood Art Center** (505-242-6367), 1114 Seventh St. NW, Albuquerque. Open Mon.–Thurs. 9–5, Fri. 9–4, first Fri. of the month 6–8, and by appointment. This 1925 Methodist girls' boarding school was refurbished as a community arts center, and the Art School at Harwood now offers an impressive calendar of arts classes, yoga, and dance. With five galleries and 45 artists' studios, the place is an artists' haven, with frequent exhibitions and many shows of new work.

**Old Town Albuquerque** (505-243-3215), south of I-25 near Rio Grande Blvd., or I-25 to Rio Grande Blvd. exit, then south. Or take Central Ave. west. The original site of Albuquerque, Old Town is a must-see for visitors who will enjoy museums, shops, restaurants, a traditional plaza, and Southwestern architecture.

**Sandia Man Cave** (no phone), NM 165, 5 miles southeast of Placitas. Rumored to be a hoax dreamed up by members of the University of New Mexico Anthropology Department, this cave in the Sandia Mountains is reputed to be the site holding evidence of ancient man. It has, by and large, been discredited as an ancient site.

THAT'S NOT CHIANG MAI. IT'S A
BUDDHIST NEW YEAR CELEBRATION
AT AN ALBUQUERQUE TEMPLE.

**San Felipe de Neri Catholic Church** (505-243-4628), 2005 N. Plaza St. NW, Albuquerque. Open daily. Museum open Mon.–Sat. 10–4. Founded in 1706 and in almost continuous use for 300 years, this Old Town landmark maintains a strong community today. Mass is held in English and Spanish. Free.

**MUSEUMS** ✎ **Albuquerque Balloon Museum** (505-880-0500), 9201 Balloon Museum Dr. NE Albuquerque, Balloon Fiesta Park. Open Tues.–Sun. 9–5. Closed Mon. Open 6 AM–6 PM during Balloon Fiesta. Named for pioneering Albuquerque balloonists Maxie Anderson and Ben Abruzzo, who completed the first manned crossing of the Atlantic Ocean in 1978, this museum has exhibits that highlight the development of hot-air and gas balloons in military, science, aerospace research, and for recreation. $4 adults, $3 New Mexico residents, $2 seniors, $1 children ages 4–12, under age 4 free.

**Albuquerque Museum of Art & History** (505-243-7255), 2000 Mountain Road NW, Albuquerque. Open Tues.–Sun. 9–5. Closed Mon. and city holidays. This premier city museum features art of the southwest, vintage Albuquerque, four centuries of Rio Grande Valley history, a sculpture garden, café, museum shop, and walking tours, as well as major traveling exhibitions. $4 adults, $3 New Mexico residents, $2 seniors, $1 children ages 4–12, under age 4 free. Free Sun. 9–1 and first Wed. each month.

✎ **American International Rattlesnake Museum and Gift Shop** (505-242-6569), 202 San Felipe NW, Albuquerque. Open Mon.–Sat. 10–6, Sun. 12–5. In Old Town you will find the largest exhibit of rattlesnake species, art, and artifacts in the world. $5 adults, $4 students, seniors, military; $3 children.

✎ **Explora** (505-224-8323), 1701 Mountain Rd. NW, Albuquerque. Open Mon.–Sat. 10–6, Sun. noon–6. This is a science center where families can explore science, technology, and art through interactive activities and 250 hands-on exhibits. $8 adults, $5 seniors, $4 children ages 1–11.

**516 Arts** (505-242-1445), 516 Central Ave. SW, Albuquerque. This "museum-style" gallery is two floors of ambitious, adventurous, and notable national, local, and regional work. Somewhat avant-garde, it remains intelligent and accessible. Tues.–Sat. 12-5. Free.

**Indian Pueblo Cultural Center** (505-843-7270), 2401 12th St. NW, Albuquerque. Open daily 9–5. There is no better place to learn about New Mexico's 19 pueblos than this museum, owned and operated by the pueblos. Two permanent exhibits showcase the history, culture, and artistic traditions of the pueblos. In addition, view exhibits of contemporary artists of painting, sculpture, and pottery. Browse the extensive gift shop that features authentic jewelry and Indian arts, plus books, music, and videos on tribal life. The Pueblo Harvest Cafe & Bakery serves Native American cuisine. Enjoy dance and artist demonstrations every weekend for the price of admission. $6 adults, $5.50 seniors, $3 students, $3 children ages 5–17, under age 4 free.

MAGNIFICENT OLD COTTONWOODS HAVE DEEP ROOTS IN THE ACEQUIAS (DITCHES) OF ALBUQUERQUE'S NORTH VALLEY.

**Maxwell Museum of Anthropology** (505-277-4405), 500 Redondo West Drive NE University of New Mexico, Albuquerque. Open Tues.–Sat. 10–4. Closed Sun. With over 10 million items in its collection, the Maxwell is considered one of the leading anthropological museums in the United States. Free.

KIDS GET HANDS-ON FUN AT EXPLORA.

**National Hispanic Cultural Center of New Mexico** (505-246-2261), 1701 Fourth St. SW, Albuquerque. Open Tues.–Sun. 10–5. Closed Mon. This splendid facility has bloomed as a center for music, dance, theater, and exhibits of art of the contemporary Hispanic world. Community events, including Día de los Muertos, Globalquerque, Latin Dance Festival, and Cinco de Mayo, are celebrated here as well. La Fonda del Bosque is the on-site restaurant, and La Tiendita, the gift shop, has a good selection of books on related subjects. $3 adults, $2 seniors, under age 16 free. Free Sun.

**National Museum of Nuclear Science and History** (505-245-2137), 601 Eubank SE, Albuquerque. Open daily 9–5. Closed Jan. 1, Easter, Thanksgiving, and Christmas. This museum is a resource for nuclear science, with exhibits, artifacts, and documentaries telling the story of the atomic age and its pioneers, as well as many related scientific topics. $8 adults, $5 seniors, $5 ages 7–17, free under age 5.

**New Mexico Holocaust and Intolerance Museum and Study Center** (505-247-0606), 616 Central Ave. SW, Albuquerque. Open Tues.–Sat. 11–3:30. Closed Sun. and Mon. The museum offers informational exhibits about genocide around the world. Admission by donation.

✿ **New Mexico Museum of Natural History and Science** (505-841-2800), 1801 Mountain Rd. NW, Albuquerque. Open daily 9–5. Closed Thanksgiving and Christmas. With a live volcano, huge dinosaurs, hands-on exhibits, natural history of New Mexico, a café, and an entertaining gift shop, this museum is guaranteed fun for the whole family. Starry Nights programs are given many

NEW MEXICO MUSEUM OF NATURAL HISTORY AND SCIENCE APPEALS TO KIDS OF ALL AGES.

Friday nights at the Planetarium ($7). Lockheed Martin DynaTheater ($10) shows hourly 10–5 daily. $7 adults, $6 seniors, $4 children ages 3–17, under age 3 free.

✍ **Rio Grande Nature Center** (505-344-7240), 2901 Candelaria NW, Albuquerque. Grounds open daily 8–5, Visitor Center 10–5. This small museum (really, an expanded visitors center) provides information on the flora and fauna of the bosque, as well as blinds for viewing waterfowl. It is a major entryway to the bike and walking paths of Rio Grande Valley State Park. Educational events and festivals are held throughout the year here. $3 per vehicle.

**Turquoise Museum** (505-247-8650), 2107 Central Avenue NW, Albuquerque. Open Mon.–Fri. 9:30–4.; Sat. 9:30–3. Closed Sun. Exhibits from 60 turquoise mines around the world, as well as the geology, mythology, and history of

✍ **Albuquerque Biological Park** (311 or 505-768-2000). Open daily 9–5, Sat. and Sun. 9–6 in summer. Closed Jan. 1, Thanksgiving, Christmas. This complex consists of an aquarium, botanic garden, and zoo (as described below), and the Tingley Beach fishing lakes (see under "Fishing" in *To Do* and under *Green Space*). $7 teens and adults ages 13–64, $3 seniors and ages 3–12. Combo tickets, with admission to aquarium, garden, and zoo, sold Tues.–Sun. before noon, $12 adults and bargain rates for children. Tickets entitle participants to ride the Rio Line train between the aquarium and the zoo, and the Thunderbird Express, a loop around the zoo.

**Albuquerque Aquarium** (505-764-6200), 2601 Central Ave. NW, Albuquerque. Exhibits trace Rio Grande from the Rockies to the Gulf Coast, with saltwater fish, invertebrates, and habitats of the Gulf of Mexico. There is a shark tank, reef fish, and turtles. Summer concerts Thurs. nights June–Aug. 7. See above for rates.

**Rio Grande Botanic Garden** (505-768-2000), 2601 Central Ave. NW, Albuquerque. Open Mon.–Fri. 9–5, Sat. and Sun. 9–6. Conservatory exhibits xeric plants of desert and Mediterranean climates, formal walled gardens, medicinal plants, Children's Fantasy Garden, Heritage Farm, and a Japanese garden. The PNM Butterfly Pavilion is open summers. Summer concerts are held Thurs. nights June–mid-Aug. at 7 PM, and holiday light festival is open evenings during Dec. See above for rates.

✍ **Rio Grande Zoological Park** (505-764-6200), 903 10th St. SW, Albuquerque. More than 1,000 animals are shown in their natural habitats. Those on the park's 64 acres include elephants, rhinos, giraffes, gorillas, wolves, polar bears, big cats, seals, tigers, amphibians, and reptiles. Zoo Music Concerts June–July, Fri. at 7. See above for rates.

turquoise, plus a lapidary room and gift shop, make this an irresistible stop. $4 adults, $3 seniors and ages 7–12, age 6 and under free.

**Unser Racing Museum** (505-341-1776), 1776 Montaño NW, Los Ranchos de Albuquerque. Open daily 10–4. Four generations of racecars, antique cars, winning pace cars, and uniforms that display the Unser family's racing accomplishments. $10 adults, $6 seniors, under age 16 free.

## ✷ To Do

Check www.itsatrip.org for the latest sports activities in and around the city.

**AMUSEMENT PARKS** ✿ **Cliff's Amusement Park** (505-881-9373; www.cliffsamusementpark.com), 4800 Osuna NE, Albuquerque. Roller coasters, water park, arcade, rides, and more rides: Cliff's is Albuquerque's answer to Disneyland.

**BICYCLING** Contact the **NM Touring Society** (president@nmts.org; www.nmts.org) for events.

The **City of Albuquerque** (311; www.cabq.gov/bike) provides maps for its many interconnecting bike paths.

**Rio Grande Valley State Park** has the 16-mile, practically level, Paseo del Bosque bike path through the bosque and parallel to the Rio Grande. (See *Green Space.*)

**CLIMBING Stone Age Climbing Gym** (505-341-2016), 4201 Yale NE. Climbing school, group events, and guided climbs in the Sandias.

**FARMERS' MARKETS** Early July–late Oct. Sat. mornings 7–noon.

BIKING ALONG THE PASEO DEL BOSQUE TRAIL.

**Albuquerque Downtown Market** (505-243-2230 ext.127), Eighth and Central SW, Robinson Park.

**Albuquerque Uptown Growers' Market** (505-865-3533), NE Corner Uptown parking lot, Louisiana and Uptown Blvd.

**Village of Los Ranchos Growers' Market** (505-890-2799), Los Ranchos City Hall, 6718 Rio Grande Blvd. NW.

**FISHING Tingley Ponds.** For generations preceding the polio scare of the 1950s, Tingley Beach was a popular swimming spot for Albuquerqueans. Includes a model boat pond. Restored as a fishing area with snack bar and train service running between here and the Biopark, Tingley Ponds is a good place to walk as well as fish for stockers. Boats and bike rentals available Memorial Day–Labor Day.

**GOLF Arroyo del Oso Golf Course** (505-884-7505), 7001 Osuna Rd. NE. Named for the Bear Canyon Arroyo, where it is located, the sloping topography of the 27-hole course makes it best suited to intermediate-advanced players. $15.75–31.50.

**The Championship Golf Course at the University of New Mexico** (505-277-4546), 3601 University Blvd. SE, Albuquerque. I-25 south to Rio Bravo exit, go left and continue half a mile. Open year-round, weather permitting. Soft spikes and collared shirts are required at this highly regarded, 18-hole public course known as UNM South or "the Monster." It has been ranked among the Top 25 public courses and boasts rolling fairways, panoramic views of the city, and undulating greens with a three-hole beginner course and driving range. $36–52.

**University of New Mexico North Course** (505-277-4146), 2201 Tucker NE. Play a midday nine holes on midcity greens shaded by tall trees. The perimeter of the course is also a popular walking and jogging path, adding up to 4 miles once around. $14–21.

**HIKING Elena Gallegos Park** (505-452-5217), 7100 Tramway Blvd. NE. This vast mountain park offers a variety of trails, plus panoramic views of the city. Trails permit hiking, biking, and horseback riding. This is a nice place for a summer evening picnic. Free.

**Juan Tabo Campground** (505-281-3304), 10 miles northeast of Albuquerque at NM 556 and FR 333. Open year-round. 22 picnic sites. $3.

**La Luz Trail** (505-281-3304). The trailhead is at the end of FR 444, or you can access the trail from Juan Tabo Campground. This 15-mile challenging round-trip hike to Sandia Crest over switchbacks is only for the very in-shape. Still, it is *the* Albuquerque hike. The trail goes through four life zones and rises over 3,000 feet to an altitude of 10,500 feet. As they say, you can always take the tram down. Some prefer to take the tram up and down. Travel well prepared for rapid weather change. Every summer, someone hikes up on a hot August afternoon, then gets hypothermia when the temperature falls 40 degrees and a hailstorm comes in. $3 per car.

**HORSEBACK RIDING Del Sol Equestrian Center** (505-873-0888), 6715 Isleta Blvd. SW. Horse boarding and lessons.

**Flying Horse School of Horsemanship** (505-822-8473), 9500 Wilshire Blvd. NE. Horse boarding and lessons.

**HORSE RACING The Downs at Albuquerque** (505-266-5555), Expo New Mexico, 300 San Pedro NE. Open daily 10–"late." Racing in season, with year-round simulcasting and slot machines providing excitement.

**ICE SKATING** ✍ **Outpost Ice Arena** (505-856-7594), 9530 Tramway Blvd. NE. Open daily. Lessons, public sessions, and group events are scheduled. Call for more information. $7–10; skate rental $3.

**ROLLER-SKATING** ✍ **Roller King** (505-299-4494; www.rollerkingabq.com), 400 Paisano NE. Northeast corner of I-40 and Juan Tabo. Open daily. Call for specific events and hours. $4 admission; skate rental $2.

**SKATEBOARDING** ✍ **Los Altos Municipal Skate Park** (505-291-6239), 10140 Lomas, west of Eubank, east of Easterday. Open daily, sunrise–sunset. Considered "the fastest skate park in the West," Los Altos demands that you wear a helmet. Free.

**SPECTATOR SPORTS Albuquerque Isotopes Baseball Club** (505-924-2255), 1601 Avenida Cesar Chavez, at intersection of University Blvd. SE. Take I-25 to Avenida Cesar Chavez, go east. The farm team for the Los Angeles Dodgers, the Isotopes are a Triple-A member of the Pacific Coast League. Isotopes Stadium is a classic ballpark with an abundance of dining and treat opportunities. Take me out to the ball game! $6–24.

**UNM Lobos and Lady Lobos Basketball** (505-925-LOBO or 505-925-5626), corner of Avenida Cesar Chavez and University Blvd. SE. Both the men's and ladies' teams play throughout the season in the Pit, or University Arena, a stadium that slopes 37 feet down toward the floor, where 18,000 fans dressed in Lobos red enjoy intimidating visiting teams and giving the Lobos their home court advantage. $12–27.

**WALKING TOURS Albuquerque Museum** (505-242-4600) offers walking tours of Old Town Tues.–Sun., 11 AM. **Walk Albuquerque** (505-344-9742; www.walkalbuquerque.org) has plans for several self-guided walking tours in neighborhoods all over town.

**WINERIES Anderson Valley Vineyards** (505-344-7266), 4920 Rio Grande Blvd. NW, Albuquerque. Tasting room hours Tues.–Sun. noon–5:30. One of the

CASA RONDEÑA WINE TASTING ROOM IN THE NORTH VALLEY.

first contemporary vineyards in New Mexico, founded in 1973, featuring Red Chile Cabernet and Balloon Blush, as specialties.

**Casa Rondeña Winery** (505-344-5911), 733 Chavez Road NW, Albuquerque. Tasting room hours Mon.–Sun. noon–7. Winemaker John Calvin has created a splendid Tuscan estate in Albuquerque's North Valley to frame his award-winning creations. Lovely picnic spot.

**Gruet Winery** (505-821-0055), 8400 Pan American Freeway NE, Albuquerque. Proprietors are the Gruet family. Tasting room hours Mon.–Fri. 10–5, Sat. noon–5. Closed Sun. Fine sparkling wine and still wines, such as pinot noir and Chardonnay.

**St. Clair Vineyards** (505-243-9916), 901 Rio Grande Blvd. NW, Albuquerque. Tasting room hours Sun.–Thurs. 11–9, Fri.–Sat. 11–10. A sixth-generation winery (its original location in Deming), its Albuquerque Old Town location is a bistro with a spacious outdoor patio, fine service, and excellent food, with wines used as menu ingredients.

## ✳ Green Space

**Rio Grande Valley State Park** (505-452-5200), 2901 Candelaria NW, Albuquerque. Open daily 8–5. Visitors center open daily 10–5. Closed Thanksgiving, Christmas, and New Year's Day. Two easy, approximately 1-mile trails through the center; a 3-acre observation pond with waterfowl, turtles, and dragonflies; demonstration gardens; wetlands; and interpretive nature trails make this a friendly place to explore the river, forest, and riparian environment. It is a migratory bird sanctuary that sponsors many events to celebrate the inhabitants. In addition, it provides access to the paved walking and bike path that extends 15 miles through the city along the bosque, or cottonwood forest. $3.

**Tingley Ponds** (505-764-6200), 1800 Tingley Dr. Open daily, sunrise to sunset. Opened during the 1930s, the city's Tingley Beach was a popular place to swim, until the polio epidemic scare shut it down. In recent years, Tingley Ponds have been restored as 18 acres of pond and wetlands that are stocked and open to public fishing. Free.

**PARKS Hyder Park.** In the beautiful southeast at the corner of Richmond and Santa Monica SE is a beloved neighborhood park with mature shade trees, benches, and a walking and running path around the circumference.

**Roosevelt Park.** Coal and Spruce SE. A lovely, large, unfenced off-leash dog park. Bring your own water. For a complete list of all off-leash parks, go to www.abqdog.com.

**Tiguex Park.** 1800 Mountain Rd. NW. With shady old cedar trees and gently rolling paths, this Old Town green space between the Albuquerque Museum and the Museum of Natural History makes a nice respite where you can get some fresh air and sunshine and stretch your legs.

## ✷ Lodging

**BED & BREAKFASTS, MOTELS, AND HOTELS Hiway House** (505-268-3971; www.hiwayhousemotel.com), 3200 Central Ave. SE, Albuquerque. If you're craving a taste of the old road, that is Old Route 66, consider this vintage remnant of what was a classic Southwest motel chain once owned by Ramada Inn founder Del Webb. You'll be in the proximity to Nob Hill, with plentiful dining and shopping choices, walking distance to the University of New Mexico, and super close to the Sunport without staying in a chain airport motel. The 60 rooms are plain but serviceable. The motel is set back a bit from Central Ave., so you'll have a bit of protection from traffic noise. Not a bad place for those seeking the character of a road experience. $75.

**Hotel Andaluz** (505-242-9090; www.hotelandaluz.com), 125 Second St. NW, Albuquerque. A $30-million renovation of the old downtown Hilton (where Conrad Hilton brought his bride, Zsa-Zsa Gabor, for their honeymoon) created a green LEED-certified oasis. Standard rooms are smallish, bedding is grand. The rooftop Ibiza Bar offers a grand sweep of city lights and the Sandia Mountains. Best of all is the nostalgia of the Spanish-style lobby. Another delightful boutique hotel. $159.

**Hotel Blue** (505-924-2400; www.thehotelblue.com), 717 Central Ave. NW, Albuquerque. Definitely the place to stay Downtown, Hotel Blue is a fairly recently renovation of tasteful mid-century modern design with a hip ambience. The place provides unexpected attention to details and is both business and family-friendly. Your hosts brag on their state-of-the-art mattresses and attention to guest comfort. You can walk anywhere Downtown from here, and you can catch a bus to anywhere else you might want to go. There's a buffet breakfast bar to get you going, plus a 24-hour coffee room. $77.

**Hotel Parc Central** (505-242-0040; http://hotelparqcentral.com), 808 Central SE. A 1926 Italianate hospital is restored to a deluxe urban oasis. In excellent walking distance to Downtown, this boutique hotel offers 74 guest rooms and the Apothecary Lounge, a hot rooftop bar, the Apothecary Lounge, worth visiting on its own. $159–179.

♂ ⚅ **Los Poblanos Historic Inn and Organic Farm** (505-344-9297; www.lospoblanos.com), 4803 Rio Grande Blvd. NW, Albuquerque. For a sense of the expansive history of Albuquerque, a stay in this John Gaw Meem–designed masterpiece of classic Territorial Revival architecture overlooking fields of lavender and an organic farm will be a memorable one. The beauty of the former Simms estate has been preserved by the owners, and every detail of the property evokes its rich past. For an extra-special stay, consider the Girard Guest House, a two-room casita decorated with Mexican folk art. Twenty different lodgings are available. The organic breakfast is a grand affair, prepared with seasonal local produce and eggs directly from Los Poblanos Organics. Throw in free WiFi, complimentary *New York Times*, and concierge service, and you have the premier Albuquerque lodging

experience. $140–360 (expect to pay around $250). Weddings!

**Sarabande Bed & Breakfast** (505-345-4923; www.sarabandebb.com), 5637 Rio Grande Blvd. NW, Albuquerque. For a charming North Valley retreat, you couldn't do better than Sarabande, named for the rose that grows in its courtyard. *Quiet, gracious*, and *relaxing* are all words that well apply to the mood you will find here. Lap pool open May–Oct. Green consciousness year-round. $109–179.

**Spy House** (505-842-0223; www .albuquerquebedandbreakfasts.com /spy-house-rooms.htm), 209 High St. SE. This meticulously restored 1912 Craftsman bungalow in Huning Highlands district near downtown was once the residence of David Greenglass, brother of convicted Los Alamos spy Ethel Rosenberg. A gourmet breakfast is included here and at sister property, Heritage House, prepared and served by caring and knowledgeable hosts. Comfort, nostalgia, and all the conveniences expected at newer lodgings. A wonderful alternative to standard lodging choices. $119–139.

## ✳ Where to Eat

**DINING OUT Antiquity** (505-247-3545), 112 Romero St. NW. Dinner daily, starting at 5 PM. Lamb roasting on the grill greets you on entering this cozy warren of an Old Town hideaway that is charming in all seasons. Make reservations and arrive early—the specials tend to sell out. There is always a fresh fish special; fresh lobster and scallops; five delicious cuts of steak, including châteaubriand for two with béarnaise sauce; and the French onion soup is the best. Reasonable wine by the glass. All in all, a good value. Expensive.

**Artichoke Cafe** (505-243-0200), 424 Central Ave. SE. Dinner nightly, lunch Mon.–Fri. Closed Sun. For going on three decades, Pat and Terry Keene have set the standard for fine dining in Albuquerque. The simplest dishes here—steamed artichoke, roast chicken, and salmon of the day—are always well prepared and beautifully presented, with just the right seasoning, intriguing sauce, and side dishes. The restaurant seats 120 but feels more intimate. When excellent service is a must, the Artichoke will do the job and do it right. Expensive.

**Chez Bob** (505-872-9097), 7610 Carmel NE. Dinner only, Tues.–Sat. What a deal! Offering affordable authentic French and Italian food in the NE Heights in casual style, Bob continues to delight fans with his famous Nutella crêpe as well as the savory mouth-watering seafood crêpe and his array of authentic French delights. You'll find an ex–Bellagio Vegas chef in an unassuming strip mall location—in my book, that's a find! Inexpensive–Moderate.

**El Pinto** (505-898-1777), 10500 Fourth St. NW. Open Mon–Thurs. 11–9; Fri.–Sat. 11–10; Sun. 10:30–9. When you want to impress your out-of-town guests with Mexican food that won't burn, take them to a really nice place for dinner. El Pinto, at the north end of the North Valley, is where to go. Salsa, chips, splashy margaritas on the patio, and barbecue ribs on the side go well with the enchiladas and chiles rellenos. The owner speaks tequila. Moderate.

**Jennifer James 101** (505-884-3860), 4615 Menaul Blvd. NE. Dinner Tues–Sat. Remarkable. Reservations a must.

The place to bring the foodie in your life. With ever-changing seasonal menus (eight times a year), the renowned JJ (often voted Albuquerque's best chef and a 2013 James Beard Award nominee) is always inventive and surprising. Shrimp and grits and fried chicken are favorites, but there is so much more. No closing hour, so you can shut the place down. Private dining available. Expensive.

**La Crêpe Michel** (505-242-1251), 400 San Felipe NW. Open Tues.–Sun. lunch; Tues.–Sat. dinner 6–9. The founder holds a PhD in anthropology, but more to the point, year after year she turns out authentic crêpes and quiche and classic French dishes in this enduringly romantic spot down a winding back alley in Old Town. Take a seat close to the fireplace and enjoy. Pâté and imported cheese, chicken and mushroom crêpes, *duck à l'orange*, *filet de boeuf*, and then *crêpe au chocolat* for dessert. It's fun to share! It can be a bit chilly on a cold night, so bring a wrap. Reservations are essential. Moderate.

**Paisano's** (505-298-7541), 1935 Eubank Blvd. NE. Dinner daily, lunch Mon.–Fri. Fresh pasta, daily specials, and you can get half-orders. Love the wild mushroom lasagna and capellini with seared scallops and the piquant house marinara. Decent house wines by the glass. Best of all, Paisano's caters to gluten-free diets (the owner is gluten-free himself) so delicious house-made pasta is available for special diets. "We cook like your Italian Grandma" is Paisano's motto. Good value. Moderate.

**Paul's Monterey Inn** (505-294-1461), 1000 Juan Tabo Blvd. NE. Lunch, dinner, Mon.–Sat. Take a time trip back to the 1970s. Slide into one of Paul's plush red booths, or sip a dry martini in the lounge. Be prepared to be spoiled rotten in this dim, classic, utterly consistent steakhouse, where women are still "dames" wearing red lipstick, seamed stockings, and stilettos. The best tournedos I've ever eaten. Known for prime rib and prime service. You will be called "Sweetheart." Quite good business lunch menu. Moderate.

**Scalo Northern Italian Grill** (505-255-8781), 3500 Central SE. Dinner daily, lunch Mon.–Fri., brunch Sat. and Sun., Intermezzo menu at bar 2:30–5. White linen sets the mood, crispy fresh bread to dip in flavorful olive oil, pasta perfectly prepared, and a nice glass of wine. Scalo remains, after almost 30 years, one of the city's top addresses for a business lunch or birthday celebration. A good place to meet with a good friend or someone you haven't seen in ages, as you can count on the service. The wine list has over 300 selections; there's a full bar that is a chic hangout on its own, plus occasional live jazz. Expensive.

**Vernon's Hidden Valley Steakhouse** (505-341-0831), 6855 Fourth St. NW. Dinner only. Open daily 4:30–9:30. Vernon's is the place for relaxing with a drink and a good steak after a workweek or for celebrating an anniversary. The service is impeccable, and the classic American food is beautifully prepared and delicious. Vernon's is for serious red meat eaters only, whether you crave a slab of prime steak or Colorado lamb chops. The sides are luscious, too, especially the "adult" mac and cheese. It's hard to choose between the French onion soup and the lobster bisque. Recommended for a special occasion. The Black Diamond Lounge is a great jazz

club, if you like the real thing. Very expensive.

**Vinaigrette, A Salad Bistro** (505-842-5507), 1828 Central SW. Open daily, lunch, supper. Be prepared to pay close to $20 for a farm-grown salad. Impressive variety, wildly popular. You can also be naughty with the mac and cheese; sides of protein, such as "hibiscus-cured duck confit," are available. Soups and sandwiches, too. The original is in Santa Fe on Cerrillos Rd.

**Yanni's** (505-268-9250), 3109 Central NE. Open Mon.–Thurs. 11–10; Fri.–Sat. 11–11; Sun. 11:30–9. Popular Yanni's and Opa Bar is a regular Nob Hill hangout and watering hole, as well as a power lunch spot. Greek specialties are served here, including an especially good vegetable moussaka. Moderate.

**Zacatecas** (505-255-8226), 3423 Central NE. Open daily. Lunch, dinner. Compound chef Mark Kiffin does it again, finding the winning formula for Nob Hill. Authentic Mexican-style flavorful tacos and tequilas are embraced by Duke City denizens ready to go a bit upscale from their tried-and-true New Mexican chile-slingin' mom-and-pop cafés. Moderate–Expensive.

**EATING OUT Blake's Lotaburger** (505-243-8343; www.lotaburger.com). Open daily. Recently voted #4 burger in the nation by *National Geographic Traveler.* Breakfast burritos at some locations; lunch, dinner. Hours vary by location. This New Mexico fast-food chain, with dozens of outlets throughout the state, serves the Lotaburger special with fries that half the town runs on. Characters in Tony Hillerman's novels pack Lotaburgers when they go out to solve mysteries. Once you try it, you will be hooked. As a word of caution, the Lotaburger on Rio Grande in Old Town can be slow during busy lunchtimes; however, the Lotaburger at 6210 Fourth St. in the North Valley (505-345-0402) is open 24 hours a day to serve you whenever the craving hits. Inexpensive.

**Cheese & Coffee Café** (505-883-1226), 2679 Louisiana NE; and (505-242-0326), 119 San Pasquale NW, near Old Town. Open Mon.–Sat. Lunch 10–3. This is the quintessential lunch stop, a deli with giant sandwiches, salads almost too big to be believed, and a New York–ish bustle generated by working folk and shoppers. The Old Town location is lower key, but if you're out shopping in the malls, go to the Louisiana locale. The salad trio is hard to pass up. Chicken salad is the best. Inexpensive.

**Farina Pizzeria** (505-243-0130), 510 Central SE. Open daily. Lunch, dinner. Dinner only Sat. and Sun. This EDO (East of Downtown) pizza café in a renovated brick building is perfect for exactly what it offers: an intimate bar, excellent crispy-crust made-to-order pizzas, and fresh salads. Can get pretty crowded on Friday nights as the university crowd meets up with Downtown. Don't expect to conduct a private conversation, unless you go for a really late lunch. Go for the *funghi* pizza with house-made sausage. Farina Alto is now in a Northeast Heights location (www.FarinaAlto.com).

**Frontier Restaurant** (505-266-0550), 2400 Central Ave. SE. Located across Central from UNM, open daily 5 AM–1 AM, the Frontier is an Albuquerque institution. Known for fragrant cinnamon rolls, freshly squeezed orange juice, green chile–smothered huevos rancheros, and soft chicken tacos, as well as its home-made tortillas, the bustling Frontier serves as a citywide social scene and study hall in addition to restaurant. Try the Frontier burger, with hickory smoke sauce, Thousand Island dressing, and onion. Not as cheap as it used to be, however. Inexpensive.

**I Love Sushi Teppan Grill** (505-883-3618), 6001 San Mateo NE, Ste. F4. Open Mon.–Sat. Closed Sun. Lunch, dinner. The Japanese food artists will dazzle you as they turn your dinner preparation into a performance at the grill. And you can't beat the sushi. Prices here are very reasonable. Beer and wine, too.

**Il Vicino Wood Oven Pizza and Brewery** (505-266-7855), 3403 Central SE. Open daily. Lunch, dinner. Open late. The dozen varieties of crispy, thin-crust pizza turned out in the wood-fired ovens here are perennially excellent, and when savored with a fresh spinach salad, one of Nob Hill's best budget dining experiences. Other locations as well. Panini and baked lasagna are also worth trying. Microbrews add to the experience. It's generally busy here and a tad rowdy, in a good way. This site is the original, and it still has the buzz.

**☙ Mannie's Family Restaurant** (505-265-1669), 2900 Central Ave. SE. Breakfast, lunch, dinner Mon.–Sun. Aside from its dependable hours, easy parking, central Nob Hill–university location, reliable WiFi and diverse menu, why dine here? Could be because of the reasonable prices, good service, fresh muffins, and bottomless cup of coffee. Go for the "66 Pile-Up." The place is hopping of a

Sunday morning, when platters of house-made corned beef hash and eggs rule. Daily specials. Inexpensive.

**Monte Carlo Steak House** (505-831-2444), 3916 Central SW. Open Mon.–Sat. Closed Sun. Lunch and dinner. Go here for the experience as much as the food. Enter through the liquor store, and then step down into the deep, dim hideaway replete with bar, red leather booths, and 1970s-era kitsch, even Elvis on velvet. Daily specials; the Thurs.–Fri. evening prime rib special is a good deal, as are the steak dinners with mounds of french fries, swell Greek salads, and the best baklava in town. The place is full of characters that may or may not slightly resemble those you've seen on The Sopranos, in a setting appropriate to *Mad Men*. Featured on *Diners, Drive-ins and Dives*. Moderate.

**Orchid Thai Cuisine** (505-265-4047), 4300 Central Ave. SE. Lunch, dinner daily. The best of the lot of Thai restaurants in this part of town. I'm always happy here, and so are my friends, as we dine on pad thai and a big bowl of lime-coconut-lemongrass soup. Lunch specials. Many vegan options. Inexpensive.

**Owl Cafe** (505-291-4900), 800 Eubank Blvd. NE. Open Mon.–Thurs. 7–10; Fri.–Sat. 7–11. Closed Sun. Breakfast, lunch, dinner. The city cousin of the San Antonio original, this Owl, which is quite recognizable from the highway, has a comfy 1950s atmosphere and serves a different all-you-can-eat special nightly for under $10, such as the famous burger and fries or spaghetti and meatballs. The menu lists just about every homey dish you remember from childhood. Nostalgia all the way. Inexpensive.

**Paddy Rawal's OM** (505-899-4423), 7520 Fourth St. NW. Lunch, dinner daily. Wine and beer. The town has not been the same since OM opened in late 2012 in the former Annupurna North Valley site. Of the dozen Indian restaurants in Albuquerque, OM is now acclaimed as the top-ranking, serving transcendent and original food that remains traditional. Buffet is fantastic, and Paddy will explain it all. Its Santa Fe sibling is Raaga, with a similar menu. Gluten-free-friendly. Inexpensive.

**The Quarters BBQ** (505-843-7505), 801 Yale Blvd. SE. With locations on the West Side and NE Heights. Open Mon.–Fri. 11–9. Sat. noon–9. Closed Sun. Lunch, dinner. When there is an argument about where to get the best barbecue in Albuquerque, many old-timers are likely to bet on the Quarters. It's dark and rowdy, being somewhat of a university hangout, and people bring their children here generation after generation. Lunch specials. The Quarters has some of the best wine and beer selections. Inexpensive.

**Route 66 Malt Shop & Grill** (505-242-7866), 3800 Central Ave. SE. Lunch, dinner daily. The very height of Route 66 retro, with the best blue cheese–green chile cheeseburgers in the city (some say, along the entire Mother Road!), meat loaf with grilled onions, homemade soups, house-made root beer (voted one of 10 best in United States), Frito pies, freshly squeezed limeade, Coke floats, and what more do you want? Chocolate malts, of course. Proprietors, "mom and pop" Eric Szeman and Diane Avila, do everything in their power to make sure you have a wonderful time and a great lunch. They elevate lunch counter food to new levels. Inexpensive.

**Siam Café** (505-883-7334), 5500 San Mateo NE #101. Open Mon.–Sat. 11–9. Others come and go, but we return here for authentic Thai. Lunch specials under $10. Green curry, drunken noodles, pad thai, and hot and sour chicken soup—a family favorite of ours—are consistent and served with aplomb. Just about every dish on the menu can be ordered vegetarian. I have been to cooking school in Chiang Mai, and the food here is indistinguishable from the real thing. Inexpensive.

**66 Diner** (505-247-1421), 1405 Central Ave. Open Mon.–Fri. 11–11; Sat. 8 AM–11 PM; Sun. 8 AM–10 PM. Perhaps the best chicken-fried steak in town, with real mashed potatoes and pie for dessert. Definitely worth the carbs. The Route 66 motif is so large and colorful, you long for your poodle skirt. Daily Blue Plate specials, ingenious pies, especially those with peanut butter. Inexpensive.

**Street Food Asia** (505-260-0088), 3422 Central Ave. SE. Mon.–Sun. Lunch, dinner. Stylish, raucous and crowded, in a way that makes the scene lively but difficult to conduct intimate conversation as you pretty much need to shout to be heard, SFA is a cool place for lunch or dinner. While reviews from my associates are mixed, I happen to adore the pan-Asian noodle dishes, satays, and wok delights as well as the chilled fruity beverages. Inexpensive.

**Sushi King Sushi & Noodles** (505-842-5099), 118 Central SW. Open daily. Lunch, dinner. Open late Fri.–Sat. For après-cinema sushi or noodle soup, you'll love this place, with its urban feel and superb tastes. And it has beer and wine. Check on other locations around town. Moderate.

**Thai Vegan** (505-884-4610), 5505 Osuna Rd., NE and Nob Hill location at 3804 Central SE. Open daily. Lunch, dinner. Elegant yet informal spot for tasty vegetarian and beyond vegetarian fare. A local favorite lunch stop. Beautiful presentation. Love the spicy eggplant with the signature heart-shaped mound of brown rice. You may wish to dabble in the faux chicken, fish, and other dietary preparations, all authentically spiced. Inexpensive.

🍲 **Tomato Cafe Gourmet Italian Food Bar** (505-821-9300), 5920 Holly NE. Open daily 11–8:30. Lunch, dinner. All you can eat! Yes, it is a buffet, and yes, it is a bargain. But the food doesn't taste like buffet food. Unlimited handcrafted pizza; pasta with a choice of homemade sauces, such as roasted tomato garlic; giant meatballs; garlicky green beans; minestrone soup; fresh salad; spinach and ricotta ravioli; and much more make this a fine place to bring teenagers with a bottomless stomach, or just yourself and your honey after a workout at the gym, when you just can't stand to cook or don't have time to put a real meal on the table. You'll spend less than if you shopped and cooked. Moderate.

## BREWPUBS AND WINE BARS

**Kellys Brew Pub** (505-262-2739), 3222 Central Ave. SE. On summer nights, it sometimes seems the entire town is sipping a brew on Kellys Nob Hill patio, and it just may be. In other towns, a place like Kellys might just be a college hangout, but this establishment rises above that designation. This historic building, the

1939 Jones Motor Co., was renovated to keep its Route 66 feel, and the food is surprisingly good, especially the green chile stew and the Albuquerque Turkey, with house-roasted turkey, green chile, and cheese. With over 20 in-house brews on tap, no wonder this place is usually jammed. Inexpensive.

**Marble Brewery** (505-243-2739; www.marblebrewery.com), 111 Marble Ave. Definitely the place to sip suds and hang out Downtown. Known more for beer than food. Food trucks are parked out front. Check the website for music and entertainment events. Also now on Santa Fe Plaza.

**O'Niell's Irish Pub** (505-255-6782), 4310 Central Ave. SE; another location in the NE Heights at 3301 Juan Tabo Blvd. NE. Lunch, dinner, late night Mon.–Sun. Pub food taken to an art form. The fish-and-chips are especially good, as is the Caesar salad.

Vegetarians can be happy here, too. Open mic, frequent live entertainment, happening patio. A comfortable place to meet up with a pal or hang out on your own at the bar. Incredible selection of beers on tap. Geeks who Drink is wildly popular and attracts crowds on Wed. nights. NE Heights location, too. Inexpensive.

**Zinc Wine Bar & Bistro** (505-254-9462), 3009 Central Ave. NE. Open daily. Lunch and dinner till 11. Sun. brunch only. Wine cellar open 5 PM–1 AM nightly, closed Sun. The chic upscale restaurant is on the main floor and mezzanine, but the real hangout is the wine bar downstairs, where you may purchase wine flights and interesting bar food. You could be in Seattle, or even Paris. Expect bistro food, seasonal, leaning locavore. Sunday brunch chicken and waffles ($9) is a treat. And the live entertainment is top-notch. Expensive.

MARBLE BREWERY PATIO

DOWNTOWN FLYING STAR CAFÉ.

**CAFÉS Flying Star** (505-344-6714; www.flyingstarcafe.com), 4026 Rio Grande Blvd. NW; (505-244-8099), 723 Silver SW. The Bernsteins started on a shoestring, and now they run a tidy chain of locally owned, popular cafés all over town, each a different style. The newer ones, such as the one on Eight and Silver, Downtown, and in Bernalillo, make the most of color and clean modern design. "You're never far from a Flying Star" is indeed true. Its baked goods are out of sight, particularly the towering Key lime pie, carrot cake, or strawberry-rhubarb pie. The burgers and fries are excellent, and the daily lunch and dinner specials go quickly. The Bernsteins brag that everything is made from scratch, and you will pay a little more for that. WiFi restricted during busy hours, and not always the easiest to connect. Moderate.

**Java Joe's** (505-765-1514), 906 Park SW. If your tastes hanker to a bygone era—shall we say the 1960s?—and you love good coffee and great scones and cinnamon rolls, by all means come on down to this Downtown hangout, where live folk and jazz transpire over much of the weekend. Scruffiness is encouraged; tattoos, while not required, are omnipresent, and the bagels and lox are just fine, thanks. Homemade soup and famous egg salad available daily. Inexpensive.

**Michael Thomas Coffee Roasters** (505-255-3330), 1111 Carlisle Ave. SE. Some folks in "the Q" prefer to drink the Fair Trade Guatemalan coffee fresh roasted in this locally owned small café. This off-the-beaten path spot is a favorite with the "mature" set, who may sit undisturbed as a cat in a sunny corner with the *New York Times* and a mug of coffee, or

## EIGHT FAVORITE ALBUQUERQUE MEXICAN RESTAURANTS

**Barelas Coffee House** (505-843-7577), 1502 Fourth St. SW. Open daily. Breakfast, lunch. Closed Sun. Politicos and TV celebrities come here to mingle with the working folk. You never know whom you'll run into. It's best known for its thick, burning red chile and delectable slow-baked *carne adovada*, but the huevos rancheros are not to be missed. For serious chile lovers and those who swear they know their chile. Try to come at off hours, or be prepared to wait in line. Then you'll have your choice of seating, including the pocket-size enclosed patio. It's a short walk to the National Hispanic Cultural Center from here. Inexpensive.

**Casa de Benevidez** (505-897-7493), 8032 N. Fourth St. NW. With its pretty green patio, waterfall, fountains, and full bar, Casa B's is a longtime favorite of North Valley residents. HOME OF THE SOPAIPILLA BURGER, reads the marquee, but that doesn't really describe the experience. The side café, geared to takeout, is a popular morning hangout and serves up a contender for the best breakfast burrito, with chorizo. The fajitas are among the best, too. It's a bit pricey for Mexican food, but the portions are immense. A nice place to take the folks for dinner or a special occasion. You'll find lots of locals unwinding here on Fri. evening with a margarita. Moderate–Expensive.

**Casa de Ruiz Church Street Café** (505-247-8522), 2111 Church St., Old Town. Open Sun.–Wed. 8–4; Thurs.–Sat. 8–8. Claiming to be located in the oldest building in Old Town, dating to the 1700s, the Church Street Café does for sure serve delicious Mexican food prepared from family recipes. In addition, there are sandwiches, salads, wine, and beer.

**Charlie's Front Door and Back Door** (595-294-3130), 8224 Menaul NE. Serving a winning margarita along with old-fashioned traditional Mexican cooking that includes such side dishes as *quelites* (greens) rarely found outside Grandma's kitchen, this is a favorite haunt of Albuquerque old-timers, who, believing they have found the best, have no need to experiment with new restaurants. The cozy step-down bar with its big black booths feels like the 1970s. Charlie's *carnitas* were recently voted Albuquerque's best. And they are tender and tasty when served with red chile blue corn enchiladas. Swell margaritas. Moderate.

**Duran's Pharmacy** (505-247-4141), 1815 Central Ave. NW. Open Mon.–Sat. 10–5. Weave your way through the cosmetics and household goods to the back, where you will find a line waiting for a seat at the legendary lunch counter or on the patio, or for one of the half-dozen tables, to taste the tortilla soup and what is likely the most delicious fresh tortillas, hot off the grill and doused in butter. Portions are immense, so unless you are famished, be prepared to share. Inexpensive.

**El Patio** (505-268-4245), 142 Harvard Dr. SE. Open daily. Lunch, dinner. This slightly funky beloved university area restaurant has been serving the same reliably fluffy light sopaipillas and savory green chile chicken enchiladas (my standy) for over 30 years. How pleasant to sip an ice tea on the shady, well-trodden patio on a hot summer day and taste the flavors of New Mexico. In fall, when the chile crop comes in, the green is over-the-top with heat. No matter how many others come and go, this place remains a top favorite. Inexpensive.

**Garcia's Kitchen** (505-842-0273), 1736 Central SW. Don't start your East Coast friends out on the red chile here. Only experienced chile eaters need apply. It takes a true chile addict to ooh and aah over the roasty green chile stew served with homemade fresh tortillas, and you can easily become addicted to the brisket tacos and the *carnitas* breakfast. You've just gotta have it! Of the many Garcia's around town, the one on Central near Old Town, with its carnival décor, is probably the best. But we each have our favorite. Daily specials are a good deal. Open late. Inexpensive.

**Mac's La Sierra Restaurant** (505-836-1212), 6217 Central Ave. NW. Open daily. Breakfast, lunch, dinner. If you can find a better deal than Mac's red enchiladas with steak fingers for $3.95, by all means go for it. Between the battered Naugahyde booths, dim lighting, neighbors who've been eating here for an eternity, and waitresses always in a hurry, hoisting trays of nothing fancy but plain old reliable tasty Mexican food, you've got yourself an authentic experience on the far end of Old Route 66. By the time you finish eating here, you'll feel like one of the gang. Inexpensive.

meditatively on the patio. Say hello when you see me there.

**Satellite Coffee** (505-254-3880), 2300 Central Ave. SE. Several locations around the city. If you long for a quieter place to check your e-mail, sip a latte, study, or read the paper, ease on into one of these Flying Star siblings, where you can also grab just a little bite to eat and a comfy easy chair. WiFi hot spot, for sure. Moderate.

**BAKERIES Le Chantilly Fine Pastries** (505-293-7057), 8216 Menaul Blvd. NE. Impeccable croissants, brioche, cheese sticks, and napoleons are the order of the day here at this classic French bakery. Now with gluten-free offerings. You'll feel secure with a hostess or host gift from here.

**Golden Crown Panaderia** (505-243-2424), 1103 Mountain Rd. NW. Home of the green chile cheese bread, this longtime neighborhood favorite can supply your dinner party with a bread sculpture of a turtle or armadillo, or a turkey for your Thanksgiving. Empanadas, *biscochitos*, New Mexican wedding cookies, and other local favorite sweets fill the display cases. And you can lunch on the bakery's beloved "bakery-style" pizza, sandwiches, and latte at the in-house café. Featured in *Gourmet* magazine.

**Great Harvest Bread Co.** (505-293-8277), 11200 Montgomery Blvd. NE. Folks drive from all over town to stock up on the hearty, whole-grain breads that Great Harvest turns out in delectable varieties. Artisan and homestyle breads and buns, as well as cookies, bars and sweets. Different varieties baked daily. Montana stone-ground red wheat available for your

own baking. Gluten-free selections available. Go to www.ghabq.com /sched.html for the baking schedule.

**CHOCOLATE, COFFEE, AND TEA Candy Lady** (505-243-6239), 524 Romero St. NW. Notorious for her "backroom" selection of adult, erotic, anatomic chocolates, the Candy Lady excels at imported candies, chocolate-dipped strawberries and apricots, truffles, and turtles. Locals say her sugar-free treats are the best around. Plus, she has 21 varieties of homemade fudge and homemade black licorice, her signature peanut butter crunch, and chocolate-free doggie treats in her Old Town shop.

**Moons Coffee & Tea** (505-271-2633), 1605 Juan Tabo Blvd. NE. Ste. F. You're likely to hear about a place like Moons at your book club. Let the knowledgeable Mrs. Moon be your guide through the fine coffees, such as Jamaica Blue Mountain and Kona, the flavored coffees, and Many Moons, the house blend, as well as the dozens of varieties of exquisite teas, including chai and rare white teas.

**New Mexico Tea Company** (505-962-2137), 1131 Mountain Rd. NW. This tiny shop is packed with several dozen elegantly arrayed varieties of fine imported teas, the exotic and the rare, as well as New Mexico–grown organic herbals and medicinals. Shopping here is a most pleasant experience, where you can you can deepen your tea experience and knowledge and find excellent teaware.

**Theobroma Chocolatier** (505-293-6545), 12611 Montgomery Blvd. NE. Come here when you want the good stuff, the very best-quality chocolate, in interesting thematic shapes, such as footballs and chocolate heart-shaped boxes, or such flavors as chocolate-covered ginger. The dark chocolate is sinfully luscious and creamy and irresistible.

**Whiting Coffee Co.** (505-344-9144), 3700 Osuna Rd. NE. Closed Tues. and Sun. It's worth a drive to this small strip mall for the finest freshly roasted coffee beans, original blends, a fine selection of loose teas, brewing devices, imported spices, chocolates, and cookies. There's always a free sample cup brewing. Where many discriminating Albuquerqueans insist on obtaining their coffee. For those who are picky about their morning brew—like you and me.

**GROCERIES La Montanita Co-op** (505-265-4631), 3500 Central SE. Five locations, including Gallup and Santa Fe. Pay $15 a year to join, and you support a member-run food co-op that is a small supermarket featuring organic, local and sustainably produced edibles. The take-out deli selections can be a tad unfamiliar, but if you are vegan or vegetarian, you'll think you can't live without this place. Your membership fee entitles you to a rebate at the end of the year and specials, too. Shop here and feel good about where you're spending your money.

**Natural Grocers** (505-292-7300), 4420 Wyoming (also on the West Side). Formerly known as "Vitamin Cottage," this is a Colorado-based chain that stocks the freshest organic, and for my money, most reasonably priced produce around. If you care to eat healthy, you can stock up on freshly ground flour, nuts, and spices for your kitchen, and purchase your

nutritional supplements and beauty products at the same time. Well-trained, friendly consultants are on hand to assist. Like shopping in the small family-owned grocery of old. West Side location also.

**TaLin Market World Food Fare** (505-268-0206), 88 Louisiana Blvd. SE. The most exotic grocery shopping experience in town, with aisles dedicated to India, Thailand, China, and the Caribbean. If you can't find the ingredient you're looking for, it probably doesn't exist. The produce and fresh fish sections are also geared to cooks of Asian cuisine. The store offers bargain prices on produce and there's a café and cooking lessons. What more could a foodie want? Food trucks assemble here in a giant pod Wed. 10–2. Also now in Santa Fe.

**Trader Joe's** (505-796-0311), 8928 Holly Ave. NE (off Paseo del Pueblo Norte). Uptown location also. Albuquerque became a city the day Trader Joe's opened its doors. Snacks and nuts, prepared salads, and take-out meals; bargain wines; and variety of frozen foods make this the favorite place to have fun while spending the weekly grocery budget. Every reason to look good in the kitchen is here, and a stop here is essential for party planning. Daily 9–9.

**Whole Foods Market** (505-856-0474), 5815 Wyoming Blvd. NE. The concept of grocery shopping as entertainment has come to Albuquerque with a glorious Whole Foods. Expensive, for sure, but the fish is delivered daily and the produce is the most beautiful around. Shopping in-house brands will lower your tab. The cheese and wine sections, as well as the bakery, make this a worthwhile stop. Carlisle location also.

## PET GOURMET AND BOUTIQUE

**☙ Canine Country Club and Feline Inn** (505-898-0725), 7327 Fourth St. NW. Both you and your beloved pet will be treated well here, whether your pup is in for grooming, boarding, or "doggie day care." You'll get a report card, too.

**Clark's Pet Emporium** (505-268-5977), 4914 Lomas Blvd. NE. This fine local pet shop has been catering to its clientele with the best in bird, fish, dog, and cat supplies for 40 years. They stock everything you could possibly need, provide personal attention, and all in a store that is definitely not a big box. You can trust this place to provide the best for your pet and there are helpful, knowledgeable salespeople about.

**☙ Gourmet Dog Bakery & People Coffee Bar** (505-797-9663), 7610 Carmel Ave. NE. A congenial pet-friendly hangout.

**☙ Three Dog Bakery** (505-294-2300), 9821 Montgomery NE. Organic dog biscuits, fancy and fanciful doggie pastries and birthday cakes, doggie wear, and "Yappy Hour" make this a popular stop for large dogs and their human companions. Ask about discounts!

**WINE SHOPS Jubilation Wine & Spirits** (505-255-4404), 3512 Lomas Blvd. NE. Not the biggest, but perhaps the best wine shop in town, with an in-depth selection that will tempt you to try a new one. The emphasis is on service. Wine tastings bring in knowledgeable instructors. Always busy.

**Kelly Liquors** (505-296-7815), 2226 Wyoming Blvd. NE. A huge selection of wines, beers, and liquors at discount prices makes this a good stop before a dinner party. Other locations in North Valley and Rio Rancho, 11 in all around town.

**Quarters Discount Liquors** (505-247-0579), 801 Yale Blvd. SE. Notice the two important words in the name: "discount" and "liquors." This place has a wide array of imported beers in stock. Other locations, too.

## ✳ Entertainment

**Adobe Theater** (505-898-9222), 9813 Fourth St. NW. A dedicated band of theater lovers produce a variety of consistently high-quality performances on this tiny out-of-the way stage.

**Albuquerque Little Theater** (505-242-4750), 224 San Pasqual Ave. SW. One of the oldest ongoing community theaters in the country, the Little Theater continues to draw an audience of dedicated and loyal followers, typically to a playbill of conventional, established theater favorites, usually very well done. There's a strong children's theater program here as well.

**Aux Dog Theater** (505-254-7716), 3011 Monte Vista Blvd. NE. This theater has not only survived, it's thrived. An intimate stage with reliably quality and engaging productions of little-known works.

**The Cell** (505-766-9412; www.fusion abq.org), 700 First St. NW. The FUSION Theatre Company is a top-notch provocative new theater that competes well with any other form of entertainment out there. Expect that chances will be taken and boundaries will be stretched.

**Filling Station** (505-243-0596), 1024 Fourth St. NW. Home of the Mother Road Theater Company in an historic Route 66 garage. Dynamite! I've

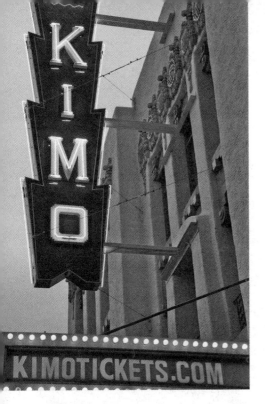

THE NAME "KIMO" MEANS "KING OF ITS KIND," AND IS FITTING FOR DOWNTOWN ALBUQUERQUE'S PUEBLO DECO THEATER.

loved every play I've seen here. The season of Irish playwrights was killer. In a funky neighborhood, get there early to park. Not shy about taking on complex or underperformed masterpieces. The production of Arthur Miller's *A View from the Bridge* was breathtaking. (As of late 2013–early 2014, Mother Road's new home will be Keshet Center for the Arts, a 30,000-square-foot building, just east of Interstate 25 and north of Interstate 40, at 4121 Cutler NE.)

**Journal Pavilion** (505-452-5100), 5601 University Blvd. SE. Bobby Foster Rd. I-25 to Rio Bravo exit or S. University Blvd. The big-name acts show up here every summer. The venue is enormous. Take your time leaving, as traffic tends to pile up.

**KiMo Theater** (505-768-3522), 423 Central Ave. NW. Originally built in 1927 as a movie palace in the flamboyant Pueblo Deco style, which used

CLASSIC PUEBLO DECO KIMO THEATER DOWNTOWN IS HOME TO SYMPHONY CONCERTS.

Indian ornamentation on art deco, the restored landmark KiMo is worth a visit on its own or to take in a concert, film, dance, or theater production. Go upstairs to see the Von Hassler murals.

**Outpost Performance Space** (505-268-0044), 210 Yale Blvd. SE. This simple intimate space is the place to come and hear a variety of live music, including jazz, folk, world music, local acts, and touring companies, as well as spoken word. Check out the outstanding New Mexico Jazz Festival.

**Popejoy Hall** (505-925-5858), 302 Cornell Dr. SE. University of New Mexico's Popejoy Hall, with 2,000 seats, is the city's premier stage venue for the New Mexico Symphony and big-stage road show musicals. The university offers a regular schedule of theater events, from Broadway road shows to student-produced work. Emmylou Harris, Sweet Honey in the Rock, and Ralph Stanley are some of the great acts to appear on this stage. Several other smaller theater spaces are in this building as well, including Keller Hall for classical music performances, Rodey Hall for smaller theater pieces, and the Experimental Theatre.

**South Broadway Cultural Center** (505-848-1320), 1025 Broadway Blvd. SE. A library, exhibition space, and beautiful small theater space, the cultural center is a stage for live theater and touring world music acts.

**Tricklock Theater Company** (505-254-8393), 1705 Mesa Vista NE. Now the resident theater company of the University of New Mexico, Tricklock is a solid and intelligent group of young theater people who perform exciting, new, and experimental work and tour internationally. They

produce the annual International Theater Festival each January.

**Vortex Theatre** (505-247-8600), 2004 Central SE. For 35 years, the Vortex has been home to the offbeat, the avant-garde, the edgy kind of theater designed to make you think.

## ✳ Selective Shopping

**Albuquerque Flea Market** (505-222-9700), 300 San Pedro NE, Expo New Mexico. With acres of booths to survey, you can find everything and anything from bargains on CDs, blankets, pots and pans, and everything you didn't know you needed, from sets of long-handled iced-tea spoons to handmade soaps to calico cat cookie jars. You're bound to go home with a sack full of something you love, feeling very proud of yourself.

**Dan's Boots & Saddles** (505-345-2220), 6903 Fourth St. NW. Even the real cowboys shop here, but if all you want to do is find the right pair of jeans, western shirt, boots, or hat, by all means get yourself to this store that's been selling feed and saddles since 1938.

**Man's Hat Shop** (505-247-9605), 511 Central Ave. NW. Over a half-century in business, with well-earned high marks in service and quality, this Downtown landmark has a great selection of hats from Panama to Stetson for the man in your life.

**Mariposa Gallery** (505-268-6828), 3500 Central Ave. SE. The finest, most adventurous, and well made in crafts, many by local artisans, grace the walls and shelves of this long-established gallery, including glass, jewelry, sculpture, pottery, and ceramics, in all price ranges. If you have time for only one gallery, make this the one.

**The Palms Trading Co.** (505-247-8504), 1504 Lomas Blvd. NW. Stop in here, near Old Town, for deals on handmade Indian jewelry, antique Indian pots, and all other manner of Native American wares. You may not find the absolute top-of-the-line, but you are bound to find something you like.

**The Yarn Store at Nob Hill** (505-717-1535), 120 Amherst Dr. NE. Extensive assortment of fine yarns, plus everything the needlecrafter needs for any project at all. Knitting lessons, too.

**INDEPENDENT AND USED BOOKSTORES Book Stop** (505-268-8898), 526 Washington St. NE. Since 1979 offering an in-depth selection of browsable used, fine, and rare books. In its latest incarnation, the venerable Bookstop retains an intellectual book-lover's air.

**Bookworks** (505-344-8139), 4022 Rio Grande Blvd. NW. Specializing in children's books, service, and the latest in current events books, plus a schedule of book signings, from national stars to local personalities, to fill the calendar, Bookworks has managed to survive the changes in the book business. The North Valley loves to browse here, then meet friends adjacent Flying Star Café.

**Page One** (505-294-2026), 11018 Montgomery Blvd. NE. Over 30 years of independent bookselling in the NE Heights. Open mic nights, events, new and used, and good deals at www.page1book.com/coupon.

**Title Wave Books** (505-294-9495), 3218 Wisconsin St. NE. Somehow, Title Wave keeps rolling along with an intelligent selection of used books that is both wide and deep. This is that rare bookstore where you will find just what you are looking for as well as the next big thing that you had no idea you were interested in, until you spotted it here.

**SHOPPING CENTERS ABQ Uptown**, Louisiana and Indian School NE. Albuquerque's newest 25,000-square-foot shopping center has become the favorite place to shop. It is designed for walking outdoors browsing upscale retailers Coldwater Creek, Anthropologie, Chico's, Pottery Barn, Williams-Sonoma, the Apple Store, and many other desirable national chains. Here you have every opportunity to be fashionable and really spend some money. For a break, try the Elephant Bar, which is a fine and reasonable restaurant and bar.

**Nob Hill Shopping Center**, Carlisle and Central SE. Built in 1937, this vintage shopping center was the first "mall" constructed west of the Mississippi. Today, the art deco center houses an engaging variety of galleries, chic home furnishings stores, a shoe store, a paper store, jewelry shops, a trendy salon, La Montanita Food Co-op, a bar, and a Scalo's restaurant. Free parking one block south of the center.

**VINTAGE AND RECYCLED Buffalo Exchange New and Recycled Fashion** (505-262-0098), 3005 Central Ave. NE. If you are stylish, trendy, or want to be, you can trade in wardrobe items you are tired of and cash in on the huge supply of both men's and women's fashions and accessories that fill the racks at Buffalo Exchange. Both styles and sizes appear geared to the university set.

**My Best Friend's Closet** (505-298-4099), 2810 Eubank Blvd. NE. An in-depth assortment of seasonally well-chosen, gently worn, generally reasonably priced apparel is available here, sold on consignment. From sportswear and sweaters to evening-wear, bargains abound.

## ✳ Special Events

Check 311 or the local paper for information on the monthly Friday evening **ARTSCrawl** (505-244-0362;

RIDING THE FERRIS WHEEL GETS YOU INTO THE STATE FAIR SPIRIT.

www.artscrawlabq.org), when various gallery districts open their doors.

*January:* **Revolutions International Theater Festival** (505-254-8393), National Hispanic Cultural Center, 1701 Fourth St. SW.

*March:* **Rio Grande Arts and Crafts Festival—Spring Show** (505-292-7457), Expo New Mexico. **National Fiery Foods and BBQ Show** (505-873-8680), Sandia Resort and Casino, I-25 and Tramway Blvd.

*April:* **Gathering of Nations Pow-wow** (505-836-2810), the Pit, University of New Mexico. **Albuquerque Isotopes** baseball games (505-924-2255), Isotopes Park, 1601 Avenida Cesar Chavez SE. Apr.–Sept

*May:* **Cinco de Mayo Concert Celebration** (505-246-2261), National Hispanic Cultural Center, 1701 Fourth St. SW.

*June:* **Festival Flamenco Internacional de Albuquerque** (505-242-7600), 214 Gold Ave. SW. **NM Arts and Crafts Fair** (505-884-9043), **Sizzlin' Summerfest** (311) offers musical themes from a variety of cultures each Saturday night in Civic Plaza Downtown.

*July:* **Mariachi Spectacular de Albuquerque** (505-255-1501); www.mariachispectacular.com/Sandia Resort & Casino.

*September:* **New Mexico Wine Festival** info@newmexicowinefestival.com, Bernalillo, Labor Day Weekend. **New Mexico State Fair** (505-222-9700), Expo New Mexico, held for two weeks each September. Livestock, home arts, Indian and Hispanic arts, food, midway with rides. The fair celebrates all things New Mexican. **Globalquerque.** Neal@globalquerque.org, **National**

BUNNIES TAKE THE PRIZE AT THE STATE FAIR JUNIOR LIVESTOCK AUCTION.

**Hispanic Cultural Center**, 1701 Fourth St. SW, at Avenida César Chávez.

*October:* **Albuquerque International Balloon Fiesta** (505-821-1000), 4401 Alameda Blvd. NE, Balloon Fiesta Park, I-25 and Alameda NE. Held first two weeks of October, this is the world's largest hot-air balloon gathering, with over 500 balloons from all over the world, including special shapes, lifting off each weekend morning in mass ascensions. Balloon glows, special shapes rodeo, fireworks, gigantic midway.

*November:* **Día de los Muertos** (505-246-2261), National Hispanic

Cultural Center, 1701 Fourth St. SW. **Marigold Parade** (505-314-0176), Westside Community Center, 1250 Isleta Blvd. SW. **Weems International Artfest** (505-293-6133), Expo New Mexico, 300 San Pedro NE.

*December:* **River of Lights** (505-764-6200), Rio Grande Botanic Garden, Nov. 24–Dec. 29.

DÍA DE LOS MUERTOS (DAY OF THE DEAD) IS CELEBRATED IN ALBUQUERQUE'S SOUTH VALLEY WITH THE MARIGOLD PARADE.

# North Central New Mexico: Georgia O'Keeffe Country

## 3

## TAOS AND THE ENCHANTED CIRCLE
Taos, Questa, Red River, Angel Fire,
Taos Ski Valley, Arroyo Seco

## HIGH ROAD COUNTRY
Chimayo, Truchas, Cordova, Peñasco,
Dixon

## RIO CHAMA COUNTRY
Abiquiu, Española, Tierra Amarilla,
Los Ojos

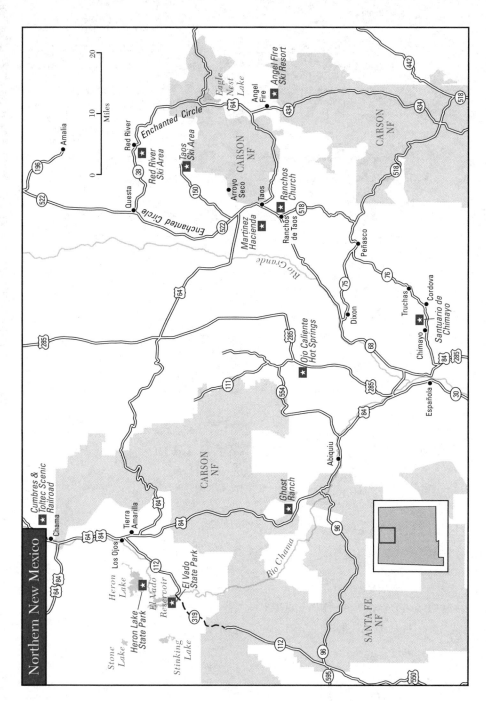

Northern New Mexico

# INTRODUCTION

There is something about northern New Mexico that speaks to our deepest image of the state. Perhaps it is the adobe houses shaded by grandmother cottonwoods, the scent of piñon smoke, or the figures of saints hand painted on the altars of High Road mission churches. Then there is the rush of water through an ancient *acequia,* the sight of snow on Taos Mountain, the curve of the buttress on the Ranchos Church, the rhythms of drum and rattle at an Indian dance, the wind-sculpted red rocks of Abiquiu . . .

Whatever it is, in northern New Mexico we catch our breath around every bend in the road as we wind through the Rio Grande canyon on the way up to Taos or follow the Rio Chama northward. Perhaps we learned this love by looking at the art of the Cinco Pintores and the Taos Moderns, those captivated by northern New Mexico light.

Here is where the four seasons unfurl themselves most deliciously, from the stillness of a snow-covered landscape overlooking the Mora Valley, to the green bursting forth from Velarde apple orchards, to the busy summer season in Santa Fe, with rainbows stretching across the sky, to, as writer John Nichols titled one of his books, "the last beautiful days of autumn" in Taos.

The changing seasons renew the enduring traditions, as each season brings its own: clearing the *acequias* in spring, the farmers' markets, fly-fishing, chopping wood, and retreating to the warmth of the fire and the simple pleasure of a pot of beans and chile on the stove.

Northern New Mexico reminds us that this can be a sustainable way of life in harmony with the land, where one eats what one grows and warms oneself through the labor of one's hands. The crafts of weaving and carving are more than decorative; they are life essentials. Take away the asphalt and the television satellite dishes, and the High Road, along with many mountain villages of New Mexico, has changed very little in the past three or four centuries; however, a road expansion is planned.

This section of the state offers much variety: retreat at artist Georgia O'Keeffe's Ghost Ranch, visit traditional weavers at Chimayo or Los Ojos, enjoy artists' studio tours during the fall at Dixon and Abiquiu, attend the Santa Fe Opera, and immerse in all the cultural events of that extraordinary capital city.

VIGIL'S IN CHIMAYO IS A PLACE TO FIND HANDMADE NORTHERN NEW MEXICO CRAFTS.

To facilitate your travel and allow you to focus on the delights of each area, think of it in three geographic sections: Taos and the Enchanted Circle Country of Questa, Red River, and Angel Fire; High Road Country of Chimayo, Truchas, Cordova, Peñasco, and Dixon; and the Rio Chama Country of Española, Abiquiu, Tierra Amarilla, Los Ojos and Chama, Ojo Caliente, and El Rito. US 84/285 parallels the course of the Rio Chama north to the Colorado border.

# TAOS AND
# THE ENCHANTED CIRCLE
## TAOS, QUESTA, RED RIVER, ANGEL FIRE, TAOS SKI VALLEY, ARROYO SECO

Warning: the beauty and magic of the Taos area may change your life. Taos Mountain is famous for doing that—as well as bringing out the dreams and creativity you have yearned to express. Add art, history, Native American and Hispanic culture, fine dining, and outdoor activities of hiking, skiing, rafting, and fishing for the sum of a destination with four-season appeal. You are guaranteed to love this region whenever you visit—and may it be soon.

**GUIDANCE Angel Fire Convention and Visitors Bureau** (575-377-6555; www.angelfirefun.com), 3365 NM 434, Angel Fire.

**Red River Visitor's Center** (575-754-2366; www.redrivernewmex.com), Red River Convention Center, Red River.

**Taos County Chamber of Commerce** (575-751-8800; www.taoschamber.com), 1139 Paseo del Pueblo Sur, Taos.

**Village of Taos Ski Valley Chamber of Commerce** (800-517-9816; 500-776-1413; www.taosskivalley.com). 122 Sutton Pl., Taos Ski Valley.

**MEDICAL EMERGENCY Christus St. Vincent Regional Medical Center** (505-983-3361) 455 St. Michaels Dr.

**Española Hospital** (505-753-7111), 1010 Spruce St., Española.

**Holy Cross Hospital** (575-758-8883), 1397 Weimer Rd., Taos.

**Los Alamos Medical Center** (505-662-4201), 3917 West Rd., Los Alamos.

**GETTING THERE** From Santa Fe, go north on NM 68. It's a slow 67 miles to Taos. From Taos, take NM 522 north, about 25 minutes, to Questa and the Enchanted Circle. Also from Taos, take NM 150 to Taos Ski Valley, a half-hour drive.

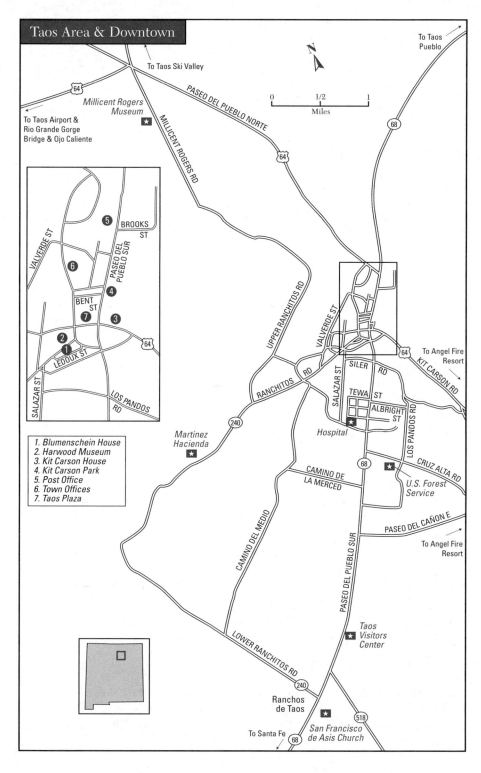

## Taos Area & Downtown

To Taos Ski Valley

To Taos Pueblo

64

*Millicent Rogers Museum*

To Taos Airport &
Rio Grande Gorge
Bridge & Ojo Caliente

PASEO DEL PUEBLO NORTE

64

68

0   1/2   1
Miles

MILLICENT ROGERS RD

BROOKS ST

VALVERDE ST

PASEO DEL PUEBLO SUR

BENT ST

LEDOUX ST

SALAZAR ST

LOS PANDOS RD

64

UPPER RANCHITOS RD

VALVERDE ST

RANCHITOS RD

SALAZAR ST

SILER RD

TEWA ST

ALBRIGHT ST

*Hospital*

To Angel Fire Resort

KIT CARSON RD

LOS PANDOS RD

CRUZ ALTA RD

*U.S. Forest Service*

240

*Martinez Hacienda*

CAMINO DE LA MERCED

68

PASEO DEL CAÑON E

To Angel Fire Resort

CAMINO DEL MEDIO

PASEO DEL PUEBLO SUR

*Taos Visitors Center*

LOWER RANCHITOS RD

240

*Ranchos de Taos*

To Santa Fe

68

518

*San Francisco de Asis Church*

1. Blumenschein House
2. Harwood Museum
3. Kit Carson House
4. Kit Carson Park
5. Post Office
6. Town Offices
7. Taos Plaza

# ✳ To See

**TOWNS  Angel Fire.** A town of many second-home condominiums and rentals with a resort at the center, yet also with a community of year-round citizens. It is a good place to stay and play year-round. It was the fall meeting grounds of the Ute and took its name from the Indian "breath of spirits," later Christianized by Franciscan friars to "breath of angels." Hiking, mountain biking, cross-country skiing, snowboarding and tubing, as well as a zip-line, are its leading attractions, in addition to skiing. It is also home to Vietnam Veterans Memorial State Park.

**Arroyo Seco.** This pretty little village on the road to Taos Ski Valley has cafés, shops, and a historic church.

**Questa.** The drive north of Taos to Questa along NM 522 passes several interesting potential explorations, including the valley of Arroyo Hondo and Lama Mountain, where the Lama Foundation—an ecumenical retreat center founded in the 1960s, still survives. Questa was for many years primarily a mining community where molybdenum, an agent used for hardening steel, reigned, but it is now home to a combination of artists, organic growers, and multigenerational Hispanic families.

**Red River.** A family resort town created for fun, with a ski area, plenty of lodging, cafés, and shopping that is a pleasant four-season family escape. At 8,750 feet, it is the highest town in the state. Founded in 1892 by homesteaders; prospectors followed suit and found their way to the settlement. The Red River takes its color after rains due to the high mineral content.

PRAYER FLAGS WAVE OVER THE RIO GRANDE GORGE ATOP LAMA MOUNTAIN.

**Taos.** The legendary town of artists and the home of multistoried 1,000-year-old Taos Pueblo has a magnetism and mystique like nowhere else. Established in 1615 as a northern outpost of New Spain, it was the site of the annual autumn rendezvous and trade fair of mountain men who hunted and trapped. The town itself is a historical composite of three parts: Ranchos de Taos on the south, Don Fernando de Taos in the central part of town radiating out from the Plaza, and Taos Pueblo. Eventually, these three sections grew together to form a unit we think of today as Greater Taos. In addition to its arts, Taos is also known as the home of larger-than-life characters, such as Kit Carson, Padre Martinez, Mabel Dodge Luhan, and D. H. and Frieda Lawrence.

**Taos Ski Valley.** Located in the old mining area of Twinings, TSV is the state's premier ski resort, internationally known for its challenging runs. Summer activities, such as concerts by Taos School of Music, are scheduled along with winter fun, including snowboarding.

**HISTORIC LANDMARKS, PLACES, AND SITES Hacienda de los Martinez** (575-758-1000), 708 Hacienda Way, off Lower Ranchitos Rd., Taos. Two miles south of plaza on NM 240 or 4 miles west of Ranchos de Taos on NM 240. Open Mon.–Sat. 10–5, Sun. noon–5; call for winter hours, likely to be closed Wed. and open only until 4. If you want to see what a 19th-century hacienda looks like, come here and experience the fortresslike restored building designed to keep out Comanche and Apache raiders. Exhibits explain trade on the Camino Real, and Spanish colonial culture of New Mexico. It is furnished authentically, with demonstrations of quilting, *colcha* embroidery, weaving, and other traditional crafts. $8 adults, $4 under age 16, under age 5 free.

**Kit Carson Cemetery** (no phone), Kit Carson Park. History makes strange bedfellows Stroll this historic cemetery in the center of town to find graves of Mabel Dodge Luhan, Padre Martinez, and Kit Carson within a stone's throw of one another.

**Picuris Pueblo** (575-587-2519), NM 75 at MM 13, Peñasco. Attractions at this tiny Pueblo on the High Road to Taos include a museum, the ancient Pot Creek Pueblo site, and historic restored church. The Pueblo is known for its golden-flecked mica pottery. The haunting Matachine dances are performed here Dec. 24–25.

**Pot Creek Cultural Site** (575-587-2519). Nine miles from Taos on NM 518. Open late June–early Sept. Wed.–Sun. An easy 1-mile trail leads to a reconstructed pueblo that includes a ceremonial kiva. This site was inhabited by the Ancestral Pueblo people between A.D. 1100 and A.D. 1300. Many pots were found here when the Spanish arrived, hence the name. Free.

**Rio Grande Del Norte National Monument** (www.blm.gov/nm/st/en/fo/taos_field_office.html) One of the nation's newest national monuments. In March 2013, President Barack Obama declared these 27 million acres of Rio Grande Rift and Taos Plateau a nationally significant landscape to be preserved permanently. Encompassing several Native American pueblos, rock art, wildlife, native grasslands, geologic features formed over 70 million years and much more, the area is a haven for hiking, rafting, fishing, hunting and sightseeing.

MUDDING THE RANCHOS DE TAOS CHURCH IS AN ANNUAL SPRING COMMUNITY EVENT.

**Rio Grande Gorge Bridge** (no phone), at intersection of NM 68 and NM 150 (Taos Ski Valley Rd.), go left 17 miles on US 64. Completed in 1965, at 650 feet above the Rio Grande, this bridge is the nation's second-highest span: 2,000 feet from rim to rim across the gorge. The winding Rio Grande below and view of the Taos Plateau is a look into the deep heart of New Mexico. From this height, river rafters on the Taos Box look like tiny specks. Hang on to your hat! The wind always blows hard up here. Free.

**San Francisco de Asis Church ("Ranchos Church")** (575-758-2754), Ranchos de Taos. Four miles south of Taos on NM 68. Open Mon.–Sat. 9–4. The most frequently painted and photographed church in the United States was built sometime between 1776 and 1813. Its massive adobe walls change appearance with the changing light. $3 to see video and Mystery Paintings in Parish Hall.

**Taos Pueblo** (575-758-1028), 2 miles north of Taos off NM 68. Feast days: Sept. 29–30, San Geronimo. Open daily 8–4:30. Closed during private Pueblo events. Pueblo may be closed during Feb.–Mar. and Aug. Taos was well established long before Europe emerged from the Dark Ages, and the ancestors of today's people have been in this area for a thousand years. About 150 live on the Pueblo full-time, and about 2,000 are living on Taos Pueblo lands. This is the only living American Indian community that is both a UNESCO World Heritage Site and a National Historic Landmark. The present Pueblo has been occupied since about A.D. 1450. To honor the residents' traditions, there is still no indoor plumbing or electricity at the Pueblo. The Rio Pueblo, running from the sacred Blue Lake in the Sangre de Cristo Mountains, courses through the Pueblo. The Feast of San Geronimo is a highlight of the year, as is Christmas Eve. Pueblo artists are known for their micaceous, gold-flecked pottery, which is sold on the Pueblo. Entrance fees include a guided tour. It is appropriate to tip your guide. $10 adults, $5 seniors and students, under age 12 free. $5 per camera. Parties of 10 or more, $8 per person.

**Vietnam Veterans Memorial State Park** (575-377-6900), 34 Country Rd., Angel Fire. 24 miles east of Taos on US 64. Visitors center open daily 9–5. Chapel open daily, 24 hours. Established in 1971 by Dr. Victor Westphall to honor his son, David, killed in Vietnam in 1968, this is the only state park in the country dedicated as a Vietnam Veterans Memorial. The 6,000-square-foot visitors center offers informative and deeply touching videos, exhibits, and memorabilia. Architect Ted Luna designed it with the idea "such that no person entering it could leave with quite the same attitude toward peace and war." Free.

**MUSEUMS Ernest L. Blumenschein Home** (575-758-0505), 222 Ledoux St., Taos. Mon.–Sat. 10–5, Sun. noon–5; call for winter hours. Taos Society of Artists founders Ernest and Mary Greene Blumenschein lived and worked in this 1797 Spanish colonial adobe. Recently restored, the house appears much as it did in their day, with the original colors and artwork brought back to life. $8 adults, $4 under age 16, under age 5 free.

**Harwood Museum of Art** (575-758-9826), 238 Ledoux St., Taos. Open Mon.–Sat. 10–5, Sun. noon–5. Closed holidays. Here is a treasury of Taos art, housed in an exemplary 19th-century Spanish-Pueblo adobe structure. Founded in 1923, the Harwood contains the work of the artists who made Taos famous: Victor Higgins, Ernest Blumenschein, Andrew Dasburg, and Patrocinio Barela, as well as that of contemporary artists, such as Larry Bell, Fritz Scholder, Anita Rodriguez, and Melissa Zink. Of special note is the Agnes Martin Gallery,

TAOS PUEBLO IS THE PLACE TO FIND GENUINE MICACEOUS POTTERY.

FOLK LIFE FESTIVAL AT THE MILLICENT ROGERS MUSEUM.

where seven canvasses of the nation's most acclaimed minimalist and Taos resident, Martin, hang for contemplation in a light-filled chamber. $10 adults, $8 seniors and students.

**Kit Carson Home and Museum** (575-758-4945), 113 Kit Carson Rd., Taos. Open daily 11–5. Closed Thanksgiving, Christmas, New Year's, and Easter. Famed mountain man and Indian scout Kit Carson and his wife, Josefa, lived in this 12-room adobe for a quarter-century. It is authentically furnished, and guides in period costume give tours. Next door is the Carson House Shop, an excellent showcase of Indian and folk art, jewelry, Christmas ornaments, and the work of Taos artist Valerie Graves. $5 adults, $4 seniors, $3 teens, $2 children, under age 6 free.

**Millicent Rogers Museum** (575-758-2462; www.millicentrogers.org), 1504 Millicent Rogers Rd., Taos. Four miles north of Taos off NM 522. Turn left on Millicent Rogers Road and follow the museum signs. Open daily 10–5. Closed Mon., Easter, Thanksgiving, Christmas, New Year's. This outstanding private museum was founded in 1953 by relatives of Millicent Rogers, a model, heiress, and socialite who moved to Taos in 1947. Her love of regional architecture and Indian and Spanish colonial art, including Penitente Brotherhood artifacts, inspired an extensive collection of jewelry, textiles, basketry, pottery, and paintings. Here find one of the most important collections of black pottery by San

Ildefonso Pueblo artist Maria Martinez and her family. A trip here makes a great immersion into the art of the region. $10 adults, $8 seniors, $6 students. Group rates available. Fantastic gift shop.

**Taos Art Museum and Fechin House** (575-758-2690), 227 Paseo del Pueblo Norte. Open summer Wed.–Sun. 10–5; call for winter hours. A Russian-style adobe home designed by artist Nicolai Fechin features his woodwork, paintings, collection of Asian and Russian art, plus many fine works by members of the Taos Society of Artists. $8 adults.

## ✳ To Do

**BICYCLING US 64 between Taos and Angel Fire.** An approximately 25-mile ride through narrow Taos Canyon (which can be backed up with traffic) and over 9,100-foot Palo Flechado Pass. Several hairpin turns as you travel around the mountain down into Angel Fire.

**CLIMBING Mallette Park**, Red River. At the west end of town three blocks from Main St. is a granite face with six bolted routes. The wooded park also has a disc golf course.

**FARMERS' MARKET Taos Farmers' Market** (575-751-7575), in back of the county courthouse at Civic Plaza at Town Hall parking lot. Mid-May–late-Oct., Sat. 8–1. Northern New Mexico and southern Colorado growers from the San Luis Valley sell the most remarkable array of produce, baked goods, flowers, preserves, bath products, and beans.

**FISHING Costilla Creek/Valle Vidal.** Open July 1–Dec. 31. Catch and release of the native Rio Grande cutthroat.

**Latir Lakes.** It takes a moderate 4-mile hike—at least—to reach the nine glacier lakes that form the Latirs, which hold trophy cutthroats. The views and the wildflowers make it a worthwhile trek. The Latirs are the headwaters of the Rio Costilla.

**Rio Grande.** The confluence of the Rio Grande and Red River near Questa and just below John Dunn Bridge in Arroyo Hondo.

**Rio Hondo.** Parallels NM 150 from Arroyo Hondo up to Taos Ski Valley.

**GHOST TOWNS Elizabethtown**, 4 miles north of Eagle Nest on NM 38. The first incorporated town in NM in 1868, E-town, named for a founder's daughter, was a boom-and-bust gold mining settlement. The ruins of several buildings and the cemetery survive. It now is home to the **Elizabethtown Museum**, and your best chance for finding it open is summer weekends.

**GOLFING Angel Fire Golf Course** (575-377-3055), Angel Fire Resort. Usually open mid-May–mid-Oct. You can golf in an absolutely gorgeous setting up here. At 8,600 feet, this is one of the highest and most lushly wooded regulation courses in the world. It's an 18-hole, par-72 course. $65.

**Taos Country Club** (575-758-7300), 54 Golf Course Dr., Ranchos de Taos. Open year-round, weather permitting. Tee times are required and take up to a seven-day advance reservation. Open to the public, at 7,000 feet this is a forgiving desert course of 18 holes. $65–75.

**HIKING West Rim Trail** (575-758-8851). From the Plaza, north on Paseo del Pueblo Norte 4 miles. Left at signal at the intersection with US 64, west 7 miles. Cross the bridge and turn left at the rest stop immediately west of the bridge. A well-maintained bathroom and water are available. Nine miles each way—go as far as you like—are flat, easy to moderate views of clouds and mountains. Recommended as a beginning mountain biking trail. Careful in summer, snakes are common; can be especially dangerous for your four-footed friends.

**Williams Lake.** The trailhead is above Taos Ski Valley, past the Bavarian Restaurant about 1.3 miles. The best time to go on this classic Taos hike, rated moderate, is during July–Aug., when the wildflowers are at their peak. Plan for 4 miles on a well-marked trail, at an altitude of 11,450 feet to Williams Lake at the base of Wheeler Peak.

NATIVE CUTTHROATS ROVE THE RIO COSTILLA.

**Wild Rivers and Orilla Verde Recreation Areas** (www.blm.gov/nm/st/en /prog/recreation/taos/orilla_verde.html), 16 miles south of Taos off NM 68. Twenty-two miles of rim and river trails, easy to intermediate, amid rocky lava flows and following the winding path of the Rio Grande. Plenty of riparian areas with good birding and wildlife viewing.

**HORSEBACK RIDING Cieneguilla Stables** (575-751-2815), 13 miles south of Taos Visitor Center on east side of NM 68, near Pilar. Custom rides or ride to the miner's cabin Rio Grande Gorge canyon country.

**Taos Indian Horse Ranch** (800-659-3210), Miller Rd. on Taos Pueblo, Taos. Horseback rides, sleigh rides, cookouts, Indian storytellers, and Taos Mountain music. Reservations required. About $103 per person for a two-hour ride.

**MOUNTAIN BIKING** For detailed information, visit the **BLM Pilar Visitor Center** (575-751-4899), 15 miles south of Taos on NM 68 or the **BLM Taos office** (575-758-8851) on Cruz Alta Rd.

**Rio Grande Gorge West Rim Trail**, the Rio Grande Gorge Rest Area at US 64. An easy 9-mile one-way trip with great rewards. Check out the Rio Grande Gorge from the bridge south to NM 567.

**Wild Rivers Recreation Area**, 35 miles north of Taos on NM 378 east of Cerro. From the 6-mile Rinconada Loop Trail and the 5-mile Red River Fault Trail to the 2-mile Red River Fault Trail, this trailhead offers rides from easy to difficult. Maps are at the Wild Rivers Visitor Center or any BLM office. $3 day use.

**NATURAL HOT SPRINGS Blackrock (John Dunn) Springs** are located on the west bank of the Rio Grande just below the John Dunn Bridge. From Taos Plaza, go north on US Highway 64. Continue straight onto New Mexico 522 at the traffic signal where US Highway 64 turns left. Six miles past the intersection with US 64, just over a small bridge on the Rio Hondo, turn left onto the paved County Road B005. Drive slowly through the village of Arroyo Hondo. In 1 mile, the pavement ends. Cross another bridge and climb a short hill. Bear right in 0.1 mile and ignore the many side tracks as the main road snakes to the top of the hill before descending into the Rio Hondo Canyon. The road into the canyon is rough but passable. Cross the Rio Grande on John Dunn Bridge and continue 0.2 mile.

**Manby (Stagecoach) Springs** are located on the east bank of the Rio Grande. Access is from US 64, then onto a private road. From Taos, drive north on US Highway 64 to the intersection with New Mexico Highway 522. Continue straight on New Mexico Highway 522. In 5.3 miles, just before the road begins a long descent, turn left on County Road B007. Continue 2.3 miles on this gravel road, and turn left onto a very rutted dirt road. From this point, a high-clearance vehicle or mountain bike is recommended. Follow the main track, taking care to stay out of driveways along the way. After a half-mile on the rutted track, take the left fork, then the right fork in another 0.8 mile. Reach the parking area on the rim of the Rio Grande Gorge at the unmarked trailhead in another half-mile,

BUFFALO THUNDER IS A STUNNING RESORT OUTSIDE SANTA FE.

1.8 miles from County Road B007. Note that the roads to the trailhead are impassable during wet weather.

**RIVER RAFTING** The **Taos Box** and the **Racecourse** are two of the most popular white-water stretches on the Upper Rio Grande. If runoff is good, you can be on the river from May through July. Adrenaline is the name of the game. Be prepared for Class IV rapids.

**SCENIC DRIVES** **Enchanted Circle Scenic Byway** (877-885-3885). US 64 and NM 522 and 38. Setting out from Taos, the Enchanted Circle links the communities of Angel Fire and Eagle Nest, circling Wheeler Peak, the state's highest mountain. Return to Taos via Bobcat Pass through Red River and Questa. The best time to do the 84-mile Enchanted Circle is when the aspens are turning, usually the last weekend in September, but it's beautiful any time. The road takes you over Bobcat Pass, with its 9,820-foot summit, so named for the many bobcats that lived there. This was once all part of the Maxwell Land Grant, the largest private land holding in the Western Hemisphere during the 19th century.

**High Road to Taos** (no phone). Pick up the High Road by driving north on NM 68 out of Santa Fe through Española. Go right at NM 76 and continue on through the towns of Chimayo, Truchas, Ojo Sarco, Peñasco, and on to Taos on NM 75. Cordova is a jog to the right between Chimayo and Truchas. This is a scenic drive any time of year, during a golden fall, a green spring, or a snowy winter, but always be alert to weather reports and fast-changing weather, whatever the season. Pack a picnic, binoculars, camera, and fishing gear, and bring your hiking boots and multiple layers of outdoors wear. Each village has its historic Spanish colonial church, and each village lives much as it has for

SANTA FE PLAZA MAKES A FINE SPOT TO ENJOY THE AFTERNOON.

centuries, making them almost living history museums. The Sangre de Cristo Mountains offer heart-stopping views. Investigate the galleries, cafés, roadside stands, and historic churches along the way. Easily an all-day trip, particularly for shutterbugs.

**River Road to Taos.** From Española, continue north on NM 68 for 47 miles to Taos. The road follows the course of the Rio Grande and swoops past the green agricultural villages of Alcalde and Velarde, then Embudo, then past the landmark Ranchos Church in Ranchos de Taos. In fall, produce stands along the way are filled with the new harvest—local apples, cider, plums, pears, squash, melons, and preserves. From late May on through midsummer, you are likely to see river rafters down below. It's fun to stop at the little store and café in Pilar, a.k.a. the Pilar Yacht Club, where rafters put in. If you have time and inclination, you can turn right on NM 76 toward Dixon and take the remaining High Road to Taos through Peñasco, Ojo Sarco, and on into Taos along NM 76-75.

**Wild Rivers Back Country Byway** (575-758-8851), 26 miles north of Taos, goes west on NM 378 off NM 522, north of Questa. This is a phenomenal 13-mile ride that parallels the Rio Grande and Red rivers along NM 378, with access to Wild Rivers Recreation Area north of Taos. Scenic overlooks above the Rio Grande Gorge into the canyon will have you in a state of wonder. You must return the same way you drove in. A word of caution: If you are thinking of hiking down to the river, be prepared for a Grand Canyon–Bright Angel Trail–style return—in other words, the hike up and back is only for those in shape, wearing good hiking boots. While it is not a difficult hike, it is extremely steep and seems to become longer with every step. And there are no mules to come rescue you.

**SKIING Angel Fire Resort** (575-377-6401), 22 miles east of Taos via US 64 and NM 434. Known as a "cruiser's mountain" with long, well-groomed trails, up to 3.5 miles, Angel Fire is a comfortable place for beginning and intermediate skiers. The waits are not long. Snowmaking capabilities guarantee 2,000 vertical feet. Tubing, polar coaster, cross-country skiing, ski school, and snowboarding. The Nordic Center has 10 miles of groomed cross-country ski trails with three loops from easy to moderate to more difficult. With over 3,000 beds, this is one of the most affordable lodging bases in the state. $66.

✍ **Red River Ski Area** (575-754-2223). Claiming to offer the best value among Rocky Mountain ski areas, Red River caters to juniors, teens, small children, and families. There's tubing, snowboarding, and a well-respected ski school. You can enjoy excellent skiing on the 10,350-foot mountain, which rises from the middle of town toward the Old Western mining sites of the 1800s. High in the southern Rockies, skiers tackle 57 powder-covered runs. Gaining popularity is the "Moon Star Mining Camp," where the family can ski to a replica of the Moon Star Mine of the 1890s. $65.

**Taos Ski Valley** (575-776-2291), north of Taos on NM 150. The news is out: TSV has finally abandoned its long-standing policy against them and now allows snowboards. Ten chairlifts; a vertical drop of 2,612 feet; challenging runs; and 110 downhill runs, over half of which are advanced; eye-popping views; moguls galore; rentals of everything you will need; and over 300 inches of snow annually make this ski area what many consider the premier skiing experience in the state.

LOVERS OF ROADSIDE MEMORABILIA WON'T WANT TO MISS THE CLASSICAL GAS OUTDOOR MUSEUM ALONG THE RIVER ROAD TO TAOS.

While it attracts experts, it does accommodate novices and intermediates as well. $75.

**SNOWMOBILING A.A. Taos Ski Valley Wilderness Adventures** (575-751-6051).

**Carson National Forest.** Access from Angel Fire tour from Forest Rd. 76 or the Elliot Barker Trail on Palo Flechado Pass.

**Red River.** Greenie Peak and Midnight Meadow are north of town.

**SNOWSHOEING** See **Angel Fire**, **Taos**, **Red River**, and **Enchanted Forest** ski areas for snowshoeing fun. Many trails are located in the Carson National Forest as well, which are often shared with cross-country skiers and snowmobilers. Also, guided snowshoe tours of Taos Ski Valley may be arranged (575-776-3233).

**UNIQUE ADVENTURES Gold Prospecting Excursion**. Enchanted Circle Gateway Museum (575-377-5978). $200.

## ✳ Lodging

**BED & BREAKFASTS, MOTELS, AND HOTELS Angel Fire Resort** (575-377-6401), 10 Miller Ln., Angel Fire. With 157 rooms, Angel Fire Resort is by far the biggest lodging establishment in town. The décor is contemporary Southwestern, and the

THERE'S A BIG FRENCH BRASS BED AT CASA EUROPA B&B.

ski area is right outside the window. The inn has two restaurants, a lounge, and an indoor pool and hot tub. It is quite comfortable. $99–220.

  &#x267F; ✿ **Casa Europa** (575-758-9798), 840 Upper Ranchitos Rd., Taos. For a true Taos getaway, this 18th-century adobe lodge—which contains the oldest door in Taos, views of Taos Mountain from a pastoral valley setting, and all the New Mexico romance of cottonwoods and kiva fireplaces—is simply the best. Hosts Joe and Lisa McCutcheon provide a scrumptious breakfast of juice, fruit, yogurt, scones, and interesting egg dishes, plus freshly baked goodies for afternoon tea; and they see to your every comfort without being intrusive. The rooms are furnished in European period and Southwestern décor, but it all goes together. Whether you are contemplating a ski vacation or an anniversary celebration, this is a good choice. Two-night minimum. $115–195.

**Dreamcatcher Bed & Breakfast**
(575-758-0613), 416 La Lomita Rd.,
Taos. Owners Prudy and John Abeln
are the best hosts one could ask for.
They know and love Taos, they cook
up a storm, and they will make you
feel so at home you won't want to
leave. $140.

🐾 **El Pueblo Lodge** (575-758-8700),
412 Paseo del Pueblo Norte, Taos.
Centrally located, pet-friendly, fireplaces in some rooms, warm, inviting,
well-worn, quiet. Clean hot tub. Have
stayed here often. Continental breakfast, good access to ski valley, Pueblo,
and Plaza. $75.

🐾 ♿ **Inn on the Rio** (575-758-7199;
www.innontherio.com), 910 Kit
Carson Rd., Taos. Brilliant flower
gardens and brightly painted flowers
adorn this charmingly renovated
22-room 1950s vintage motor court
inn with heated outdoor swimming
pool and hot tub, all beautifully
tended. The breakfast of quiche,
lemon poppy-seed cake, and other
hearty dishes prepared and served by
hostess Julie and host Robert are rich
enough to spoil you. The inn is worth
the press it gets as a choice comfortable destination. You are certain to be
happy here. $100–150.

♿ **Mabel Dodge Luhan House**
(575-751-9686), 240 Morada Ln.,
Taos. Set on 5 acres at the edge of the
Taos Pueblo, this rambling three-
story, 22-room quintessential Taos
adobe hacienda was the property of
Mabel Dodge Luhan, the arts patron
who arrived in Taos in 1918, married
Taos Pueblo native Tony Lujan, then
proceeded to import such artists as
Georgia O'Keeffe and D. H. Lawrence to town for their first taste of
New Mexico. Intellectuals and lumi-
naries, such as Carl Jung, Aldous
Huxley, and Willa Cather, all visited
here. Following Mabel's death, it was
purchased by Dennis Hopper, who
lived here during the filming of *Easy
Rider.* You can soak it all up with a
stay in this meticulously furnished and
decorated B&B that is romantic to
the core. And the lodge is now niched
as "offering supportive solitude for
creative reflection," so bring your
journal. $130–150.

♿ 🐾 **San Geronimo Lodge Bed
& Breakfast Inn.** (575-751-3776),
1101 Witt Rd. Welcome to Old Taos.
Bottom-floor rooms are pet-friendly.

EL PUEBLO LODGE IS A COMFORTABLE,
REASONABLY PRICED PET-FRIENDLY B&B.

MABEL DODGE LUHAN'S HOME, LOS GALLOS, IS NOW A TAOS BED & BREAKFAST.

Swim in Taos's only chile-shaped pool. Classic Taos art and architecture. Substantial hot breakfast served in the breakfast room, where the host may play piano. Dates to 1925, secluded, very romantic. Labyrinth on the premises. Very classy, a top choice. $179.

**Sun God Lodge** (575-758-3162), 919 Paseo del Pueblo Sur, Taos. The Sun God is the place for bargain hunters. The 53 rooms are decorated in Southwest style, and with colorful tile accenting the rustic Taos wood furniture. It is quiet despite its location on a busy strip mall across from Walmart. Still, it is best to ask for a room toward the back and away from the main drag. Also, it is possible to encounter problems with the heat—be forewarned. Pet-friendly. $69.

**Taos Inn** (575-758-2233), 125 Paseo del Pueblo Norte, Taos. Stay here and you'll be signing the same guest register as Greta Garbo, Thornton Wilder, and D. H. Lawrence. Each of the 37 guest rooms in this National Historic Landmark property has a distinct personality—most have a pueblo fireplace. Taos-style antique furniture and several rooms open onto the balcony overlooking the lobby. Choose a room in the main building if you prefer a historic experience; the motel-like rooms out back are lighter and brighter. $75–275.

**Taos Mountain Lodge** (575-776-2229), Taos Ski Valley. Located on a south-facing mountainside, Taos Mountain Lodge has 10 condominium split-level A-frame suites that hold four to six. Eight have a fireplace. All are tastefully decorated in Southwest décor. Indoor and outdoor whirlpools can be a blessing after skiing. Here you are completely surrounded by the Carson National Forest, with only a seven-minute trip to the lift. A good deal for a family or small group. $120–275.

**CAMPING** See **Carson National Forest** (page 147), where you can camp virtually anywhere.

**Questa Lodge** (575-586-9913), 8 Lower Embargo Rd., Questa. Open May–Oct. On the Red River, only a quarter-mile off NM 522, there is a motel and RV park with 26 full-service hookups, five cabins, and tent sites. $32 RV site; $60–150.

**Roadrunner RV Resort** (575-754-2286), 1371 E. Main St., Red River. Open May 1–Sept. 15. A 28-acre campground has it all, including almost 100 full hookups, laundry, tennis court, wildlife, and playground. $32–37.

## ✳ Where to Eat

**DINING OUT Lambert's of Taos** (575-758-1009), 123 Bent St., Taos. Open daily. Lunch and dinner, Sunday brunch. If you crave a memorable splurge, and perhaps one of the finest dinners you will ever set a fork into, make a reservation here. House special pepper-crusted lamb loin with red wine demiglaze, medallions of beef tenderloin with blue cheese mashed potatoes, and pistachio-crusted chicken breast with roasted shallot sherry sauce are a few of the luscious options. The menu changes seasonally, and the wine list is one of the most complete and intriguing in town. Expensive–Very Expensive.

**Love Apple** (575-751-0050), 803 Paseo del Pueblo Norte, Taos. Tues.–Sun. Dinner. Dine by candlelight in an antique church for a sense of the faraway and magical. Suitable date night locale. Strictly local and organic, the menu can be limited, and a bit offbeat, but whatever you order, it will be delicious. Not at all typical. It works better here if you don't have expectations of a regular three-course meal. You may prefer two appetizers and a dessert, or a perfectly fresh composed salad. The steak is always good. Even everyday staples, such as corn bread, are lifted into sublime deliciousness. A bit pricey for what you get. No credit cards. Expensive.

**Martyrs Steakhouse Restaurant** (575-751-3020), 146 Paseo del Pueblo Norte, Taos. Open daily. Lunch, dinner. White linen, excellent beef, fancy cocktails, and elegant service fill a dining void Taos didn't know it had. Oysters, veal, local lamb, and free-range chicken are all served with otherworldly side dishes. Whether you choose the lovely patio or indoor dining room, you will enjoy fine dining here. The prime rib is especially succulent, and unless you've just been skiing all day, the serving is generous enough to share. You'll better your chances of having your marriage proposal accepted here. Expensive.

**Old Martina's Hall** (575-758-3003), 4149 NM, Ranchos de Taos. Open daily, breakfast, lunch, dinner. Finally! The long-awaited and much-anticipated, very expensive restoration of the former Ranchos de Taos 68 roadside eyesore does not disappoint. The food is French-ish, or you might say, "American continental," creative, and exquisitely presented. Stop in for a meal or wine and *moules*. Gorgeous bar. Superb baked goods. A great addition to the Taos dining and entertainment scene. If you beg, they will make you schnitzel off the menu. As with so many restaurants, it helps if you like chèvre. I celebrated my most recent birthday there, and everyone in the party, who ordered from tuna to tenderloin, enjoyed it immensely. Moderate.

**Trading Post Café & Gallery Italian Restaurant** (575-758-5089), 4179 NM 68, Ranchos de Taos. Lunch, dinner. Closed Sun., Christmas, and New Year's. Located in the former favorite general store and meeting place in town; this is a place to choose on a chilly night, in front of the fireplace or at the bar. Order a glass of fine wine and peruse the extensive menu that includes salads, fish, pastas, soups, roast duck, chicken Vesuvio, paella, and a large selection of daily specials. In warm weather, try the patio. This is the spot for casual sophistication. Moderate–Expensive.

**EATING OUT Dragonfly Café & Bakery** (575-737-5859), 402 Paseo del Pueblo Norte, Taos. Breakfast, lunch, dinner Wed.–Sat. Breakfast, lunch Sun. Happiness is weekend brunch on this whimsical patio—count on the best omelets and coffee cake. The very best place for a pastry indulgence. Also serving East Indian food—occasionally. The hours can be confusing—sometimes Dragonfly is closed for what seems like a random reason.

DRAGONFLY CAFÉ SERVES A LOVELY SUNDAY MORNING BRUNCH ON THE PATIO.

**Elevation Coffee** (575-779-6078), 1110 Paseo del Pueblo Norte, Taos. Conveniently located on the way to Taos Ski Valley, Elevations is the current "in" spot, serving creamy lattes that are a work of art.

🌸 **Graham's Grille** (575-751-1350), 106 Paseo del Pueblo Norte, Taos. Open daily. Lunch, dinner, weekend brunch. Chef-owner Lesley Fay has given us a stylish eatery just off the Plaza that accomplishes the seemingly miraculous: food with flair at an affordable price. They do a deservedly brisk business with locals and take-out orders. The crab-corn chowder, applewood-smoked BLT, and the signature creamy, dreamy mac and cheese with bacon and green chile are mouthwatering. The lamb with fresh mint is divine. Everything is cooked and served with care. Warning: Winter dining can be chilly if you are seated near the doors. Go for the eggs Benedict on the Sunday brunch menu. Moderate.

**Hatcha's Grill of Angel Fire** (575-377-7011), 3453 Mountain View Blvd. Ste. D, Angel Fire. Mon.–Sun., breakfast, lunch, dinner. I discovered Hatcha's when it was located in Mora on the High Road; now it serves at both locations. Angel Fire is fortunate indeed to have the hearty blue corn enchiladas, fresh guacamole, aged rib eye, slow-simmered *carnitas*, and fajitas, plus burgers and steaks for the gringo palate. When in Angel Fire, eat here.

**The Hole Thing Donut Shop** (575-754-2342), 601 W. Main St., Red River. Open daily 7–2. Breakfast and lunch. If you're a sucker for fresh homemade doughnuts, with or without bacon and eggs smothered in gravy, you'll get up early and hightail it over here. It's the real thing, for sure, and the shop's comfort food is a great way to begin a day on the slopes. Moderate.

**Orlando's** (575-751-1450), 1.8 miles north of plaza on left, off Paseo del Pueblo Norte, 114 Don Juan Valdez Ln., Taos. Open Mon.–Sat. 10:30–3, 5–9. Closed Sun. and Christmas. From its humble beginnings as a hot-dog cart on the Plaza, Orlando's mother's authentic northern New Mexico recipes, minus the lard, is what you'll get here in this colorful café that Frida Kahlo might have decorated. Try the chile bowl "with everything" or the Frito pie. Summer dining on the patio is a joy, day or night, but avoid peak times to dodge the crowds. If you can save room, try the homemade carrot cake. Inexpensive.

**Shotgun Willie's** (575-754-6505), 403 W. Main St., Red River. Homemade barbecue by the pound, hand-breaded catfish, and New Mexican cuisine hearty enough to appease any starving skier. Looking, as it does, like a small shack of a place, you might be tempted to pass Shotgun Willie's by. Don't make that mistake. This place serves by far the best barbecue (and remember, there are a lot of Texans in Red River) and the fattest breakfast burritos, and the paper plates don't hurt a bit. Inexpensive.

🍦 **Taos Cow Ice Cream Scoop Shop Café & Deli** (575-776-5640), 485 NM 150, Arroyo Seco. Open daily 7–6. You might think you're in a time warp here with the longhairs and Rastafarians, but we all know a good thing when we see it. If you're an ice cream lover, head up the Taos Ski Valley Road to the ice creamery that has the creamiest, most exquisite

## GAMING

In addition to serving as venues for Las Vegas–style gaming and dining, Indian-run casinos are popular venues for celebrity performers.

**Camel Rock Casino** (800-GO-CAMEL or 800-462-2635), 10 minutes north of Santa Fe on US 84/285. Run by Tesuque Pueblo, Camel Rock offers slots, blackjack, bingo, roulette, and a restaurant.

**Cities of Gold Casino** (800-455-3313), 15 miles north of Santa Fe on US 84/285. Cities of Gold is run by Pojoaque (po-ah-kay) Pueblo and has more than 700 slot machines, plus an extravagant 24-hour buffet spread.

☀ **Hilton Santa Fe Buffalo Thunder** (505-455-5555), 20 Buffalo Thunder Trail, Santa Fe. Actually located out of town on US 84/285, this is the newest and most deluxe resort in the area, with a knockout art collection, revolving tower gallery, four great restaurants, lovely pool, spa, fabulous golf course, and accessible casino. The only glitch is it is difficult to pin down rates, which are highly negotiable depending on occupancy and time of week and year. Rates are a tightly held secret, and no rate sheet exists.

**Ohkay Casino** (877-829-2865), just north of Española on US 84/285. Operated by Ohkay Owingeh (formerly San Juan) Pueblo, this casino is known for its breakfast buffet, lounge, and new 100-room hotel.

**Taos Mountain Casino** (575-737-0777), Taos Pueblo. This is the only nonsmoking casino in the state, offering slots but no bingo.

BUFFALO THUNDER CASINO & RESORT HAS AN EYE-POPPING ART COLLECTION.

all-natural and rBGH-free ice cream you've ever tasted, in delectable seasonal flavors, such as peach and lavender, and the chocolate variations will win your heart. Freshly roasted organic Fair Trade coffee and WiFi, too. Sandwiches and soups will satisfy your lunch cravings. Inexpensive.

🍴 **Taos Diner** (575-758-2374), 908 Paseo del Pueblo Norte, Taos; Taos Diner II Paseo del Pueblo Sur. Breakfast, lunch daily. Nothing fancy here. Just good wholesome American fare, freshly prepared, and lots of it. One of the best burgers in town, made with local beef, excellent omelets, fantastic homemade biscuits and hot red chile. Huge salads. Wine and beer at the Southside location, which also serves dinner, but I am a fan of the original. Inexpensive.

**Taos Pizza Out Back** (575-758-3112), 712 Paseo del Pueblo Norte, Taos. Open daily May–Sept. 11–10; during the winter, 11–9 weekdays. Closed Thanksgiving, Christmas. You may think you've had the best pizza, but this really is the best. You may have to hunt a bit to find it—it really is out back—but you'll remember where it is and what it is—a funky, hip, wood-warm busy spot. It specializes in "Taos-style gourmet pizza" lovingly made to order from organic Colorado wheat. I love the Florentine, with chicken, garlic, and herbs sautéed in white wine. A slice of pizza with a salad will satisfy most appetites. Lovely hot soups and desserts, too. Inexpensive.

**Tim's Stray Dog Cantina** (575-776-2894), 105 Sutton Pl., Taos Ski Valley. Open daily 8–9 winter, 11–9 summer. This is the place for a lively, if not rowdy, après-ski libation. Plenty of big portions of standard American fare

and "famous margaritas" await. Inexpensive.

**Wired? Coffee Cyber Café** (575-751-9473), 705 Felicidad Ln., Taos. Open daily. Right in back of Albertson's, Wired? is the essence of Taos, with a meandering indoor, porch, and outdoor seating, hodgepodge of hilarious gifts, used books, and basic chile, salads, and burritos. Quiet laptop space provided.

**Zeb's Restaurant & Bar** (575-377-6358), 3431 Mountainview Blvd., Angel Fire. Open daily. Lunch, dinner. This big pub serves up Mexican food, burgers, steaks, and salads at reasonable prices. It may remind you of your college hangout, but there's no problem feeding a hungry family after a day of skiing. It's not gourmet fare, but it's been around a long time. Inexpensive–Moderate.

## ✳ Entertainment

**Alley Cantina** (575-758-2121), 121 Teresina Ln., Taos. Said to be Taos's oldest building, the place draws crowds of tourists and locals who dance into the late hours to the live music every night. Happy hour is a bargain.

**Best Western Kachina Lodge** (575-758-2275), 413 Paseo del Pueblo Norte, Taos. Local bands play here weekend nights.

**Bull O' The Woods Saloon** (575-754-2593), 401 E. Main St., Red River. Live music nightly at 9. Dancing, too. This is *the* nightlife scene in Red River. It's a historic bar with shuffleboard, pool, and karaoke.

**Caffe Tazza** (575-758-8706), 122 Kit Carson Rd., Taos, often has live poetry and spoken word performances, on Fri.–Sat.

**Don Fernando de Taos Hotel** (575-758-4444), 1005 Paseo del Pueblo Sur, Taos. Live music and karaoke sound off at the Hideaway Lounge, and complimentary appetizers are served during happy hour Mon.–Fri. 4–6.

**El Taoseno Restaurant and Lounge** (575-758-4142), 819 Paseo del Pueblo Sur, Taos. If you want to mingle with the locals, hang out here on a Friday night. One of them might ask you for a turn on the big dance floor.

**Eske's Brew Pub and Restaurant** (575-758-1517), 106 Des Georges Pl., Taos, is still the best place to relax with a microbrew, brats, and green chile stew.

**Metta Theater** (575-758-1104), 1470 Paseo del Pueblo Norte, Taos. Innovative, offbeat, premier, and serious theater featuring true local talent. Worth checking out.

**Sagebrush Inn** (575-758-2254), 1508 Paseo del Pueblo Sur, Taos. Live music most nights at 9, with some of the best local country and western performers and dancing.

**Taos Center for the Arts** (575-758-2052; www.taoscenterforthearts.org), 133 Paseo del Pueblo Norte, Taos. The Taos Community Auditorium here is a venue for music, theater, exhibitions, film, and concerts of all varieties.

**Taos Inn** (505-758-2233; www.taosinn.com), 125 Paseo del Pueblo Norte, Taos. Long considered "Taos's living room," there is a huge variety of live entertainment here most nights in the Adobe Bar to accompany your margarita. Walk right in and make yourself at home. The place can get elbow-to-elbow on weekend evenings.

In warmer weather, the streetside patio is divine.

## ✳ Selective Shopping

**Arroyo Seco Mercantile** (575-776-8806), 488 NM 150, Arroyo Seco. Anyone who loves to shop will adore this 1895 general store stocked with vintage textiles, quilts, toys, gifts, books, and garden ornaments. So much fun it should be illegal!

**Artemesia** (575-737-9800), 117 Bent St., Taos. Warning—highly addictive! Stupendous selection of one-of-a-kind handmade wearable art ("artwares"), including hats, scarves, jewelry, wraps, and jackets, of wool, silk, linen. Some amazingly good deals online. If you want to make a statement or change your look, pop in here. You have to start someplace! Compliments guaranteed.

**Fenix Gallery** (575-758-9120), 208-B Ranchitos Rd., Taos. Intriguing displays of contemporary-verging-on-cutting-edge sculpture, painting, mixed media, and the work of many of the area's best known artists, including Bea Mandelman, Alyce Frank, Earl Stroh, and Suzanne Wiggin.

**Francesca's Clothing Boutique** (575-776-8776), 1018 Paseo del Pueblo Norte, El Prado (also in Arroyo Seco). "A great time to be a girl," is the motto here at this stylish, reasonably priced popular boutique. At Francesca's, it also helps to be a tiny girl. Nowhere else captures the essence of the hip Taos look quite so well. Rich display of online offerings as well.

**The Good Sole** (575-737-5000), 1033 Paseo del Pueblo Sur, Taos. Can a shoe store change your life? Maybe not completely, but the right combi-

ARROYO SECO GENERAL STORE HAS JUST ABOUT EVERYTHING.

nation of style and comfort, complimented by Annie's custom-fitted orthotics, could make a huge difference in how you feel about it. Give yourself a meaningful present and get your feet in here.

**Jackie's Trading Post** (575-751-3466), 311 Paseo del Pueblo Norte, Taos. I recommend shopping at this reputable family establishment for your turquoise and silver Southwest-style earrings and bracelets. Plenty of pottery and Indian artifacts to tempt you, plus paintings by well-known contemporary artists.

✐ **Moby Dickens Bookshop** (575-758-3050), 124 Bent St., Taos. Moby Dickens is one of the very best independent bookstores anywhere. In addition to a brilliantly selected two floors of books for browsing, the upstairs has a section devoted to the rare and out of print. Although it recently changed hands, the new owners have vowed to keep it as is.

**Moxie Fair Trade & Handmade** (575-758-1256), 216B, Paseo del Pueblo Norte. There are trinket shops and there is Moxie. Looking for an affordable gift for yourself or a pal—such as a felted hat from Katmandu or a beaded bracelet from Guatemala? This is a fun place to browse and even buy without breaking the piggy bank.

**Open Space: An Artist-Owned Gallery** (575-758-1217), 103 E. Plaza #B, Taos. This mature artist-run co-op gallery showcases a deep treasure chest of fine local pottery, jewelry, photography, and contemporary fine art.

**Overland Fine Sheepskin & Leather** (575-758-8820), 1405 N.

NM 522. Shearling coats to get you through the coldest winters, fine Italian leather coats, fringed and embroidered suede outfits, hats, slippers, mittens, and more. Uggs, too. Of course it's pricey, but think of it as an investment. I do. The midwinter sales, around Valentine's Day, are worth a trip to Taos.

**Steppin' Out** (575-758-4487), 120 Bent St., Taos. Two floors of fine leather goods, including many, many shoes you will want, plus belts and handbags. The high-end waterproof boots turn bad weather into an opportunity for chic. Has branched out into stylish clothing as well. Save your allowance before you go.

**Taos Fiber Arts** (575-758-8242), 108A Dona Luz, Taos. This adorable mother-daughter team of Julie and Ashley Cloutman are business and artistic partners. They have created an inspiring scene in their gallery that includes all you need for weaving, felting, unique wearable art fashion, and classes. Delicious colors and textures of wool and fibers. I have taken felting classes from them and enjoyed every moment. They will customize a class for you and your friends. Truly Taos!

✍ **Tiovivo** (575-758-9400), 226 Ranchitos Rd., Taos. *Tiovivo* means "lively uncle," or, in Taos, the name refers to a venerable carousel that is taken out on special occasions. This shop is a kids' dream come true.

✍ **Twirl Toystore and Playspace** (575-751-1402), 225 Camino d la

TAOS FIBER ARTIST AND TEACHER JULIE CLOUTMAN MODELS ONE OF HER CREATIONS.

EACH PONY ON THE VENERABLE CAROUSEL KNOWN AS TIOVIVO WAS DECORATED BY A WELL-KNOWN TAOS ARTIST.

TWIRL IS A TOY STORE WHERE KIDS CAN REALLY PLAY.

Placita, Taos. Amazing collection of toys and games for all ages plus a fantasy-come-true of an outdoor playground.

**Wabi Sabi** (575-758-7801), 216 Paseo del Pueblo Norte, Taos. You'll be offered a cup of tea as you browse this fine Asian-inspired boutique. Imported scarves, handmade papers, home décor, wearables, much that is irresistible. The place to find the gift for the one who has it all. Inspiring.

**Weaving Southwest** (575-758-0433), 487 NM 150, Arroyo Seco. New location! After achieving international fame as a weavers' gallery, Weaving Southwest has refocused on weaving supplies and classes. Yarns are all hand-dyed outdoors, over wood-burning fires, using acid dyes. Unsurpassed color and quality.

# HIGH ROAD COUNTRY

## CHIMAYO, TRUCHAS, CORDOVA, PEÑASCO, DIXON

Take away the satellite dishes and asphalt, and you might think you've landed in an 18th-century mountain village. Little has changed here over the centuries. Many descendants of original settlers still farm and live sustainably, getting by with bartering, wood cutting, hunting, and fishing on land granted their families by the Spanish crown. Crafts of woodcarving and weaving still thrive here, along with the tried-and-true way of life. Isolated in small villages within high mountain ranges, people are polite but not overly friendly to outsiders. The mission churches of Truchas and Chimayo are not to be missed. A new road is in the offing, so change is on the way.

**GETTING THERE** From Santa Fe, take US 68 north to Española. From Española, go right on NM 76 on up the High Road to Chimayo.

## ✳ To See

**TOWNS Chimayo.** Ten miles east of Española on NM 76. The name comes from the Tewa Indian, meaning "good flaking stone." The village, founded near here in the early days of the Spanish Reconquest in 1692, is famous as the home of El Santuario de Nuestro Señor de Esquipalas, commonly called El Santuario, known for its healing dirt, miraculous cures, and as a Good Friday pilgrimage site. The nearby shrine dedicated to Santo Nino de Atocha is also considered holy. There is a local "belief" that says Santo Nino must have his shoes replaced, as he wears them out traveling about the village at night performing good deeds. The Plaza del Cerro is the only original fortified plaza in the southwest.

**Cordova.** Fourteen miles east of Española on NM 76, 1 mile south of NM 76. Traditional woodcarving is the essence of this village's soul. It's what everyone does. The Cordoba style is unpainted aspen and cedar. You can walk into anyone's studio and find exquisite tree of life, Noah's ark, nativities, and *santos* for purchase.

131

**Dixon.** Twenty miles northeast of Española, 2 miles east of NM 68. Named for the town's first schoolteacher, this village on the Embudo River has an idyllic appeal. With its Victorian architecture intermixed with adobe homes, it is a cozy community of artists, old-timers, and agricultural folk, who appear to share a vision of neighborliness. There's a sweet co-op grocery store in the middle of town next to the library, where you can pick up supplies and a decent cup of coffee.

**Peñasco.** Two miles SE of Picuris Pueblo on NM 75. This is probably the largest village on the High Road, where you can find an ATM, a couple of cafés, and gas. Families have lived here for generations, and everyone is either related to or certainly knows everyone else. Much of the life of the town still revolves around barter and living off the land.

**Truchas.** Eighteen miles northeast of Española on NM 76. Known as the place where the movie *The Milagro Beanfield War*—based on the novel set in Taos by John Nichols—was filmed; it is named for the Rio de Truchas, "trout river," nearby. Set in the high Sangre de Cristos, it is the quintessential isolated High Road village, sprinkled with galleries, with an active *morada*, the home of the Penitente Brotherhood. Warning: Packs of untended dogs roam the streets. And those who live here are not really crazy about those who do not.

## ✷ To Do

**BALLOONING** **Eske's Paradise Balloons** (575-751-6098), P.O. Box 308, El Prado, offers valley and Rio Grande Gorge balloon flights year-round. Each includes an hour aloft and a champagne brunch. Ultralight flights are also available. $240.

**CAMPING AND FISHING** See **Carson National Forest** on page 147.

**MOUNTAIN BIKING** **Carson National Forest** trails off US 64 will take you all the way to Angel Fire.

**Picuris Peak**, access off NM 518, is an intermediate-to-difficult route with a steep grade and a great view.

**Rio Chiquito**, a long forest service road off NM 518 that connects with Garcia peaks, is a favorite of families and includes beaver ponds and good picnicking.

**UNIQUE ADVENTURES** **The Tower at Crawford's Garlic Farm** (575-579-4288), Dixon. Stan and Rosemary Crawford have built an interesting life in rural New Mexico. The author and former president of the Santa Fe Farmers' Market and his wife bring their garlic and fresh produce to sell in town Tues. and Sat. They have constructed "The Tower," a guest house on their farm, where guests are free to forage for vegetables and flowers during growing season. Hiking, biking, kayaking, and skiing are all nearby. Two-night minimum. $95.

THE LOVELY BLACK MESA WINERY MAKES A WORTHWHILE STOP ON THE ROAD UP TO TAOS.

### WINERIES AND WINE SHOPS **Black Mesa Winery** (505-852-2820),

1502 NM 68, Velarde. Open Mon.–Sat. 11–6, Sun. noon–6. Jerry and Lynda Burd live on the road to Taos in fruit country where grapes have been cultivated for centuries. Their best known wine is probably their Black Beauty, a chocolate-flavored dessert wine, but if you prefer something less sweet, their Viognier, Antelope, and several others, especially their big reds fermented in oak barrels, are superb. This fine winery has recently added a tasting room and gallery in Taos at 241 Ledoux St.

BLACK MESA WINERY TASTING ROOM.

**Kokoman Fine Wines & Liquors**
(505-455-2219), 34 Cities of Gold Rd., Pojoaque. Twelve miles north of Santa Fe. An exceptional selection of 2,500 wines, 161 tequilas, and 400 beers are sold here at very

## HIGH ROAD CHURCHES

The hand-carved and painted altar screens and *santos* (saints) found in the High Road Spanish colonial churches represent some of the most striking examples of folk art, created with natural materials, found in New Mexico. A *retablo* is a two-dimensional *santo*, while a *bulto* is three-dimensional. Those who created them are known as *santeros*. Many remain anonymous or nearly so, though numerous explanatory books are available. Check the reading room of the Santa Fe Public Library to learn more.

**El Santuario de Chimayo** (575-351-4889), 25 miles northeast of Santa Fe on US 84/285 to Española. Turn east on NM 76. Follow signs to Chimayo.

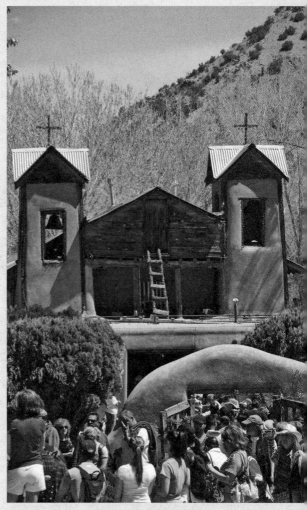

THOUSANDS OF PILGRIMS GATHER EACH GOOD FRIDAY AT EL SANTUARIO DE CHIMAYO.

The site of this chapel, known as the "Lourdes of America" for its "healing dirt," is believed to be a healing place of Pueblo Indians. It was built in 1813–16 by Bernardo Abeyta, who constructed the Santuario to commemorate the remarkable healing he received here. A variation of the legend says there was a cross that was taken from here that kept returning, and on the spot where it returned, Abeyta built the church. Pilgrims arrive with prayers for healing all year long, but on Good Friday it becomes a pilgrimage destination for thousands who walk here.

**Nuestra Señora del Sagrada Rosario** (no phone), Truchas. Constructed around 1805, this beautiful church is not often open. It may be appreciated from the outside, however, or perhaps you will be lucky and find it unlocked.

**San Jose de Gracia de Las Trampas** (575-531-4360), NM 76, 40 miles northeast of Santa Fe. Open daily 8–5 in summer. Considered one of the most beautiful, if not the most architecturally perfect and best-preserved Spanish colonial churches in New Mexico, it was constructed between 1760 and 1780. If you arrive and find the church locked, ask at one of the gift shops on the plaza for the person who keeps the key, or call the parish number above to arrange a tour. Donations accepted.

**Santa Cruz de la Canada** (505-753-3345), NM 76, Santa Cruz, 3 miles north of Española. One of the most venerable High Road churches, located in a community founded by Governor De Vargas in 1695.

ALONG THE HIGH ROAD, THE SAN JOSE DE GRACIA CHURCH IN LAS TRAMPAS IS AN OUTSTANDING EXAMPLE OF SPANISH MISSION ARCHITECTURE.

competitive prices. A well-informed staff will assist you in your selection.

**La Chiripada Winery** (505-579-4437), 3 miles east of NM 68 at 1119-8 NM 75, Dixon. Open Mon.–Sat. 11–6, Sun. noon–6. At 6,100 feet, this is the highest commercial vineyard in the United States. Hearty grapes: two pinot noir hybrids, for example, ripen into intense flavor right here. A signature favorite is the Primavera, a blend of Riesling and French hybrids.

**Vivác Winery** (575-579-4441), 2075 NM 68, Dixon. Twenty-five miles south of Taos at the intersection of NM 75 and US 68. Open Mon.–Sat. 11–6, Sun. noon–6. A showy place with an adobe tasting room built by the owners, colorful flower beds, colorful art, jewelry, and hand-painted chocolates. The wines are interesting, too, and the owners project themselves and their wines as "young and edgy." Their V. Series represents their highest-quality reserve blends and best varietals.

LA CHIRIPADA WINES ARE AVAILABLE IN TAOS, IF YOU'RE LOOKING FOR FINE NEW MEXICO WINE.

## ✳ Lodging

**BED & BREAKFASTS Rancho de Chimayo Hacienda** (505-351-2222), 297 Juan Medina Rd., Chimayo, 25 miles north of Santa Fe off NM 76. A converted rural hacienda owned by the Jaramillos is your home away from home. Seven guest rooms with Spanish-Victorian flair, all with fireplaces and some with balconies. And it's right across the street from Rancho de Chimayo. $95.

❀ **Rancho del Llano** (505-689-2347), 371 County Road 0078, Truchas. This three-bedroom guest house also offers a comfortable stall where your pony can bed down. With so

much mountain and valley trail riding through piñons and meadows, with panoramic overlooks, this is a place where you can get as close as you like to nature. "A guest ranch on a high grassland at the foot of Truchas Peak." Two-night minimum. $100–150.

♂ **Rancho Manzana Bed and Breakfast** (505-351-2227), 26 Camino de Mision, 24 miles northeast of Santa Fe off NM 76. This establishment is a working 4-acre farm known especially for the lavender and apples watered by an ancient *acequia*. The lodging is a 2-foot-thick adobe dating to the 18th century. Gourmet full breakfasts are served outdoors under the grape arbor, weather permitting. There's a hot tub and outdoor pond for dipping, and a separate garden cottage in addition to the two guest rooms in the adobe. It doesn't get any more romantic. Weddings. Cooking school. $105.

## ✴ Where to Eat

**DINING OUT Rancho de Chimayo Restaurante** (505-351-4444), 300 Juan Medina Rd., Chimayo. Open daily. Lunch, dinner. Closed Mon. Nov.–May. After experiencing the beneficial effects of the "holy dirt" of the Santuario, try some of the "holy chile" served here. You will fall in love as you sip a margarita by the fireplace on a chilly winter afternoon. And if you have only one New Mexico classic restaurant to sample, do not miss this beauty. The chile is on the mild side, but that does not detract from its tastiness. This beautiful adobe ranch house has been in the Jaramillo family since the 1880s. With its wooden floors, whitewashed walls, vigas, and terraced patio, you couldn't be anywhere but northern New Mexico. Flavor and service are consistent. Try the crispy nachos; the sopaipilla stuffed with beef, beans, and rice; and the Chimayo chicken, with flan for dessert. Moderate.

**EATING OUT 🐌 Sugar Nymphs Bistro** (575-587-0311), 15046 NM 75, Peñasco. Be advised to call first, as hours are not strictly adhered to. Lunch, dinner daily, Sun. brunch. Locavore alert. Here's a gourmet experience where you least expect to

MEET AT THE VISITOR CENTER FOR A TOUR OF OFF-THE-GRID EARTHSHIPS.

find one. Freshly baked bread and homemade mushroom soup, pizza, and calzones made to order. Interesting combinations of wholesome contemporary American flavors are put together by a San Francisco–trained chef. Save room for the signature chocolate-pecan pie. This tiny way off the beaten track spot has been discovered by foodies from *Gourmet* and *Sunset*. Keep posted on the bistro's special dinners. Moderate.

**Sugar's BBQ & Burger** (505-852-0604), 1799 NM 68, Embudo. Open Mon. and Wed.–Sun. 11–6. Closed Tues. Lunch, dinner. When you need a quick, tasty lunch stop, come to this unpretentious little drive-in that has a national reputation for its delectable smoked ribs and a phenomenal Sugar Burger. The sausage also gets raves, as does the brisket. Hmm . . . hard to decide. Inexpensive.

## ✳ Selective Shopping

**Galeria Ortega** and **Ortega's Weaving Shop** (505-351-2288), 55 Plaza del Cerro, Chimayo. Mon.–Sat. 9–5. Closed Sun. Authentic 100 percent woolen blankets, rugs, coats, vests, and purses are handwoven here in the traditional Chimayo style. Anything you purchase here will last forever. You can watch Andrew Ortega, a seventh-generation weaver, at work in his studio. Southwest books and snacks are available as well.

**High Road Marketplace Artists' Co-op & Gallery** (505-689-2689), 1642 NM 76, Truchas. Open daily winter 10–4; summer 10–5. A mustsee for lovers of local folk art. Traditional and contemporary arts and crafts by more than 70 northern New Mexico artists, mainly High Road dwellers, from whimsical sage dolls to tinwork to fine woodcarving, are found in this nonprofit community outlet.

**Ojo Sarco Pottery** (505-689-2354), 82 County Road 73, Ojo Sarco. Open daily May–Sept. 10–5 and by appointment. Go oven to table with durable and beautiful premade or customordered dinner- and servingware that blend with just about any décor are created in this studio-gallery. Sensational multilayered glazes make for irresistible pieces by two of New Mexico's most accomplished potters.

**Theresa's Art Gallery and Studio** (505-753-4698), NM 76, Santa Cruz. Open daily 8–8. Local folk, Jewish, and Indian art, angels, tinwork, *retablos*, pottery, kachinas, and more make this extended family shop a worthwhile stop. The charm will make it difficult to leave.

# RIO CHAMA COUNTRY

## ABIQUIU, ESPAÑOLA, TIERRA AMARILLA, LOS OJOS

I f you love the paintings of Georgia O'Keeffe, this region will have special meaning to you as it reveals the landscapes and the wind-sculpted red rocks that inspired her iconic work. Outside of Española, known for its culture of cruising low-riders, much of the area is occupied by ranchers and villagers with a complex history of Native American and Hispanic relationships. These folks maintain strong pride in their heritage. Faith and tradition guide the way. Ghost Ranch makes a fine base for hiking and sight-seeing. Weavers at Tierra Wools, who work with wool of the Churro sheep, the breed originally brought by the Spanish, make Los Ojos a model of renewed sustainability.

**GETTING THERE** From Santa Fe, take US 68 north. Continue through Española, turn on US 84/285, and continue north.

**GUIDANCE** **Chama Valley Chamber of Commerce** (575-756-2306), 2372 Highway 17, Chama.

**Española Valley Chamber of Commerce** (505-753-2831), 710 N. Paseo de Oñate, Española.

## ✳ To See

**TOWNS** **Abiquiu** (ab-eh-q). Famed as the haunt and home of 20th-century America's famous woman artist Georgia O'Keeffe, Abiquiu was founded as a Spanish land grant community and became the home of people known as *genizaros*—detribalized Indians who lost their tribal identity through warfare and captivity. Here they were Christianized and given full citizenship by the Spanish Crown. Abiquiu residents received a 16,000-acre land grant for grazing and timber. In 1829 it became the trailhead for the Old Spanish Trail linking 1,200 miles between Santa Fe and Los Angeles. Along with the beauty of its landscape, which has attracted the rich and famous, descendants of the original

WEAVINGS IN THE RIO GRANDE STYLE ARE AVAILABLE AT TIERRA WOOLS IN LOS OJOS.

settlers remain proud people who continue to practice their traditions, including a contemporary revival of the Penitente brotherhood.

**Española.** Known as the territory of the low-riders, those who cruise the streets slowly in their elaborately altered and colorfully painted automobiles, Española is a crossroads and jumping off point to both the River Road and the High Road to Taos. According to local lore, the name means "Spanish woman," with local tradition referring to a woman who worked in a restaurant here and was known to railroad workers.

**Los Ojos.** A tiny community, which, during the 1960s, experienced a revival of traditional, sustainable ways through the raising of Churro sheep and the restoration of the Rio Grande weaving tradition. You'll want to visit **Tierra Wools** (575-558-7231), 91 Main St., Los Ojos, and the weaving co-op there. You can watch the weavers and observe the hand dying of the yarn.

**Tierra Amarilla** means "yellow earth," a name common to all the native people who lived here and used the yellow pigment for pottery. It is the county seat of Rio Arriba County. It gained notoriety in 1967 for the courthouse raid led by Reyes Lopez Tijerina.

**HISTORIC LANDMARKS, PLACES, AND SITES Dar al-Islam Mosque** (505-685-4515), 342 County Road 155, above Ghost Ranch. Built by the world's foremost adobe architect, Hassan Fathy, this mosque hosts the Annual North

American Muslim Pow-Wow in June. If you choose to visit, call ahead, as access
is limited.

**Echo Amphitheater**, 18 miles north of Abiquiu on US 84, is a remarkable natural sandstone amphitheater-shaped formation where echoes really resound.
Find a few campsites here and a short, easy hiking trail.

**Georgia O'Keeffe's Home and Studio** (505-946-1000; 505-685-4539),
Abiquiu. Tours are conducted by appointment only on Tuesdays, Thursdays, and
Fridays from mid-March through November, with additional tours on Wednesdays and Saturdays from June to October. All Georgia O'Keeffe tours last
approximately one hour and are limited to a maximum of 12 people. Tour office
is located next to Abiquiu Inn. $35.

**Ghost Ranch Education & Retreat Center** (505-685-4333; www.ghostranch
.org), Abiquiu. Forty miles northwest of Española on US 84. Classes and seminars in photography, writing, pottery, silversmithing, tin punching, history,
health, and spirituality are offered year-round at this 21,000-acre retreat center
in the heart of O'Keeffe's red rock country. Specialized historic and landscape
tours are also available. Operated by the Presbyterian Church, rustic Ghost
Ranch is a center of diversity. Upgraded accommodations are available, as are
simple dorm spaces and camping. Intermediate hiking trails, Kitchen Mesa and
Chimney Rock, traverse expansive desert landscape with clear views of forever.

**Pedernal** means "Flint Mountain" and is where the ancient people hunted that
valuable stone. "God told me that if I painted it often enough, He would give it
to me," said the painter Georgia O'Keeffe. She made the imposing peak hers,
regardless of who holds the deed.

**Los Brazos** means "the arms" and refers primarily to the tributaries of the Rio
Brazos. However, as you drive north on US 84, look to the right as you approach
Chama to see striking cliffs of sheer Precambrian quartzite, popular with
climbers.

**Monastery of Christ in the Desert** (801-545-8567; www.christdesert.org),
west on US 84 past Ghost Ranch Visitor's Center. Left on Forest Service Rd.
151. A 13-mile winding dirt road leads to monastery grounds. A Japanese monk
designed the primitive rock-and-adobe church of this remote Benedictine monastery along the Chama River. In the Benedictine tradition, hospitality is offered
by the community. It is possible to make a retreat here by contacting the guest-
master. You will have the opportunity to take part in the life of the monks during
prayers, which focus on the Book of Psalms, and silent meals. Two-night minimum. $40.

**MUSEUMS Florence Hawley Ellis Museum of Anthropology** (505-685-
4333), Ghost Ranch Conference Center, Abiquiu. US 84, 35 miles northwest of
Española. Open Mon.–Sat. 9–5, Sun. noon–5. Named for a pioneer anthropolo-
gist, this museum specializes in excavated materials from the Ghost Ranch Gallina digs. The Gallina culture of northern New Mexico was rooted in the people
who left Mesa Verde and Chaco Canyon during a drought around A.D. 1200.
Adjacent ✍ **Ruth Hall Museum of Paleontology** Tues.–Sat. 9–5, displays a

copy of the diminutive Coelophysis dinosaur skeleton, the official state fossil. $4 adults, $1 children and seniors.

**Ghost Ranch Piedra Lumbre Education and Visitor Center** (505-685-4312), US 84 between Mile Markers 225 and 226, just north of Ghost Ranch. Open Tues.–Sun. 9–5. Exhibits of Georgia O'Keeffe, paleontology, archaeology, geology, and the Old Spanish Trail, as well as the Jicarilla Apache. Gift shop and picnic area. Free.

## ✳ To Do

**BOATING El Vado Lake State Park** (575-588-7247), near Chama, has ramps, camping, and waterskiing, plus Kokanee salmon fishing waters.

**Heron Lake State Park** (575-588-7470) is a popular sailing lake set in a ponderosa pine forest. Cross-country skiing, fishing, camping, and hiking. Because it is a restricted no-wake lake, it is ideal for canoeing and kayaking as well. During Apr.–Nov., contact **Stone House Rentals** (575-588-7274) for boats and canoes, and kokanee salmon fishing waters.

**CLIMBING, SKIING, HIKING, AND PADDLING Bumps! Ski Shop** (575-377-3146), 48 N. Angel Fire Rd., Angel Fire.

**Cottam's Ski Shops** (800-322-8267), 207A Paseo del Pueblo Norte, Taos.

**Mountain Sports Rentals** (575-377-3490), 3375 NM 434, Angel Fire.

**Taos Mountain Outfitters** (575-758-9292), 114 S. Plaza, Taos.

**CROSS-COUNTRY SKIING Angel Fire Excursions** (575-377-6941; www.cti-excursions.com), Angel Fire.

**Bobcat Pass Wilderness Adventures** (575-754-2769), 1670 NM 38, Red River.

**Cumbres Pass**, north of Chama, is a popular cross-country spot where people pull their vehicles off the road and break their own trails.

**Enchanted Forest XC Ski and Snowshoe Area** (575-754-2374), Bobcat Pass.

**Miller's Crossing** (575-754-2374), 417 W. Main St., Red River.

**FISHING Abiquiu Lake** (505-685-4371), 65 miles northwest of Santa Fe on US 84/285; turn on NM 96. Open year-round. This large, scenic reservoir behind Abiquiu Dam offers a little of everything. Kokanee salmon fishing is fine, and, if you bring your own equipment, windsurfing, waterskiing, and canoeing are all doable. RV and tent sites here, too.

**Canjilon Lakes.** (575-684-2489). From El Rito take NM 554 to NM 129 for approximately 16 miles to these gems of small lakes for some of the best trout fishing on the Carson National Forest. Also nearby, check out Trout Lakes and Hidden Lake. The best access to Trout Lakes is off US 84 above Tierra Amarilla; go right at Cebolla for about 2 miles. Two campgrounds available at Canjilon's.

Heron Lake.

**Dos Amigos Anglers** (575-377-6226), 247 E. Therma, Eagle Nest.

**High Country Anglers** (575-376-9220), Ute Park. Orvis Guide of the Year, Doc Thompson.

**Los Rios Anglers Fly Shop & Guide Service** (575-758-2798), 126 W. Plaza, Taos.

**HIKING** **Ghost Ranch** has four popular hikes: Chimney Rock, between easy and moderate as it climbs about 600 feet, about two hours, with a stunning view of the Piedra Lumbre Basin; Box Canyon, the easiest, about 4 miles, across the arroyo in back of the main property, with a bit of rock scrambling en route; Kitchen Mesa, the most challenging at 5 miles; and the Piedra Lumbre Hike, beyond the WETLANDS sign off the main road to the left, through the bosque and over a suspension bridge crossing Canijlon Creek for a 3-mile round-trip gentle hike to the Ghost Ranch Piedre Lumbre Visitor Center. You can get maps and details at the visitor office, where you must sign in.

ABIQUIU LAKE IS A PREMIER SPOT FOR HIKING, CAMPING, AND FISHING.

CHIMNEY ROCK IS ONE OF SEVERAL OUTSTANDING HIKES AT GHOST RANCH.

**HOT SPRINGS Ojo Caliente Mineral Springs** (505-583-2233), 50 Los Banos Dr., Ojo Caliente. Open daily. Closed Christmas. The reasons to come to Ojo Caliente are to visit the hot springs, stay at the lodge, and relax. The quality and composition of these geothermally heated waters is said to be as high quality as the finest European spas. Ojo gets progressively more expensive as improvements are made, but it is still a bargain compared with taking the waters in Santa Fe. It is cheaper by far, and less crowded, during the week. Ask about Tues. specials, local bargain rates, sunset rates, and winter specials. A half-dozen pools of varying temperature and mineral composition are guaranteed to relax you, and there are private tubs, too. Massage is available. You can sweat out your toxins with the Milagro wrap ($13). The wine bar is a most pleasant place to unwind. $18–28. There is also an easy 4-mile round-trip hike. See *Lodging*.

**RIVER RAFTING Far Flung Adventures** (800-359-2627), El Prado.
**Known World Guide Service**, 2217 NM 68, Embudo (505-983-7756).
**Los Rios River Runners** (800-544-1181), 233 Paseo Del Pueblo Sur, Taos.
**Native Sons Adventures** (575-758-9342). 1203 King Dr., Taos.

**SNOWMOBILING AND JEEPING Bitter Creek Guest Ranch** (505-754-2587), Red River. Jeeps, snowmobiles, tours, and rentals, plus rustic cabins.

**Cumbres Pass** (no phone). Snowmobiles are given free rein and parking areas along NM 17 across the 64 miles of the 10,222-foot pass that borders Colorado in the Rio Grande National Forest. Be sure to travel well prepared, with maps, supplies, and water. Folks do get lost out here.

**Fast Eddie's** (575-754-3103), Red River.

*✿***TRAIN RIDES Cumbres and Toltec Scenic Railroad** (888-286-2737; www.cumbrestoltec.com), Chama. Open daily May 26–Oct. 21. This narrow-gauge steam-powered railroad runs 64 miles along 10,015 Cumbres Pass between Chama and Antonito, Colorado. It was built over 125 years ago by the Denver & Rio Grande Railway to carry the products of mining and timber out of the region. The fare includes lunch at the stagecoach town of Osier, Colorado, along the route. Hamburgers, hot dogs, hot turkey, soup, and salad bar are on the buffet. Make reservations well in advance. Autumn color tours are especially sought after. $78–171 adults, $52–69 children. Parlor car $115–129.

THE GEOTHERMALLY HEATED HOT SPRINGS AT OJO CALIENTE RANK WITH THE WATERS FOUND AT THE BEST SPAS IN EUROPE.

ALL ABOARD FOR THE CUMBRES AND TOLTEC NARROW-GAUGE RAILROAD IN CHAMA.

## ✳ Green Space

**Resting in the River Organic Farm & Natural Products** (505-820-0563), Abiquiu. Certified organic medicinal herbs are grown according to "Spiritual Agriculture." Farm tours are sometimes offered at this organic farm operated by movie star Marsha Mason, where fine herbal products are also sold. Please call for information on visiting.

**PARKS Kit Carson Memorial State Park** (575-758-8234), central Taos. This park is the site of the historic cemetery, walking paths, and a playground on its 22 acres of green space in the middle of town.

**Rio Grande Gorge Recreation Area, Orilla Verde Visitor Center** (575-758-8851), Picnic shelters and campgrounds along the road that runs beside the river. A stunning area where you (and your pets) do want to be wary of rattlesnakes.

**Carson National Forest** (575-758-6200), 208 Cruz Alta Rd., Taos. Stop in here for maps and guidance when planning a trip on this 1.5-million-acre national forest. You can find any kind of seasonal recreation you seek: snowshoeing; snowmobiling; jeeping; hiking on 330 miles of trails (which in winter become cross-country skiing trails); fishing in 400 miles of cold-water mountain streams for rainbow, brown, and Rio Grande cutthroat trout; and you can camp virtually anywhere, in a designated campground or outside one, if you prefer. The forest elevation ranges from 6,000 feet to the 13,161-foot Wheeler Peak, the state's highest. Plus, there are 86,193 acres of wilderness, limited to foot and horseback travel, including the Wheeler Peak and Latir Wilderness areas. Black bear, mountain lion, and bighorn sheep roam the old-growth forests, as do fox, deer, beaver, and smaller animals. In other words, the Carson is an outdoor paradise. Like the Gila National Forest in southwestern New Mexico, you could spend a lifetime exploring it.

**El Rito Ranger District** (575-581-4554)

**Tres Piedras Ranger District** (575-758-8678)

## ✳ Lodging
### BED & BREAKFASTS, MOTELS
**Abiquiu Inn** (505-685-4378), 21120 US 84. Abiquiu Southwest rustic luxury in a gracious lodge with restaurant and gallery. Lectures and cultural programs related to the area can be part of your stay. Expedia has deals. $85–130.

**Branding Iron Motel & Restaurant** (575-756-2162), 1511 W. Main St., Chama. Open May–Oct. This is as clean and serviceable motel as you are likely to find. It's nothing special, but it is comfortable enough, and you will be happy to have a reservation here during railroad season. $85.

☀ ♿ **Elkhorn Lodge and Cafe** (575-756-2105), 2663 US 84, Chama. This 50-year-old lodge on the bank of the Rio Chama has 22 rooms and 11 cabins. The café serves a decent breakfast and has a fine outdoor patio,

and you can fish from the Rio Chama out back on Elkhorn's 10 acres. Pet-friendly. Say hi to the resident bulldog, Jack, who blogs at travelinjacks dog-blog.blogspot.com. Low-season prices start from $45–69.

**Las Parras de Abiquiu Guesthouse & Vineyard** (505-685-4200), 21341 US 84, Abiquiu. This casita amidst the grapevines along the Chama River has two sweet bedrooms, El Jardin and El Pedernal. Note" Breakfast is not included. $130.

### LODGES AND RANCHES
**Cooper's El Vado Ranch** (575-588-7354), 3150 NM 12, Tierra Amarilla. On the Chama River below El Vado Lake. The state record brown trout resides in the grocery store here, which tells you something. Two-night minimum required during peak season; three nights on holiday

weekends. Ten comfortable log cabins on 100 acres make this an outdoors lover's getaway. El Vado is the put-in site for river rafters on the Chama, which in season gets Class II and III rapids. $114.

❧ **Corkins Lodge** (575-588-7261), 750 NM 512, Chama. A very special place, suitable for family reunions and other special gatherings, with cabins that sleep up to 12. Located in the Chama Valley on 700 acres at the foot of the Brazos Cliffs, there is no more beautiful setting. Guests may fish along a private 2.5-mile stretch of the Brazos River. Half-price specials available during the week and off-season. $195–240.

**Ojo Caliente Mineral Springs** (800-222-9162), 50 Los Banos Drive, Ojo Caliente. Remodeling is a continual state of affairs here, and several of the older cabins have received a renovation. Upscale suites with a private pool are the newest additions. You can warm yourself by the lobby fireplace or sun yourself in a rocker on the front porch, or make new friends in the wine bar. And Artesian Café serves wholesome, healthy breakfast, lunch, and dinner, with decent salads and fresh fish on the menu. $139–469.

**CABINS AND CAMPING Brazos Lodge & Rentals** (575-588-7707), 7 Sweeney Lane, Tierra Amarilla. 15 miles southeast of Chama in the Brazos Canyon on NM 512. Here find a lodge, about a dozen cabins of whatever size you need to suit your group, as well as condos with a minimum two-night stay. Three-night minimum during holidays. Pets okay. $110–225.

**Rio Chama RV Park** (575-756-2303), two blocks north of depot on

NM 17 toward Alamosa, Chama. Located along the Rio Chama, this RV park with full hookups and electric is walking distance to downtown Chama and the railroad depot. RV site $39, tent site $16.

**Sky Mountain Resort RV Park** (575-756-1100), 2743 US 84, Chama. With unobstructed views of the Rio Chama on 10 acres are 46 sites with full hookups. $27–37.

🐾 **Stone House Lodge** (575-588-7274). 95 Heron Lake Rd., Los Ojos. Off NM 84, go west on NM 95 for 14 miles. Lodge is 3 miles west of Heron Dam. The location is perfection— right between El Vado and Heron Lake State Parks. The cabins are properly rustic; however, the Stone House itself holds up to 20 people. RV hookups, too. And you can rent a boat, stock up at the grocery store, fill your propane tank, or engage a professional fishing guide. Snowmobilers can head out on 300 miles of trails, and cross-country skiers can take off to the backcountry. Pet-friendly. Cabins $100–350; Stone House $450.

✳ **Where to Eat**

**DINING OUT El Paragua** (505-753-3211), 603 Santa Cruz Rd., Espanola, or NM 76 just to the right of NM 68. Open daily, lunch and dinner, 11–9. This dark, very Spanish institution continues to serve consistently fine New Mexican and mesquite-grilled meals. If you can get past the scrumptious *carne adovada*, chiles rellenos, and chimichanga, there's the garlic shrimp in butter. No better chips and salsa, the mark of a fine establishment. Moderate.

**EATING OUT Bode's General Store** (505-685-4422), 21196 US 84.

Open daily 6 AM–8 PM. Breakfast, lunch. This is no ordinary gas station. Trader Martin Bode arrived in Abiquiu at least a century ago, and his family still operates the place, which is a combination pit stop, bakery stocked with house-baked yummies, grocery store, hardware store, and gift shop. Where else can you spot a monk from Christ in the Desert Monastery buying a shovel while you are eating a freshly baked cinnamon roll or Frito pie and reading the Sunday *New York Times*? Known for green chile cheese burgers. Wine, beer, and WiFi. Inexpensive.

**El Farolito** (575-581-9509), 1212 Main St., El Rito. I used to be able to count on this place to be open Sundays, but lately, hours have been uncertain. Do call before taking the long drive to confirm the café is actually open. The reason to drive on NM 15 to El Rito is to dine at this darling New Mexican eatery with eight tables. On my top ten green chile list. Inexpensive.

**El Parasol** (505-753-8852), 603 Santa Cruz Rd. Española. You could spot a Hollywood actress without much makeup munching an out-of-sight chicken guacamole taco at this drive-in, on one of the picnic benches along with the local Sikhs and low-riders. Don't miss this cultural mix. Best to phone in your order before you arrive if you don't want a long wait. Other Parasols now in Santa Fe and the area, but of course, the original is always best. Inexpensive.

**Foster's Hotel, Restaurant and Saloon** (575-756-2296), 393 S.

BODE'S IS A LANDMARK GAS STATION, CAFÉ, AND MERCANTILE SHIP IN ABIQUIU.

Terrace Ave., Chama. Open daily 6 AM–10 PM. Breakfast, lunch, dinner. Okay, so it's not the Ritz.; it was a Harvey House once upon a time. The big old woodstove in the middle of the café puts out the heat, and that's just fine when the temperature is 8 below and streets are lined with 3-foot snowdrifts. Standard American and Mexican fare are offered. Breakfast is probably the best meal. It's cozy, it's warm and friendly, and you can go next door to the bar after you've eaten (or before). Inexpensive.

**Three Ravens Coffee House** and **World Drums** (575-588-9086), NM 531, Tierra Amarilla. Good strong coffee, pastries, muffins, panini, wraps, salads, smoothies. Who knew? Right next to the courthouse where activist Reies Tijerina made his stand in 1967 is a WiFi- and espresso-endowed refuge from the road. Call ahead for hours. Inexpensive.

## ✳ Entertainment

**High Country Restaurant and Saloon** (575-756-2384), 2289 S. NM 17, Chama. Order a steak and take in the live country music on weekends. You might hear a dead-ringer for Patsy Cline, who once performed at the Grand Ole Opry! This cowboy bar is the place to go for an evening in Chama.

## ✳ Selective Shopping

**The Mystery Store: A Book Exchange and More** (575-756-1069), 612 S. Terrace, Chama. A little bit of a lot: good coffee, tea, pastry, book exchange, jewelry, local crafts, pet-friendly patio. WiFi free to customers.

**Rising Moon Gallery** (505-685-4271), 1 Bode's Court, Abiquiu. Located directly across US 84 from Bode's at the entrance to Abiquiu, this adorable gallery has handmade jewelry, tinwork, pottery, and works on paper that will make you exclaim with the perhaps overused, nonetheless apt description, "Charming!"

## ✳ Special Events

*January:* **Taos Winter Wine Festival** (505-946-8506), last two weeks. Wine and food events, seminars, grand tastings in Taos and Taos Ski Valley. **Chama Chile Ski Classic**

TAOS SCHOOL OF MUSIC BRINGS THE NEXT GENERATION OF CLASSICAL MUSICIANS TO LEARN AND PERFORM IN TAOS SKI VALLEY EACH SUMMER.

(575-756-2746), XC race plus *beau-coup* fun activities.

*June:* **Taos Solar Music Festival** (www.solarmusicfest.com), Kit Carson Park, last weekend. It rocks, with demos of sustainable energy projects as well as such bands as Los Lobos and stars as Lyle Lovett, plus the new music. **Toast of Taos** (575-758-3329), late June–early July. Golf tournament, gallery tours, wine dinners, and art auctions. **Taos School of Music Summer Chamber Music Festival** (575-776-2388), mid-June–mid-Aug.

*July:* **Taos Pueblo Pow Wow** (575-741-0181) and **Fiestas de Taos** (575-741-0909), midmonth.

*August:* **Music from Angel Fire** (575-377-3233). Internationally known musicians perform classical in concerts all over northern New Mexico. $25 average, with complimentary performances along the way.

*September:* **High Road Art Tour** (www.highroadnewmexico.com), last two weekends, 10–5. **San Geronimo Day** (575-741-0181), annual Taos Pueblo pole-climbing event. **Taos Fall Arts Festival** (575-758-3873).

*October:* **The Wool Festival at Taos** (www.taoswoolfestival.org), Kit Carson Memorial Park, Taos, first weekend. A celebration of the animals, textiles, fiber and fiber enthusiasts that retains its folksy feel, even as it has grown into a huge event. **Annual Abiquiu Studio Art Tour** (www.abiquiustudiotour.org), Columbus Day Weekend.

*November:* **Taos Mountain Balloon Rally** (575-758-9210). **Dixon Studio Tour** (www.dixonarts.org), first weekend. Over 50 area artists open their studios in a grand gala of arts and crafts.

*December:* **Yuletide in Taos** (taos.org), all month. Farolitos, tree lighting, open studios on LeDoux St., and lovely festivities of the season.

# Santa Fe and Beyond

4

SANTA FE, TESUQUE, LOS ALAMOS,
LA CIENAGA, GALISTEO

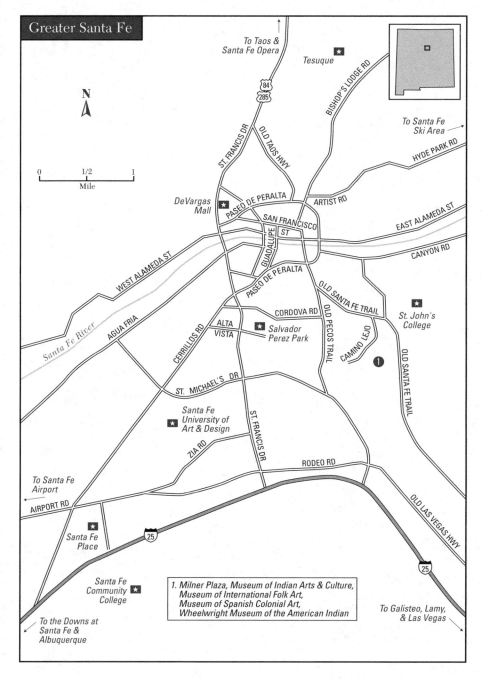

# Greater Santa Fe

To Taos &
Santa Fe Opera

Tesuque

To Santa Fe
Ski Area

N

BISHOP'S LODGE RD

HYDE PARK RD

ST. FRANCIS DR

OLD TAOS HWY

0    1/2    1
Mile

DeVargas
Mall

PASEO DE PERALTA

ARTIST RD

EAST ALAMEDA ST

SAN FRANCISCO
ST

GUADALUPE

CANYON RD

WEST ALAMEDA ST

PASEO DE PERALTA

OLD SANTA FE TRAIL

St. John's
College

AGUA FRIA

Santa Fe River

CERRILLOS RD

ALTA
VISTA

Salvador
Perez Park

CORDOVA RD

OLD PECOS TRAIL

CAMINO LEJO

OLD SANTA FE TRAIL

ST. MICHAEL'S DR

Santa Fe
University of
Art & Design

ST. FRANCIS DR

ZIA RD

RODEO RD

To Santa Fe
Airport

AIRPORT RD

OLD LAS VEGAS HWY

Santa Fe
Place

25

Santa Fe
Community
College

1. Milner Plaza, Museum of Indian Arts & Culture,
   Museum of International Folk Art,
   Museum of Spanish Colonial Art,
   Wheelwright Museum of the American Indian

25

To Galisteo, Lamy,
& Las Vegas

To the Downs at
Santa Fe &
Albuquerque

# SANTA FE, TESUQUE, LOS ALAMOS, LA CIENAGA, GALISTEO

Santa Fe. The very sound of the name conjures visions of blazing sunsets, ancient adobe buildings, romantic patios, colorful fiestas, and shopping beyond compare. This "City Different" is, after all, the oldest capital city in the United States, founded in 1610. This City of Holy Faith sits at the foot of the Sangre de Cristos, the Blood of Christ Mountains, at 7,000 feet. In fact, this city is so intriguing that it consistently places in the top three favorite U.S. travel destinations.

What distinguishes Santa Fe from other American cities are its flat-roofed, wood-beamed adobe houses and public buildings. This "Santa Fe Style" of architecture is called Pueblo Revival. The style was inspired by one building: the Museum of Fine Arts, a 1917 structure designed by architect Isaac Hamilton Rapp that stands off the Plaza, modeled originally on San Estevan Mission at Acoma Pueblo. This signature building style was subsequently enforced by city ordinance and the town fathers with the foresight, a century ago, to understand the city's mission was to attract tourists. The scale and the use of natural materials both capture and communicate the ancient essence of this place.

Stroll up Canyon Road and browse the galleries that give the city a reputation as one of the nation's top art markets, then over to Camino del Monte Sol and Acequia Madre, the path of the annual Christmas Eve farolito walk. These streets were made famous by artists who lived and worked there during the first half of the 20th century, and whose work still hangs in the Museum of Fine Arts and sells for six and seven figures in the better galleries. One of the best remembered, Will Shuster, created Zozobra, also known as "Old Man Gloom," a giant effigy that is burned at Santa Fe Fiestas every September as the season changes, in a joyous communal celebration.

And there is truth to the mystique. There is nothing like sipping a margarita on Sena Plaza when the gardens are in bloom, or brunching at Geronimo, or tailgating at the Santa Fe Opera, or maxing out your credit cards on Canyon Road.

It is also true that "bargains" are not easy to come by in Santa Fe. There is no real off-season, not in a city that receives over a million visitors a year and

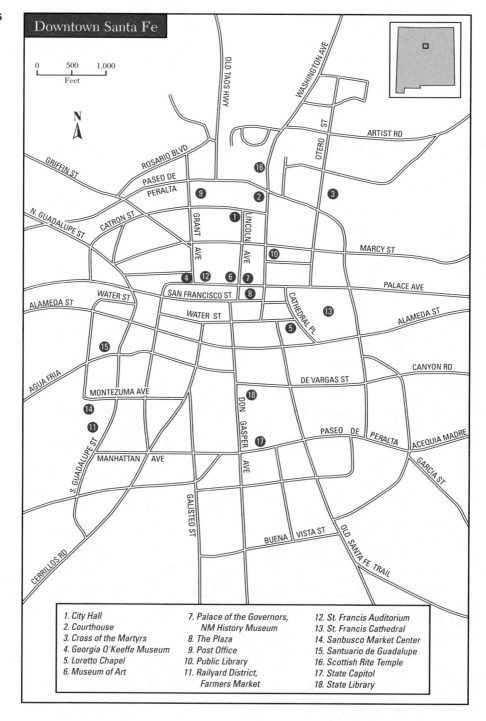

# Downtown Santa Fe

0    500    1,000
Feet

N

1. City Hall
2. Courthouse
3. Cross of the Martyrs
4. Georgia O'Keeffe Museum
5. Loretto Chapel
6. Museum of Art
7. Palace of the Governors,
   NM History Museum
8. The Plaza
9. Post Office
10. Public Library
11. Railyard District,
    Farmers Market
12. St. Francis Auditorium
13. St. Francis Cathedral
14. Sanbusco Market Center
15. Santuario de Guadalupe
16. Scottish Rite Temple
17. State Capitol
18. State Library

where retail space is reputedly higher per square foot than on Madison Avenue in Manhattan. Finding good value, and avoiding the "tourist trap" is the best you can hope.

For your choice of lodging, it is necessary to make reservations well in advance, particularly if you are interested in one of the well-known events, such as Indian Market or the International Folk Art Market. Even though Santa Fe charm has been packaged and commercialized, some say "Disney-fied," it remains and irresistible draw.

It is true that if you have to ask the price of something, you probably can't afford it. No longer are there casual artists' studios on Canyon Road. Once-Bohemian Gypsy Alley is strictly high-rent and upscale these days. The artists who once might have set up shop here have likely relocated to Albuquerque, Pecos, or Truth or Consequences because they can't afford the rent. There are no shoe shops or drugstores on the plaza anymore, only expensive boutiques and galleries and upscale chain stores, and local people have been driven farther and farther from the center of town.

If you are so charmed that you want to move here, as so many are by the looks of the sprawling developments south and east of town, keep in mind that a substantial trust fund, inheritance, pension, or reliable alimony check are

DOZENS OF GALLERIES MAKE CANYON ROAD ONE OF THE WORLD'S FINEST ART BOULEVARDS.

requirements for you to live in the style to which you would like to become accustomed.

On the other hand, a wealth of free entertainment and cultural events are available just about every night of the week. And despite the high ticket prices at the opera, there are too many free—or low-cost—concerts, lectures, book signings, gallery openings, and art festivals every day of the week to keep up.

There is no real industry, and the biggest employers are state government and public education, or the tourist business. As in many other places, and probably more so here, it is who you know, or more likely, to whom you are related, not what you know, that will get you a job.

Unlike anyplace else in New Mexico, Santa Fe is a world of its own. What other small city, with a population under 70,000, has this old-world feel, this vast historic legacy, and this concentration of culture—opera, classical music, museums, galleries—as well as shopping opportunities?

Although it is located in New Mexico, Santa Fe does not think of itself as particularly Mexican. Many of the longtime locals and those descended from old families regard themselves as "Spanish," and they are quite sensitive on this point. However, the presence of recent immigrants from Mexico is obvious when you look at who is providing service in this tourist economy and when you drive

REGARDLESS OF THE SEASON, CANYON ROAD IS A LOVELY PLACE TO STROLL.

out Cerrillos Rd. and see all the restaurants, food carts, and businesses catering to Mexican and Central American immigrants.

The Railyard District off Guadalupe St. and Paseo de Peralta has repurposed itself as an entertainment, dining, and shopping area, anchored by the year-round Farmers' Market. It's been reestablished long enough that several cafés have already come and gone.

Friday nights are the customary time for gallery openings, when in summer, especially, Canyon Road is crowded with strollers out to see what's new.

To keep up or find out what's going on, check the *Santa Fe Reporter*, a weekly newspaper published on Wednesday, or *Pasatiempo*, the weekly entertainment magazine of the *Santa Fe New Mexican*, the daily paper. And do check www.santafe.com for the latest doings.

A particularly good deal is the New Mexico CulturePass, which for $25 entitles you to a visit to each of the 14 state museums and monuments during a 12-month period. Contact www.newmexicoculture.org/index.php. Similar discounts to museum admissions are available with the Santa Fe Museum Pass and the One-Day Pass—ask about them before you begin your museum-trekking. The visitors information booth on the Plaza keeps up with the prices and deals.

In addition to its arts scene, Santa Fe, which has always drawn health seekers as well as quirky and eccentric people, is today a home of religious diversity, healing arts, and a great deal of spiritual searching. The town is by any measure very tolerant. Advocates for progressive causes seem to receive pretty unanimous support.

And of course, with its splendid location, it is a base for enjoying four seasons of recreation. Ski Santa Fe; the Dale Ball Trails, which may be accessed from town; hiking and cross-country skiing only minutes away from the Plaza are the beginning of the adventure. Appreciation for the outdoors is a way of life here.

**A FEW TIPS AND CAUTIONS** As in the rest of New Mexico, smoking in public places is not permitted.

Pets must be leashed and picked up after.

Talking on a handheld cell phone or texting while driving will get you a ticket. Stay off the phone! You do not want to tangle with the Santa Fe police, who can be very intimidating and, well . . . downright scary. If you do get stopped for any reason, expect to be delayed, insulted, and even treated like a criminal. Toward that end, keep your driver's license and insurance close at hand and ready to show at all times. Be cool, patient, and humble.

Be especially careful of your safety and your property. Be aware of your surroundings and use caution at all times. Do not leave anything of value in your car—no computers, no cameras, no jewelry. Be sure to lock your car, even if you'll only be gone "for a minute." Break-ins are epidemic.

Drivers are impatient, so be ultracautious when on the road. Wait before you step on the gas and look both ways when the light turns, as drivers frequently blast through red lights. And you will probably be honked at for your caution. Roads are narrow, just wide enough for a burro loaded with wood, so turns can be sharp. Consult a map before you go out.

Look both ways before you cross the street. Do not expect traffic to yield. Yes, tourists get killed here, even on the Plaza.

While service in high-end restaurants and lodgings is generally quite good, in many establishments you may run into staff that is new or not well trained. Exercise patience.

Santa Fe's history is wrapped up in its identity as a destination—as the end point of the Camino Real, the Royal Road from Mexico City, and as the end of the Santa Fe Trail, a great 19th-century trade route across the plains from Independence, Missouri. And it is still a destination, one of those "bucket list" places that never loses its appeal.

**GUIDANCE New Mexico Dept. of Tourism, Santa Fe Welcome Center** (505-827-7400), Lamy Bldg., 491 Old Santa Fe Trail. Open daily, summer 8–7, winter 8–5.

**Public Lands Information Center** (505-954-2002), 301 Dinosaur Trail, Santa Fe. Open Mon.–Fri. 8:00–4:30. Information about recreation on public lands statewide, maps, camping permits, hunting, and fishing licenses.

**Santa Fe Chamber of Commerce** (505-988-3279), 1644 St. Michael's Dr. Open Mon.–Fri. 8–5. Business and relocation information and visitors guide. Mid-May–mid-Oct. the Bienvenidos booth at First National Bank on the Plaza provides tourist information.

**Santa Fe Convention & Visitors Bureau** (505-955-6200; www.santafe.org), 201 W. Marcy Ave. Open Mon.–Fri. 8–5.

**Santa Fe Creative Tourism** (http://santafecreativetourism.org). An extensive listing of learning and hands-on arts, crafts, and culinary opportunities.

**GETTING THERE** *By car:* I-25 north or south is the most direct route into Santa Fe.

*By air:* The **Santa Fe Municipal Airport** (505-955-2908) is open to private aircraft and **American Eagle Airlines** (800-433-7300), which offers two nonstop daily flights between Dallas and Santa Fe and one nonstop daily flight between Los Angeles and Santa Fe. More frequent flights may be available during the summer. Flights to Denver and Phoenix are on the schedule as of this writing. Also, as of this writing, United Express flights to Santa Fe are planned.

Shuttle service is available from the Albuquerque airport, the Santa Fe airport, and the train station in Lamy about 20 miles from Santa Fe.

*By train:* The **Amtrak** *Southwest Chief* stops in Lamy, 18 miles south of Santa Fe.

*By bus:* **Greyhound Lines** (505-243-7922; 505-243-4435; 800-231-2222; www .greyhound.com/en/contactus.aspx; 320 First St. SW, Albuquerque). Serves Albuquerque from outside the state. Connect to Santa Fe via Rail Runner Express.

**GETTING AROUND Capital City Cab** (505-438-0000).

**Faust's Transportation** (505-758-3410) runs buses between Santa Fe and Taos and will pick you up and drop you off at almost any motel or hotel in Taos. The departure spot in Santa Fe is the Santa Fe Hilton, 100 Sandoval St.

**Loretto Line City Tours** (505-983-3701), Loretto Chapel, 207 Old Santa Fe Tr. Open daily, depending on weather. This open-air sight-seeing trolley ride covers an 8-mile loop and is a good way to get the lay of the land. The tour is approximately one and a quarter hours. $15 adults, $12 children under age 12. Call for departure time.

**Santa Fe Pick-Up** (505-231-2573). The Santa Fe Pick-Up shuttle service is a great way for train passengers to get around once they step off the Rail Runner Express, or others who want a fast, free way to get around downtown. Routes start and end in front of the former New Mexico Film Museum (the old Jean Cocteau Cinema) on Montezuma Avenue and run counterclockwise around downtown with stops at:

The Capitol/PERA building
The Cathedral Basilica of St. Francis of Assisi
The Main Library/City Hall
The Santa Fe Community Convention Center/Santa Fe Plaza
Eldorado/Hilton Hotel
Four stops on Canyon Road
One stop at Alameda and Paseo de Peralta

YOUR CHARIOT AWAITS FOR A GUIDED TOUR OF SANTA FE.

Stops are marked "Pick It Up Here." An entire route takes about 20 minutes. The shuttle drops off passengers at other places along the route if it is safe to stop there.

**Santa Fe Trails** (505-955-2001) provides public bus transportation around town weekdays 6:40 AM–9:50 PM, Sat. 8–8, Sun. 10–6. Pick up maps at the Public Library, 145 Washington Ave., or City Hall, 200 Lincoln Ave. $1 adults, $.50 seniors and children under age 17.

**MEDICAL EMERGENCY Christus St. Vincent** (505-913-8720), 1631 Hospital Dr., Santa Fe. Fast-track emergency room open daily 8–midnight.

## ✳ To See

**TOWNS Galisteo.** Twenty-two miles south of Santa Fe via I-25, US 285, and NM 41. The site of an ancient Indian dwelling, this became a land of sheepherders and later ranchers, starting life as a Spanish colonial outpost in 1614. Today, this funky, dusty village is home to artists, writers, healers, and the like, but its Spanish character remains predominant. It is drop-dead gorgeous.

**La Cienega.** Nine miles southwest of Santa Fe via I-25. The name means "the marsh." The winding streets maintain the feeling of the Hispanic agricultural village this once was—and still is.

**Los Alamos**, 39 miles northwest of Santa Fe via US 84/285 and NM 502, is the secret "city on the hill" where J. Robert Oppenheimer assembled the distinguished cast that produced the bomb in the Manhattan Project. Today, the county has the highest concentration of PhDs than any other county in the United States, and the Los Alamos Laboratory is still the main employer around which most of the town revolves. The name means "the cottonwoods." In 1918, Ashley Pond established the Los Alamos Ranch School for boys. During the Manhattan Project era, after the school was taken over to house project scientists, Los Alamos was rumored to be a hideout for pregnant WACs. Thus was secrecy maintained.

**Santa Fe.** The "City Different," established in 1610, has been at the heart of New Mexico history and culture for over four centuries. It is the state capital and home of the Roundhouse, where the state legislature convenes each winter.

**Tesuque** (te-Sue-kay) is 3 miles north of Santa Fe on Bishop's Lodge Rd. Named for the nearby Indian pueblo, this community dates to 1740. An exquisite village of venerable adobes and architectural gems, cottonwoods, pastoral scenes, winding roadways, and architectural masterpieces that is a pretty, quiet suburb of Santa Fe. You don't have to be rich and famous to live here, but it helps. Either that, or inherit one of these grand old places.

**HISTORIC PLACES, LANDMARKS, AND SITES Canyon Road.** One of Santa Fe's oldest and most colorful streets, Canyon Road was originally an Indian trail to the mountains. In the 1920s, East Coast artists adopted it. Now the narrow, winding street is home to dozens of galleries, boutiques, and upscale restaurants. You are likely to find represented here whatever type of art interests you.

**Cathedral Basilica of St. Francis of Assisi** (505-982-5619), 131 Cathedral Place, Santa Fe. Open daily 7–6; use the side doors. At the east end of San Francisco St. stands one of Santa Fe's most iconic and incongruous structures. Built in French-Romanesque style, it was the inspiration of Jean Baptiste Lamy, Santa Fe's first archbishop. The Hebrew inscription over the keystone is said to be a mark of Lamy's gratitude to the Jewish community for their contributions to the cathedral's building fund.

**Cristo Rey Church** (505-983-8528), 1120 Canyon Rd., intersection of Canyon Rd. and Camino Cabra. Open weekdays 8–5; call one month ahead to arrange tours; donations appreciated. An outstanding example of Spanish Colonial Mission architecture, Cristo Rey Church was designed by Santa Fe architect John Gaw Meem and built to commemorate the 400th anniversary of Coronado's arrival in the Southwest. This is one of the largest modern adobe structures in existence. The church is famous for the stone reredos (altar screen) carved by craftsmen from Mexico in 1760.

**Cross of the Martyrs Walkway.** Enter on Paseo de Peralta, between Otero St. and Hillside Ave. Always open. Only a five-minute walk from the plaza, this historic spot boasts the best view of downtown to those who brave the steep climb. A brick walkway winds up a small hill, and plaques highlight Santa Fe history. The white cross at the summit is a memorial to the 21 Franciscan monks killed in the 1980 Pueblo Revolt.

✪ **El Zaguan**, 545 Canyon Rd., Santa Fe. The home of Historic Santa Fe, this 19th-century house sits next to a Victorian garden where you can read or enjoy the flowers. Weddings

**Fuller Lodge.** Once the dining and recreation hall for Los Alamos Ranch School, after 1943 it was taken over by the U.S. government for the Manhattan Project. An impressive log building designed by John Gaw Meem, it is now a National Historic Landmark.

✪ **Miraculous Staircase/Loretto Chapel Museum** (505-922-0092), 207 Old Santa Fe Trail. Open summer Mon.–Sat. 9–6, Sun. 10:30–5; winter Mon.–Sat. 9–5, Sun. 10:30–5. Closed Christmas. Loretto Chapel was begun in 1873 and designed to look like Sainte-Chapelle in Paris. Stones came from the same quarry as those for St. Francis Cathedral, and the same French and Italian stonemasons worked on both structures. As the story goes, the sisters prayed for a staircase, and an unknown carpenter arrived and built them an amazing circular staircase, lacking both nails and visible means of support. When the job was complete, the mysterious carpenter vanished. $2, under age 7 free.

**The Plaza**, center of town. Always open. Four hundred years of history speak from the Santa Fe Plaza. It was originally laid out according to the wishes of King Philip II in 1600. It is still one of the best people-watching spots in the city.

✪ **Santa Fe Botanical Garden** (505-471-9103), 725 Camino Lejo. Open daily 9–5. Winter hours Tues.–Sun. 10–4 Over 20 years in the planning, the community's dream of a botanical garden has finally been realized on Museum Hill near the Museum of International Folk Art. An exquisite, well-designed retreat for strolling, picnicking, photographing, or just enjoying the blossoms and the views. Docent-led hikes may be requested. $5, under age 12 free.

**Santuario de Guadalupe** (505-983-8868), 314 S. Guadalupe St., Santa Fe. Open Mon.–Fri. 9–4, Sat. 10–4, closed Sun. (summer). The Santuario is a Santa Fe landmark built by Franciscan missionaries in 1776–79 with 3- to 5-foot-thick adobe walls. It is the oldest shrine in the United States dedicated to Our Lady of Guadalupe, who revealed herself in a vision to Indian worshipper Juan Diego in Mexico in 1531.

**Randall Davey Audubon Center & Sanctuary** (505-983-4609), 1800 Upper Canyon Rd. Open summer 8 AM–dusk for garden and trails; winter hours may vary; summer house tours Fri. 2–3. One of the few historic homes in Santa Fe open to the public, this center is a state office, an environmental education center, and National Audubon Society wildlife refuge. Set on 135 acres at the mouth of the Santa Fe River Canyon, it was the home of musician and artist Randall Davey. What is now the house was the original mill. An excellent bookshop is on the premises, as well as a shady picnic area (highly recommended!). $5 house tours, $2 trails, $1 children under age 12.

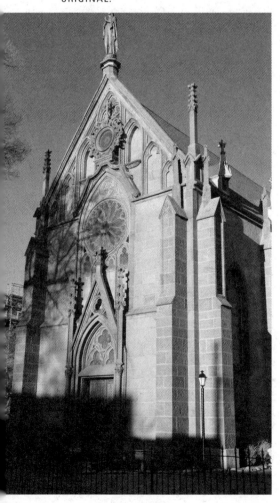

LORETTO CHAPEL, MODELED ON A PARIS ORIGINAL.

**San Miguel Mission** (505-983-3974), 401 Old Santa Fe Trail, Santa Fe. Open daily summer 9–5:30; 9–5; winter Sun. 1–4:30 year-round. Mass 5 PM. The oldest church in the United States, San Miguel was built around 1626. It stands in the Barrio de Analco, Santa Fe's oldest neighborhood, next door to the Oldest House, 215 E. De Vargas St. $1, under age 6 free.

**Sena Plaza**, 125–137 E. Palace Ave., Santa Fe. A separate world that resonates with the flavor of colonial Santa Fe, Sena Plaza is reached by an adobe passage from busy Palace Ave. Now it holds private shops and a restaurant. You can stroll around and imagine the

SPRINGTIME IN SANTA FE PLAZA.

old days as you listen to the fountain, watch the birds, and enjoy the flowers and greenery.

**MUSEUMS** **Bradbury Science Museum** (505-667-4444), 1350 Central, Los Alamos. Open Tues.–Sat. 10–5, Sun.–Mon. 1–5. Photographs and documents provide in-depth education of the unfurling of "Project Y," the World War II code name for the laboratory that developed the first atomic bomb. Displays of the lab's weapons research program and models of accelerators as well as the latest research on solar, geothermal, laser, and magnetic fusion energy. A most interesting film on the history and personalities behind the Manhattan Project is screened regularly. Free.

**Center for Contemporary Arts** (505-982-1338), 1050 Old Pecos Trail. Open daily noon–7. Innovative, creative, challenging contemporary work shown here. The highlight is the small movie theater out back, which screens hard-to-find classic, indie, and world films. Gallery free. $8 films.

**El Museo Cultural de Santa Fe** (505-992-0591), Camino de la Familia, Santa Fe. Open Tues.–Sat. 1–5. This museum showcases and promotes Hispanic arts, culture and heritage exhibits and contemporary and traditional artists of northern New Mexico through photography, weaving, tinwork, painting, and sculpture. Also here, find issue-oriented exhibits on such subjects as water and land use. The 200-seat theater features live performance with an emphasis on original work. Free for art, variable for performance. Also the site of a winter flea market on weekends. Located in the Railyard.

RANDALL DAVEY AUDUBON CENTER & SANCTUARY IS A LOVELY SPOT TO HIKE, TOUR, AND PICNIC.

✏ **El Rancho de las Golondrinas** (575-471-2261), 344 Los Pinos Rd., La Cienega. 15 miles south of Santa Fe, exit 276 off I-25 to La Cienega. Guided group tours Apr.–Oct., self-guided tours June–Sept., Wed.–Sun. 10–4. "The ranch of the swallows" has seen settlers and traders, bishops and Indian raiders in its 300-year history. It was the last stop before Santa Fe on the Camino Real. Caravans of traders, soldiers, and settlers made the six-month round-trip. The 18th-century house, defensive tower, water mills, blacksmith shop, and numerous farm animals are at their best at the spring and harvest festivals, when costumed villagers portray life in Spanish colonial New Mexico. $6 adults, $4 seniors and teens, under age 12 free. Wednesdays, June through September, are free for New Mexico residents. All other days are $2 for residents, and children age 12 and under are free. Entrance fees slightly higher for special events.

**Georgia O'Keeffe Museum** (505-946-1000), 217 Johnson St., Santa Fe. Open daily 10–5, Fri.10–7, "In New Mexico, half your work is done for you," said the famous artist, an iconoclast in life as well as her art, of the home she adopted permanently in the 1940s. Here she found the light and subject matter that built her reputation as "the most singularly original American artist before WWII." O'Keeffe's museum endeavors to show changing exhibits of the work and artists who impacted her life and art. To tour the O'Keeffe home in Abiquiu, contact the above number to arrange a tour Tues., Thurs., or Fri. at 9:30, 11, 2, or 3:30. Reservations must be made well in advance. Tours $25 adults, $20 students.

Museum $12 adults, $10 seniors, under age 18 free; New Mexico residents $6; first Fri. of the month 5–7 PM free to NM residents.

**Los Alamos Historical Museum** (505-662-6272), 1921 Juniper, Los Alamos. Adjacent to Fuller Lodge, 35 miles northwest of Santa Fe via US 285 north and NM 502 west. Open Mon.–Sat. 10–4, Sun. 1–4. Housed in a log-and-stone building originally part of the Los Alamos Ranch School attended by J. Robert Oppenheimer, the museum covers a million years, beginning with the volcanic creation of the Pajarito Plateau. The exhibit "Life in the Secret City" details through vintage photographs and original accounts the story of Los Alamos during World War II. A booklet describing a Los Alamos walking tour is available. Free.

**Museum of Contemporary Native Arts (MoCNA)** (595-983-8900), 108 Cathedral Pl., Santa Fe. Mon., Wed., and Sat.10–5. Sun. noon–5. Closed Tues. Some of the best-known names in Indian art, including Allan Houser, Fritz Scholder, and T. C. Cannon, were students or teachers at Institute of American Indian Arts (IAIA), which operates the MoCNA. The museum houses a large collection of contemporary Indian art and demonstrates the vitality and innovation of these artists. $10 adults, half-price seniors and students, under age 16 free.

**Museum of Indian Arts and Culture** (505-476-1250), 710 Camino Lejo, Museum Hill. Open Tues.–Sun. 10–5. Closed Mon. This state museum brings

THE ALTAR SCREEN AT EL RANCHO DE LAS GOLONDRINAS IS A FOLK ART CLASSIC.

MUSEUM OF CONTEMPORARY NATIVE ARTS.

together the past and present of Southwest Indian culture, including pottery, jewelry, basketry, and textile, over 50,000 artifacts assembled by the Laboratory of Anthropology. The continuing exhibit "From this Earth: Pottery of the Southwest" covers archaeological, historic, and contemporary Indian pottery. $5 New Mexico adults, $7 nonresidents, under age 17 free; Sun. free to New Mexico residents; Wed. free to New Mexico seniors with ID.

✐ **Museum of International Folk Art** (505-476-1200), 706 Camino Lejo, Museum Hill. Open Tues.–Sun. 10–5. Closed Mon., Thanksgiving, Christmas, Easter, and New Year's. Travel to all the continents and 100 countries through this amazing collection of folk art, including textiles, toys, masks, and clothing. The miniature Mexican village scenes delight children. The museum, established by Florence Dibell Bartlett in 1953, received the addition of Alexander Girard's collection in 1976. The Hispanic Heritage Wing, opened in 1989, showcases Spanish colonial and Hispanic folk art, emphasizing northern New Mexico. $5 adults; Sun. free to New Mexico residents; Wed. free to New Mexico seniors.

**Museum of Spanish Colonial Art** (505-982-2226), 750 Camino Lego, Museum Hill. Open Tues.–Sun. 10–5. Closed Mon. A visit here is an excellent introduction to New Mexico history and will make any visit to Santa Fe more meaningful. An intimate museum, housed in a Pueblo Revival adobe structure created by architect John Gaw Meem, pioneer of "Santa Fe Style," it is home to the Spanish Colonial Arts Society's 3,000-piece collection, spanning 500 years. $6 adults, under age 16 free; $3 New Mexico residents.

**New Mexico History Museum** (505-476-5200), 113 Lincoln Ave. The state's newest museum; the jewel in the crown, with rich exhibitions of all aspects of New Mexico history in a light-filled, spacious viewing area. Next door, the previous history museum, the Palace of the Governors, offers permanent exhibits largely related to Spanish colonial history in the oldest continuously occupied government building (built in 1710) in the United States. Open Tues.–Sun. 10–5, Fri. 10–8; closed Mon.; $9 nonresidents, $6 New Mexico residents, free Fri. 5–8 PM; Sun. free to New Mexico residents, Wed. to free to New Mexico senior citizens.

**New Mexico Museum of Art** (505-476-5072), 107 W. Palace Ave. Open Tues.–Sun. 10–5. Closed Mon. Sept.–May only. This is the 1917 Pueblo Revival building that kicked off the architectural design known as Santa Fe style. On permanent exhibition are works by early-20th-century New Mexico artists, such as Gustave Baumann, William Penhallow Henderson, and Jozef Bakos. The collection emphasizes 20th-century American art, particularly Southwestern. $9 nonresidents, $6 New Mexico adults, free Fri. evenings; Sun. free for New Mexico residents.

GUARANTEED AND JURIED HANDMADE NATIVE AMERICAN JEWELRY FOR SALE ON THE PORTAL OF THE PALACE OF THE GOVERNORS.

**Palace of the Governors** (505-476-5100), 105 W. Plaza. Open Tues.–Sun. 10–5. Closed Mon. Dating to 1610, this is the oldest continuously occupied government building in the United States. While the building itself is interesting enough, the artifacts—textiles, carvings, and ceramics—displayed within eloquently speak the history of the area. $6, free Fri. 5–8 PM, Sun. free to New Mexico residents.

❧ **Santa Fe Children's Museum** (505-989-8359), 1050 Old Pecos Tr., Santa Fe. Open Mon.–Sat. 10–6 Sun. noon–5. Closed Tues. Hands-on exhibits encourage children to learn by touching, moving, experimenting, and playing. Lots of ongoing interactive family programs, workshops, and performances keep things lively. $9 nonresidents, New Mexico residents $6; Sun. $5 nonresidents, $2 New Mexico residents.

**Site Santa Fe** (505-989-1199), 1606 Paseo de Peralta, Santa Fe. Open Wed.–Sat. 10–5, Sun. noon–5. Closed Mon. and Tues. This innovative museum features contemporary art

WALK BACK IN TIME AT THE SANTA FE PLAZA.

and cutting-edge exhibitions, including a challenging Biennial and works from Latin America. $10 adults, $5 students and seniors, free Fri.

**Wheelwright Museum of the American Indian** (505-982-4636), 704 Camino Lejo. Open Mon.–Sat. 10–5, Sun. 1–5. Closed Thanksgiving, Christmas, New Year's. Founded by the unlikely combination of Boston heiress Mary Cabot Wheelwright and Navajo medicine man Hosteen Klah, originally for the purpose of preserving Navajo customs and ceremonies, the 1927 museum to house their collections looks completely contemporary. The Case Trading Post, modeled after early-1900s Southwestern trading posts, is a respected outlet of Navajo weaving and jewelry. The site of lively discussion series. Free.

## ✳ To Do

**FARMERS' MARKETS Railyard Artisan Market at the Market Pavilion** Sundays 10 AM–4 PM. The 10,000-square-foot Market Hall with year-round vending plus summer outdoor sales adjacent provides shoppers with produce fresh from the farm and local and imported handcrafted items. Hundreds of growers, however, so you have no way of knowing for sure what is organic, or for that matter, home-grown. Very pricey, and in many cases, worth it . . . but not always.

Be warned: Parking is just about impossible, and you do not want a run-in with the area police; trust me.

**Santa Fe Farmers' Market** (505-938-4098; www.santafefarmersmarket.com), 1607 Paseo de Peralta, in the Railyard. Saturdays (year-round!), fall/winter: 8 AM–1 PM, summer, 7 AM–noon); May 1–Nov. 28, Tues. 8 AM–1 PM.

**GALLERIES** **Andrew Smith Gallery: Masterpieces of Photography** (505-984-1234), 122 Grant Ave., Santa Fe. The world's leading 19th- and 20th-century photo gallery. A breathtaking history of photography. You'll see familiar images and you'll also have your conceptions of documentation pushed. Ansel Adams to Annie Liebowitz, with the emphasis on Adams.

**Davis Mather Folk Art Gallery** (505-983-1660), 141 Lincoln Ave., Santa Fe. One of the best collections of New Mexico animal woodcarvings and Mexican folk art resides in this small corner gallery.

**Gerald Peters** (505-954-5700), 1011 Paseo de Peralta, Santa Fe. This international gallery, which is really a museum in its own right, contains classic Western and Taos Society of Artists, Los Cinco Pintores, plus contemporary realistic and minimalist work, as well as photography and sculpture.

MEET THE GROWERS AT THE SANTA FE FARMERS' MARKET.

**Nuart Gallery** (505-988-3888) 670 Canyon Rd., Santa Fe. You want art? This is art—deeply intriguing contemporary art of many genres that draws you in and won't let you look away. My kind of gallery.

**Pachamama** (505-983-4020), 223 Canyon Rd., Santa Fe. You can find something affordable here among this colorful collection of Latin American folk art that includes textiles, jewelry, dolls, and *milagros* (folk charms).

**Shidoni Foundry and Galleries** (505-988-8001), 1508 Bishop's Lodge Rd., 5 miles north of Santa Fe. This 8-acre sculpture garden in the lush Tesuque River Valley is internationally known, and fun to stroll. Sat. afternoon bronze pourings $5.

**Verve Gallery of Photography** (505-982-5009), 219 E. Marcy St., Santa Fe. Mostly large format local and international fine contemporary photography. Exhibits of work by people who travel to the ends of the earth and bring back beauty.

ART IS EVERYWHERE ON CANYON ROAD.

**GOLF Marty Sanchez Links de Santa Fe** (505-955-4400), 205 Caja Del Rio, Santa Fe. Open year-round, weather permitting, this public course offers a tremendous variety of golfing experiences, including an 18-hole championship course, driving range, and PGA-certified instructors. $43.

**HIKING, CROSS-COUNTRY SKIING, SNOWSHOEING, AND MOUNTAIN BIKING** An extensive system of trails that serves hikers and mountain bikers in warmer weather becomes cross-country trails when snow falls.

**Aspen Vista Trail.** Easily the most popular trial in the Santa Fe area, the moderate 10-mile Aspen Vista is especially memorable in fall when the aspens are changing. It is at the top of Ski Basin Rd., 13 miles from town.

**Borrego Trail.** A 4-mile enjoyable, slightly more challenging, but still easy round-trip hike on only a few miles beyond the Chamisa Trail. It can be crowded on the weekend.

**Chamisa Trail.** Six miles north from the Plaza on Ski Basin Rd. This is always a pleasant, as well as accessible and easy, 4.75-mile round-trip hike through rolling meadows.

**Dale Ball Trails** (505-955-2103). This relatively new trail system, better than 14 miles round-trip, may be accessed most conveniently right in town at Canyon Rd. and Cerro Gordo as well as on NM 475 at Sierra del Norte. The bike trail is

about 7 miles of single-track intermediate riding through the foothills of the San- 
gre de Cristos. The trail is generally easy but becomes more challenging as you 
go up the mountain. La Piedra Trail connects the Dale Ball Trail north to the 
Winsor Trail up near the Santa Fe Ski Basin.

**Winsor Trail.** The favorite of mountain bikers near and far; accessible from Ski 
Basin parking lot for the full thrill.

**HORSEBACK RIDING Bishop's Lodge** (505-983-6377; www.bishopslodge 
.com/horseback-riding), 1207 Bishop's Lodge Rd., Santa Fe. Two-hour guided 
trail rides within the lodge's 1,000-acre grounds start at 10:30 and 2 most days. 
Closed Sun. Call for reservations.

**LECTURES Lannan Foundation** (505-986-8160; www.lensic.com), 309 Read 
St., Santa Fe. The popular Lannan "Readings & Conversations" literary series on 
occasional Wed. evenings Sept.–May at the Lensic Theater brings in national 
and international literary stars to read and discuss their work. Tickets go fast. 
$6–15, students $3.

**Santa Fe Institute** (505-984-8800), various locations. Free, open, accessible 
occasional lectures by fellows and associates of the renowned Santa Fe Institute, 
interdisciplinary meeting ground of the world's greatest minds.

**St. John's College** (505-984-6000), 1160 Camino Cruz Blanca, Great Hall, 
Peterson Student Center, Santa Fe. Mind-blowing assortment of brilliant schol- 
arly presentations on literature and philosophy, all free.

**MUSIC Santa Fe Chamber Music Festival** (505-982-1890; www.santafe 
chambermusic.org). Season: July–Aug. One of Santa Fe's biggest draws, the fes- 
tival brings in foremost composers and musicians to play classical, jazz, folk, and 
world music.

**Santa Fe Concert Association** (505-984-8759; santafeconcerts.org), 321 W. 
San Francisco St. Season: Sept.–May. Since 1931 Santa Fe's oldest music organi- 
zation has been bringing outstanding musicians from all over the world to per- 
form a repertoire of classical and modern concert music.

**Santa Fe Desert Chorale** (505-988-2282; www.desertchorale.org). Season: 
July–Aug. and Christmas. One of the few professional choruses in the United 
States, the chorale performs a great many 20th-century works, as well as major 
music from all periods, particularly Renaissance and Baroque.

**Santa Fe Opera** (505-986-5900; www.santafeopera.org). Seven miles north of 
Santa Fe on US 285. Season: late June or July–Aug. Each season of the premier 
summer opera festival in the United States features an ambitious repertoire that 
usually includes unknown or new operas as well as popular standards and a 
revived masterpiece. The opera's mystique is amplified by its elegant amphithe- 
ater, now roofed, and the acoustics. Bring a warm coat and blankets; tempera- 
tures plummet after dark, and you'll be out past midnight.

**Santa Fe Pro Musica** (505-988-4640; www.santafepromusica.com). Most spe- 
cial are the Christmas-season Baroque ensemble concerts played on period

TAILGATING AT THE SANTA FE OPERA IS A FAVORITE SUMMER CULINARY EVENT.

instruments. If you can attend a performance in the Loretto Chapel, by all means go.

**Santa Fe Symphony Orchestra and Chorus** (505-983-3530; www.sf-symphony .org). The symphony performs various concerts at the Lensic Theater.

**RAILROADING  Santa Fe Southern Railway** (505-989-8600), 430 W. Manhattan Ave., Santa Fe. Open year-round with excursions from two to four hours. Ride the rails to Lamy and enjoy scenic and holiday train events. Closed 2013. Due to reopen March 2014.

**SCHOOLS AND CLASSES  Santa Fe School of Cooking & Market** (505-983-4511), St., 125 N. Guadalupe St., Santa Fe. Want to learn how to make a great salsa or serve an entire dinner of Southwestern cuisine? This is the place to learn from well-known chefs. Hands-on and observational classes to immerse in history and culture of regional cooking. Restaurant walking tours are popular.

**Las Cosas Cooking Classes** (505-988-3394), 181 Paseo de Peralta, Santa Fe. Enjoy hands-on cooking classes at this excellent kitchen shop with personality-plus chef Johnny Vee.

**Santa Fe Culinary Academy: Culinary Classes and Professional Chef Training** (505-983-7445), 112 W. San Francisco St., #300, Santa Fe. Whether you want to learn technique or change your life by embracing a new profession, you can't go wrong with the lively classes taught by top professionals.

## SPAS

**Absolute Nirvana Spa, Tea Room, & Gardens** (505-983-7942), 106 Faithway St., Santa Fe. Named a hot new spa by *Condé-Nast Traveler,* this is the place to purify and calm the body and mind with a range of Asian spa rituals. At $165 for an hour-and-a-half "chocolate and peppermint" revivifying massage, scrub and more, it's a bargain.

**Body** (505-986-0362), 333 W. Cordova Rd., Santa Fe. Open daily 7 AM–9 PM. This place has it all: an oasis of a one-stop shop for massage, movement, yoga, Pilates, boutique, organic, GMO-free, vegan-friendly café and spa, plus child care and children's and family classes. A nice place to meet a friend for tea or lunch, and parking is no problem.

**La Posada de Santa Fe Spa** (505-986-0000), 330 E. Palace Ave., Santa Fe. Santa Fe is a city with some great, great spas. This one may not be the most aesthetically posh, but it sets the standard on service. You can choose from a menu that includes a Chocolate-Chile Wrap and several other treatments that will move you forward on the path of enlightenment. Highly rated on Discovery Channel. Pricey, but you get what you pay for. $125 and up.

**The Spa at Loretto** (505-984-7997), 211 Old Santa Fe Trail, Santa Fe. Embracing local indigenous and Native American herbs and minerals, this spa features exquisite facials, body wraps, couples massage global rituals and treatments as well as Thai massage. Consistently ranked high nationally. Pampering to the max. $125 and up.

**10,000 Waves Japanese Spa and Resort** (505-982-9304), 3451 Hyde Park Rd., Santa Fe. Open daily 9:15–9:30. A 10-minute drive up Hyde Park Rd. is an exquisite Japanese bath-style spa that is a world of its own. It is considered a romantic, sensual date experience. There are public and private hot tubs and men's and women's scheduled tub hours, and patrons stroll about in fluffy white robes, sipping herbal tea. Hourly tub rates are reduced for anyone with a New Mexico driver's license and for frequent users. It is a lovely experience but can be quite expensive, and, more to the point, the water temperature can be a little too hot for languorous soaking. A favorite treat for locals. Limited lodging is available in The Houses of the Moon by reservation. $31 hour basic tub rate. Massage begins at $109.

**Santa Fe Photographic Workshops** (505-983-1400), 50 Mt. Carmel Rd. Workshops in all aspects of photography, taught by photographers of national and international repute, some abroad year-round. Whatever you'd ever dreamed of trying in photography, you'll find it here. Intensive workshops designed to move you to your next level and beyond. Free summer evening presentations by faculty are special events.

**SKIING Ski Santa Fe** (505-982-4429; 877-737-7366 for reservations), 16 miles northeast of Santa Fe on NM 475. Open Thanksgiving–early Apr. This is the reason why so many people love Santa Fe. With a base elevation of 10,350 feet and a 12,075-foot summit, this ski area is geared to appeal to every member of the family and is as fine a place to learn, as it can be thrilling. Terrain Park is exceptional. It also has packages for beginners, freestyle terrain, and multiday ticket bargains. Reservations are required for the adaptive ski program for both the physically and mentally challenged (505-995-9858; www.adaptiveski.org). $70–92.

**THEATER Santa Fe Playhouse** (505-988-4262), 142 E. De Vargas St., Santa Fe. Season: year-round. Founded in the 1920s by writer Mary Austin as the Santa Fe Community Theater, it remains the longest-running theater group in New Mexico, now at home in an intimate adobe theater in one of the city's oldest neighborhoods. A favorite each fall is the *Fiesta Melodrama*, a spoof staged the week of La Fiesta.

**WALKING TOURS Historic Walks of Santa Fe** (505-986-8388), La Fonda Hotel, 108 E. San Francisco St. Daily at 9:45 AM, 1:15 PM. No reservations required. Professional museum docent guides specialize in the history of Santa Fe landmarks. Ghost Walks and Spirit Walks are especially popular. Santa Fe is reputedly a highly haunted city. $12, senior discounts, under age 12 free.

**New Mexico Museum of Art** (505-476-5072). Art walking tours of Santa Fe Apr.–Nov., Mon. at 10 AM. $10, under age 18 free.

**Palace of the Governors** (505-476-5109). Daily at 10:15 except Sun. Two-hour historic walking tours conducted by the Friends of the Palace. Meet at the blue gate on Lincoln Ave. side of the Palace of the Governors. $10, under age 17 free. No tipping.

**WINERIES** & **Balagna Winery & San Ysidro Vineyards** (505-672-3678), 223 Rio Bravo Dr., White Rock. Open daily. noon–6. Sip fine wines above the clouds.

**Estrella del Norte Vineyard** (505-445-2826), 106 N. Shining Sun, Santa Fe, 15 miles north of Santa Fe on US 285 in Nambe.

## ✳ Green Space

**Bandelier National Monument** (505-672-3861). Go 46 miles west of Santa Fe on US 285 north to Pojoaque, west on NM 502, south on NM 4. Open daily, year-round. Closed Christmas and New Year's. Summer 8–6, winter 8–4:30. Ruins trails open dawn till dusk. Tucked deep into a canyon on the Pajarito Plateau is the ancestral home of many Pueblo tribes that was occupied A.D. 1100–1550. You can climb among the cliff dwellings and view village ruins and ceremonial kivas. The loop trail of Frijoles Canyon ruins is an easy one-hour walk. Rangers offer "night walks" during the summer. There are more rigorous hikes out here, which you can learn about at the visitors center. Varying restrictions regarding the monument have gone into place due to devastating forest fires. $10 per car; $10 camping.

**Frank S. Ortiz Dog Park**, 160 Camino de las Crucitas, Santa Fe, is a popular off-leash dog park where pets can run free. Acres and acres of trails with expansive mountain views make this excellent walking terrain for human companions.

**Ft. Marcy–Magers Field and Complex** (505-984-6725), 490 Bishop's Lodge Rd., Santa Fe. Fitness complex including pool is open Mon.–Fri. 6 AM–8:30 PM, Sat. 8–6:30, Sun. 10–6.

AT BANDELIER NATIONAL MONUMENT, YOU CAN CLIMB INTO AN ANCIENT CLIFF DWELLING.

This facility has picnic tables, tennis court, baseball field, indoor swimming pool, fitness room, a parcourse, and well-used walking paths. Variable fees, quite reasonable.

☿ **Hyde Memorial State Park** (505-983-7175), 740 Hyde Park Rd., Santa Fe. Eight miles northeast of Santa Fe via Hyde Park Rd. Open daily 8 AM–11 PM. Forested with aspens and evergreens, this easily accessed park is close enough for an afternoon hike or even a long lunchtime walk. In warm weather, the almost 4-mile Hyde Park Loop Trail provides stunning views of the Sangre de Cristo Mountains, although the first third of the trail is quite steep and attention must be paid to finding the correct return path. In winter, this is a closed-in cross-country skiing, snowshoeing, and tubing area. Find the trailhead in back of the visitors center. $5 day use; $8–18 camping.

**Santa Fe National Forest** (505-438-5300), 11 Forest Ln., Santa Fe. This vast national forest, measuring 16 million acres, includes much of the most beautiful scenery in northern New Mexico. It holds four wilderness areas: Pecos, San

VALLES CALDERA NATIONAL PRESERVE IS ONE OF THE STATE'S PREMIER RECREATION SITES.

Pedro Parks, Dome, and Chama River Canyon, and three Wild and Scenic River areas: 11 miles of the East Fork of the Jemez (great for cross-country skiing), 24.6 miles of the Rio Chama, and 20.5 miles of the Pecos River, plus over 1,000 miles of trails accessible to horses, hikers, and mountain bikes, as well as four-wheel-drive vehicles. Close to Santa Fe is the Black Canyon Campground, northeast on NM 475 and convenient to the Borrego Trail.

**Valles Caldera National Preserve** (866-382-5537), 40 miles northwest of Santa Fe. Continue on NM 4 past Bandelier about 15 miles. This vast, astonishing green basin—all that remains of what was once the world's largest volcano—is believed to be part of an 89,000-acre caldera, a basin formed during Pleistocene volcanic activity. Located on a 42-year-old land grant named Baca Location No. 1, it is also called the Valle Grande or Baca Location and is home to a herd of 45,000 elk. Since the area was named one of the country's newest national monuments, hiking, cross-country skiing, fly-fishing, mountain biking, night sky adventures, wildlife viewing, and hunting have become available for various fees on a reservations-only basis. Variable fees.

## ✳ Lodging

**BED & BREAKFASTS, MOTELS, AND HOTELS** ♿ **El Rey Inn** (505-982-1931), 1862 Cerrillos Rd., Santa Fe. This classic 1937 Route 66 motel gets high marks on several counts: convenient location, lovely landscaping, and classic Route 66 Southwest style; however, when I have stayed there, I found the antiquated heating system noisy enough to wake me at 3 AM. Many of the 87 rooms have flagstone floors and exposed vigas; 20 have fireplaces. There is a heated pool and indoor and outdoor hot tubs. Perhaps the passive-solar rooms might deliver a peaceful night. Or just bring your earplugs. This is an in-demand place, so book early. The Lodge can accommodate reunions and workshops. $84–140.

♿ **La Fonda Hotel** (505-982-5511), 100 E. San Francisco St., Santa Fe. There's been an inn of some sort on the southeast corner of the Plaza for almost 400 years. La Fonda is still the only hotel on the Plaza, and no other can match its rich past. The dark, old-fashioned lobby with its INDIAN DETOURS sign, the clubby bar, the lovely La Plazuela restaurant with its colorful hand-painted glass, and the French Pastry Shop designed by Mary Elizabeth Jane Colter (designer for the Fred Harvey Hotels) all conspire to trick you into thinking you have time-traveled back into Santa Fe's past. Swimming pool, hot tubs, and spa are on-site, and La Fonda features 14 "nontoxic" suites for environmentally sensitive guests. A major renovation is underway. $219–319.

♿ **Garrett's Desert Inn** (505-982-1851), 311 Old Santa Fe Tr., Santa Fe. Location, location, location. This place is pretty basic, not unpleasantly so, just not very imaginative in a city of romantic lodgings, but it is situated exactly where you want to be, in about two blocks' walking distance of the Plaza and other attractions. Despite modest prices, it remains an address with a bit of cachet. Le Chantilly café on the premises serves breakfast and lunch. Note: There's an $8 a day parking fee. $67–149.

♿ **Inn and Spa at Loretto** (505-988-5531), 211 Old Santa Fe Tr., Santa Fe. Built in 1975 on the site of Loretto Academy, a 19th-century girls' school, this inn's terraced architecture is modeled after Taos Pueblo. With 134 rooms, it includes a swimming pool, a bar with live entertainment, and a restaurant, Baleen. There is a deluxe spa "to die for" on the premises, where you can reduce your stress pronto. An automatic $10-plus-tax "hotel fee" is added to each day of your bill to pay for gratuities, newspaper, WiFi, and the like. Belongs to Destinations & Resorts properties. $249–340.

**Inn at Vanessie** (505-984-1193), 427 Water St., Santa Fe. Formerly the Water Street Inn. This handsomely restored adobe B&B has an air of romantic intimacy. It is hidden away on a side street within strolling distance of downtown. The 12 rooms are spacious with brick floors and four-poster beds. Most have a fireplace; some have private patios with fountains. Sunset views from the upstairs balcony are splendid, and hot hors d'oeuvres are served with New Mexican wines at cocktail hour. Vanessie's piano bar is across the alley. $150–185.

**La Posada de Santa Fe Resort & Spa** (505-986-0000), 330 E. Palace Ave., Santa Fe. A 19th-century mansion, known as the Staab House and built by 19th-century pioneer merchant Abraham Staab, a complex of Pueblo-style casitas, and 6 acres of huge cottonwoods and fruit trees are some of the features of this unusual inn. One drawback is you have to walk outdoors from the Staab House to your room, which is not fun in nasty weather. The casitas have classic New Mexican décor: adobe fireplaces, hand-painted tiles, Indian rugs, and skylights. Guests enjoy a good-size swimming pool and lovely courtyard for drinking and dining in nice weather. The restaurant, Fuego, achieved a Four Diamond rating; however, sad to say, I was recently underwhelmed. Best to go for the steak. The WiFi was also shaky. The service is excellent. The "resort fee" is an additional $20–30 per day, and don't forget to tip the mandatory valet. $162–274.

**Rosewood Inn of the Anasazi** (505-988-3030), 113 Washington Ave., Santa Fe. This striking 57-room hotel is as close to the Plaza as you can get without landing on a bench there. It is done in classic Pueblo Revival style, with viga and latilla ceilings throughout, stone floors and walls, and a beautiful flagstone waterfall. Exquisite simplicity highlights the fine local artwork. Service is tops, as are on-site business services: Staff will bring an exercise bike to your room or rent you a mountain bike. Offering the best sense of peace and privacy money can buy, this small luxury hotel continues to reign as the city's most chic address for visitors. Restaurant on-site. $239–349.

🐾 **Santa Fe Motel & Inn** (505-982-1039), 510 Cerrillos Rd., Santa Fe. If you are looking for an attractive, affordable motel downtown, this one is set far enough off a busy intersection to have an air of seclusion. In addition to typical motel rooms, it includes 10 adobe casitas with refrigerator, microwave, and patio entrance. Across the street, kitchenettes are available. Many will find this an excellent value. Plus, a complimentary full breakfast is included. $79–134. Only $89 per weeknight most of the winter, if you call in your reservation.

🐾 ❀ **Santa Fe Sage Inn** (505-982-5952), 725 Cerrillos Rd, Santa Fe. Surprisingly affordable and quiet centrally located lodging. Free Sage Coach shuttle service to plaza. Pet-friendly. Ask about special deals, such as buy two nights, get one free. $79.

🐾 **Silver Saddle Motel** (505-471-7663), 2810 Cerrillos Rd., Santa Fe. Vintage 1953 Route 66 motor court next door to Jackalope makes this a shopper's paradise. Absolutely reasonable with warm hospitality. Western-themed rooms are small but clean; feels like a tour back in time. Continental breakfast included. $53.

### LODGES, INNS, AND RANCHES

**Bishop's Lodge Ranch Resort & Spa** (505-983-6377), 1297 Bishop's Lodge Rd., Santa Fe. Bishop Jean Baptiste Lamy, the model for Willa Cather's classic *Death Comes for the Archbishop*, chose this magnificent spot in the foothills of the Sangre de Cristo Range for his retirement and getaway home and garden a century ago. The lodge is activity- and family-oriented. Horseback riding, tennis, swimming, trap and skeet shooting, and fishing are available in-season on 1,000 acres. The rooms have a distinctly New Mexico flavor, and the restaurant offers a fine Sunday brunch. Best of all, there's still an air of serenity here, and Lamy's private chapel stands untouched. The She-Nah Spa makes the place complete. $149–449.

🐾 ♿ **Inn on the Alameda** (505-984-2121), 303 E. Alameda, Santa Fe. This two-room inn across the street from the Santa Fe River feels a lot smaller than it is, due perhaps to the individual private courtyards surrounding rooms. (You will pay extra for a balcony.) It has two hot tubs, exercise room, full-service bar, and comfortable sitting rooms. The morning fare is a buffet breakfast feast. $125–215.

**CABINS AND CAMPING Hyde Memorial State Park** (505-983-7175), 740 Hyde Park Rd. Open year-round. Tent sites and RV hookups available. $8–18.

**Rancheros de Santa Fe Campground** (505-466-3482), 736 Old Las Vegas Hwy. Open Mar. 15–Oct. 31. Cabins, RV sites, full hookups, pool, tent sites—in short, whatever your travel style, it can be accommodated here. $20–30.

**Santa Fe National Forest** (505-438-7840; www.fs.usda.gov/santafe). Open May 15–Sept. 30. Two campgrounds in the Santa Fe area are Aspen Basin and Big Tesuque, each about 12 miles northeast of Santa Fe on NM 475. Both grounds offer RV sites with no hookups and tent sites. $10 and up.

**Santa Fe Skies RV Park** (505-473-5946; www.santafeskiesrvpark.com), 14 Browncastle Ranch. One mile off I-25 at southeast end of NM 599 on

the Turquoise Trail. Open year-round. A comfortable stop for RVers with modem hookups, too, this park boasts views of four mountain ranges. $30.

## ✳ Where to Eat

**DINING OUT Cafe Pasqual's** (505-983-9340), 121 Don Gaspar, Santa Fe. Open daily. Closed Thanksgiving, Christmas. Breakfast, lunch, dinner. Named for the saint of the kitchen, owned and operated by Kathy Kagel, organizer of a food distribution system that feeds the hungry. Consistently on the list of "Ten Best Places to Have Breakfast in the United States;" the huge, delicious, Mexican (from Mexico) breakfast is served all day. Emphasis is on flavorful organic and natural foods. Genovese omelet with sun-dried tomatoes and pine nuts, grilled salmon burrito, toasted piñon ice cream with caramel sauce. Moderate–Expensive.

♂ **The Compound** (505-982-4353; www.compoundrestaurant.com), 653 Canyon Rd., Santa Fe. Chef-owner Mark Kiffin revived this Canyon Rd. grande dame with its Alexander Girard–designed white interior. The art of service has been perfected here. Food as entertainment on the grand scale is to be expected. The beautiful people, dressed to the nines, nibbling designer Continental dishes concocted from ingredients air-freighted in from all over the world—it is truly to die for. Sweetbreads and foie gras, grilled lamb rib eye, blue corn–dusted softshell crabs, and liquid chocolate cake for dessert—one of the best chocolate items I have ever tasted. If you have one special splurge on your visit to Santa Fe, make your reservation here. A great place for a humble writer to pretend she has big bucks.

Kiffin is a James Beard nominee and Best Chef winner. Very Expensive.

**Coyote Cafe and Cantina** (505-983-1615), 132 W. Water St., Santa Fe. The granddaddy of all nouvelle Southwestern cuisine, pioneered by anthropologist-turned-chef Mark Miller, still serves inspired dishes that blend native ingredients with sophisticated flavors. Miller has moved on, and famed Geronimo chef Eric DiStefano has taken the helm as chef-owner. In warm weather, the light-hearted rooftop patio serves reasonably priced simpler, but still delicious, fare, with Mexican beer, margaritas, fabulous fire-roasted salsa, Cuban sandwiches, and more. Very Expensive.

**Geronimo Restaurant** (505-982-1500), 724 Canyon Rd., Santa Fe. Open daily. Dinner. Housed in one of the city's finest historic adobes, this restaurant is the last word in minimalist Santa Fe elegance. The menu consists of American staples updated with Southwestern and other ethnic ingredients Very, Very Expensive.

**Il Piatto Italian Restaurant** (505-984-1091), 95 W. Marcy St., Santa Fe. Lunch Mon.–Sat., dinner Mon.–Sun. I adore this place! In its incarnation as an "Italian Farmhouse Kitchen," Il Piatto continues to delight with emphasis on local ingredients. Its value bargain prix fixe lunch ($17), and three-course prix fixe dinner ($32.50) offer great flexibility of ordering. Small plates are available. Try the pumpkin ravioli with brown sage butter, slow roast breast of lamb, and so much more. Unparalleled happy hour with half-price on appetizers, small plates, and many fine wines by the glass. Late-night dining, abundant wines by the glass.

Frequently voted Santa Fe's best Italian restaurant. Moderate.

**Rio Chama Steakhouse** (505-955-0765), 414 Old Santa Fe Tr., Santa Fe. Next door to a bar that is especially lively in winter when the legislature is in session. Open daily. Lunch, dinner. Closed Christmas. Forget the cholesterol. Try this instead: prime dry-aged beef, succulent rib eyes and fillets, and Black Angus prime rib, house-made onion rings, rich creamed spinach, and shrimp cocktail. The blue cheese–green chile burgers are dripping with decadence and irresistible. Add a full bar, and you've got a real meal going. Go for the fondue.

JOY! A DINNER OF ENCHILADAS AND SOPAIPILLAS IN SANTA FE.

Two can manage lunch for under $40. Expensive.

**Taberna La Boca** (505-988-7102), 125 Lincoln Ave., Ste. 117, Santa Fe. Closed Sun. Those who remember Carlos' Gosp'l Café will be amazed by the transformation chef-owner James Campbell Caruso has wrought in this now svelte space at La Boca's sibling Taberna. Folks, this is the place to create a lively, celebratory evening with tapas, music, good sherry, featuring the incomparable Nacha Mendez on Thurs. nights, and informal dining. And bravo to Chef Campbell Caruso—winner of the 2013 James Beard Foundation Award. Moderate.

**EATING OUT Back Street Bistro** (505-982-3500). 513 Camino de los Marquez (behind Cordova Rd.), Santa Fe. Lunch Mon.–Sat. Closed Sun. Call me hooked on the creamy Hungarian mushroom soup. Select from a daily blackboard of well-simmered soups, such as creamy sweet onion and Thai chicken ginger coconut, yummy sandwiches, and salads. Vegetarian, vegan, gluten-free options, remodeled warehouse feel—in a good way. Inexpensive.

**Counter Culture** (505-995-1105), 930 Baca St.,#1, Santa Fe. Breakfast, lunch, dinner daily. The hip, the pierced, the tattooed, the artistic, and even their parents agree on the homemade fries and Asian soups of the eclectic menu served here. This little Baca St. neighborhood is sometimes called "the SoHo of Santa Fe" for its galleries, jewelry shops, and slightly edgy atmosphere. Inexpensive.

**Cowgirl Hall of Fame Bar-B-Que** (505-982-2565), 319 S. Guadalupe, Santa Fe. Open daily. Breakfast, lunch, dinner. Closed Thanksgiving,

Christmas. This place is known as much, if not more, as a hopping watering hole than as a restaurant. The décor is old-time cowgirl memorabilia. The specialty is the mesquite-smoked barbecue, but beside all the meat are vegetarian chile and butternut casserole. Try the signature dessert, the Baked Potato, which is actually a chocolate sundae disguised as a spud, or just have the peach cobbler. Moderate.

**Del Charro** (505-954-0320), 101 W. Alameda, at the Inn of the Governors. Open daily 11:30–midnight, slightly earlier closing on Sun. They said it couldn't be done. However, at Del Charro you can find a very good, not gourmet, bargain lunch, in the $5–7 range, that might be a burger, enchilada, chicken-fried steak, poblano pepper relleno, or cream of mushroom soup. Homemade potato chips, too. Choose the bright, airy atmosphere or go directly to the bar. Give your wallet a break. Inexpensive.

**Guadalupe Café** (505-982-9762), 422 Old Santa Fe Tr., Santa Fe. Open Tues.–Sun. Closed Mon. Breakfast, lunch, dinner. Either arrive hungry or be prepared to split a main dish. New Mexican food, but don't ask for the chile on the side. The salads are humongous. Absolutely the best cinnamon rolls, too, big as pie plates. Moderate.

**Jambo Café: African Homestyle Cuisine** (505-473-1269), 2010 Cerrillos Rd., Santa Fe. Lunch, dinner Mon.–Sat. Closed Sun. Open till 9 PM. Multiple-year winner of the Santa Fe Souper Bowl, famous for the sweet potato curry soup, jerk chicken, goat and lentil stew, stuffed phyllo (recommended)—love the island spice chicken coconut peanut stew.

Authentic flavors where you'd least expect to find them—in a strip mall. Recent expansion has harmed neither food nor service, and eliminated cold air blowing through every time the door was opened. Inexpensive–Moderate.

**Maria's New Mexican Kitchen** (505-983-7929), 555 W. Cordova Rd., Santa Fe. Open daily. Lunch, dinner. Closed Thanksgiving, Christmas. With over a half-century in the same location, Maria's is a Santa Fe classic that continues to draw crowds of all ages. You can watch the experts make fresh tortillas by hand. Sizzling fajitas, authentic green chile stew, and the classic blue corn–red chile enchiladas—you can't go wrong. Fresh guacamole on the side and scrumptious flan are a couple of other specialties. Owner Al Lucero has written a definitive book about margaritas, and his bartenders can concoct over 70 different kinds. Try ordering dinner in the bar. Moderate.

❦ **Pantry Restaurant** (505-986-0022), 1820 Cerrillos Rd., Santa Fe. Open daily. Breakfast, lunch, dinner. How about homemade corned beef hash (best in town), freshly baked biscuits and gravy, pancakes stuffed with fruit and whipped cream, and endless cups of coffee, in a completely unpretentious spot that locals adore for good food and reasonable prices? My go-to spot for reliable, rib-sticking fare and sweet service. Sit at the counter or grab a table. Very, very unpretentious and local. Open till 9 PM. Inexpensive.

**Piccolino Italian Restaurant** (505-471-1480), 2890 Agua Fria St. Santa Fe. Additional new location at Agora Plaza in Eldorado. Lunch, dinner daily. You may have to hunt to find it,

but when you do, you will discover down-home, unpretentious, checked tablecloth local red sauce–based real Italian food. Credible pizza, calzones, very good chicken piccata and marsala. It's packed with locals who disdain fancy-schmancy and prefer value and flavor for their dining dollars. A happy place! Save room for dessert. Inexpensive–Moderate.

**Plaza Cafe** (505-982-1664), 54 Lincoln Ave., Santa Fe. Open daily. Breakfast, lunch, dinner. When you're out and about and looking for a bite, this family restaurant is the place, with its black-and-white tile floor and old-timey counter service. You can count on excellent enchiladas, sopaipillas, diner food, salads, moussaka, and chicken-fried steak, all served as consistently and efficiently as they have been since 1918, making this the oldest restaurant in town. Restored to perfection after suffering a kitchen fire. Southside location, too. Moderate.

**San Francisco St. Bar & Grill: An American Bistro** (505-982-2044), southwest corner of the Plaza at San Francisco St. and Don Gaspar. Open daily from 11 AM. Lunch, dinner. Go upstairs to find a reasonably priced and well-varied menu of salads, sandwiches, and fresh fare that is bound to have something please any appetite. Moderate.

**Santa Fe Bar & Grill** (505-982-3033; www.santafebargrill.com), southwest corner DeVargas Center. Open daily. Lunch 11–5, dinner 5–10, Sun. brunch 11–3. Casual and warm, the place that comes to mind when you can't think where to go to meet a friend for dinner or have a business lunch where you can talk. The shopping center parking lot makes it a

GO LOCAL AND GRAB A MEAL OR JUST A FABULOUS DESSERT AT THE PLAZA CAFE.

convenient stop. Love the fish tacos with black beans, but the menu has everything from swell burgers to enchiladas and lives up to the motto, "Creative southwest cuisine." Inexpensive–Moderate.

**The Shed** (505-982-9030), 113½ E. Palace Ave., Santa Fe. Open Mon.–Sat. Lunch dinner. Closed Sun. Located in an adobe dating from 1692 and tucked away in an enclosed patio, The Shed is a landmark where you can count on consistently delicious chile, ground on the premises. Perhaps the very best red chile, blue corn enchiladas. Colorful Southwestern décor adds to the fun of eating here. Selections of fish and beef are also available. Homemade hot fudge for dessert. Take a seat by a corner fireplace in winter, or on the patio on a summer night with a glass of wine, and you know you can only be in one place, the capital of the Land of Enchantment. Moderate.

**Tecolote Café** (505-988-1362), 1203 Cerrillos Rd., Santa Fe. Justifiably famous for breakfast, Tecolote serves delicious low-cholesterol alternatives to its heaping helping of French toast and freshly baked muffins.

**Tesuque Village Market** (505-988-8848), junction of Bishop's Lodge Rd. and Tesuque Village Rd., Tesuque. Open daily. Breakfast, lunch, dinner. Wood-fired pizza, organic and all-natural meats, fabulous blue corn pancakes, amazing homemade pies and decadent chocolate desserts, and boutique wine and rare tequila selections are all here at this neighborhood hangout with heated outdoor seating.

Cowboys, artists, Hollywood types, and the president of the rose society are all at home here. Moderate.

**Tia Sophia's** (505-983-9880), 210 W. San Francisco St., Santa Fe. Open Mon.–Sat. 7:30–2. Closed. Sun. and major holidays. Breakfast, lunch. Located in the heart of San Francisco St., this is an unassuming little restaurant that serves consistently good New Mexican meals in a family atmosphere. The breakfast burritos and huevos rancheros, with red chile that has a kick, are worth ordering, and for lunch, try one of the homemade stuffed sopaipillas. Inexpensive.

### COFFEE AND TEA HOUSES

(Check the hours before you go—they can vary.)

**Chocolate Maven Bakery & Cafe** (505-984-1980), 821 San Mateo, Unit C, Santa Fe. Open daily. Breakfast, lunch, weekend brunch. Monster chocolate croissants and unbelievable sandwiches make this one popular spot, but parking is hellacious, and you have to brave the crowds before you get to a tiny table. Solution: Go early or late. Maybe it's the lighting, but the encased pastries positively glisten with goodness. Inexpensive.

**Clafoutis** (505-988-1809), 402 N. Guadalupe St. Open daily 7–4. Closed Sun. Go early or go late, but go. To paraphrase *New Yorker* writer Adam Gopnik, as with the food in Paris, it is better than it needs to be. Parking can be *très difficile*. Feast on beignets, macaroons, the best croissant in town. Omelets, meat and cheese plates, and of course, quiche. Inexpensive.

**Downtown Subscription** (505-983-3085), 376 Garcia St., Santa Fe. Good for browsing the shelves of magazines and newspapers, good for coffee, and good for hanging out on the informal patio. Inexpensive.

**French Pastry Shop** (505-983-6697), 100 E. San Francisco St., Santa Fe. Just the place for a slice of quiche, fresh strawberry crêpe, or a chocolate éclair and a latte. So many delights, in the room designed by Fred Harvey's architect, Mary Colter. Croque monsieur for lunch. 'Tis as French as a morning on the Rive Gauche. Inexpensive.

**Kakawa Chocolate House** (505-982-0388), 1050 Paseo de Peralta, Santa Fe. Preparing historic and global chocolate drinks. Want to sip the kind of chocolate Thomas Jefferson favored? Or taste the ancient brews of Mesoamerica? Expect to pay around $5 for a tiny cup of the experience.

**Ohori's Coffee, Tea & Chocolate** (505-982-9692), 1098 S. St. Francis Dr., Santa Fe. For serious coffee drinkers, please. Coffee is what it's all about here. The beans are freshly roasted, and a different coffee is brewed every time the urn is emptied. The new patio is quite the spot. Inexpensive.

**Revolution Bakery** (505-988-2100), 1291 San Felipe Avenue, Santa Fe Gluten-free cookies, cinnamon rolls, chocolate cupcakes, and more. Mon.–Fri, 8–4.

🍴 **Santa Fe Baking Co. & Cafe** (505-988-4292), 504 W. Cordova Rd., Santa Fe. Open Mon.–Sat. 6–8, Sun. 6–6. Breakfast, lunch, dinner. Read the paper; check your e-mail on the free reliable WiFi; go for a breakfast of bacon and eggs, or the breakfast burrito special, smothered with green chile, plump and sustaining, served all day; or drool over the pastry counter.

Everyone else does! A comfortable hangout. Inexpensive.

**The Teahouse** (505-992-0972), 821 Canyon Rd., Santa Fe. The aesthetic is Zen, the tea choices are in the dozens, and Tara's ice cream is creamy, organic, and comes in outrageous flavors, such as mango ginger, saffron, and chocolate tarragon. Many are fans of the serious porridge served here for breakfast. Go for the panino or steamed eggs. Plenty of gluten-free variety. Inexpensive.

## ✳ Entertainment

You can hear live music on various nights at the Santa Fe hot spots below:

**Eldorado Court & Lounge** (505-988-4455), 309 W. San Francisco St., has flamenco on weekends and a piano bar during the week.

**El Farol** (505-983-9912), 808 Canyon Rd., Santa Fe's oldest restaurant and cantina, also has nightly live entertainment in summer. In winter, salsa lessons are followed by Cuban music on Wed. nights and world music on Sun. evenings.

**El Meson** (505-983-6756), 213 Washington Ave., Santa Fe. Come for the tapas and fine aged sherry, stay for the jazz. A favorite weekend hangout for my friends and me.

**Evangelo's** (505-982-9015), 200 W. San Francisco St., offers live country, jazz, and rock bands Fri.–Sat. nights.

**Gig Performance Space** (www.gig santafe.com/contact.html), 1808 Second St., Ste. H. Intimate venue for a grand variety of local and national musicians. Folk, Americana, jazz workshops, even cameos by actor Alan Arkin.

**La Café Sena Cantina** (505-988-9232), 125 E. Palace Ave., has wait staff who belt out Broadway musical tunes.

**La Fonda's La Fiesta Lounge** (505-982-5511), 100 E. San Francisco St., is a favorite of locals and visitors, with country dancing on the intimate dance floor plus jazz and flamenco on various evenings.

**Lensic Performing Arts Center** (505-988-1234; www.lensic.com; www.ticketssantafe.org), 211 W. San Francisco St., Santa Fe. Built originally as a grand motion picture palace, the 1930 Lensic is a fantastic creation in a faux Moorish-Renaissance style and boasts a silver chandelier from New York's Roxy in the lobby, along with the crests of Santa Fe's founding families. State-of-the-art sound equipment makes this a popular performing venue for an extraordinary variety of events, including Aspen Santa Fe Ballet, Big Screen Classics, and Live from the Met.

**Maria Benitez Teatro Flamenco** (505-982-1237), 750 N. St. Francis Dr., Santa Fe. June–Sept. No one who has seen diva María Benitez perform her passionate versions of flamenco can forget her powerful energy. Her troupe is among the finest you will ever experience. This is a summer in Santa Fe must-do you will always remember.

**Second Street Brewery** (505-982-3030), 1814 Second St. An award-winning microbrewery, this is a relaxed pub serving fish and chips, soups, and salads, with live weekend entertainment. A second location at the Railyard is a popular entertainment venue.

**Secreto Lounge at Hotel St. Francis** (505-983-5700), 210 Don Gaspar Ave., Santa Fe. Mixology supreme.

**Staab House** (505-986-0000), 330 E. Palace Ave. The home built by Abraham Staab for his family is now a cozy night spot with live music of an evening. Nacha Mendez, diva of international Spanish song, performs most Friday nights.

**Tiny's Restaurant and Lounge** (505-983-9817), 1015 Pen Rd. Open daily. Closed Sun., except during football season. The lounge is the heart and soul of Tiny's, where you can get great *carne adovada*, chicken guacamole tacos, and *posole*. Here is where country and western meets Frank Sinatra. Live entertainment Thurs.–Sun. and dancing on weekends. It is a time capsule that never changes.

**Vanessie of Santa Fe** (505-982-9966), 434 W. San Francisco St., has a cocktail lounge atmosphere and live piano nightly.

## ✳ Selective Shopping

**Back at the Ranch Cowboy Boots** (505-989-8110), 209 E. Marcy St., Santa Fe. You might actually go ga-ga when you look upon the fabulous selection of wild and fanciful cowboy boots. Expect to blow the budget on a lifetime purchase.

**Design Center Santa Fe** (www .designcentersantafe.com), 418 Cerrillos Rd., Santa Fe. Here is some diverting browsing turf, a veritable bazaar, where you can stumble upon the unexpected piece of art, furniture, or antique that makes your entire trip worthwhile. It's also the site of some offbeat ethnic and vegetarian eateries.

✄ **Doodlets Shop** (505-983-3771), 120 Don Gaspar Ave., Santa Fe. A

SECOND STREET BREWERY IS A RAILYARD HIGHLIGHT, WITH MICROBREWS AND LIVE MUSIC.

shop for kids of all ages, Doodlets stocks tin mermaids to chocolate sardines and all the postcards, stickers, Victoriana, and miniatures in between.

**Jackalope** (505-471-8539), 2820 Cerrillos Rd., Santa Fe. "Folk art by the truckload" is the motto here. Whether you have a yen for handmade furniture from Mexico, chile lights, or a birdbath from the more than 2 acres of imported pottery, you will have fun shopping here. There's a patio restaurant, carousel, outdoors market, and plenty to amuse you for hours.

**Jacqueline's Place** (505-995-1150), 233 Canyon Rd., Santa Fe. American-made jewelry and stylish women's clothing, reasonable prices, excellent selection of contemporary looks for young girls, treasure trove of turquoise and silver. One-of-a-kind look. Why not shop here?

**Keshi: The Zuni Connection** (505-989-8728), 227 Don Gaspar, Santa Fe. For the best selection of guaranteed authentic Zuni fetishes, inlay and needlepoint jewelry, displayed brilliantly, with excellent advice, don't fool around, come here.

**Lucille's** (505-983-6331), 223 Galisteo St., Santa Fe. This store is hung from floor to ceiling with racks crammed full of soft, loose, ethnic-y dresses and separates in rayon, cotton, and other breathable fabrics. You can get a broomstick skirt here, for sure. Lucille's is moderately priced and has a good selection of roomy, larger sizes.

**Maya** (505-989-7590), 108 Galisteo St., Santa Fe. Deliriously diverse and choice selection of timeless international imported clothing, jewelry, art, and embellishments. Don't expect a bargain, however.

**Palace of the Governors Portal** (www.palaceofthegovernors.org/index .php), north block of the Plaza. Open daily. One of the best places in town to shop for traditional Indian jewelry is beneath the portal of the Governors' Palace. Here prices are reasonable for a huge array of guaranteed authentic handmade Indian wares.

**Purple Sage** (505-954-0600), 110 Don Gaspar, Santa Fe. When a Santa Fe woman wants to splurge on a special-occasion outfit, she is likely to go to the Purple Sage for an ensemble in their luscious handwoven and hand-painted fabrics.

**Santa Fe Flea Market** (no phone), 10 miles north of Santa Fe on US 84/285. Open seasonally Fri.–Sun. 8–5. Although not the bargain-hunter's paradise this once was, the market, now operated by Tesuque Pueblo, still has a vast display of leather goods, jewelry, furniture, masks, and so much more.

**Fashion Outlets of Santa Fe** (505-474-4000), 8380 Cerrillos Rd., 8 miles south of Santa Fe. More than 40 outlet stores with bargain prices on name brands.

**The Shops at Sanbusco** (505-989-9390), 500 Montezuma St., Santa Fe. Located in the Railyard area, this is an indoor arcade of high-end dress, accessory, and gift shops.

SHOPPING AND ROMANCE GO HAND IN HAND IN SANTA FE.

**Silver Sun** (505-983-8743), 656 Canyon Rd., Santa Fe. Offering jewelry from 25 turquoise mines for over 30 years, Silver Sun promises that what is sold here is the finest quality, and you will receive reliable, informed guidance. Prices are fair (not cheap), and there are sales. Look in back.

**Sun Country Traders** (505-982-0467), 123 E. Water St. Specializing in Zuni beadwork, this reputable shop is well-stocked with the irresistible, the beautiful, and the well-crafted in Native jewelry, wood, pottery, and intriguing household objects, such as hand-beaded wineglasses.

**Todos Santos** (505-982-3855), 125 E. Palace Ave. #31, Santa Fe. Chocoholic alert. The most beautiful, imaginative artisanal chocolates, made in Santa Fe and arrayed from around the world are displayed in this jewel box of a shop in Sena Plaza. Pricey!

**BOOKSTORES** **Ark Books** (505-988-3709), 133 Romero St., Santa Fe. The New Age lives and thrives here, in these six rooms of books specializing in healing, world religions, magic, and mythology. Tapes/CDs, Tarot, jewelry, and incense make for a serene browse. Look for the hidden alcove with bargain books.

**Collected Works** (505-988-4226; www.collectedworksbookstore.com), 208-B W. San Francisco St., Santa Fe. This is the city's oldest and most complete independent bookstore. Check

SO MANY BOOKSTORES, SO LITTLE TIME!

FINE CRAFTSMEN FROM ALL OVER THE WORLD ATTEND SANTA FE'S INTERNATIONAL FOLK ART MARKET.

**Photo-Eye Books & Prints** (505-988-5152), 376 Garcia St., Santa Fe. Self-dubbed "the world's largest photography bookstore"; if you can't find it, the staff will order it.

## ✳ Special Events

*July:* **Pancake Breakfast on the Plaza** (505-982-2002), July 4. **Spanish Market** (505-982-2226), Santa Fe Plaza, last weekend. A juried show of traditional Spanish Colonial artwork created by artists of Spanish descent. **International Folk Art Market** (505-992-7600), Milner Plaza, Museum Hill, second weekend. **Rodeo de Santa Fe** (505-471-4300), Rodeo Grounds, 3237 Rodeo Rd., second weekend.

*August:* **Indian Market** (505-982-5333), Plaza. Weekend closest to Aug. 19. The world's largest sale of Native American arts.

*September:* **La Fiesta de Santa Fe** (505-913-1517) is the oldest ongoing festival (since 1712) in the United

the calendar for frequent events, readings and signings. This new location has a cozy fireplace and coffee bar. No finer place to spend a wintry afternoon.

**Garcia Street Books** (505-986-0151), 376 Garcia St., Santa Fe. With such an assortment of well-selected titles, you can't possibly walk out of here without a wonderful find.

**Nicholas Potter Bookseller** (505-983-5434), 211 E. Palace Ave., Santa Fe. This antiquarian Santa Fe classic has survived it all. A must-visit for book lovers. A dream of a shop.

**op.cit.** (505-428-0321), 500 Montezuma Ave., Santa Fe. The indie bookstore that took over where Borders left Sanbusco is a hit. New and used books; satisfying browsing.

SANTERA MARIE ROMERO CASH DISPLAYS HER CARVINGS AT SPANISH MARKET.

States; second weekend. **Thirsty Ear Festival** (www.thirstyearfestival.com), Eaves Movie Ranch, first weekend. **Santa Fe Wine and Chile Fiesta** (505-438-8060; www.santafewineand chile.org), last week.

*November:* **Winter Indian Market** (505-982-5333).

*December:* **Winter Spanish Market** (505-982-2226), first weekend. **Santa Fe Film Festival** (505-988-5225), emerging and established artists. Various venues. **Baumann Marionettes** (505-476-5072). Annual treat for children at St. Francis Auditorium, New Mexico Museum of Art. **Christmas at the Palace** (505-476-5100), hot cider and an old-fashioned celebration at the Palace of the Governors, midmonth. **Las Posadas** (santafe. org), midmonth, is a reenactment of a traditional holiday play around the Plaza. **Canyon Road Farolito Walk** (www.santafe.org), sunset–midnight, Dec. 24.

# Northwest New Mexico: Ancestral Pueblo Country

5

**SKY CITY COUNTRY**
Acoma Pueblo, Crownpoint, Laguna
Pueblo, Gallup, Grants, Ramah, Zuni
Pueblo

**CHACO COUNTRY**
Aztec, Bloomfield, Cuba, Farmington,
Shiprock

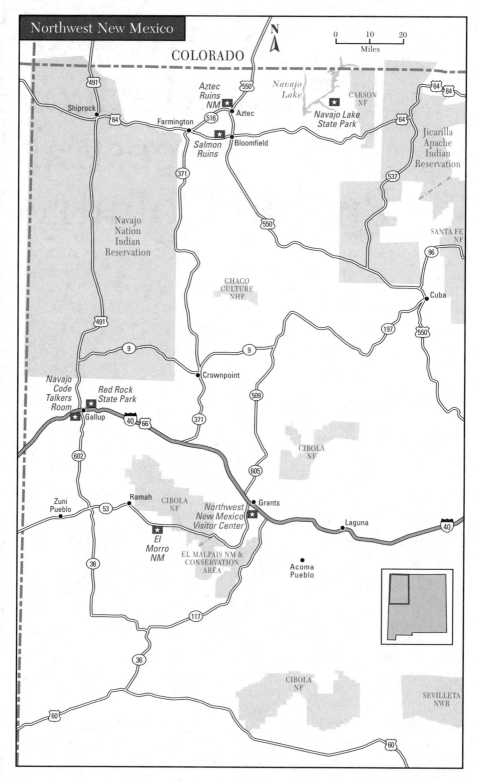

**Northwest New Mexico**

COLORADO

N

0    10    20
Miles

Shiprock

Aztec Ruins NM ★

Aztec

Farmington

Salmon Ruins ★

Bloomfield

Navajo Lake

Navajo Lake State Park

CARSON NF

Jicarilla Apache Indian Reservation

Navajo Nation Indian Reservation

SANTA FE NF

CHACO CULTURE NHP

Cuba

Crownpoint

Navajo Code Talkers Room ★

Red Rock State Park ★

Gallup

CIBOLA NF

Zuni Pueblo

Ramah

CIBOLA NF

El Morro NM ★

Northwest New Mexico Visitor Center ★

Grants

Laguna

EL MALPAIS NM & CONSERVATION AREA

Acoma Pueblo

CIBOLA NF

SEVILLETA NWR

# SKY CITY COUNTRY

## ACOMA PUEBLO, CROWNPOINT, LAGUNA PUEBLO, GALLUP, GRANTS, RAMAH, ZUNI PUEBLO

Making a journey to northwest New Mexico is as close as a traveler can get to the mysteries of a civilization that thrived, then vanished, long before Europeans dreamed of setting foot on this continent. The monumental structures of Chaco Canyon, the restored Great Kiva at Aztec Ruins, and the solstice marker precise as a Swiss watch at Salmon Ruins provoke awe and wonderment in even the most worldly traveler.

The sight of these magnificent ruins raises more questions than we can answer. Was Chaco Canyon a trading or ceremonial center? Or the home of a priestly class? Were its arrow-straight roads, which lead to outliers throughout the Four Corners region, also related to religious traditions? How far did trading extend—to Mesoamerica, to the Andes? Did the inhabitants depart their homes because of drought, illness, or war? The best we can do is speculate and continue asking questions.

Once known as the Anasazi, now referred to as the Ancestral Pueblo, the people who lived here are now believed to be the forbears of contemporary New Mexico Pueblo Indians. Yet in this region one encounters, with the exceptions of Acoma, Laguna, and Zuni, not the Pueblo, but the Navajo, whose reservation extends throughout four states. For those who admire the fine weaving, silver and turquoise jewelry, and sand paintings of the Navajo, there are no better places to see these wares and shop for them than in the trading posts of Gallup and Farmington, or at the monthly Crownpoint Rug Auction.

To savvy fly-fishermen, the San Juan River outside Farmington is a holy grail, which is not to underestimate the attractions of the region for golfers, hikers, cavers, birders, and mountain bikers.

The rich, multilayered history of the exploration of the Southwest is vividly recorded on El Morro, or Inscription Rock, which bears the signs of those who passed by this water source. Petroglyphs, signatures of Spanish conquistadors, of

CHACO CANYON IS ALWAYS WORTH THE JOURNEY.

U.S. Calvary, of homesteaders and miners, tell a centuries-old story. From the time Coronado passed through in 1540 on his search for the fabled "Seven Cities of Cibola" in his quest for gold, this harsh high-desert landscape, with its black lava, rich farming land, red buttes, and its resources of wood, coal uranium, natural gas, and oil, has held out the promise of fortunes to be made.

The name "Cibola" refers to a mythic city. In medieval Europe, a popular legend told of Seven Cities of Antilia located across the Atlantic Ocean. Spanish explorers came here searching for legendary cities, in hopes of discovering the same riches of gold as they had found in the southern hemisphere, among Mayan, Aztec, and Incan cities. In 1539, explorer Cabeza de Vaca first saw Zuni, and his report fueled Coronado's quest. Zuni was believed to be the smallest of the fabled cities.

In this region you can stand at the point where four states meet, cross the Continental Divide, witness the all-night winter ceremonial of Shalako at Zuni Pueblo, and travel long stretches of the Mother Road, Old Route 66. Many of the sights and experiences that make the West the West are found here. Best of all, these experiences can be had on a personal scale. These places remain true to themselves. They are not overwhelmed with or by tourism, but somehow manage to absorb visitors in a comfortable fashion, still moving at their own pace. While ample selections of amenities are available, this is not an area of high-end lodges, upscale boutiques, or fine dining opportunities. Rather, it is a place to chat with old-timers in a local café, watch sunsets flame the sky, bask in the quiet of really wide open spaces, and, if you are lucky, see a mountain lion leap across the road. It is a place where adventure and discovery are still possible.

By making a giant loop, it is possible to travel through Ancestral Pueblo country without going over the same territory twice. However, this country may also be traveled conveniently in two sections: Sky City Country, linked by I-40 and anchored by Acoma Pueblo with Gallup as a base destination; and Chaco Country, linked by US 550 and anchored by Chaco Canyon with Farmington and surrounds as a base.

**GUIDANCE** **Sky City Travel Center** (505-552-5700), Acoma.

**Gallup Convention & Visitors Bureau** (800-242-4282 or 505-863-3843), 201 E. Historic Route 66, Gallup.

**Gallup/McKinley Country Chamber of Commerce** (575-722-2228), 103 W. Route 66, Gallup.

**Grants/Cibola County Chamber of Commerce** (505-287-4802), 100 N. Iron Ave., Grants.

**Indian Country New Mexico** (www.indiancountrynm.org).

**Laguna Pueblo** (505-552-6654), Laguna Pueblo.

INSCRIPTION ROCK IS MARKED WITH THE SIGNATURES OF NEW MEXICO EXPLORERS AND CONQUISTADORS.

**New Mexico Route 66 Association** (www.rt66nm.org).

**Northwest New Mexico Visitors Center** (505-876-2783), 1900 East Santa Fe Ave., off I-40 at exit 85, Grants. Open 8–5 MST, 9–6 MDT (summer). This stop is a must-do for trip planning to Chaco, El Morro, El Malpais, and all the area attractions, with an abundance of maps, books, and experience available.

**Zuni Tourism** (www.zunitourism.com).

**GETTING THERE** From Albuquerque, take I-40 west 221 miles to Gallup, passing Acoma Pueblo, Laguna Pueblo, and Grants, while following the direction of Route 66.

**MEDICAL EMERGENCY** **Cibola General Hospital** (505-287-4446), 1016 Roosevelt Ave., Grants.

**Rehobeth McKinley Christian Hospital** (575-863-7000), 1901 Redrock Dr., Gallup.

## ✳ To See

**TOWNS AND PUEBLOS** **Acoma Pueblo, or Sky City**, is said to be the oldest continuously inhabited community in North America. Acoma people have lived here for 2,000 years. After exiting I-40 at exit 102, 65 miles west of Albuquerque, follow Indian Route 23 south to Sky City Cultural Center. Tours with native tour guides take you by bus to the top of the 357-foot-high mesa, the original village site of 300 adobe structures, and the remarkable San Esteban del Rey Mission Church. Acoma is especially well known for its fine pottery, which may sometimes be purchased from the makers on the pueblo tour and during feast days. Feast days and traditional observances open to the public are Dec. 24–28, Sept. 2, Aug. 10, and the first or second weekend in February.

**Crownpoint** is situated 24 miles north of the Thoreau exit off I-40 on NM 371 and is notable for its second Fri. of the month Navajo rug auction. From here, it is about 40 rough miles farther on unpaved NM 57 to the south entrance of Chaco Canyon.

**Gallup** claims title as "the Indian jewelry capital of the world" with over 100 trading posts. It is the home of the annual Intertribal Ceremonial, held in late July or early August, as well as a noted Route 66 stop, and in its heyday, it was a coal mining and railroading center. The town is a gateway to the Navajo Reservation, a base for exploring Canyon de Chelly and Monument Valley, as well as a trading, shopping, medical, and educational center for the Navajo and Zuni.

**Grants**, a Route 66 stop and formerly "the uranium capital of the world" at the base of Mt. Taylor, is a good place to rest en route to Chaco Canyon and Crownpoint Rug Auction.

**Laguna Pueblo** Inhabited as early as 3000 B.C., this area has been occupied by Mesa Verde migrants since the 1300s. Laguna was named for a lake, which no longer exists and was first mentioned in accounts of Coronado's 1540 exploration party. Old Laguna Village is now the ceremonial center of several neighboring

ZUNI OLLA MAIDENS IN THE GALLUP INTERTRIBAL CEREMONIAL PARADE.

villages. Feast days are Mar. 19 and Sept. 19. The stone San Jose de la Laguna Mission Church and Convento is a landmark seen from the north side of I-40 about 35 miles west of Albuquerque.

**Ramah**, chiefly a Mormon and Navajo town with one small museum, located along NM 53, is the home of Ramah Navajo Weavers Association, and Ramah Lake is 2.5 miles northeast of town. The Ramah Museum, open Fri. 1–4, tells the story of the town.

**Zuni Pueblo**, 32 miles south of Gallup on NM 53. The first Native American village encountered by Coronado on his search for the Seven Cities of Gold, it is believed Zuni was the inspiration for this conquistador legend. Shalako, the annual all-night winter ceremony held late Nov. or early Dec., is noted for the dancing of the 10-foot-tall Shalakos representing guiding spirits. Today's Zuni dwellers are known for fine inlay and turquoise needlepoint jewelry, their fetishes carved of semiprecious stones, and, of course, their hand-carved kachina figures. This is the largest of the pueblos, and the people speak their own language, Zuni, unrelated to any Pueblo languages. The restored mission church, Nuestra Señora de Guadalupe de la Candelaria de Halona, originally established 1630–66, has life-size restored murals.

## HISTORIC LANDMARKS, PLACES, AND SITES **Continental Divide.**
Approximately 170 miles west of Albuquerque on I-40 is the pinnacle of a geological ridge that separates the nation's waterways. East of the Divide all waters flow east to the Atlantic Ocean, while those west of the Divide flow towards the Pacific.

**El Morro National Monument** (505-783-4226), 42 miles southeast on NM 53 from Grants. Closed Christmas and New Year's Day. Visitors center open daily

Oct. 2–DST 9–5; trails open 9–4. Check for summer hours. El Morro is also known as Inscription Rock for its 2,000 inscriptions and prehistoric petroglyphs. In 1640, Francisco Coronado wrote *"Paso por aqui"* (I passed by here) in the sandstone formation. It is the pool, the reliable water source beneath the huge boulder, that caused travelers to stop here throughout history. There is a paved 0.5-mile loop trail from the visitors center to Inscription Rock and a two-hour round-trip moderate hike to the mesa-top, 13th- and 14th-century pueblo ruins. $3, under age 16 free.

**MUSEUMS A:shiwi A:wan Museum and Heritage Center** (www.ashiwi-museum.org), 02 E. Ojo Caliente Rd., Zuni. Open Mon.–Fri. 9–5. Closed during religious ceremonies. The heritage center displays artifacts retrieved when the ancient city of Hawikku was excavated in 1920. The center is located on the site of one of Zuni's first trading posts. Tours, exhibits, and programs about the village and the environment make this a sensible place to begin a visit. Free.

**Atchison, Topeka & Santa Fe Railway Depot/Gallup Cultural Center** (505-863-4131), 201 E. Historic Route 66, Gallup. Open Mon.–Fri. 10–4. This restored depot contains exhibits and a gift shop, plus the Storyteller Museum and Gallery of the Masters. Indian dances are performed nightly at 7 in summer. Free.

**Navajo Code Talkers Room** (505-722-2228), 103 W. Historic Route 66, Gallup. Open Mon.–Fri. 8:30–5. During World War II, members of the Navajo Nation volunteered for a special mission. They translated intelligence into Navajo, and the Japanese never broke this code. Memorabilia and photos commemorate their contributions. Free.

**New Mexico Mining Museum** (800-748-2142), 100 N. Iron Ave., Grants. Open Mon.–Sat. 9–4. Visit the world's only underground uranium mining museum, learn about rocks of the region, and ride "the cage" down an actual mineshaft. $3 adults, $2 seniors and children.

**Rex Museum** (505-863-1363), 300 W. Historic Route 66, Gallup. Open Mon.–Fri. 8–3. Housed in a century-old stone building, the former home of the Rex Hotel, the museum displays memorabilia and history of this railroad and coal mining community. $12 adults, $5 children.

**Sky City Cultural Center and Haak'u Museum** (505-552-5700). Mesa tours are available daily on the hour May–Sept. 8–6 (last tour 5) and Oct.–Apr. 8–4:30. Please call ahead to confirm hours. The beautiful new cultural center displays pottery, jewelry, exhibits of history, and significant individuals of Acoma. Cultural center free. Tours $23 adults, $20 seniors, $15 children, $13 still camera permit.

**NATURAL WONDERS Bandera Volcano and Ice Cave** (888-423-2283), 25 miles southwest of Grants off NM 53. Open daily from 8 until one hour before sunset. The temperature in the ice cave is 31 degrees Fahrenheit year-round, kept that way by 20-foot-thick ice on the cave floor. Bandera is the largest of 29 extinct volcanoes in the region. It is a 40-minute hike to the volcano, and a 20-minute hike into the ice cave. Both are reasonably easy, but the ice cave involves some intense stair climbing. There is an old-time trading post on the premises. $11 adults and teens, 10 percent off for seniors and military, $5 ages 5–12.

**La Ventana Natural Arch** (www.explorenm.com/hikes/LaVentana/). Access from NM 117. *La ventana* means "the window," and that is exactly what this 165-foot-wide natural golden sandstone arch appears to be, a window onto the sky. Free.

**SCENIC DRIVES** **Ancient Way** (http://byways.org/explore/states/NM), NM 53 as it parallels the ancient trade route between Acoma and Zuni pueblos and the route originally taken by Coronado. Take exit 81 off I-40 for a 73-mile scenic drive to Zuni Pueblo that leads en route to El Morro, or Inscription Rock. En route, pass the villages of San Rafael, San Mateo, and Cebolleta.

**Old Route 66.** Driving east on I-40 between Albuquerque and Gallup affords many opportunities to get off the interstate and hop onto original stretches of Route 66, the Mother Road, as author John Steinbeck named it, with several Route 66 markers, such as the Rio Puerco Bridge, in evidence. The road from Chicago to Los Angeles was opened in 1926, then it was realigned in 1937 and subsequently made famous by songs and television shows that celebrated it as a road of freedom and discovery for postwar America.

**Zuni Mountain Historic Auto Tour** (505-287-8833). From Santa Fe Ave. in Grants, go west to NM 53, cross I-40, and go right on Zuni Canyon Rd. This tour leads 60 miles as it winds through Zuni Canyon to Agua Fria Valley to the historic town of Sawyer, and loops back to Grants via Bluewater Lake. It follows Forest Service dirt roads to trace the history of logging and railroading in Cibola National Forest with old railroad grades, town sites, and trestle remnants en route.

## ✳ To Do

**BICYCLING** For trail maps and information on area races, call 800-448-1240.

**Aztec Mountain Biking and Hiking Trails** (505-334-7632; www.scout.me /mountain-bike-trails-near-aztec-nm) includes three main trails: Aztec Trails, Mountain View Trails, and Alien Run. The system starts near the city limits and leads to Hart Canyon, the site of the alleged 1948 UFO crash.

**BOATING** See the state parks under *Green Space.*

**FISHING** **Ramah Lake** (no phone), 2.5 miles northeast of Ramah. Fishing, boating, and picnicking.

**San Juan River/Quality Waters** (505-326-7602; www.sanjuanriver.com/River Upper.htm), 26 miles northeast of Aztec off NM 173 and NM 511. Year-round fishing in 12 miles of open water. Sought-after trophy trout fly-fishing in the waters west of Navajo Lake Dam brings fishermen to the San Juan to catch the big ones. But those big ones swimming around your waders are wily, as they have been caught and released so many times. Enormous rainbow trout that feed well makes this one of America's top 10 trout fishing waters. A section of the river for 6 miles south of the dam flows through a magical, scenic sandstone

## WILDER PLACES

**Angel Peak Recreation Area** (505-564-7600), 30 miles southeast of Farmington on US 550. Take the 6-mile gravel road northeast into the site. No water or services, but accessible camping and picnic areas are available, as are hiking trails and wildlife viewing. Angel Peak is a striking 40-million-year-old, 7,000-foot-high geologic formation crowning 10,000 acres of rugged wilderness. Fossils and petrified wood visible in these badlands formations. An amazing perspective on the history of the planet. This area is not recommended for RVs. Free.

**Bisti Badlands/De-Na-Zin Wilderness** (505-599-8900; www.blm.gov/nm/st /en/prog/wilderness/bisti.html). Roughly 50 miles south of Farmington off NM 371, 2 miles down gravel road #7297. Remote, 42,000 acres administered by the BLM. This wind-sculpted shale and sandstone formation with its fantastic, colorful landforms might well be a journey to the moon. The best formations may be reached by hiking 2 miles east from parking area. Motorized vehicles not permitted. Primitive camping is possible, but no services. Best to visit late spring or fall. Free.

**Cabezon Peak** (505-761-8700; www.blm.gov/nm/st/en/prog/recreation/rio _puerco/cabezon_peak.html). Go west on US 550 onto CR 279, approximately 20 miles northwest of San Ysidro. Continue 12 miles past village of San Luis to Cabezon turnoff onto BLM road 1114. The pavement ends just beyond San Luis. At intersection of CR 279 and BLM Road 1114, pass the ghost town of Cabezon. Follow 1114 for 2.9 miles to a dirt road that leads to a trailhead. Check road conditions before attempting this journey. *Cabezon* translates as "big head," and it is the most prominent volcanic neck in the Mt. Taylor lava fields, rising 8,000 feet above sea level. This is considered a sacred site by Pueblo and Navajo peoples. It is not recommended for children or pets. The trail, only for the fit and the adept, involves some Class 3 climbing and is accessible year-round, and this is a popular climb for the well-prepared and experienced. Caution: Rattlesnakes are active in warmer weather. Primitive recreation. Camping for 14 days or less is okay. Free.

**Mount Taylor** (575-287-8833). An 11,301-foot-high volcano visible from Albuquerque, Mount Taylor is a sacred site known as Turquoise Mountain in Navajo culture and within Cibola National Forest. The Mt. Taylor Quadrathlon is a grueling 44-mile race held every Presidents' Day weekend, starting from downtown Grants to the summit and back. The race includes biking, running, skiing, and snowshoeing. Trail 77 is a moderate 6-mile round-trip hike near the top—with phenomenal views. Go north on First St. in Grants to NM 547 (Lobo Canyon Rd.) for 13 miles, right on FR 193 for 5 miles to trailhead.

**Ojito Wilderness** (575-761-8700; www.blm.gov/nm/st/en/prog/wilderness/ojito .html). From Albuquerque, go north on I-25 for 16 miles, then exit on US 550 at second Bernalillo exit. Go 20 miles northwest toward Cuba on US 550. Two miles before San Ysidro, turn left onto Cabezon Road (CR 906), follow the left fork 10 miles to the Ojito Wilderness sign. This remote, austere, quiet place is a roadless area with no facilities, no services, and no water. The 11,000 acres are full of steep canyons and rugged cliffs to challenge experienced hikers. Horseback riding and primitive camping are allowed in this increasingly popular exploration site. You might see fossils, petroglyphs, petrified trees, and even seashells. Free.

**Wild Spirit Wolf Sanctuary** (505-775-3304; wildspiritwolfsanctuary.org), 378 Candy Kitchen Rd., Ramah. Go 2 miles past El Morro on NM 53 (approximately 50 miles southeast of Grants), left on BIA 125 for 8 miles, right on BIA 120 for 4 miles; sanctuary on left. Open Tues.–Sun. Closed Mon. Guided tours at 11, 12:30, 2, 3:30. Meet wolf dog and wolf captive born in the Zuni Mountains and wolf and wolf dog rescues. $7 adults, $6 seniors, $4 children, under age 7 free. $15 camping.

BISTI BADLANDS SUGGESTS A REMOTE MOONSCAPE.

canyon. There are four wheelchair-accessible fishing piers along the river and an easy hiking trail that runs for 1.5 miles along the north side of the San Juan River. Quality waters have special restrictions. Free.

**FLOATING AND KAYAKING** See *Green Space*.

**HIKING Pyramid Rock**, in Red Rock Park. At the summit one can see 50 miles on a clear day. The 3-mile round-trip takes you through amazing rock formations, with a summit elevation of 7,487 feet. Church Rock Trail begins at Outlaw Trading Post parking lot, with great views of Church Rock Spires. From Gallup, go 6 miles east on Route 66/NM 118. Turn north onto NM 566 for 0.5 mile. Turn left into Red Rock Park, follow the signs. Check with the visitors center for maps.

**Zuni-Acoma Trail** in El Malpais National Monument traverses the Continental Divide, which stretches from Canada to the southern border of the United States. You need strong shoes to hike from cairn to cairn across the lava of this ancient trade route, a segment of an old Indian trail connecting Acoma and Zuni pueblos. Bring lots of water for this lifetime hike. It will take five or six hours and is quite strenuous, ranging from easy to moderate to difficult.

**MOUNTAIN BIKING Farmington Lake** has many trails through all types of terrain that can be accessed off the Road Apple Trail.

**Farmington Trails** (505-326-7602) include **Road Apple Trail**, behind San Juan College, with sandy washes and arroyos, hilly jumps, and steep climbs; **Kinsey's Ridge**, at the end of Foothills Drive, with 6 miles of rolling hills and great views; and **Pinon Mesa**, 3 miles north of Main St. on NM 170, with a trailhead marked by a large cottonwood on the west side of the highway.

**High Desert Trail System.** A new mountain bike trail on the high mesas northwest of Gallup has a stacked loop trail with trailheads near Gamerco and Mentmore, former coal mines. To get to Gamerco, go 2 miles north of I-40 on US 491, and left at Chino Loop traffic signal; the trailhead is on the left just after the curve. The trail heads west for 2.25 miles around the mesa top with expansive viewpoints. Or turn right at Six Flags, continuing on to Second Mesa. The third mesa is higher to the south. Challenging.

See **Zuni Mountain Historic Auto Tour** under *To See*, "Scenic Drives." Many of these old logging roads along the way are suitable for mountain biking.

**SNOW SPORTS** Best to check out opportunities at nearby **Durango Mountain Resort** (www.durangomountainresort.com) and **Wolf Creek Ski Area** (www.wolfcreekski.com).

**WINERIES Wines of the San Juan Tasting Room** (575-632-0879), 233 NM 551. Open Mon. and Wed.–Sat. 10–6, Sun. 2–6. Closed Tues. Find this rustic tasting room 6 miles below Navajo Lake State Park on NM 511 at Turley. The San Juan region is the ideal microclimate to produce these rich, fruity wines.

# ✳ Lodging

## BED & BREAKFASTS, INNS, AND MOTELS

♿ **Cimarron Rose, Zuni Mountain Bed & Breakfast** (800-856-5776; www.cimarronrose .com), 689 Oso Ridge Rd., 30 miles southwest of Grants on NM 53. To preserve your solitude and privacy, breakfast is delivered to your room. Local artists display their wares for sale in this true retreat and "green" lodging located on the Great Divide. Each of the three rooms has its own bath. $90–185.

**El Rancho Hotel** (505-863-9311), 1000 E. Historic Route 66, Gallup. One block south of I-40 at exit 22. With 24 rooms, each named for a movie star, and the mezzanine deco-rated with black-and-white photos of all the stars that stayed here while shooting movies, this 1937 hotel is the epitome of Hollywood gone western nostalgia. The hot pink neon beckons you to stop, and the pool, lounge, and quite decent restaurant serving break-fast, lunch, and dinner make this the top choice for a Gallup stay. Most of the rooms are on the small side; you can stay, however, for a not unreason-able price, in the Presidential Suite (a.k.a. the Ronald Reagan Room). The open lobby with curving wooden staircases on either side, decorated in Navajo rugs and rustic western fur-nishings, with a floor-to-ceiling stone fireplace, is one of the most welcom-ing sights along the road. $104–132.

**The Inn at Halona** (505-782-4547; www.halona.com), 23 Pie Mesa Rd., Zuni. Located in the middle Zuni Pueblo in the historic 1940 home of trader Bernard J. Vanden Wagen and operated by his granddaughter, Elaine, this eight-room bed & break-fast imparts a sense of a faraway

adventure, in comfort. Several of the rooms are graced with comfortably furnished private patios. Breakfast is included. $79.

## RANCHES AND LODGES

**Apache Canyon Ranch B&B Country Inn** (505-908-8220), 4 Canyon Dr., Laguna. Bordered by Indian lands, not far from Old Route 66, the ranch's views and the peace and quiet are unmatched. It's somewhat surprising to find an upscale lodging all the way out here, but there you are. The inn sits on several acres, and the main quarters has rooms and courtyards, a grand parlor for tea, a six-hole putting green, and a guest cottage with a whirlpool tub and kiva fireplace. Of course, the breakfast is gourmet qual-ity, and dinner, should you choose to remain on the premises rather than zip over to the Route 66 Casino, may be prepared on request. $250–200.

**Stauder's Navajo Lodge** (505-862-7553), Continental Divide, 20 miles east of Gallup. Seasoned innkeepers Sherwood and Roberta Stauder share their hospitality and love of this place in their quarters, filled with Indian arts and antiques. With only two rooms, each with private bath, guests are certain to feel catered to at this old-fashioned (in a good way), deeply western lodge whether en route to Chaco Canyon or Crownpoint Rug Auction. There's a pretty courtyard and mind-blowing views of the red rock bluffs. Peach sauce from the lodge's own peach trees graces your scrumptious breakfast. Delightful! $85–95.

✂ **Z Lazy B Mountain Retreat** (888-488-2007), Ft. Wingate. Open year-round, weather permitting. The descendant of the original homesteaders on this land now lives here with her husband, and together they raise horses in this somewhat desolate and wild Zuni Mountain area that was formerly a busy logging territory. There are five comfortably and completely furnished log cabins, nothing shabby here, each sleeping 8–10, each with kitchen, bath, lounging, and private areas, and guests may choose to have the staff cook for them or prepare their own meals. A hearty meat and potatoes freshly cooked breakfast is included, at any rate. The lodge is also known for horseback riding, offering trail, pony, and wagon rides May–Oct. And they will cook all meals for you, on request. $120 night double occupancy, $15 each extra person.

**CABINS AND CAMPING El Morro RV, Cabins, & Ancient Way Café** (505-783-4612), 4018 NM 53, Ramah. Open year-round. Just down the way from El Morro National Monument are cozy cabins in the pines at the base of San Lorenzo Mesa with sleeping accommodations for four, and full hookup RV sites in a pet-friendly place with free WiFi. The friendly café serves home-cooked breakfast, lunch, and dinner and is a gathering place where locals mingle with visitors for plenty of storytelling. Perfection! $79–94 cabin; $25 camping.

## ✴ Where to Eat

**DINING OUT Don Diego's Restaurant and Lounge** (505-722-5517), 801 W. Historic Route 66, Gallup. Open Mon.–Sat. 8–9. Closed Sun. Breakfast, lunch, dinner. Nightlife, such as it is, may be found here, along with pretty tasty New Mexican food and good hot red chile. Inexpensive.

**EATING OUT Eagle Cafe** (505-722-3220), 220 W. Historic Hwy. 66, Gallup. Open Mon.–Sat. 7–7. Closed Sun. Breakfast, lunch, dinner. You can still hear the trains rolling in on the tracks across Old 66. Sink into one of the old-time booths and order mutton stew with local traders and Navajo. The Eagle has been here since 1904, and from the looks of the place, nothing much has changed. Inexpensive.

🍴 ♿ **Earl's Family Restaurant** (505-863-4201), 1400 E. Route 66, Gallup. Open daily. Breakfast, lunch, dinner. Rightly called "Gallup's living room," this is the place to eat reasonably priced green-chile-smothered enchiladas, but if you're not accustomed to the local cuisine, plenty of real mashed potatoes and gravy are served with delicious daily specials of fried chicken and meat loaf. Shop while you eat, as vendors circulate showing off their wares. If you don't care to be bothered, you can get a sign indicating so from the management. If you have time for only one meal in Gallup, by all means eat at this 40-year-old family restaurant. Inexpensive.

**Ranch Kitchen** (505-722-2328), 3001 W. Hwy. 66, Gallup. Open daily. Closed Easter and Christmas. Breakfast, lunch, dinner. Here is Southwestern cooking, somewhat cowboy style, in a place that comfortably accommodates the long-distance travelers who know it well. Love those big plates of smoky barbecue, and the Navajo tacos are mighty fine. The gift shop is a treasure chest of Route 66 memorabilia. For a feeling of road trip, come here. Inexpensive.

**Uranium Cafe** (505-285-4550), 519 W. Santa Fe, Grants. Irregular hours. "Our food will blow your mine" is the motto at this Route 66–era café, where it's catch as catch can to find them open. The rear end of a Cadillac, with fins, serves as the salad bar. Inexpensive.

**Virgie's Restaurant & Lounge** (505-863-5152), 2720 W. Old Hwy. 66, Gallup. Closed Sun. Open Mon.– Sat. 7 AM–9 PM. Breakfast, lunch, dinner. In the glow of Virgie's neon, feast on enchiladas in true Old 66 splendor. Virgie's is at least as much a roadside institution as it is a restaurant serving steaks and Mexican food. Virgie's beef stew and the chico steak smothered in green chile and cheese are favorites. Or go for the crème de la crème, the crispy chicken taquitos. This fine family restaurant started serving its homemade pie around 1960. Love Virgie's! Inexpensive.

## ✳ Entertainment

**Summer Theater Series in Lions Wilderness Amphitheater** (877-599-3331; www.fmtn.org/sandstone). June 20–Aug. 2. Repertory Theater under the stars in a natural golden sandstone arena. A most pleasant venue for light and family-oriented productions. $10 adults, $7 seniors, $5 children.

VIRGIE'S RESTAURANT & LOUNGE SERVES SOME OF THE MOST AUTHENTIC AND FLAVORFUL NEW MEXICAN FOOD IN THE STATE.

**Totah Theater** (505-327-4145), 315 W. Main, Farmington. A renovated 1948 movie house downtown. The facility books performances by local theater groups, such as Theatre Ensemble and traveling performers.

## ✳ Selective Shopping

**Old School Gallery** (505-783-4710), 53 NM 46. Open Thurs.–Sun. 11–5. An enterprise of the El Morro Area Arts Council, here you can find current exhibits and work of local artists in diverse media for sale. Lectures, workshops, cook-offs, tarot classes, yoga, Zumba, and special events and celebrations also go on at this gallery. A busy schedule. Call for exact directions and schedule of events.

**Richardson's Trading Co.** (505-722-4762), 222 W. Historic Hwy. 66, Gallup. Open Mon.–Sat. 9–5. The selection of the best turquoise, coral, and silver Navajo and Zuni jewelry; Navajo rugs; sand paintings; pottery; and old pawn fills every nook and cranny of this creaky trading post established in 1913. As much a museum as a store. The staff is patient and knowledgeable, and

RICHARDSON'S TRADING POST HOSTS NAVAJO WEAVING DEMONSTRATIONS.

Richardson's is as reliable a place (with fair prices) to make a purchase as you can find. There are treasures here at all price levels. Be prepared to take your time—it's difficult to choose!

# CHACO COUNTRY

## AZTEC, BLOOMFIELD, CUBA, FARMINGTON, SHIPROCK

Two activities of major interest dominate this region: visiting monumental ancient ruins and the opportunity to land the big trout on the San Juan River. If your senses are truly open, you might catch a faint drum beat or a whiff of fry bread on the wind. There is a sense of being in uncharted territory, almost at the end of the world, which is highlighted in places like no other such as the Bisti Badlands or the area around Shiprock. The place is haunting and unforgettable.

**GUIDANCE** **Aztec Chamber of Commerce & Tourist Center** (505-334-9551; www.aztecchamber.com), 110 N. Ash, Aztec.

**Bloomfield Chamber of Commerce** (505-632-0880; www.bloomfield chamber.info/index.php/event-calendar), 224 W. Broadway Ave., Bloomfield.

**Cuba Area Chamber of Commerce** (575-289-3514), 41 Martinez Dr., Cuba.

**Farmington Convention and Visitors Bureau** (505-326-7602; www .farmingtonnm.org), 3041 E. Main St., Farmington.

**Farmington Field Office, BLM** (505-564-7600), 6251 College Blvd., Farmington.

**Navajo Nation Tourism** (928-871-6436); www.discovernavajo.com), P.O. Box 663, Window Rock, Arizona.

**Northwest New Mexico Visitor Center** (505-876-2783), 1900 E. Santa Fe, Grants. Open daily 9–6 MDT, 8–5 MST.

**MEDICAL EMERGENCY** **San Juan Regional Medical Center** (505-609-2000), 801 W. Maple St., Farmington.

**GETTING THERE** From Albuquerque, go 180 miles northwest on I-25 north to Bernalillo, then US 550 to Bloomfield, then US 64 to Farmington. Along the way pass Cuba, the road to Chaco Canyon, Bloomfield, and the Salmon Ruins.

# ✳ To See

**TOWNS AND PUEBLOS Aztec** is 14 miles northeast of Farmington on US 550. Supporting the early belief that the nearby Ancestral Pueblo ruins were of Aztec origin, the town's founders in 1890 named their village for them. Aztec maintains a sense of civic pride in its homesteading past. Main Street Historic District is charming and well preserved, as are the Victorian residences, which form the core of the town.

**Bloomfield.** Located on the San Juan River at the junction of US 550 and US 64, 11 miles east of Farmington, this oil and gas center is a convenient place to make a quick stop for gas and groceries.

**Cuba** is 102 miles southeast of Farmington on US 550. This little town was not named for the Caribbean country by veterans of the Spanish-American War, as is sometimes said. Rather, the name refers to a geographical feature and means "sink," or "draw" in Spanish. Several cafés and gas stations cater to travelers. The ranger station on the south end of town offers permits and information about hiking, camping, cross-country skiing, and fishing in the nearby Santa Fe National Forest (505-289-3264; P.O. Box 130, Cuba, NM 87103).

**Farmington** is 180 miles northwest of Albuquerque on US 550. Totah, "among the rivers," is the Navajo name for this gateway city where three rivers—the Animas, La Plata, and San Juan—come together. But English-speaking settlers named it for its fine agricultural produce, recognizing it as a "farming-town." The economy has gone boom and bust with the oil, gas, and uranium industries for the past 60 years, and today there are two Farmingtons—the nicely preserved and still busy downtown, with its trading posts, cafés, and antiques shops, and the "parallel universe" of strip malls and shopping centers. In addition to making a great base for exploring the area, Farmington serves as the entertainment, shopping, and recreational center of the region, with summer theater, museums, an aquatic center, number-one-rated municipal golf course, and plenty of family activities.

**Shiprock** is 29 miles west of Farmington on US 64. Taking its name from its unforgettable landmark, the imposing "rock with wings," Shiprock is mainly a center of Navajo tribal business and services. The annual Northern Navajo Fair, held each fall, is an exceptional gathering of rugs, rodeo, and tradition.

**MUSEUMS** ✐ **Aztec Museum and Pioneer Village** (505-334-9829), 125 N. Main Ave., Aztec. Open Apr.–Sept. 10–5; Oct.–May 10–4. Closed Sunday. Here find a wealth of pioneer Americana, plus oilfield, military, and farm equipment exhibits. $3 adults, $1 children ages 12–17, age 11 and under free.

✐ ♿ **E-3 Children's Museum & Science Center** (505-599-1425), 302 N. Orchard, Farmington. Open Tues.–Sat. noon–5. Closed Mon. The kids will love the hands-on, science-related, and exploration exhibits found here. Free.

**Farmington Museum & Gateway Center** (505-599-1174), 3041 E. Main, Farmington. Open Mon.–Sat. 8–5. Closed Sun. Maps and trip planning; exhibits related to the history of the West and the Farmington area. Free.

✄ ⚕ **Riverside Nature Center** (505-599-1422), off Browning Pkwy. in Animas Park, Farmington. Open Tues.–Sat. 10–6. Tuesday morning bird-watching. Wetlands! Wildlife viewing; butterfly walks; hands-on exhibits of tracks, bones and seeds; xeriscape gardens; herb garden; history walks; and stargazing. Free.

**NATURAL WONDERS** **Four Corners Monument** (928-871-6647; www .navajonationparks.org), 30 miles northwest of Shiprock off US 64 and US 160. Open daily Oct.–May 7–5, June–Sept. 7 AM–7 PM. Erected in 1912, the Four Corners Monument is the only place in the United States where four states intersect: Arizona, New Mexico, Utah, and Colorado. You will find an Indian marketplace with handmade crafts as well. $3.

**Shiprock Pinnacle** (no phone; www.discovernavajo.com), 10 miles southwest of Shiprock off US 491. This signature western landmark, a mass of igneous rock flanked by walls of solidified lava, was given its apt name by early area settlers. Known to the Navajo as "rock with wings," this volcanic rock formation rises 1,700 feet above the desert floor. Because it is a sacred site to the Dine, or Navajo, only viewing is permitted. There is no access.

SHIPROCK, THE "ROCK WITH WINGS," IS A NAVAJO SACRED SITE.

## ANCIENT RUINS

**Aztec Ruins National Monument** (575-334-6174, ext. 230; www.nps/gov
/azru), 84 CR 29, Aztec. Ruins Road, 0.75 mile north of NM 516. Open Memorial Day–Labor Day 8–6; remainder of year 8–5. Closed Thanksgiving, Christmas, New Year's Day. These dwellings, dating to A.D. 900 and abandoned by
A.D. 1300, were inhabited as a Chaco outlier for 200 years. The inhabitants
were related to Mesa Verde as well as Chaco. A 700-yard paved trail winds
through the West Ruin, passing through several rooms with intact original
roofs. The centerpiece is the reconstructed Great Kiva, the only one in the
United States. $5 adults, under age 15 free (good for seven days).

**Chaco Culture National Historical Park** (505-786-7014, ext. 221; www.nps
.gov/chcu), Nageezi. The best access is off US 550 from the north at
Nageezi, via County Rd. 7900. Or take Thoreau exit off I-40 for 25 miles to
Crownpoint; 3 miles farther, turn east on Indian Highway 9. Continue to
Pueblo Pintado. Go north on NM 46 to CR 7900/7950 to reach the visitors
center. Visitors center open daily 8–5. Closed major holidays. Park open
daily 7 AM–sunset. Four-wheel drive is a necessity in difficult weather conditions. A word of caution: Call the ranger number above if in doubt. Both dirt
roads in are slow, rutted, and dangerously slippery when wet or icy. That
said, a visit to this ancient trade and ceremonial center that linked over 100
communities in the Four Corners area is a must. There are no services, but
there is a campground, and it is possible to make the moderate hike to the
top of mesas where the entire complex of ruins that were deserted by A.D.
1200 may be viewed. A 9-mile self-guided paved road offers a tour of five
major ruins, including massive great houses with hundreds of rooms. The
Chacoan culture is believed to have been the ancestral origins of today's
Pueblo Indians. While formerly known as "Anasazi," the current preferred
term is "Ancestral Pueblo."

Just a few of the mysteries involve how these ancient people of this
complex civilization created their remarkable astronomical alignments, their
masonry construction, and the arrow-straight outliers, as the roads visible
from the air leading to related settlements throughout the Four Corners
region are known. Was this a dwelling place or a spiritual or trade center?

We still do not know. $8 per vehicle (good for seven days); $4 per individual (good seven days); $10 camping.

**Salmon Ruins/Heritage Park, Archaeological Research Center and Library** (505-632-2013; www.salmonruins.com), 10 miles east of Farmington on US 64. Open daily 8–5. Closed major holidays. An eleventh-century pueblo built in Chacoan style, plus pioneer homestead. Ancestral Puebloan pottery, jewelry, tools, and hunting equipment are on display. Customized tours with professional archaeologists available. $3 adults, $2 seniors, $1 children ages 6–16.

AZTEC RUINS NATIONAL MONUMENT.

✳ **To Do**

**GOLF Pinon Hills** (505-326-6066), 2101 Sunrise Pkwy., Farmington. Open year-round, weather permitting. This Ken Dye–designed course is rated by a Golf Digest readers' poll as "America's best golf bargain . . . with large terraced greens, sculptured serpentine fairways and challenging sand bunkers. #1 munici-pal golf course in the nation." Special rates are available for those who live within a hundred-mile radius. $35–49.

**SWIMMING** ♂ **Farmington Aquatic Center** (505-327-7701), 1151 N. Sulli-van, Farmington. Call for hours. This is a full-fledged 150-foot Olympic pool, open year-round, with a 150-foot double loop water slide. Rates vary; $2.50 lap swims.

✳ **Green Space**

**Bluewater Lake State Park** (505-876-2391), 30 Bluewater Rd., Prewitt, is a lovely oasis of rolling hills encircling a 7-mile lake stocked with trout and catfish year-round. Boating, wildlife watching, camping, and hiking are popular pastimes here, as well as ice fishing, waterskiing, swimming, and hiking. $6 day use; $10–18 camping.

**Navajo Lake State Park** (505-632-2278; www.nmstateparks.com or www .emnrd.state.nm.us/nmparks), 1448 NM 511 #1, Navajo Dam, 45 miles east of Farmington on NM 511. Boat slips, fishing and boating supplies, and houseboat and ski boat rentals supplement this year-round boating opportunity on the 15,590-surface-acre lake. In addition, find three recreation areas with fishing and camping, and directly below the dam is the famous San Juan River fishing area. Here see blue herons, bald and golden eagles, red-tailed hawks, a variety of ducks, and Canada geese. Altogether, there are 150 miles of shoreline fed by the San Juan, Pine, and Piedra rivers. Accessible. Seasonal closures. $6 day use; $10–18 camping.

**Red Rock State Park** (505-722-3839), 7 miles east of Gallup, exit 31 north of I-40, off NM 118. A surprisingly interesting, tucked-away area of history may be found here in the Heritage Canyon display at the visitors center. High, wind-sculpted red sandstone formations frame this 640-acre park that is the site of the Gallup Intertribal Ceremonial on three sides. From the parking area, a hiking trails lead to views of Pyramid Rock and the spires of Church Rock. There's a welcome mat out for horses at the Horse Park. $6 day use; $10–18 camping.

**River Corridor** within Red Rock State Park, is 5 miles of multipurpose trails accessed off Browning Pkwy. south of Animas River, and at Scott Ave. and San Juan Blvd., behind the motels; **Woodland Trails**, found here, make excellent jogging and bicycling paths, with picnic areas with grills along the way.

**Riverside Park** (505-334-7670), on the Animas River outside Farmington at US 550 and NM 574, 500 S. Light Plant Rd., Aztec. There's excellent bird-watching year-round with wintering bald eagles fishing the Animas River, one of the last undimmed rivers in the West, and historical and wildlife interpretative signs lend depth to the experience.

Hwy., 1 mile east of Farmington on US 64. Go right. The 12,000-acre Bolack
Ranch is a private wildlife preserve, an experimental farm, and a working farm
and ranch. Two museums feature farm machinery, wildlife, and generating
equipment. Tours by appointment.

## ✷ Lodging

**BED & BREAKFASTS, INNS, AND MOTELS** **Casa Blanca Inn & Suites** (505-327-6503; www.4corners bandb.com), 505 E. La Plata St., Farmington. This gracious, red-tiled Mediterranean-style home high on a bluff in town is the ideal spot for either the visitor or business traveler. It's quiet the way rich people might be quiet, and the gardens are well tended. When you taste the rich breakfasts of crêpes Benedict, Belgian waffles with fresh raspberry sauce, or orange almond French toast, you might wish you could stay longer. $149–269.

**D's Bed & Breakfast at Navajo Dam** (505-632-0044; www.dsbandb .com), 10 Country Road 4265, Navajo Dam. You can walk right down to the river here, but you may have to share a bathroom. Only two of the six accommodations have a private bath at D's. It's a fishing delight, only 5 miles from Navajo Reservoir, a few hundred yards from San Juan River fishing. The lodging has grand river views and a two-story wraparound porch. $85.

**Kokopelli's Cave Bed & Breakfast** (505-326-2461), 5001 Antelope Junction, Farmington. Stay in a plush-carpeted, man-made cave inspired by the Cliff Dwellings at nearby Mesa Verde. Carved into 65-million-year-old sandstone, this single lodging is located 70 feet below the surface on a west-facing vertical cliff face granting you a 360-degree view of the Four Corners' outstanding geologic features. The bedroom balcony overlooks La Plata River Valley 250 feet below. What a sunset! Imagine, a waterfall-filled hot tub. Meals are not served, but the refrigerator is stocked and dinner may be catered. This is an experience that can make your cocktail party talk for years to come! $269.

**Silver River Adobe Inn B&B** (800-382-9251 or 505-325-8219; www .silveradobe.com), 3151 W. Main St., Farmington. Rustic yet elegant, the B&B perches on a sandstone cliff looking over the confluence of the San Juan and the La Plata rivers. There's a nature reserve with hiking paths, so good birding and grandmother cottonwoods are part of your stay. Plus, enjoy the library and salon-style breakfast. You couldn't ask for a more serene getaway. The three rooms each have a private bath and entrance. In-house massage available. $115–175.

**CABINS AND CAMPING** 🐾 **Abe's Motel & Fly Shop** (505-632-2194), 1791 NM #173, Navajo Dam. Open daily year-round, 7–7. Abe's, a landmark since 1958, is the fisherman's mecca on the San Juan. Over time, the fly shop has added RV parking and full hookups, a restaurant and lounge, grocery store, gas station, and boat storage facilities. Most rooms have two double beds and kitchenette, but it is easier to bring your own utensils. The motel rooms feel more like rustic cabins, but they are clean and within walking distance of the river. El Pescador Restaurant, which serves Mexican and American food, is open seasonally. The fly shop is the place for all your needs on the river, and it's where you can book guided tours with Born 'n Raised on the San Juan. Pets allowed. Motel $45–105; RV $18.95.

**Cottonwood–Navajo Lake State Park Pine Site and Main Campground.** See *Green Space*.

**Ruins Road RV Park** (505-334-3160), 312 Ruins Rd., Aztec. This completely pleasant campground quite close to the Aztec Ruins and the Animas River offers remote tent sites as well as 53 RV hookups. You will do well here. $10 tent; $20 hookup.

## ✳ Where to Eat

**EATING OUT Boon's Family Thai BBQ** (505-325-5556), 321 W. Main St., Farmington. Open daily. Lunch, dinner. Craving authentic green curry? Believe it or not, you will be impressed by the quality of this cuisine. Full Thai menu.

**Dad's Diner** (505-564-2516), 4395 Largo St., Farmington. Open daily. Breakfast, lunch, dinner. A local, family-run place that serves decent milk shakes and French dip sandwiches. It looks just like a real, old-time gleaming silver diner. It is a fun place to hang out, and all you "diner experience" collectors won't be disappointed. Breakfast served all day. Inexpensive.

ABE'S FLY SHOP IS A MUST-DO WHEN FISHING THE SAN JUAN RIVER.

**Hiway Grill** (505-334-6533), 401 NE Aztec Blvd., Aztec. Open Mon.–Sat. Breakfast, lunch, dinner. Closed Sun. Cute 1950s–'60s cruising theme for a restaurant and bar serving American fare of burgers, salads, and the like. The food is a standard, nothing adventurous, and a bit bland—don't expect anything but iceberg lettuce in your salad. Reasonable family dining option. All-you-can-eat homemade soup and salad for $8. Live entertainment in the bar. Inexpensive.

**St. Clair Winery & Bistro** (505-325-0711), 5150 E. Main St., Farmington. French country cooking, delightful wines, live jazz Thurs.–Sat. A casual, upscale dining spot was just the ticket for Farmington. Moderate.

🍖 **Spare Rib BBQ Company** (505-325-4800), 1700 E. Main St., Farmington. Open Tues.–Sat. Lunch, dinner. Closed Mon. Order at the counter delicious hickory-smoked beef, ribs, sausage, chicken, homemade coleslaw, and cobbler. It's all served on picnic tables covered in red-checked cloths. You can be happy here. Very happy. Inexpensive.

🍺 **Three Rivers Brewery Block** (505-325-6605), 111 E. Main, Farmington. Open Mon.–Sat. Lunch, dinner. Closed Sun. A friendly family hangout serving microbrews, homemade sodas, huge menu, kid's menu; play area. In a 1912 building that housed the first newspaper in town. The original restaurant has expanded to the entire block and now includes a tap and game room and pizzeria. Investigate which atmosphere you prefer before you are seated. Plenty of good cooking goes on here, resulting in soups and big salads, and you can't go wrong with the burger that made the brewery famous. It's a great place to cool off with a root beer float, made with house root beer, and the Friday night specials, such as crab boil, are a good deal. Inexpensive.

## ✳ Special Events

*Monthly:* **Crownpoint Navajo Rug Auction** (505-786-7386), Crownpoint Elementary School, 72 miles south of Farmington on NM 371. Third Fri. of the month 4–6 PM rug viewing; auction at 7. Plenty of arts and crafts and food vendors await. This monthly auction of 300–400 hand-woven Navajo

THREE RIVERS BREWERY IN FARMINGTON MAKES AN EXCELLENT STOP FOR A MICROBREW OR A ROOT BEER FLOAT.

rugs sponsored by Crownpoint Rug Weavers Association affords an excellent opportunity to meet weavers and get great bargains, though you will be competing with collectors and dealers. The school carnival atmosphere, with Frito pies and fry bread, plus crafts such as jewelry, make this a bargain hunter's paradise. Usually held the second Fri. of the month.

*March:* **The Aztec UFO Conference** (505-334-7698; www.aztecufo .com) is held annually to investigate the reported UFO crash in Hart Canyon, 12 miles outside Aztec, and is hosted by Friends of the Aztec Public Library.

*June:* **Aztec Fiesta Days** (www .aztecchamber.org). During the first weekend in June, this "All-American City" bids summer welcome with a parade, crafts, a carnival, and the burning of Old Man Gloom.

*August: ♂* **Connie Mack World Series** (conniemackworldseries@ gmail.com), Rickett's Park, Farmington. Aug. 4–11. Teams from the United States and Puerto Rico play in front of pro scouts and college officials at this world amateur baseball event. **Gallup Inter-tribal Ceremonial** (http://theceremonial.com) Parade down Old Route 66, Gallup; Red Rock State Park All-Indian Rodeo; indoor and outdoor marketplace; contest powwow; ceremonial

Indian dances; native foods. An enormous "gathering of nations" dating back over 80 years—not to be missed!

*September:* **Totah Festival Indian Market & Powwow** (800-448-1240), Farmington Civic Center, 200 W. Arrington. First weekend. Annual American Indian fine arts show, rug auction, and powwow.

*October:* **Northern Navajo Nation Shiprock Navajo Fair** (505-368-4301), Shiprock Fairgrounds, Shiprock. Parade, fair, arts, crafts, rodeo, powwow, traditional food, song and dance, "the oldest and most traditional" Navajo fair.

*November:* **Aztec Fantasy of Lights** (www.aztecfantasyoflights.com), Fri. after Thanksgiving–New Year's Eve, 6 PM. A driving tour of two dozen lighted sculptures in Aztec's Riverside Park. $4 per vehicle.

*December:* **San Juan College Luminarias** (505-326-3311), San Juan College, 4601 College Blvd., Farmington. Dec. 1, sunset. The campus is illuminated with 50,000 luminarias for the largest nonprofit display in New Mexico. **Navajo Nativity** (505-325-0255), 2102 W. Main, Farmington. Dec. 23, 6–8 PM. This living nativity with native Navajo costumes and live animals is presented by children at the Four Corners Home for Children.

# Southwest New Mexico: Ghost Town Country

6

**CAMINO COUNTRY**
Socorro, Truth or Consequences, Elephant Butte, Hatch, Las Cruces, Mesilla

**OLD HIGHWAY 60 COUNTRY**
Magdalena, Datil, Pie Town, Quemado

**GHOST TOWN COUNTRY**
Hillsboro, Glenwood, Reserve, Columbus, Silver City, Deming

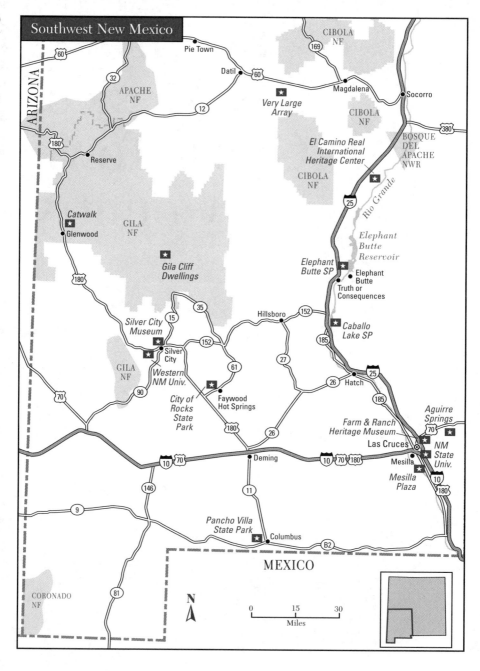

## Southwest New Mexico

ARIZONA

MEXICO

60
32
APACHE NF
12
180
Reserve

Pie Town
Datil
60
Magdalena
CIBOLA NF
169
Socorro
380
25

Very Large Array

El Camino Real International Heritage Center

CIBOLA NF

CIBOLA NF

BOSQUE DEL APACHE NWR

Rio Grande

Catwalk
Glenwood
GILA NF

Gila Cliff Dwellings

180

Elephant Butte Reservoir

Elephant Butte SP
Elephant Butte
Truth or Consequences

Silver City Museum
15
35
Hillsboro
152
185
Caballo Lake SP

Silver City
GILA NF
152
61
27
26
Hatch
25
185

Western NM Univ.
90
70

City of Rocks State Park
180
26

Faywood Hot Springs

Aguirre Springs
Farm & Ranch Heritage Museum
Las Cruces
NM State Univ.
Mesilla
Mesilla Plaza
70
10
180

10
70
Deming
10
70
180

146
11
9

Pancho Villa State Park
Columbus
B2

81

N

0    15    30
Miles

CORONADO NF

# INTRODUCTION

Driving on I-25, in only a few hours the New Mexico landscape transforms from ponderosa pine mountain forests and piñon-juniper covered hillsides of northern New Mexico into the creosote landscape south of Albuquerque. Here, on the northern edge of the Chihuahuan Desert, the hot, dry climate creates a different ecology, where the scarcity of water is a fact of life that historically has determined where and how people live and travel. The desert is culturally different as well.

The rural way of life is the predominant mode, and agriculture and ranching are the economic mainstays. Grapes, chile, alfalfa, and cotton grow abundantly in this river valley, where farmers depend on water released from Elephant Butte Dam and cattle and horses graze in open fields. The drought of recent years is impacting everyone who lives here.

There is less sense of urgency among people, who seem to make more time for visiting, baking, and caring for each other and their place. A different sense of time—a proudly mañana attitude—prevails in the small towns off the superhighway. Here folks either accept life and have made peace with it, or they are resigned to its limitations. Things are never done in a "New York minute." Life moves slowly, people run late, and phone calls may not be returned in what is, in the big city, considered a timely manner.

As this area is geographically closer to Mexico, the influence of that country south of the border—its language, food, religion, and strong family ties—has remained in force. Some believe the border itself is an artificial line drawn through the ancient kingdom of "Atzlan," and that the southern region of New Mexico and northern Mexico really belong together as one country.

Immigration issues are visible. You will see, and be required to pass through, Border Patrol stations along the way. There really is no way to travel through this area without experiencing these inspections, but they usually just consist of a quick look at you and your vehicle by an agent as you drive through the station, and past an armed guard.

The past is well preserved in the hot, dry New Mexican desert. That goes for the 400-year-old trail markings of the Camino Real, the Royal Road, still visible from the air. It once took oxcarts three years to make that round-trip between Mexico City and Santa Fe. This is the path taken by the conquistadors, by Juan de Oñate, in 1598, and it is the same path the Spanish followed when they fled to El Paso in 1680 after the Pueblo Revolt. It is the road Don Diego de Vargas took when he returned with his followers at the Reconquest 12 years later and retook Santa Fe for the Spanish crown.

Like much of the rest of the state, southwest New Mexico includes a vast area that can be thought of in distinct regions, shaped by location and resources, and the history that resulted from the uses people made of those features. Probably each of them, depending on your personal pace, can be at least seen in a good long weekend. These three regions are the Camino Real Country, the Old Highway 60 Country, and the Ghost Town Country.

This region includes towns accessible from I-25 from Socorro, Truth or Consequences, Elephant Butte, Las Cruces, and its next-door neighbor, Mesilla. It flows in more or less a straight line north to south, following the path of the ancient road along the river. Where it diverged from the river into the Journada de Muerto, the "dead man's journey," is a waterless stretch that tested the survival skills of those who dared cross it.

Old US Highway 60, often referred to as a link in the Ocean-to-Ocean Highway, the first paved transcontinental road, begun in 1912. It bisects southern New Mexico and remains the slow road from east to west, a two-lane with a 65 mph speed limit and no billboards, chain restaurants, or chain motels. Get on Highway 60, which still follows its original alignment through New Mexico, south of Socorro and travel to the Arizona border in a half-day passing through Magdalena, the old cattle railhead; seeing Kelly, the mining town up above it; on to Datil; Pie Town, with its remains of a 20th-century homesteading community; the Very Large Array radiotelescope installation, and Quemado; then on to Springerville, Arizona.

Let it be known that residents of Catron County, along old US 60, object to two things in particular: environmentalists and the Mexican gray wolf conservationists are trying to bring back. This is an area of staunch independent thinkers, with strong Old West roots, and outsiders with nonlocal opinions and beliefs partial to endangered species are not favored. Enough said.

It is possible, with any show of polite curiosity, to connect with the old-timers who still live along the road, who run the mom-and-pop shops, cafés, and motels. They have long memories and don't mind sharing their stories. There is not much going on, and days are fairly alike, so you yourself may provide the break in routine that is needed at the moment. This is where history still lives. With curiosity and a camera, you can experience the real West down to its bones. People are often willing to share information about historical characters, the legends of their place, their families, their special places, the best places to fish, those landmarks that aren't in the books, but where someone once lived, or where someone was once killed, or where a treasure is supposedly buried, and what ghosts haunt which buildings.

People out here are generally as friendly as their sharp ability to judge character instantly allows them to be. If they feel you are a decent person, they will literally give you the shirt off their back and the story of their lives. They will extend trust and invite you home to see their family photo albums. The locals you encounter can be much better sources of information about a place than the initial pointers you will receive at the visitors center. This may be true for travelers in general, and it is especially true in rural New Mexico, where kindness is the currency. Those who have moved from other places, in general, prefer their privacy. A surprising number of artists manage to live out here by running an Internet business.

Traveling west over NM 152 through the Black Range to Silver City, pass by Hillsboro and Kingston. Much of this area has gold, silver, and copper mining in its past. Some towns, like Silver City, where mining has recently resumed, have reinvented themselves as tourist towns with service economies. Others, like Winston, Chloride, and Kingston, have faded into true ghost town status. If you treasure the silence, the crumbling buildings of splintered wood and adobe, the ruins of former banks and jailhouses, and the spirit of place that evokes the past far more eloquently than any history book, you will find plenty to intrigue you in Ghost Town Country.

Much of the country is still pretty wild, and it was among the last part of the United States to be taken from the Indians. This is the territory of Geronimo, Mangus Colorado, and the great woman warrior, Lozen, and other great Apache warriors, who fought hard for their homeland against the encroachment of the Americans. The vanished ancestors, the Mimbres, who made distinctive black-on-white pottery, and the people who built the Gila Cliff dwellings, left much to wonder about and be amazed at. They settled in the hospitable river country.

This is also the part of the world that inspired the first national wilderness area, named for the naturalist Aldo Leopold, who was inspired to push for the establishment of the Gila National Forest.

Another character who occupies a great deal of psychic space, Pancho Villa, made his foray over the border into the United States at Columbus, where old-timers continue to hold on to their versions of the raid. General Black Jack Pershing gave chase through Mexico, but he never managed to catch up with Villa. Pershing then went on to command the U.S. forces in Europe during World War I.

There is a sense in much of this place that life can still be hard. Folks' survival depends as much on their ability to trust as it does on their ability to read the rain clouds, and there's not much that escapes them.

If you like your history real, you crave immersion in the stuff of legends, and you don't mind the taste of grit or standing out in the wind, you will find much to appeal to you in southern New Mexico.

For convenience's sake, *Green Space* for all of southwest New Mexico is listed toward the end of the chapter, and all *Medical Emergency* information for the area is given at the beginning.

NO, PANCHO VILLA NEVER SLEPT HERE.

# CAMINO COUNTRY

## SOCORRO, TRUTH OR CONSEQUENCES, ELEPHANT BUTTE, HATCH, LAS CRUCES, MESILLA

Big skies and wide open spaces define this area, as do the green chile fields of Hatch and the "six flags" that have flown over Mesilla Plaza. History is everywhere, in the faded advertisements painted on the sides of brick buildings, the thick adobe walls, and the WPA-era buildings. There is no forgetting that this is an area linked by road—yesterday's Camino Real, today's I-25. Beside the road, like a great ship, is the fantastic El Camino Real International Heritage Center. You will find a variety of experiences—starting with Bosque del Apache National Wildlife Refuge, to bustling Las Cruces, growing with amenities migrants and retirees, and the traditional small farming villages south of Mesilla. However, no matter how many Santa Fe and Albuquerque artists flee to quiet Truth or Consequences to open galleries and boutiques, and despite the construction of the Spaceport, change comes slowly. Refreshingly, Camino Country refuses to join the modern world completely.

**GUIDANCE Elephant Butte Chamber of Commerce** (575-744-4708), 503 NM 195, Elephant Butte. Open Mon.–Sat. 10–2.

**Greater Las Cruces Chamber of Commerce** (575-524-1968), 505 S. Main St., Las Cruces.

**Hatch Valley Chamber of Commerce** (575-267-5050), 210 W. Hall St., Hatch.

**J. Paul Taylor Visitor Center** (575-524-3262 ext. 117), 2231 Avenida de Mesilla, Mesilla.

**Las Cruces Convention and Visitors Bureau** (575-541-2444), 211 N. Water St. Las Cruces.

**Socorro County Chamber of Commerce** (575-835-0424), 101 Plaza, Socorro.

**Socorro Heritage and Visitor Center** (575-835-8927), 217 Fisher Ave., Socorro.

**Truth or Consequences/Sierra County Chamber of Commerce** (575-894-3536), 400 W. Fourth Ave., Truth or Consequences.

**GETTING THERE** Take I-25 south out of Albuquerque. Taking this road south to Las Cruces, you'll find all the towns and attractions listed in Camino Real Country en route. To reach US Highway 60 country, take I-25 to exit 127 south to Socorro, then go west on US 60. To reach Ghost Town Country, take I-25 south to exit 63 onto NM 152.

**MEDICAL EMERGENCY Gila Regional Medical Center** (575-538-4000), 1313 E. 32nd St., Silver City.

**Memorial Medical Center** (575-522-8641), 2450 S. Telshor Blvd., Las Cruces.

**Mountain View Regional Medical Center** (575-556-7600), 4311 E. Lohman Ave., Las Cruces.

**Sierra Vista Hospital** (575-894-2111), 800 E. Ninth Ave., Truth or Consequences.

**Socorro General Hospital** (575-835-1140), 1202 Highway 60 West, Socorro.

## ✳ To See

**TOWNS Elephant Butte** is 79 miles south of Socorro on I-25. With the construction of Elephant Butte Dam in 1912–16, a recreational area was born that today is home to marinas, vacationers, and year-rounders who enjoy the 40-mile

VISITORS TO LAS CRUCES ARE SERENADED WITH TRADITIONAL MARIACHI MUSIC.

WELCOME TO HATCH, CHILE CAPITAL OF THE WORLD.

lake and the 200 miles of shoreline that make it one of New Mexico's most popular state parks. If you look carefully—you may have to tilt your head or squint a bit—and use your imagination, you will see the silhouette of an elephant in a prominent butte.

**Hatch** is 34 miles south of Truth of Consequences on I-25. This agricultural town is known for three things: chile, chile, and chile! This is the home of the famous "Hatch chile," New Mexico's leading export and favorite food. Whether you favor red or green, this is the place to pull off the highway (I-25 at exit 41) and buy some. The best time to come here is August–October, when you can smell the aroma of roasting chiles and see the ripe red ones drying on rooftops and in strings of crimson chile ristras all over town.

**Las Cruces** is 223 miles south of Albuquerque on I-25. The unofficial capital of southern New Mexico, this growing town near the border has been discovered by retirees and others seeking to relocate and is now a bona fide boomtown. It is home of New Mexico State University, and Aggies football and basketball are promoted and followed with much enthusiasm. With its climate, medical facilities, university, and a feeling of small-town well-being and family-friendliness, Las Cruces' attractions continue to grow.

**Mesilla.** One mile south of Las Cruces on University Blvd. With Rio Grande *acequias* running through it, a historic plaza over which the flags of six nations have flown, and venerable adobe homes on streets wide enough for a burro cart to pass through, this sister city and next-door neighbor to the south of Las Cruces is the archetype of a historic village. The little town has plenty of galleries, cafés, and boutiques arrayed around the plaza, and it is fun to walk or jog along the ditch banks. The name "Mesilla" means "little table" and refers to the geographic spot where the town is located in the Mesilla Valley of the Rio Grande, a rich agricultural area where chile, cotton, onions, cotton, and pecans flourish.

**Socorro**, 72 miles south of Albuquerque on I-25, received its name from conquistador Juan de Oñate in 1598 because he and his party were given much help and aid there by the native Piros. Today it is the home of a fine college, New Mexico Institute of Mining and Technology, a legacy from the days when it was the center of a rich mining district.

**Truth or Consequences** is 79 miles south of Socorro on I-25. When television host Ralph Edwards made the offer to bestow the name of his program, *Truth or Consequences*, to the American city that would change its name to that of the show, the little New Mexico town of Hot Springs jumped at the opportunity and became the town of Truth or Consequences, New Mexico. True to his word, Ralph Edwards returned every year for over 50 years to lead the parade in the annual May festival. Today the town is experiencing something of a renewal, with the arrival of artists and artistically and community-minded folks from Albuquerque and Santa Fe looking for a cheaper place to live and express themselves. New Age–tinged paths of healing continue the older healing traditions of the place. The main street is now dotted with boutiques, cafés, and a Black Cat bookstore as a result of the younger population's influence. The town sits on a 110-degree hot spring aquifer and bills itself as the "Hot Springs Capital of the World," with many spa establishments. It also claims to be the most affordable spa town in the country.

**HISTORIC LANDMARKS, PLACES, AND SITES Elfego Baca Monument** (no phone), Henry's Corner, N. Main St., Reserve, commemorates a legendary lawman known for his solo David-and-Goliath three-day standoff against hundreds of invaders.

**Fort Craig National Historic Site** (575-835-0412), 32 miles south of Socorro, I-25 exit 124, 901 S. NM 85. A remote station on the Rio Grande, Fort Craig, commissioned 1854–85, was a base for U.S. Army campaigns against Native Americans and Confederates during the Civil War. Free.

**Fort Selden State Monument** (575-526-8911), 1280 Fort Selden Rd., Radium Springs. I-25 exit 19. Twelve miles north of Las Cruces. Open Wed–Mon. 8:30–5. Closed Tues. The second Sat. of every month brings a living history program, plus Dutch oven cooking most Saturdays. The fort is so quiet now, the visitor would never imagine the activity it saw during the Civil War and the days of the Indian Wars. Perhaps its most famous resident was Captain Arthur MacArthur, its commanding officer in 1884, and his son, Douglas MacArthur, who became supreme commander of the Allied forces in the Pacific during World War II. $3 adults, children free; free Wed. New Mexico seniors, free Sun. New Mexico residents.

**MUSEUMS Branigan Cultural Center** (575-541-2155), 501 N. Main St. Exhibits and activities related to local and regional history. Free.

DUTCH OVEN COOKING IS STILL THE FAVORITE WAY TO FEED COWBOYS.

**El Camino Real International Heritage Center** (575-854-3600), 35 miles south of Socorro, I-25 exit 115. Open Wed.–Sun. 8:30–5. Closed Mon.–Tues. This state monument sits on the Camino Real like a magnificent ship out on the desert and tells the story of the road's 400-year history powerfully with state-of-the-art technology. Its magic conveys the story of the road as trade route, link between cultures, and lifeline from New Mexico to the rest of the world, to all ages. It must be seen by anyone who seeks to know this place. $5 adults, age 16 and under free; free Wed. New Mexico residents and seniors.

**Geronimo Springs Museum** (575-894-6600), 211 Main St., Truth or Consequences. Open Mon.–Sat. 9–5. Closed Sun. Located beside Las Palomas Plaza, where Native Americans came to bathe in the hot springs, the museum has exhibits of each of Sierra County's cultures, from prehistoric times to the present day. Here get a good historical overview, from mastodon and mammoth skulls to the Apache room; Hispanic Heritage Room, with a diorama of the Jornada del Muerto; to the exceptional pottery room; and best of all, the Ralph Edwards Room, with memorabilia on the Annual Fiesta. $3 adults, $1.50 students ages 6–18, under age 6 free, $7.50 families.

**Las Cruces Museum of Art** (575-541-2155), 501 N. Main St., Las Cruces. Traveling exhibits, art with a New Mexico focus. Free.

**Mineral Museum** (575-835-5140), 801 Leroy Place, southeast corner of Canyon Rd. and Olive Ln., on the New Mexico Tech campus, Socorro. Open Mon.–Fri. 8–5, Sat. and Sun. 10–3. Nicknamed "Coronado's Treasure Chest," this museum has an amazing display of gold, silver, fossils, mining artifacts, and precious gems, as well as top-quality mineral specimens found all over New Mexico. So worth a visit! Free.

*◊* **Museum of Nature & Science**
(575-541-2155), 501 N. Main St., Las
Cruces. An entirely delightful and
user-friendly new museum designed
to appeal to all ages, specializing in
geography and natural history of the
area. Free.

*◊* **New Mexico Farm & Ranch
Heritage Museum** (575-522-4100),
4100 Dripping Springs Rd., Las Cruces. Take the university exit 1 off I-25
and travel east, toward the Organ
Mountains. Open Mon.–Sat. 9–5,
Sun. noon–5. This impressive ranch-
style museum maintains exhibits on
agriculture in the West, and the best
may be seen outside the galleries at
daily blacksmithing demonstrations;
the barns of sheep, cattle, and other
animals; the Antique Equipment
Park; and regular demonstrations of
dowsing, milking, weaving, and quilting. There is ample vehicle access.
The Green Bridge, New Mexico's sec-
ond-oldest highway bridge, was
moved here from the Rio Hondo and

SATURDAY MORNING AT LAS CRUCES
MUSEUM OF NATURE & SCIENCE IS
MULTIGENERATIONAL FUN.

installed over Tortugas Arroyo. You'll also find exhibits of local photography and
art. $5 adults, $3 seniors, $2 children ages 5–17, age 4 and under free.

**NMSU Center for the Arts** (575-646-4515), University Blvd., Las Cruces. The
new home of NMSU arts programs is a big wow of a sophisticated building that
includes the jewel of the Medoff Theater. Quality live theater productions found
here.

## ✷ To Do

**BIRDING Bosque del Apache National Wildlife Refuge** (575-835-1828), 9
miles south on I-25 to exit 139, east 0.25 mile on US 380 to flashing light at San
Antonio, turn right onto NM 1, continue south 9 miles to visitors center. Visitors
center open Mon.–Fri. 7:30–4, Sat. and Sun. 8–4:30, Tour Loop 1 hour before
sunset-1 hour after sunset. This premier winter day trip involves a drive to the
bosque for the fly-in of thousands of cranes and geese at sunset. Winter is also
the best time to spot bald eagles. Mid-Nov.–mid-Feb. is the peak time for viewing these migrants. Many varieties of birds winter here along the Rio Grande
Flyway. Every season offers birding opportunities: summer is the time to see
nesting songbirds, waders, shorebirds, and ducks; spring and fall warblers and
flycatchers show up. Bicycling is encouraged as a way of experiencing the
bosque, and many bike paths have been upgraded and made accessible. Bring

your bike for miles of level cycling along the ditches, lakes, and wetlands, and don't forget the binoculars. Fifteen-mile auto tour loop. $5 per vehicle.

**Mesilla Valley Bosque State Park** (575-523-4398), 5000 Calle del Norte, between Mesilla Dam and NM 538, is a brand-new day-use park state park on the banks of the southern Rio Grande, with a visitors center and interpretive programs highlighting birds and wildlife of the bosque, as well as beautiful trails for walking, jogging, and biking. $5 per vehicle.

OLD TIME MUSICIANS PERFORM FREQUENTLY AT FARM & RANCH HERITAGE MUSEUM EVENTS.

**CANOEING AND KAYAKING**
**Leasburg Dam State Park** (575-524-4068), 15 miles north of Las Cruces on I-25 or NM 185. Mar.–mid-Oct., enjoy canoeing and kayaking on the Rio Grande. $5 per vehicle day use.

**CLIMBING** **Box Canyon** (no phone), I-25 exit 147 at Socorro, go west on US 60 for 6.8 miles, immediately after bridge go east. Second left is gravel road to parking area. This is a favorite red rock climbing and rappelling area west of Socorro.

NM FARM & RANCH HERITAGE MUSEUM.

**FARMERS' MARKETS Las Cruces Farmers & Crafts Market** (575-541-2288), 300 Main St., Downtown Mall, Las Cruces. Open-year round Wed. and Sat. 8 AM–12:30 PM. Several blocks of fresh produce and clever crafts, jewelry, handmade jams, soaps, and things you can't possibly find anywhere else make this one of the best farmers' markets. Plus, some of the best coffee you'll find anywhere, custom brewed by "Beck," and crafts galore: jewelry, glass, ceramics, textiles, woodwork, photography. I found a cast-iron jalapeño roaster here. Named #1 American Farmers Market by American Farmland Trust.

**Socorro Farmers' Market** (575-312-1730), Socorro Plaza. July–Oct., Tues. 5 PM–7 PM, Sat. 8 AM–sellout. Fresh corn, watermelons, eggs, and all the glorious produce of the season sold in a neighborly, festive market.

**GOLF New Mexico State University Golf Course** (575-646-3219), 3000 Herb Wimberly Dr., Las Cruces. Framed by the rugged Organ Mountains and the Mesilla Valley, the course challenges all skill levels by combining desert and traditional golf on this 18-hole course that is home to the Aggies' golf team. Very reasonable.

**Red Hawk Golf Club** (575-373-8100), 7520 Red Hawk Golf Rd. The newest, and many say, the best, golfing in southern New Mexico is here on this 200 acre links-style course. Reasonable.

BECK BREWS CUSTOM CUPS AT HER OUTDOOR LAS CRUCES FARMERS AND CRAFTS MARKET CAFÉ.

**HIKING Dripping Springs Natural Area** (575-525-4300), 10 miles east of Las Cruces. From exit 1 on I-25, take Dripping Springs Rd. to the end. At the base of the rugged Organ Mountains, this is the favorite hiking area of Las Cruces, with a 4.5-mile moderate-difficult hike. $3.

See also **Aguirre Springs**, under "Mountain Biking."

**HOT SPRINGS Truth or Consequences** (575-894-3536). The dozen natural hot mineral springs in the downtown Historic District are geothermally heated with temperatures between 95 and112 degrees Fahrenheit. With a dozen public bathhouses, ranging from funky to deluxe, mostly built in the 1920s, many nicely updated, you have quite a choice of how you will experience getting into hot water here. Some have large tiled tubs, some have pebble-bottomed pools, and most have healing services such as massage, facials, aromatherapy, and hot rock treatments.

THE RESTORED RIO GRANDE THEATER IS A BUSY DOWNTOWN VENUE.

**MOUNTAIN BIKING Aguirre Springs** (575-525-4300), 22 miles east of Las Cruces on I-70. Mountain biking and camping, with a variety of trails that are part of the National Recreation Trail System. $3.

**PARKS Chihuahuan Desert Nature Park** (575-524-3334), 56501 N. Journada Rd., east of Las Cruces on I-70, Mesa Grande exit to Jornada Rd. Tues.–Sat. 7–5. Closed Sun.–Mon. A 960-acre park with a 1.5-mile walking trail that has plant identification is a sweet education on the diverse ecosystems of the Chihuahuan Desert. Free.

**WINERIES Blue Teal Winery** (877-669-4637), 1710 Avenida de Mesilla. Mon.–Sat. 11–6, Sun. noon–6. Hand-painted wine bottles and exhibits of local artists accompany tastings of award-winning reds.

**La Vina** (575-882-7632), 4201 S. NM 28. Twenty miles south of Las Cruces. Open Thurs.–Tues. noon–5. What a serene drive it is down south to the oldest winery in the state, which hosts the oldest wine festival every October and a jazz festival in April.

ORGAN MOUNTAINS, LAS CRUCES.

**Vintage Wine Bar** (575-523-9463), 2461 Calle de Principal, Mesilla. How is this for happiness: cozy wine bar, 50 wines by the glass, tapas, chocolates, cigars, jazz, Latin jazz, flamenco guitar, live music Fri. and Sat. and WiFi, too.

**Wines of the Southwest** (575-524-2408), next to the Fountain Theater in Mesilla. Open Mon.–Thurs. 11–6, Fri.–Sat. 11–8., Sun. noon–6. When you need (or want) to pick up a bottle of wine to enjoy, come here for the best selection of New Mexico wine.

## ✳ Lodging

### BED & BREAKFASTS, MOTELS, AND INNS Blackstone Lodge

(575-894-0894), 410 Austin St., Truth or Consequences. Consistently voted #1 lodging in Truth or Consequences, the Blackstone's serene rooms, each styled for a period TV series (*Twilight Zone, Golden Girls*) contain private tubs. Unlike many of the remodeled old motor court lodgings in town, Blackstone feels clean and fresh. Affordable luxury. $95–135.

🐾 **Elephant Butte Inn** (575-744-5431), 401 NM 195, Elephant Butte. I-25, exit 83. From here, enjoy views of the lake and desert, spot wildlife, have a drink in the Ivory Tusk Tavern, perhaps a massage at the Ivory Spa, and hike to Elephant Butte Lake. Heated outdoor pool. Pet-friendly, handicapped accessible. A deluxe continental breakfast is included. Golf and spa packages as well. A particularly good deal is stay Sat. and get Sun. half-price. Very pleasant. $100.

♂ **Josephine's Old Gate** (575-525-2620), 2261 Calle de Guadalupe, Mesilla. Café, wine bar, and small luxury lodging a block from Mesilla Plaza. The big four-poster bed and secluded quarters make it ideal for honeymoon or anniversary. A place to inspire dreams or be transported to another era, long before e-mail or even the horseless carriage came along.

🐾 **Riverbend Hot Springs** (575-894-6183), 100 Austin, Truth or Consequences. Three outdoor soaking pools and one rock pool overlooking the Rio Grande, facing Turtleback Mountain, for $10 per person per hour. Open daily 8–7. Mineral soaks used to be free with lodging, but if you are only staying the night, you must pay your $10. Prices have gone up here, as the place has gained popularity and is gradually shedding its old hippie ambience. Also, if you are looking for some peaceful time, you may prefer to reserve a private tub for $15 per person. Pet-friendly. $70–135.

**Sierra Grande Lodge and Spa** (575-894-6976), 501 McAdoo St., Truth or Consequences. The town's most upscale address, a restored 1929 lodge with deluxe rooms featuring sunken tubs and well-chosen art, with complimentary outdoor tubs (one brief soak per visit per day) as well as public facilities with massage and reflexology. Spa packages may be reserved in advance. This lodge was recently purchased by Ted Turner, said to be keeping something of a headquarters here. $99–169.

**CABINS AND CAMPING Caballo Lake RV Park** (575-743-0502), Caballo. Exit 59 off I-25, north 1 mile on NM 187 to Mile Marker 22. Quiet, WiFi, enjoyable fishing and birding, walking distance to the Caballo Lake beach, tours of remote ghost towns, and prospecting and gold panning are in easy reach here in this desert campground. $15 plus electric hookup.

**Hacienda RV Resort** (575-528-5800), 740 Stern Dr., Las Cruces. This is the life! Complimentary breakfast bar, concierge service, large patio, and hydrotherapy pool, plus WiFi. Spacious, top-of-the-line sites, cable TV. $34–39.

## ✳ Where to Eat

**DINING OUT Café BellaLuca** (575-894-9866), 303 Jones St. Truth or Consequences. Lunch, dinner Wed.–Mon. Closed Tues. Upscale Italian in Truth or Consequences in an industrial chic setting. Love the eggplant, but everything pasta is delectable. Clean, modern décor. My caveat: The many fine wines are served in teensy-weensy portions at big prices. *Wine Spectator* Award of Excellence. You can wear your jeans, but put on a clean shirt, *por favor*. Moderate–Expensive.

**Double Eagle Restaurant** (575-523-6700), 2355 Calle de Guadalupe, Mesilla Plaza. Daily 11–10. Within the oldest building on the plaza—and the most haunted; photos of the ghosts are on the walls—is the most elegant dining in the area in Victorian splendor. Go for the opulent Sunday brunch (the Double Eagle claims the finest buffet in the Southwest, and we won't argue about it!); well-aged steaks, with the only dedicated beef aging room in the state; fine wine from the extensive wine list; or just order a margarita at the long, ornate mirrored bar. *Wine Spectator* Award of Excellence. At least have a margarita at the baroque bar. Expensive.

**La Posta Restaurant** (575-524-3524), 2410 Calle de San Albino, Mesilla Plaza. Tues.–Thurs. and Sun. 11–9, Fri.–Sat. 11–9:30, also open Mon. during summer. For a tourist restaurant, this place does a respectable job of keeping up with the crowds that include plenty of locals. In fact, it serves one of my favorite chiles rellenos plate, southern New Mexico style, lightly sautéed in egg batter, not breaded, so the taste and texture of the chiles sing forth. Located in the old Butterfield Stage Building, the place is saturated in historic Southwest atmosphere. They boast of the largest tequila selection in the Southwest, and of course, the best margaritas. The ghost was created by a pranksters' hoax. If you must wait, you can shop for salsa or commune with the parrot. Moderate.

**Los Arcos Steak & Lobster** (575-894-6200), 1400 N. Date St., Truth or

LA POSTA, POPULAR WITH LOCALS AND VISITORS, ON MESILLA PLAZA.

Consequences. Sun.–Thurs. 5–9 PM; Fri.–Sat. 5–10:30 PM. This well-established grown-up, scotch-and-steak sort of place is good for a splurge or a quiet conversation. A place with classic—think 1970s—restaurant atmosphere, where service is as important, or more so, than the food, which is usually very good. No need to break the budget. Early-bird specials are a good deal, and Los Arcos serves a fine green chile cheeseburger. Moderate–Expensive.

**Pacific Grill** (575-894-7687), 800 N. Date St., Truth or Consequences. Lunch, dinner. Closed Mon., Wed. I usually end up having a meal here when I am in Truth or Consequences, and I love to spend winter weekends soaking in the hot springs. Freshest salad bar in town, unique homemade soups and desserts, fine curry, diverse, mixed Asian menu, care given to preparation and service. Moderate.

**St. Clair Winery & Bistro** (575-524-0390), 1720 Avenida de Mesilla, Mesilla. Open daily. Lunch, dinner. This lively spot immediately became a favorite for locals. Outdoor patio, live jazz Thurs.–Sat. Delightful New Mexico wine selection. Lovely addition to Southern New Mexico dining scene, featuring French country cooking.

**EATING OUT** **Andele Restaurant** (575-526-9631), 2184 Avenida de Mesilla. Open daily. Breakfast, lunch, dinner. The fresh salsa bar is the attraction here. Alas, Andele's may have gotten too big. It used to be spectacular, now it is just down a notch. Stay away from the chicken, as it is generally overcooked and dry. The Dog House, across the street, serves the same food, with a bar and a rollicking patio. Inexpensive.

**Arrey Cafe** (575-267-3822), Arrey. Daily 8–8. Is it the local beans and chile of this tattered homespun spot in the road, where chile growers are chowing down on the good stuff that makes this place such a find, or is it merely that it is so out of the way on a dusty deserted street that it could be the restaurant version of *The Last Picture Show* that makes it so special? Drive the back road, NM 185, north of Hatch and find out. Inexpensive.

**The Bean of Mesilla** (575-523-0560), 2011 Avenida de Mesilla, Mesilla. Open Mon.–Fri. 6:30–9, Sat. 7–9, Sun. 7–5. Breakfast, lunch, dinner. How pleasant it is to sip the fresh, strong coffee at a table on the sunny patio, munch a freshly baked chocolate croissant, and leaf through the Sunday paper. This no-frills café has WiFi, and you can catch performances of local musicians Thurs.–Sat.

The Bean is a top-notch hangout or meetup café. Inexpensive.

**Buckhorn Tavern** (575-835-4423), 68 US 380, San Antonio. Closed Sun. Lunch, dinner. Located just across the street from the Owl; the decision about where to dine is challenging. However, I am here to say the green chile burgers here are among the best. Fabulous fries, too. You'd better be hungry or prepare to split yours. Since the chef-owner Bobby Olguin won his smackdown with Bobby Flay, this place has become a pilgrimage site. Sit at the bar if it's just too crowded. Inexpensive.

**CDM** (575-652-3019), 2051 Calle de Santiago (off Mesilla Plaza). Breakfast, lunch. Sometimes open evenings. The essence of a charming café housed in an ancient adobe. Lovely service. Coffees, ice cream, treats. Inexpensive.

BOBBY OLGUIN'S BUCKHORN BURGER IN SAN ANTONIO BEAT BOBBY FLAY'S.

**Caliche's** (575-674-5066), 590 S. Valley Dr., Las Cruces. Open daily. Good news—the frozen custard is still the best. Where else can you get a green chile pecan sundae? With a hot dog. If you can ever tear yourself away from the custard, try the mango Desert Ice to cool off. Free doggy cones! Inexpensive.

**Carmen's Kitchen** (575-894-0006), 1806 S. Broadway, Truth or Consequences. Breakfast, lunch, dinner Mon.–Fri.; Sat. breakfast, lunch only. Closed Sun. My husband's favorite red chile, excellent breakfast spot, now open till 8 with generous dinner specials several times a week. Like eating in Grandma's kitchen. Carmen hand selects her chile from Hatch, and she does not compromise. Inexpensive.

**Chope's Bar & Cafe** (575-233-3420), NM 28, La Mesa. Open Tues.–Sat. 11 AM–2 PM and 5:30–8:30.

Closed Sun. and Mon. Why are people standing in line out here in La Mesa, 12 miles south of Las Cruces, at lunchtime? If you guessed because the food served in this humble outpost is worth the long drive, you'd be right. There's a good chance there was a Chope's before you were born, way back in 1940, and it is still in the founder's Benavidez family. It had a well-deserved reputation as a political hangout in the early days, and you can see several generations of families enjoying the red chile enchiladas and beef tacos together. Inexpensive.

**Cuchillo Creek Cafe** (575-743-2233), 659 NM 52, Cuchillo. Fri. 4–7; Sat. 11–7; Sun. 11–7. It's not open often, and this simple whitewashed house is not exactly a four-star Michelin destination, but when it is, the stuffed sopaipillas are worth the drive off the interstate. Each entrée comes with a bottomless basket of

RED CHILE LIKE MAMA MADE IS SERVED WITH A SMILE AT CARMEN'S KITCHEN IN TRUTH OR CONSEQUENCES.

CHOPE'S HAS BEEN SERVING LA MESA SINCE BEFORE YOU WERE BORN.

hot, fluffy sopaipillas, and you can't resist eating more than your fill. Red chile over anything is the way to go here. And the fries are homemade, too. This would be a ghost town, but people actually live and work here. Finding this place and eating here gives you bragging rights with those who think they know New Mexican food. Inexpensive.

🍽 **Dick's Cafe** (575-524-1360), 2305 S. Valley Dr., Las Cruces. Open daily 7 AM–8 PM. The college crowd mixes with bikers, truckers, and city employees to make this a classic casual stop with the locals. The chile cheeseburger is substantial and all-day sustaining. I love to wake up to the breakfast burrito doused in red, and the coffee has guts. There's a bit of turnover in the staff, and sometimes the service can be a little ditzy, but who cares? Relax, have another cup of coffee, and read the paper, like the

rest of the locals. A graduate of NMSU who confessed she got through school on the burgers, homemade fries, and delicious beans here introduced me to Dick's. Warning: The green chile is really hot. Inexpensive.

🍽 **Frank and Lupe's El Sombrero** (575-835-3945), 210 Mesquite, Socorro. Open daily. Lunch, dinner. Enjoy a wine margarita or imported beer with your fajitas or chicken mole enchiladas. A friendly, long-established family-oriented local favorite. The pleasant patio is enclosed. Inexpensive.

**Happy Belly Deli** (575-894-3354), 313 N. Broadway, Truth or Consequences. Breakfast, lunch. Open daily. Sun. brunch only. Fri. night pizza. Love the breakfast, great coffee, decent lox and bagels. Local and snowbird hangout par excellent. Dine on the funky patio or stay inside.

**International Delights Cafe** (575-647-5956), 1245 El Paseo Rd., Las Cruces. Breakfast, lunch, dinner Mon.–Sun. Open till 11 PM during the week; midnight weekends. In the far corner of a strip mall, find this chic yet comfortably worn treasure trove of pastries, Middle Eastern food— shish kebab, couscous, early morning bagel and lox, and fine Turkish coffee. Imported groceries, too!

🦪 **La Nueva Casita** (575-523-5434), 195 N. Mesquite St., Las Cruces. Breakfast, lunch, dinner Mon.–Sat. Breakfast, lunch Sun. The last time I visited the Las Cruces' historic Mesquite District, I saw two ancient ladies wheeling an aged Pomeranian in a baby carriage. I also followed a fire truck crew into La Nueva Casita, and I was not disappointed. This is my new favorite Mexican restaurant. This family café been around for 70 years, so it must be doing something right. Best chiles rellenos! Best green chile! Four stars! A find and a bargain. Inexpensive.

**Maria's Mexican Restaurant** (575-894-9047), 1990 S. Broadway, Truth or Consequences. Breakfast, lunch, dinner Mon.–Sun. Comfortable place, generous portions, authentic flavors. Inexpensive.

**Nellie's Cafe** (575-524-9982), 1226 W. Hadley Ave., Las Cruces. Open Tues.–Sat. 8–2 Nellie's is one of those local institutions that have helped the city establish and keep its reputation. Fluorescent-linoleum in feel; the minimal atmosphere only highlights the main attraction: the seriously delicious and seriously hot Mexican food of this "joint." It's all good! Nellie's started out as a burrito wagon in 1962. Inexpensive.

**Owl Bar & Cafe** (575-835-9946), US 380 and NM 1, San Antonio. Open Mon.–Sat. 8 AM–9 PM. Closed Sun. Home of the world-famous green chile cheeseburger, the Owl began when Manhattan Project scientists first came to the area to test the bomb on the nearby Trinity Site. The Owl is a New Mexico institution. The only thing to do is slide into a booth and order that burger with the homemade fries. Inexpensive.

**Passion Pie Cafe** (575-894-0008), 406 Main St., Truth or Consequences. Breakfast, lunch. Vegetarian and vegan, light and bright WiFi, out-of-this-world scones and pastries, lunch specials of quiche, homemade soup, and more—what's not to love? Inexpensive.

**Pepper Pot** (575-267-3822), 207 W. Hall St., Hatch. Breakfast, lunch, dinner. Have a nice sit-down lunch, with tablecloths on the tables, where everyone seems to know one another, and you might even run into someone you graduated from college with, and order a big combination plate. Red or green, you can't lose. But this is green country, amigo. Inexpensive.

**Si Señor Restaurant** (575-527-0817), 1551 E. Amador Ave., Las Cruces. Lunch, dinner Mon.–Sun. So many good Mexican restaurants, so little time. I inevitably feel that way in Las Cruces. I believe I've tried them all, and Si Señor still scores high, with its welcoming selection of fresh chips and four salsas, keen service, and fair prices. Love the location for a post– mall shopping trip lunch; lunch specials are a particularly good deal. Inexpensive–Moderate.

**Socorro Springs Brewing Co.** (575-838-0650), 1012 N. California St.,

Socorro. Open daily. Lunch, dinner. This pleasant local brewpub serves good pizza, calzones, salads, and sandwiches. Its menu has enough variety to please everyone in a relaxed atmosphere. Former New Mexico Tech grads started with a little place on the plaza, and it was so popular, it grew into a main street attraction. Inexpensive–Moderate.

**Sparky's Burgers, Barbeque and Espresso** (575-267-4222), 115 Franklin St., Hatch. Lunch, dinner Thurs.–Mon. Closed Tues. and Wed. One of NM's destination cafés. Famous green chile cheeseburgers, fabulous coffee, decent barbecue—Sparky's has it all! Worth it for the funky décor, much of it discarded cultural icons, such as Big Boy and the Colonel. Live music weekends. Inexpensive.

**White Coyote Café** (575-894-5160), 113 Main St., Truth or Consequences.

Breakfast, lunch. Thurs.–Sun. Organic, vegetarian, and proud of it, this charming, sunny, corner 1920s-era building with the original red-oak floors has yummy homemade baked goods. Salads, omelets, and wraps make this a place to enjoy light, fresh fare. Go for the savory quiche. The menu has become limited of late, but food is still wholesome, even if pre-prepared. Inexpensive.

**Zeffiro Pizzeria** (575-525-6757), 136 S. Water St., Las Cruces. Lunch, dinner Mon.–Sat. Closed Sun. So much more than pizza. Excellent pasta, bread and wine. All is fresh and delicious. A downtown bistro at which to meet friends or enjoy a casual post-ramble dinner Fri. evening. I challenge you to give Olive Garden a break in favor of this local family-run establishment. Sibling pizza place near University. Inexpensive–Moderate.

YOU CAN GET JUST ABOUT ANYTHING YOU WANT AT SPARKY'S RESTAURANT IN HATCH.

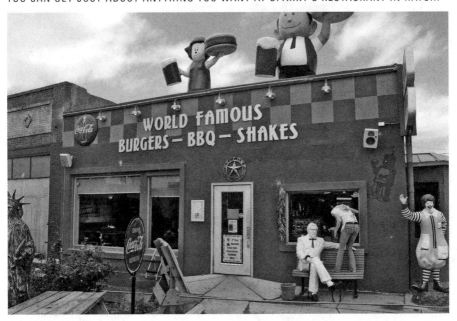

# ✳ Entertainment

**Capitol Bar** (575-835-1193), 110 Plaza, Socorro. This 1896 watering hole presents live entertainment on the weekends. With its bulletholes in the ceiling, shadows of jail cell bars, and having survived Prohibition, this is still the place to go in Socorro.

**Fountain Theater & Mesilla Valley Film Society** (575-524-8287), 2469 Calle de Guadalupe, half a block south of Mesilla Plaza. Screenings nightly at 7:30 and Sun. matinees can catch you up and keep you current with cinema. This is virtually the only place south of Albuquerque where you can catch independent, foreign, and alternative films.

**Manzanares St. Coffeehouse** (575-838-0809), 110 Manzanares Ave., Socorro. Lively hangout, perfect for a road trip coffee and pastry stop and a stroll around the plaza; or, you could be lucky, as I was one Sunday afternoon, to drop in on a women's knitting circle and Irish fiddle music.

**New Mexico Tech Performing Arts Series** (575-835-5688), Macey Center, NM Tech, Socorro. Sept.–May. Macy Center. Live and symphonic and world music, dance, performance, and film brighten the nights in southern New Mexico.

# ✳ Selective Shopping

**Black Cat Books and Coffee** (575-894-7070),128 N. Broadway St., Truth or Consequences. Fri.–Mon., 8–5. Help! I can't get out of this place. Between the captivating and intelligent used book selection, the house-roasted organic coffee, the Sunday *New York Times*, and the neighborliness of the folks sitting around

SUNDAY MORNING MARKET ON MESILLA PLAZA.

formica tables, gabbing . . . Owned and operated by a bookseller who knows her business and loves books. Sunday live poetry readings. Inexpensive.

**Del Sol** (575-524-1418), 2322 Calle Principal, Mesilla. This Mesilla Plaza import shop is a treasure trove of lucky finds, in the way of wearables, household art, and décor. Casual, imports, natural fabrics, plenty of rayon and cotton for Southwest comfort, denim and hats, belts and jackets to accessorize, with good prices and good sales on styles that don't go out of style makes this one of my favorite places to shop.

**Hatch Chile Express** (575-267-3226), 622 N. Franklin, Hatch. Surprise your favorite chilehead with a gift from this well-stocked kitschy bazaar of chile-related and themed kitchenware, foodstuffs, and gifts, from a red chile spoon rest to chile-print boxers and ties. Jo Lytle, proprietor, holds the Guinness World Records title for raising a 13.5-inch Big Jim chile.

**La Vieja Antiques and Vintage** (575-526-7875), 2230 Avenida de Mesilla, Mesilla. Omigosh! Vintage shopper alert! La Vieja, just off Mesilla Plaza, is crammed with one-of-a-kind wearables that, if paired properly, can make a memorable outfit for the opera or a potluck. My best find here: a fringed hot pink suede jacket for $20! My friend found an elegant embroidered green Chinese tunic she wears to the theater over black slacks with ballet flats.

**Moon Goddess** (575-744-0011), 415 Broadway, Truth or Consequences. Imagination rules at this boutique of fanciful feminine repurposed,

upcycled vintage textile wear, lacy underthings, cards, and irresistible glittery gewgaws. The shop is a work of art. A bit pricey.

**Rio Abajo Antiques** (575-835-2872), 1783 Main St, San Antonio, one block south of Owl Bar. Open Sun.–Wed. 10–4, June–July by appointment. A complete surprise en route to Bosque del Apache is this tiny shop packed with to-die-for classic silver and turquoise jewelry, maps, regional artifacts, religious items, books, postcards, and just about anything else worth collecting. The shop is a work of art to warm the heart of any true pack rat.

**Stahmann's Country Store** (800-654-6887), 22505 NM 28 S., 6 miles south of Mesilla. Open daily 9–5. Drive through the world's largest pecan orchard to this shop, where you can taste the products of the world's largest family-owned pecan business all produced right here. Over 128,000 trees produce from 8 to 10 million pounds of pecans a year. Candies, cookies, chile-flavored pecans, and chocolate-covered pecans, plus kitchenware and other goodies, are sold here. This is a great stop for gifts—who do you know who wouldn't love to receive a gift pack of chile pecans or chocolate pecan turtles? Tours may be scheduled to view the shelling process and candy plant.

## ✳ Special Events

*Monthly:* **Truth or Consequences Art Hop**, second Sat., 6–9 PM, Downtown. **Las Cruces First Friday Art Ramble**, 5–8, Downtown.

*February:* **Cuchillo Pecan Festival**, Rich's Pecan Orchard, NM 52,

Cuchillo. **Festival of the Cranes** (575-835-1878), Bosque del Apache National Wildlife Refuge.

*March*: ♪ **Cowboy Days** (575-522-1232), NM Farm & Ranch Heritage Museum.

*April*: **La Vina Wine Festival** (575-882-7632), 4201 NM 28, La Union.

*May*: **Truth or Consequences Fiesta** (Ralph Edwards Day) (575-894-6673), Truth or Consequences. **Southern New Mexico Wine Festival** (www.nmwine.com), Southern New Mexico Fairgrounds, west of Las Cruces.

*September*: **Hatch Chile Festival** (www.hatchchilefest.com), Labor Day Weekend.

*November:* ♪ **Renaissance Artsfaire** (575-523-6403), Young Park, Las Cruces. **El Día de los Muertos** (575-647-2639; calaveracoalition@q.com), Mesilla. **International Mariachi Conference** (www.lascrucesmariachi .org), Las Cruces.

MERRIMENT ABOUNDS AT LAS CRUCES RENAISSANCE ARTSFAIRE.

# OLD HIGHWAY 60 COUNTRY
## MAGDALENA, DATIL, PIE TOWN, QUEMADO

Along Old US Highway 60, nicknamed the "Pieway," you can find, in addition to many slices of fine homemade pie, sources of fascination from one end of the spectrum—cowboy country and wide open spaces—to the other, the very high-tech Very Large Array radiotelescope. In a sense, this slow road, without chain stores or billboards, is a microcosm of New Mexico. The new and the old find the place big enough and accommodating enough to coexist and go their own distinct ways.

**GUIDANCE Magdalena Chamber of Commerce** (866-854-3217; www .magdalena-nm.com), P.O. Box 281, Magdalena, NM 87825.

## ✹ To See

**TOWNS Datil**, 35 miles west of Magdalena on US 60, was named for the nearby Datil Mountains. The name translates to "date" (perhaps a wild fruit that grew here). There's not too much to see here, but the Eagle Guest Ranch has been a convenient pit stop for travelers since folks first took to the road in automobiles. Gas, food, and lodging are still available.

**Magdalena** is 27 miles west of Socorro on US 60. Supposedly the face of Mary Magdalene is visible on the mountainside at the eastern edge of town. The truth is, this was the cattle shipping railhead of the "Hoof Highway," or the "Beefsteak Trail," where cowboys rounded up and drove cattle in from ranches 125 miles west to Arizona and across the Plains of San Augustin and shipped them out on the railroad. The second weekend in July is "Old Timers' Day," when the old storytellers return and the Queen, who must be over 70, is celebrated on a float in the parade.

**Pie Town** is 21 miles northwest of Datil on US 60. This 20th-century homesteader town baked its way out of the Depression by selling homemade pies to cowboys. Pies are still baked here, with a couple of cafés open, with irregular hours, at what is largely a wide place in the road. Do get there early in the day if you want pie, because things tend to shut down by 3 PM.

**Quemado** is 43 miles west of Pie Town on US 60. Last chance! You're only 33 miles from the Arizona border here, so if you're heading west, you might think of gassing up and stopping for some home cooking in a local café before leaving. The name of the town means "burned" in Spanish, but no one is really certain how or why this name was given to the place.

**HISTORIC LANDMARKS, PLACES, AND SITES** **Lightning Field** (212-989-5566 or 505-898-3335), Quemado. An installation of 400 polished steel poles by American sculptor Walter De Maria that catches the changing light, and the lightning, of New Mexico's isolated high desert. You will be brought to the location, 45 miles outside Quemado, and permitted to stay overnight one night in a rustic cabin that sleeps six. You may be bunking with strangers. For reservations, contact Dia Art Foundation, 535 W. 22nd St., New York. $150 May–June, Sept.–Oct.; $250 July–Aug.

**Very Large Array** (575-835-7000), 50 miles west of Socorro on US 60. Visitors center open 8:30–sunset. Closed major holidays. Did you see *Contact*, starring Jodie Foster? If so, you will recognize the 27 giant dish antennas of the VLA, a.k.a. the National Radio Astronomy Observatory, on the barren Plains of San Augustin between Magdelena and Datil. The visitors center shows a video and has exhibits explaining the VLA telescope and radio astronomy. An easy

VERY LARGE ARRAY RADIO TELESCOPE ON THE PLAINS OF SAN AUGUSTIN.

MAGDALENA, TRAIL'S END.

self-guided walking tour goes to the base of one of the antennas. Guided tours first Sat. each month 11 AM–3 PM. Free.

**MUSEUMS** **Box Car Museum** (575-854-2361), 108 N. Main St., Magdalena. A collection of vintage photos and artifacts of frontier life are housed here. Call for hours and fees.

## ✷ To Do

**CAMPING** **Datil Well Campground** (575-835-0412), Datil. US 60 at Datil, south 1 mile on NM 12. You will find 1 mile of moderate hiking trails through piñon-juniper and ponderosa pine at this site of one of 15 wells that supplied water along the 1880s cattle driveway between Magdalena and Springerville, Arizona. Twenty-two campsites; firewood provided. $5 camping.

**FISHING** **Quemado Lake Recreation Area** (575-773-4678). From Quemado, west on US 60 for 0.5 mile, south on NM 32 for 16 miles to NM 103. Quiet and truly unspoiled, here are 800 acres of ponderosa pine that border a 131-acre man-made trout lake with three-season fishing. The area is regulated by the Quemado Ranger District of the Gila National Forest and contains seven campgrounds, two ADA fishing piers, and 7 miles of hiking trails. The Quemado Lake Overlook Trail is a moderate 1.5-mile hike one-way with about a 1,000-foot elevation gain and is quite a photogenic trail with birding opportunities. Several easy-moderate hikes crisscross the area.

# ✳ Lodging

## BED & BREAKFASTS, MOTELS

**Rancho Magdalena Bed & Breakfast** (575-854-3091), US 60, Mile Marker 109, west of Magdalena. "For Horses and their People," located right on the historic cattle driveway. Hunting and guide services are also available here. Providing rustic elegance, peace and quiet, and biscuits and coffee delivered to your room each morning. A getaway for those in need of deep R & R. $115.

**Western Motel and RV Park** (575-854-2417), 404 First St., Magdelena offers three kinds of accommodations, including its 1956 knotty pine motel, or if you prefer, a Victorian room in old "Grandma Butter's" adobe home that served as a hospital during the 1920s. Fourteen RV sites. $41–60.

# ✳ Where to Eat

**EATING OUT Eagle Guest Ranch** (575-772-5612), US 60 and NM 12, Datil. This roadhouse began as a gas station and grocery shop and dates back to the early 20th century. It is still in the family. Steaks and burgers are the order of the day, and the Mexican food served Friday only will heat your bones. Expect to rub elbows with cowboys and hunters. Inexpensive.

**Good Pie Cafe** (575-722-2700), Pie Town. Open Mon.–Fri 8–4. Breakfast all day, lunch, Fri. dinner specials. Closed Sat. and Sun. Order an entire pie with 48 hours' advance notice. Home cooking on the Great Divide, and as they say, "It's all downhill from here." It's hard to say just who makes the best pie on this stretch of US 60, but this is an argument worth having. From the flaky crust to the flavorful fillings, the pies served here are divine. You can also get a very good home-cooked lunch and a great burger. This place is just fun! Inexpensive.

**Pie-O-Neer** (575-772-2711), US "Pieway" 60, Pie Town. Open Fri.–Mon. 10–3. Eat homemade pie on the Continental Divide. You have your choice of a dozen varieties; coconut cream is a big fave. Kathy Knapp bakes and feeds the wood stove as well as happy customers, who come from several counties. Homemade lunch as well. It's worth the trip! Inexpensive.

KATHY KNAPP HAS BEEN DELIVERING LEGENDARY PIES IN PIE TOWN FOR ALMOST TWO DECADES.

PIE-O-NEER CAFÉ, PIE TOWN.

## ✳ Entertainment

**London Frontier Theatre Company** (575-854-2519; www
.londonfrontiertheatre.com), 502
Main at Fourth St., Magdalena. Open
select weekends Mar.–Dec. With over
a dozen seasons under its belt, and
now housed in its historic WPA theater, the London Frontier Company
regularly receives enthusiastic notices
from all who experience it. The season centers on original ensemble
plays related to the West and its history, with the Christmas offering in
December as a highlight. $5 adults,
$3 children.

## ✳ Selective Shopping

**Blue Canyon Gallery** (575-854-
2953), 602 First St., Magdalena.

**Elvires Rock Shop & Saw Shop**
(575-854-2324), E. Hwy. 60,
Magdalena.

**Route 60 Trading Post and Gal-
lery** (575-854-3560), 400 First St.,
Magdalena. Authentic jewelry made
by Navajo living in nearby Alamo is
sold here, along with cowboy art.
You'll also find information on US
Highway 60 here.

## ✳ Special Events

*May:* **Magdalena Festival Arts &
Crafts Sale and Studio Tour** (575-
854-2261), Magdalena. Also held in
fall.

*July:* **Magdalena Old Timers'
Reunion** (575-854-2261), Magdalena.

*Sept.:* **Pie Festival** (www.pie-o-neer
.com), Pie Town.

*December:* **Christmas Theater program** (575-854-2519), Frontier Theatre, Magdalena.

# GHOST TOWN COUNTRY

## HILLSBORO, GLENWOOD, RESERVE, COLUMBUS, SILVER CITY, DEMING

**GUIDANCE** **Columbus Chamber of Commerce** (575-531-3333), P.O. Box 350, Columbus, NM 88029.

**Deming-Luna County Chamber of Commerce** (575-546-2674), 800 E. Pine, Deming.

**Glenwood Area Chamber of Commerce** (575-539-2711), P.O. Box 183, Glenwood, NM 88039.

**Silver City Chamber of Commerce** (575-538-3785), 201 N. Hudson St., Silver City.

## ✳ To See

**TOWNS** **Columbus** is 32 miles south of Deming on NM 11. Not quite deserted enough to be classified as a true ghost town, Columbus still receives plenty of visitors seeking to learn more about Pancho Villa's Mar. 9, 1916, border raid as well as those touring Pancho Villa State Park. It is only 3 miles north of the Mexican border crossing at Palomas.

**Deming**, 61 miles west of Las Cruces on I-10, is convenient to both City of Rocks State Park and Rockhound State Park, and the town bills itself as "Rockhound's Paradise." The big annual event is the annual Rockhound Roundup held in March. It is another small town you will generally spend time in because you are on your way to somewhere else, unless you are one of the many "snowbirds" who regularly winter here. There are over 30 restaurants, many of them chains, to serve the population. It has ample motel accommodations and low overhead, but there isn't much to do in the town itself, aside from touring the very worthwhile, recently remodeled Deming Luna Mimbres Museum.

**Glenwood.** Sixty miles northwest of Silver City on US 180. Driving into Glenwood on a sun-dappled autumn day is like coasting into a lovely little piece of paradise, or a film set from the 1940s. Its proximity to the Catwalk has made it a pleasant stop for gas and a visit to any of the cafés you might happen to find open—usually one is.

**Hillsboro.** Once the center of gold mining activity, Hillsboro, 17 miles on NM 152 from the I-25 exit, was well on its way to becoming a true ghost town when it was discovered by a few urbanites who moved in and fixed up the old houses or built new ones to look just like the old ones. It's a pretty place with a decent café, and it really is the gateway to the Black Range. Cowboys drew from a hat for the honor of naming it, and it used to be the center of an apple-growing region. Alas! The Apple Festival is no more.

**Mogollon.** A former silver and gold mining town in the Mogollon Mountains, now with a scattering of cafés, antiques shops, and several well-weathered, photogenic wooden buildings. Still, a ghost town at heart. Silver Creek runs through the town.

**Reserve** is 36 miles north of Glenwood via US 180 and NM 12. Welcome to cowboy country, ma'am. A couple of bars, a gas station, and, if absolutely necessary, a motel, can provide for your immediate needs. This is not the place to share your feelings with strangers. A retreat to your motel room with a good book is the best advice.

**Silver City.** Seventy-two slow miles across Emory Pass west of exit 63 off I-25, Silver City makes an excellent base for exploring the Gila Cliff Dwellings, attending any of the many annual area festivals, and enjoying the birdlife and wildlife, and it is a good enough stop on its own, with two museums, plenty of galleries, and some restaurants that will not disappoint you, plus an historic downtown. Founded in 1870 and named for the rich silver deposits west of town, its period architecture is well preserved. Recent visits have demonstrated

NOTHING MUCH HAS CHANGED IN MOGOLLON FOR A CENTURY OR SO.

that Silver City is a foodie destination waiting to be discovered.

**HISTORIC LANDMARKS, PLACES, AND SITES Gila Cliff Dwellings National Monument** (575-536-2250), 44 miles north of Silver City on NM 15. Memorial Day–Labor Day 8–6, visitors center 8–5; the rest of the year 9–4, visitors center 8–4:30. Closed Christmas and New Year's Day. Contact the visitors center for information on guided tours. A short drive from the visitors center along the West Fork of the Gila River, a 1-mile loop trail leads through the dwellings, natural caves that were made into 40 rooms with stone quarried by these indigenous people. They were farmers who raised squash, corn, and beans on the mesa tops and along the river. We know them by these dwellings and for their exquisite black-and-white pottery. We do not know why they abandoned their homes and can only speculate that they may have joined other pueblos. They were the home of the Mogollon people who lived here from the 1280s until the early 1300s. The trail is steep in places, as there is a 180-foot elevation gain. For camping information, inquire at the visitors center. $3 individual, $10 family.

GILA CLIFF DWELLINGS. REMOTE AND WORTH THE TRIP.

**Pancho Villa State Park** (575-531-2711), 35 miles south of Deming via NM 11, Columbus. Open daily. Visitors center daily 9–5. This is the only U.S. park named for a foreign invader! Here you can tour an extensive desert botanic garden; see the ruins of Camp Furlong, site of the attack; and view a display of early-20th-century military equipment. Birding is excellent, and camping is available. The new 7,000-square-foot exhibit hall showcases vehicles from the 1916 raid on Columbus in which 18 Americans were killed. This spot marks the site of the only ground invasion of American soil since 1812. The visitors center is housed in the 1902 Customs Service Building, and it is where you can learn from historic photos and exhibits all about Francisco "Pancho" Villa's attack, though many locals continue to tell their own versions of the event, if you show a bit of curiosity. $5 day use; $18 camping.

**MUSEUMS Black Range Museum** (575-895-5233), NM 152, Hillsboro. Closed Jan. and Feb. Call for hours. This was once the home of British-born

A DELIGHTFUL COLLECTION OF ANTIQUE DOLLS AND DOLLHOUSES IS ON DISPLAY AT THE DEMING LUNA MIMBRES MUSEUM.

madam Sadie Orchard, the archetypal lady of the night with a heart of gold. She served the town during epidemics and donated to good works. Now her home tells the story of the early days of Sierra County, with an emphasis on mining. Donation.

**Columbus Historical Society Museum** (575-531-2620), corner of NM 9 and NM 11, Columbus. Open daily 10–4. A restored 1902 Southern Pacific Railroad depot is the repository of collections on Columbus history, the Villa raid, and the railroad. Free.

**Deming Luna Mimbres Museum** (575-546-2382), 301 S. Silver, Deming. Open Mon.–Sat. 9–4; Sun. 1:30–4. Closed Thanksgiving, Christmas. Americana lovers, this is your new favorite place. Visit the Quilt Room; the Doll Room, with over 600 antique dolls; the ladies' fashion room; the military room, with mementos of the Pancho Villa raid; and the Indian Kiva, with outstanding Mimbres pottery and native basketry. This newly remodeled 1916 armory now has 25,000 feet of exhibit space and a motorized chairlift. Contributions welcome.

**Percha Bank Museum** (www.sierracountynewmexico.info/.../percha-bank -museum-kingston/), Main St., Kingston. Open Sat. and Sun. 10–4 or by appointment. Hard as it is to believe, in 1890 this ghost town, population 30, was New Mexico's largest city, with 7,000 people. This museum offers an education on those days. Donation.

**Silver City Museum** (575-538-5921), 312 W. Broadway, Silver City. Open Tues.–Fri. 9–4, Sat. and Sun. 10–4. Closed Mon. Open Memorial Day, Labor Day, and July 4. The museum, a brick Mansard-Italianate style home built by prospector Harry Ailman in 1880, showcases exhibits on local history. This is one of the most beloved and best-curated and maintained local history museums in the Southwest. $3.

**Western New Mexico University Museum** (575-538-6386), Fleming Hall, 1000 W. College, Silver City. Open Mon.–Sat. This recently renovated hidden treasure of a museum houses the largest collection of prehistoric Mimbres black-on-white pottery in the nation. It will leave you breathless. Also on exhibit are Casas Grande pottery, mining artifacts, and prehistoric tools and jewelry. Open according to the university's schedule. Call for hours. Free.

**WILDER PLACES Catwalk**, Glenwood. Take US 180 from Silver City to Glenwood; go right at NM 174 for 5 miles. Originally constructed by miners in 1889, this high walkway and suspension bridge leads to a waterfall through narrow Whitewater Canyon and over the Whitewater River in the Gila National Forest. You can easily imagine the ancient people who lived here, as well as Geronimo and Butch

SILVER CITY MUSEUM.

Cassidy hiding out here. The sycamore trees and rock walls make this place special any time of year, though especially in fall. The Catwalk follows the path of a pipeline built in the 1890s to deliver water to the mining town of Graham. The trail itself is easy, though there is some mild up and down. Free. Disassembled due to flood. Please check on status.

## ✳ To Do

**FARMERS' MARKETS Silver City Farmers' Market** (575-388-9441), 1400 US 180 E., Silver City. Open May–Oct., Sat. 8:30–noon.

**FISHING Lake Roberts** (575-536-3663), US 180 north from Deming to City of Rocks turnoff. Continue on NM 61, then NM 35 for 66 miles to the intersection of NM 15 and NM 35. Or take NM 35 north from Silver City. Open year-round. This sweet trout fishing lake, which appears like a surprise on the side of the road in the Gila National Forest, has three campgrounds. $7 camping.

PICKNICKING NEAR THE CATWALK IN GLENWOOD.

**GOLF Rio Mimbres Country Club and Golf Course** (575-546-9481), Deming. Eighteen-hole public golf course, east end of Deming with views of Cookes Peak and the Floridas, with pleasant lakes and paths. Inexpensive.

**Silver City Golf Course** (575-538-5041), NM 90 west from downtown, left on Ridge Road. Open year-round, weather permitting. A challenging 18-hole championship public course with high desert vistas, natural vistas, and mild weather. $16–21.

**HORSEBACK RIDING Gila Wilderness Ventures** (575-539-2800; www .gilawildernessventures.com). Take US 180 for 3 miles north of Glenwood, then go 3 miles east on NM 159. Leah Jones is a well-seasoned veteran outfitter on the Gila Wilderness. Whether you prefer a day ride, pack trip, custom trip, or drop camp, it can all be arranged to your liking. Leah's talents include Dutch oven cooking.

**WolfHorse Outfitters** (575-534-1379), Santa Clara. Within the Gila National Forest, create a horseback adventure with this Native American guide service. Rides through the wilderness, lodge to lodge, to the ruins, and in the moonlight.

**HOT SPRINGS Fayewood Hot Springs** (575-536-9663; www.faywood.com), next to City of Rocks State Park on NM 61, halfway between Silver City and Deming. Open daily 10–10. Despite rumors Fayewood has closed or been sold to the mine, it is alive and well. There are over a dozen shaded, outdoor, natural, geothermal mineral water soaking pools, some public, some private, and some for overnight guests, who may use the public pools all night. "Limp in, leap out" is the motto here. Cabins, RV, and tent sites are available. $12.50 per adult per day; $25 per hour private tub.

**PARKS Big Ditch Park**, behind Bullard St., Silver City. The flood of 1895 roared through Silver City with 12-foot-high waters, leaving behind a ditch 35 feet below street level. The subsequent flood of 1903 lowered the "Big Ditch" 20 feet more. It is now a pleasant town park for strolling and picnicking, directly behind downtown.

**WILDLIFE REFUGES Wolfsong Ranch/Painted Pony Ranch** (575-557-0082), 41 Painted Pony Rd., Rodeo. Sitting near the New Mexico–Arizona border in the San Simon Valley, on 440 acres in the "boot heel" country of Hidalgo County. Habitat preservation, education, and experimental learning opportunities abound, and many of these animals have been injured or orphaned. This is a

## SCENIC DRIVES

**Geronimo Trail Scenic Byway** (575-894-6600), 211 Main St., Truth or Consequences, is the site of the trail's interpretive and visitors center. Open Mon.–Sat. 9–5. The geology, flora and fauna, history, and events of the area are available here. Travel a loop starting from Truth or Consequences up the Mimbres across steep, winding Emory Pass of the Black Range, passing through geological and cultural eons, and certainly, traveling in Geronimo's footsteps. The trail loops back at San Lorenzo on NM 152. This is an all-day trip at 220 miles, and you might want to overnight in Kingston.

**Gila Cliff Dwellings/ Trail of the Mountain Spirits Scenic Byway.** Take NM 15 north from Silver City into the Gila National Forest to the Cliff Dwellings for 110 miles, through Pinos Altos, Lake Roberts, the Mimbres River, and the Santa Rita open pit copper mine to the Cliff Dwellings. Allow plenty of time, as the road is slow and there is much to see.

**Lake Valley Back Country Byway.** Go east from Deming to Truth or Consequences via Hillsboro. Take NM 1521 and 27 for 47 miles. Slow going and well worth the trip. You'll see ghost towns and unparalleled views of the mountains south of Truth or Consequences.

**NM 185 Back Road.** Go north from Las Cruces or Dona Ana to San Antonio through pecan groves and chile fields for a view of the wilder side of the Rio Grande you can't get any other way. You can avoid the interstate all the way along this scenic two-lane. Glorious!

## GHOST TOWNS

**Bayard Historical Mining District** (575-537-3327). Now owned by the Phelps Dodge Mining Co., the six underground shafts with head frames of this once-busy mining district, which produced more gold, silver, copper, lead, zinc, iron, manganese, and molybdenum than all the other mining districts in New Mexico combined, may be toured by automobile. This area is popular with mountain bikers, horseback riders, and birders. The Buffalo Soldiers, the African American unit of the Ninth Cavalry, was stationed here 1866–99. Get tour information at the Bayard City Hall.

**Chloride** (575-743-2736), Main St., Chloride. California retirees Don and Dona Edmund were inspired to purchase the entire town of Chloride, and they have, through the saintly labor of their own hands, been restoring it building by building. The general store has become the Pioneer Store Museum, open daily 8–5. Open for tours. All the original stock is still in place. You have to really want to come here, and it is an effort to reach this place, but you won't soon forget it, either.

**Kelly** While the rumor is that Monsieur Gustave Eiffel, of Eiffel Tower fame, constructed the mining head frame here, it turns out to be a colorful story only. Once a booming mining town of 3,000 located 2 miles north of Magdalena where zinc, copper, then silver were mined, Kelly is a ghost town made for exploring. Artists come here to retrieve materials, and care must be taken because not all the old buildings or mine shafts are well protected. However, even if you don't actually see the ghosts said to roam here, you can certainly feel their presence.

**Kingston.** Nine miles west of Hillsboro on NM 152. The home base of Sadie Orchard, the British madam with a heart of gold who made her fortune here, Kingston was a rip-snorting place with dozens of brothels and saloons and banks during the silver mining heyday. Hard to believe now, but it was once home to 7,000. Today, population 30. The old Victorio Hotel and Percha Bank still stand. Now it is quiet, picturesque, and the home of one delightful Black Range Lodge (see *Lodging*), and where javalinas roam Percha Creek.

**Mogollon** (mo-go-yone). Two hours north of Silver City on US 180, right on NM 159 between Glenwood and Alma. Calling all hard-core explorers: what is termed New Mexico's most remote ghost town, and, I must say, one of its most haunting, is accessible only by a 9-mile road that climbs 2,080 feet via switchbacks, without guardrails. The last 5 miles become a one-lane road. Founded in 1895, this gold rush boomtown was the state's leading mining district by 1915. While accommodations and attractions (aside from exploring and photographing on your own) come and go, at last moment before press time, the **Silver Creek Inn** (866-276-4882) was a functioning bed & breakfast, and the **Mogollon Prehistoric Native Museum** (575-539-2016) was open during summer weekends. Do check road conditions carefully before you go.

**Pinos Altos.** Six miles north of Silver City on NM 15, this town sits directly on the Continental Divide. The Old West lives on here in a mining town where the Hearst Mine supplied the gold for the Hearst Castle. It is fun to photograph the splintering, wooden buildings, some housing the occasional gallery or ice-cream parlor, at sunset in their splendid decay; perhaps spot an elk wandering across the road; and order a steak at the Buckhorn Saloon.

**San Antonio.** Fourteen miles south of Socorro at the junction of NM 1 and US 380 off I-25 exit 139 east, San Antonio is known as the hometown of hotelier Conrad Hilton, whose father ran a boardinghouse here. It is also the gateway to Bosque del Apache National Wildlife Refuge and on the main road east to Lincoln and Billy the Kid country. Today it is the home of two famous burger houses: the Owl Cafe and the Buckhorn.

**Shakespeare** (575-542-9034), 2.5 miles southwest of Lordsburg. I-10 from Lordsburg at Main St. exit 22, go south and follow the signs. Open a few days each month. Guided tours available. Shakespeare, which bills itself as "the West's most authentic ghost town," might well call itself Phoenix. Owned and operated since 1935 by the Hill family, it has recovered from the ashes of a terrible fire in 1997 and is again offering 90-minute guided tours by Janaloo Hill as well as shootouts and special events for slightly high admission. Shakespeare, named for the mining company that held silver claims, was a stagecoach and mining town in its day, and here you can see the assay office, old mail station, saloon, general store, and much more. $4 adults, $3 children ages 6–12.

WHIMSICAL SILVER CITY DOORWAY.

**Winston** (no phone) is so close to Chloride that the two towns are generally visited on the same trip. Both towns are at the base of the Black Range.

refuge for unwanted and abandoned wolves, wolf dogs, and other wild animals. Horseback tours are available. Donations recommended.

**WINERIES St. Clair Vineyards** (575-546-5394), 1325 De Baca Rd., Deming. I-10 west from Las Cruces about 60 miles. Open Mon.–Sat. 9–6, Sun. noon–5. No appointments are needed for the tours offered Sat. and Sun. Grapes grown in the vineyards right here produce lovely Cabernet, Chardonnay, and Zinfandel. St. Clair also operates restaurants and tasting rooms in Albuquerque's Old Town, Las Cruces, and Farmington.

## ✳ Green Space

Elephant Butte State Park, Caballo Lake State Park, and Percha Dam lie like three separate but neighboring versions of a similar geography, all fed by the Rio Grande, arrayed from north to south.

**Caballo Lake State Park** (575-743-3942), 16 miles south of Truth or Consequences at exit 59 off I-25. Named for the wild horses descended from the horses brought here in the 1540s by the Spanish, at Caballo find a recreation area and lake against the background of the Caballo Mountains just south of Elephant Butte, and it is much, much quieter, with excellent bass and walleye fishing. The champion striper from Caballo Lake weighed 51 pounds. There is plenty of camping available here. This is just about your best bet to see migrating bald and golden eagles. We have spotted a few during the winter, and about 50 are known to reside in the area. $5 day use; $10–18 camping.

---

### GILA NATIONAL FOREST

3005 E. Camino del Bosque, Silver City (575-388-8201). Ranger office open Mon.–Fri. 8–4:30. Measuring over 3.3 million acres—the nation's sixth-largest national forest—the vast Gila is incomparable in its diversity and the opportunities it offers for outdoor recreation. Its varied terrain ranges from high desert at 4,200 feet to rugged mountain and canyon lands at 10,900, and four of the six life zones of planet Earth are found here. Your best bet is to contact the number above to plan your trip around your specific interests. The forest, named for the Spanish corruption of a Yuma Indian word meaning "running water that is salty," is accessible from many of the small towns in southwest New Mexico, including Quemado, Glenwood, and Reserve. Whether your interests include birding, hiking, camping—which is mostly primitive, but does include RV hookups—ATV-ing, fishing, rafting, mountain biking—it is all here, at all levels of challenge. Nearly 400 species of birds make this their home or nesting area. The forest includes the Gila Wilderness and the Aldo Leopold Wilderness, the nation's first, founded in 1924. A section of the Continental Divide Trail lies within the forest. You could spend a week here, a summer, or a lifetime.

**City of Rocks State Park** (575-536-2800), US 80 24 miles from Deming west toward Silver City, then 4 miles northwest on NM 61. Open daily 7 AM–9 PM. With the feel of a natural Stonehenge, this state park is an astounding array of pillars of 34.9-million-year-old wind-sculpted volcanic ashes, some up to 40 feet tall. Paths run between the rock columns like the streets of a "city." There's an astronomy observatory and starry-night programs. This could be the state's premier dark-skies opportunity. $5 day use; $10–18 camping.

**Elephant Butte State Park** (575-744-5923), I-25 exit 83, 5 miles north of Truth or Consequences. Open daily, 24 hours a day. It is huge, with 200 miles of shoreline and hundreds of campsites. This is a place for water sports of all kinds: wind surfing, fishing, and waterskiing, in addition to fishing, birding, and rockhounding. Elephant Butte Lake is the largest body of water in New Mexico, and it is well known for trophy fish, including striper, bass, and walleye. There are no elephants, only the eroded core of a volcano in the middle of the lake that somehow reminded someone of an elephant.

CITY OF ROCKS STATE PARK RESEMBLES STONEHENGE IN ITS OWN WAY.

SAILING ALONG AT ELEPHANT BUTTE LAKE STATE PARK

The park hosts close to 1.7 million visitors annually. Be forewarned, Memorial Day, Fourth of July, and Labor Day can draw between 80,000 and 100,000 visitors. The U.S. Bureau of Reclamation built the dam from 1912 to 1916, primarily for irrigation purposes; the reservoir capacity is 2.2 million acre feet. Boats and Jet Skis are available for rental at the two marinas. Public tours of the power plant are available. $5 day use; $10–18 camping. Houseboat, pontoon, ski boat rentals (888-736-8240).

**Percha Dam State Park** (575-743-3942). Just south of Caballo Dam. Known for its handicapped-accessible playground and spectacular bird-watching, this park, with its huge cottonwoods, usually remains quiet, as it is still somewhat undiscovered. There are no developed hiking trails, only paths to the river, and walking along the dirt roads is a fine way to go. $5 day use; $10–18 camping.

**Rockhound State Park/Spring Canyon** (575-546-6182). From Deming, go south 5 miles on NM 11, then east on NM 141 for 9 miles. Open daily 7:30–sunset. Set on the western slope of the Little Florida Mountains, the visitors center here has displays pertaining to the geology and history of the area. Known as a rockhounder's paradise; every visitor is permitted to take 150 pounds of rocks home. There are good pickings in jasper and perlite, and you can find some geodes or thunder eggs, as they are known. $5 day use; $10–18 camping.

## ✳ Lodging

**BED & BREAKFASTS, MOTELS, AND INNS** ☕ **Black Range Lodge** (575-895-5652; www.blackrangelodge .com), 119 Main St., Kingston. When Catherine Wanek and her new husband drove out from Los Angeles on their honeymoon, they spotted this old mining hotel, fell in love with it, and decided to buy it on the spot. Since that fortuitous day, this rather dark, massive lodge has turned into a merry B&B. Massive stone walls and log-beamed ceilings date to 1940, but the original dates to the 1880s, when it was built to house miners and cavalry. Despite improvements in the seven guest rooms, the original character of the place has not been tinkered with. Cyclists and tourists come from all over the world to stay and enjoy the informality of the buffet breakfast with homemade bread, waffles, and home-raised jams and fruit. It has the feeling of a hostel, with shared clawfoot tubs. The new luxury guest house has a jetted hot tub and complete kitchen and wraparound deck. The Percha Creek House has five bedrooms, kitchen, dining, living room, and large deck. Catherine has become an expert and author on straw bale construction, and there are several straw bale buildings on the premises, including an all-natural meeting room that occasionally hosts live music and events. $79–95.

**Casitas de Gila Guesthouses** (575-923-4827), 310 Hooker Loop, Gila. Five private guest houses in perfect Southwest style and comfort are perched on a ledge overlooking Bear Creek and the Gila Wilderness. The experienced innkeepers, Becky and Michael O'Connor, used to run a bed & breakfast in Ireland, and privacy and peace and quiet are what you can expect here. The gallery displays a good selection of folk art, icons, and jewelry. Bring your binoculars to spot the bighorn sheep across the river.

Also, bring your own food to cook in the fully equipped kitchens. WiFi, too, but no TV. Great stargazing, though. This spot frequently makes the list of "most romantic spots in New Mexico." $125–200.

**The Hideaway at Gallery 400** (575-313-7015), 400 N. Arizona, Silver City. A downtown lodging located in an art gallery. Or an art gallery tucked away in an historic lodging? No matter. Urbane, comfortable, casual place to stay with an atmosphere that will be instantly recognizable to world travelers and visitors from metro areas. Light continental breakfast, coffee and tea bar, discounts to Vicki's Eatery across the street for breakfast. $90–110.

**Inn on Broadway** (575-388-5485), 411 W. Broadway, Silver City. Three guest rooms and a Garden Suite conjure the glories of this 1883 merchant's home with marble fireplaces

and hand-carved imports from Germany. There's a shady front veranda in this grand home. $125–140.

**Murray Hotel** (575-956-9400), 200 W. Broadway St., Silver City. Retro five-story streamline art deco hotel in the heart of Silver City's Historic Downtown Arts & Cultural District is refurbished and open for business. Another of this town's magnetic attractions.

**Palace Hotel** (575-388-8111), 106 W. Broadway, Silver City. Every town has a grand old hotel, and the 1900 Palace is Silver City's. Although rather more diminutive than grand, it is where to stay if you collect historic hotel experiences. The 22 rooms are small, and, facing directly on a busy street corner, it is not the quietest place in the world. The healthy continental breakfast will get you going. But it is comfortable, it has been restored, and if you are not expecting the Holiday Inn

THE RUSTIC BLACK RANGE LODGE.

THE REMODELED ART DECO MURRAY HOTEL IN SILVER CITY SHOWS OFF ITS INVITING LOBBY.

and don't mind carrying your luggage up and down a couple of flights of stairs, all will be well. And all of downtown is in walking distance. $51–82.

### RANCHES AND LODGES ❀ Bear Mountain Lodge (575-538-2538), 2251 Cottage San Rd., Silver City. I am really partial to Bear Mountain Lodge; in fact, it would have to be on my choice of top three places in NM to spend a week relaxing, regardless of the season. This 11-room lodge is a birder's dream come true, especially during hummingbird season in July–Aug., when numerous varieties descend on Silver City. Pet-friendly. $115–185.

### CABINS AND CAMPING Bear Creek Motel and Cabins (575-388-4501). 88 Main St., Pinos Altos. Bordering Bear Creek at the gateway to

the Gila National Forest are some comfortable furnished cabins with porches and balconies among the tall pines. $99–119.

**Continental Divide RV Park** (575-388-3005), 4774 NM 15, 6 miles north of Silver City on NM 15, Pinos Altos. Smack in the middle of an apple orchard with views of the Gila National Forest, this site accommodates RVs. Cabins and tent sites available, too. Please call for rates.

**Gila Hot Springs Ranch & Doc Campbell's Post** (575-536-9551), Gila Hot Springs. Enjoy a real kick-back time in a motel-like room; bring your RV or camp by the river. Natural hot pools and jetted tub, horseback riding, and fishing make this a real vacation. $50–75.

**Lake Roberts Cabins & General Store** (575-536-9929), 5 Chestnut St., Lake Roberts, Silver City. The cabins are fully furnished with kitchens or kitchenettes, so you can catch it and cook it. $69–99.

## ✳ Where to Eat

**DINING OUT Buckhorn Saloon & Opera House** (575-538-9911), 32 Main St., NM 15, Pinos Altos. Open daily 6–10 PM, dinner only. Saloon opens at 3. Closed Sun. Live music sometimes. This 1860s establishment is a necessary New Mexico experience. The Old West saturates the foot-and-a-half-thick adobe walls, and the Buckhorn radiates romance in its dimmed lights. In fact, this place may have invented "character." You're guaranteed to meet memorable characters at the bar, if that is your choice. The steaks are excellent, prepared perfectly, and served with fresh baked sourdough bread and all the trimmings, including house-made

dressings for your salad. Love that filet mignon! Steak is not the only item on the menu, however. There is now a variety of dishes to please any palate. Reservations are a very good idea, especially on weekends. Weekend entertainment as well. Moderate–Expensive.

**Curious Kumquat** (575-534-0337), 111 E. College Ave., Silver City. Gourmet by night, beer garden by day. Lunch, dinner Tues.–Sat. Closed Sun. and Mon. Recently voted 39th of *Saveur* magazine's 100 top restaurants. Chef Rob Connoley awakens at 6 AM to forage ingredients in the Gila Wilderness. Incredibly interesting. He specializes in what is known as the art of molecular gastronomy, creating kinesthetic experiences from wild food. Also on the menu is 4-H raised lamb, elk, rabbit, and duck. Very reasonable—even a college student can

NOTHING BEATS CURLING UP BY THE FIRE AT BEAR MOUNTAIN LODGE IN SILVER CITY.

save up for a date here. You will be astounded. Moderate.

**❀ Diane's Restaurant and Bakery** (575-538-8722), 510 N. Bullard St., Silver City. Lunch Tues.–Sun. 11–2, brunch Sat. and Sun. 9–2, dinner Tues.–Sat. 5:30–9. No matter how many times you eat at this lovely downtown bistro, the food and service are impeccable. Fish, chicken, steak, and more light, harmonious, sophisticated fare, thoughtfully prepared, with just the right spicing and saucing, at a reasonable price—what more could you ask? Try the roast Asian duck with sweet sesame glaze, juicy meat loaf with garlic mashers, or pesto pasta. Diane's son Bodhi is busy in the kitchen, a happy chef. Moderate.

**Shevek and Co.** (575-534-9168), 602 N. Bullard St., Silver City. Open Thurs.–Tues. Lunch, dinner weekdays; breakfast, lunch, dinner weekends. Closed Wed. One special feature of this excellent restaurant is that you may order the same dish in one of three sizes: tapa, meze, or entrée, depending on your appetite or your desire to sample several tastes. This is a vegetarian-friendly place: feta-stuffed roasted pepper, Cabrales blue cheese and apple crostini are served along with orange and coriander duck, lobster mousse, and tournedos of beef with sautéed wild mushrooms and lemon-mint roasted potatoes. You find a level of sophisticated and authentic Mediterranean taste, along with an extensive wine list, that you would expect in a big city. Cooking classes available. Consistently voted most popular restaurant in town. Extremely caring service. Moderate–Expensive.

**EATING OUT ❀ Adobe Deli Steakhouse** (575-546-0361), 3970

DINE ON FORAGED SPLENDOR AT THE CURIOUS KUMQUAT—NAMED 39TH IN *SAVEUR'S* TOP 100.

THE BUCKHORN SALOON IN PINOS ALTOS HAS AN EXPANDED MENU AND LIVE MUSIC ON WEEKENDS.

Lewis Flats Rd. SE, Deming. Lunch, dinner Mon.–Sun. If you watch any food TV, you've probably encountered this place, as notable for the old barn/mounted heads décor as for the food. They serve as perfect a sandwich as you can find in these parts, with freshly baked bread and generous stacks of tasty meats. The signature onion soup is truly yummy, and the steaks are worth the drive. At the bar, you'll not only see the Wild West characters—here you become one. Oxygen Bar upstairs. Moderate.

**Jalisco Cafe** (575-388-2060), 100 S. Bullard St., Silver City. Lunch, dinner. Open Mon.–Sat., Closed Sun. When I first ate here about 20 years ago, there were lace curtains on the windows of a one-room establishment. When Silver City rancher friends brought me here recently, the place had expanded to three colorful rooms of folks enjoying the hot fluffy sopaipillas, green chile chicken enchiladas, and zippy salsa on the warm, house-made chips. Inexpensive.

**La Fonda** (575-546-0465), 601 E. Pine St., Deming. Enjoy the fresh warm chips, deliciously spicy salsa, fluffy sopaipillas, and delicious enchiladas at this very friendly and welcoming local spot. Inexpensive.

**Millie's Bake House** (575-597-2253), 215 W. Yankie St., Silver City. Out of the kitchen of this tidy, unpretentious bungalow come soups, salads, sandwiches, and baked goods, oh my, all with the taste of homemade. Death by Chocolate is a big favorite. Inexpensive.

**Vicki's Eatery** (575-388-5430), 315 N. Texas, Silver City. Open Mon.–Sun., breakfast, lunch. Perfect little café with super omelets, just the place to chow down, conveniently located in an historic brick building in the heart

THE ADOBE DELI IN DEMING IS A FOOD NETWORK STAR.

of town. Stylish, spacious, light, with homey food, good value. A local favorite. Inexpensive.

## ❋ Entertainment

**Copper Creek Ranch** (575-538-2971), 20 Flury Ln., Silver City. Four and a half miles east of Silver City on US 180 east. Open daily, rain or shine, late May–early Sept., Fri.–Sat., 6–closing. This particular chuckwagon BBQ supper and western show gets good reviews even from locals. Live music is provided by Silver City's Copper Creek Wranglers.

**Pinos Altos Melodrama Theatre** (575-388-3848), Opera House, 18 Main St., Pinos Altos. Fri.–Sat. at 8 most of the year. Reservations are usually necessary for this slapstick melodrama. Enter through the Buckhorn Saloon.

## ❋ Selective Shopping

**Gila Hike & Bike** (575-388-3222), 103 E. College, Silver City. This is the place to come when preparing a bike trip of any kind, to get equipment, service, maps, and rentals.

**Seedboat Gallery** (575-534-1136), 214 W. Yankie St., Silver City. Ever walk into a place and feel like you could take home anything and be happy? The guiding hand of exquisite sophisticated taste is apparent when you walk in the door. Art off and on the wall, jewelry, sculpture, mixed media, ceramics.

**Silver City Trading Company's Antiques Mall**. (575-388-8989), 205 W. Bdwy. The largest collection of vintage vinyl you'll find outside of a major metro, western memorabilia, jewelry, furniture, textiles. Easy to get lost. You may not land on the

*Antiques Road Show* after a visit here, but you'll feel like you could!

**Southwest Women's Fiber Arts Collective/Common Thread** (575-538-5733), 107 Broadway, Silver City. This grassroots cottage industry markets the work of fiber artists in the rural Southwest. On the Fiber Arts Trail.

**Yankie Street Artist Studios** (575-313-1032), 103 W. Yankie, Silver City. Various local artists display their pottery and paintings here.

## ✳ Special Events

*February:* **Cuchillo Pecan Festival** (575-894-0707), 211 Main St., Cuchillo. I-25 exit 83, west on NM 54 for 15 miles. This tiny family-owned pecan orchard puts on a great big party with orchard tours, homemade chocolates, food, and crafts booths; evokes the old days.

*March:* **Border Book Festival** (575-524-1499). Comprehensive celebration of Southwest literature, including children's and Spanish literature, with authors, book signings, music, special events all over town, and a book fair on Mesilla Plaza. **Rockhound Roundup** (575-267-4399), Southwestern New Mexico Fairgrounds, 4750 Raymond Reed Blvd., Deming. Second weekend.

*May:* **Tour of the Gila Bike Race** (800-548-9378), Silver City, first week. This event is billed as America's most popular five-day stage race. **Southern New Mexico Wine Festival** (575-522-1232), Southern New Mexico State Fairgrounds. Live entertainment and sampling of New Mexico wines. Last weekend: **Silver City Blues Festival** (575-538-5555).

*July:* **Magdalena Old Timers' Reunion**, weekend after Fourth of July. Cattle drive, parade, rodeo,

MESILLA PLAZA.

barbecue, fiddlers' contest; and a good time is had by all (575-854-2261).

*August:* 🐎 **Great American Duck Race** (575-544-0469), 202 S. Diamond, Deming. Fourth weekend. Has it come to this? It sure has. **Silver City Clay Festival** (575-538-5555).

*September:* **Hatch Chile Fiesta** (www.hatchchilefest.com/events.php), Labor Day Weekend, despite its popularity and longevity, retains its down-home authenticity with food and craft booths, live music, and, of course, lots of freshly roasted chile to sample and buy. **Whole Enchilada Festival** (575-526-1938), Meerscheidt Recreation Center, Las Cruces. Having set

PRETTY SENORITA DANCES ON MESILLA PLAZA.

the Guinness World Record for the biggest enchilada, this festival has evolved into one for-sure big old street party. **New Mexico Wine Harvest Festival** (575-522-1232), Southern New Mexico State Fairgrounds, Labor Day weekend. **Pickamania** (575-538-5555), Silver City.

*October:* **Geronimo Days** (575-894-6600), Truth or Consequences, second week, is a celebration of the many cultures that have sought the healing waters.

*November:* **Festival of the Cranes** (www.festivalofthecranes.com), Bosque del Apache National Wildlife Refuge, weekend before Thanksgiving. Workshops, tours, special birding events. **Día de los Muertos** (Day of the Dead) (calaveracoalition@q.com), Mesilla Plaza, Mesilla. First weekend. Following the Mexican custom of building altars and feasting on the graves of departed family members, Mesilla Plaza is now filled with altars and craft booths at this time, and the custom has been revived here during the past 10 years to include a procession to the cemetery.

**Renaissance Artsfaire** (www.las -cruces-arts.org/events/renaissance -artsfaire/), Young Park, Las Cruces. Second weekend. Joust on, all ye lords and ladies, knights and maidens, in costume, please.

*December:* **Tamal Fiesta** (575-538-5555), Silver City. Most towns and many state parks and monuments have luminaria tours during the month. Please check individual listings.

# Southeast New Mexico: Billy the Kid Country

## 7

**BILLY'S STOMPING GROUNDS**
Capitan, Fort Sumner, Lincoln,
Carrizozo, Tularosa, Alamogordo,
Ruidoso, Roswell, Cloudcroft, Clovis

**CAVERN COUNTRY**
Carlsbad, White's City

**OIL PATCH COUNTRY**
Artesia, Hobbs, Lovington, Portales

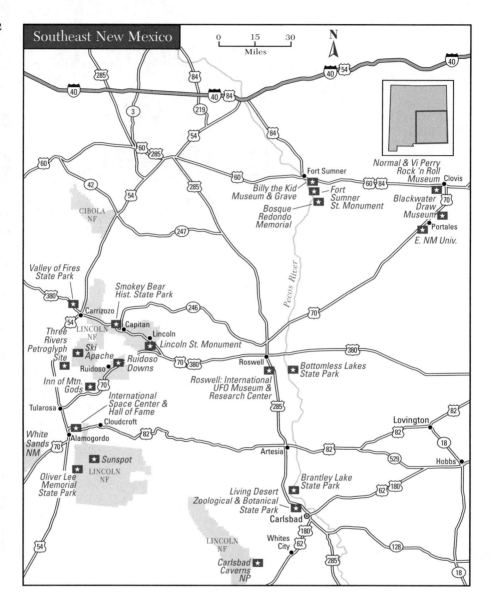

## Southeast New Mexico

0   15   30
Miles

N

# INTRODUCTION

Like a hidden canyon where exposed walls reveal the earth's turbulent formation, southeast New Mexico tells the tumultuous story of the West's natural and social history. In this accessible region, it is possible to experience within a few days the history of the West, from the prehistoric petroglyphs of Three Rivers to one of the West's most notorious battles, the Lincoln County War, starring William H. Bonney, a.k.a. Billy the Kid. In addition, southeast New Mexico displays the beginnings of the Atomic Age at the Trinity Site and the visual record of space travel at the New Mexico Museum of Space History in Alamogordo. Along the way are enduring legends and unsolved mysteries, agricultural festivals, and Apache ceremonials, all highlighted by eye-popping natural beauty.

Entering southeast New Mexico off I-25 south of Socorro and heading east, the visitor traverses the Valley of Fires State Park, a glistening black rock landscape, known as *malpais* (badlands), created by a lava flow as recently as 1,000 to 1,500 years ago. The landscape is relieved by the 10-foot-high yucca stalks.

As microcosms of evolution, critters living on the black lava flows have evolved to blend in, as creatures that dwell in the White Sands, such as the earless lizard, have evolved to white.

A user-friendly, well-maintained road system links towns and sites efficiently while granting the traveler continuous access to the area's varied natural beauty. Getting on and off the more traveled highways onto two-lane and scenic byways is easy.

As in other areas of New Mexico, it is always wise to be aware of rapid changes in weather, particularly afternoon thunderstorms that may cause flash floods. Temperatures may vary by as much as 40 degrees from day to night, so it is advisable to dress in layers and travel with warm jackets and rainwear, even if the sun is shining and the thermometer reads 80 when you set out. Good hiking boots or sturdy walking shoes are essential. Sunscreen, ample water, and a solid spare tire with proper installation tools are a must.

In this region, the mysterious vastness of the White Sands National Monument and the World Heritage Site of Carlsbad Caverns, with its fantastic crystal formations, coexists with the stomping grounds of the West's most notorious outlaw, Billy the Kid. Vibrant Apache initiation ceremonials still take place in Mescalero, and the *acequias* (irrigation ditches) hand dug by pioneers, still flow with water from 12,000-foot Sierra Blanca through the streets of Tularosa's historic district.

Memories are long here, and it is possible to run into Lincoln County old-timers who grew up hearing versions of the Lincoln County War and its participants that never appeared in history books. To many natives, Billy the Kid is regarded as more of a likeable Robin Hood than a violent thug. Questions about "the Kid" still evoke passionate debate: Did he really kill one man for each of his 21 years? Or was he simply doing what was just, at least according to the "law west of the Pecos," avenging the honor of his comrades, resulting in no more than three murders by his own hand?

The disappearance of attorney Albert Fountain and his son Henry in the White Sands more than a century ago, to this day New Mexico's leading "unsolved mystery," still evokes strong opinions about "who done it" among locals. And somewhere out there, supposedly, is a cache of Spanish gold waiting to be discovered.

THE SOUND OF RUNNING WATER IS EVERYWHERE, AS IT FLOWS THROUGH HAND-DUG ACEQUIAS (DITCHES) IN HISTORIC TULAROSA.

ANOTHER THEFT OF BILLY THE KID'S GRAVESTONE IN FORT SUMNER SEEMS UNLIKELY.

In addition, southeast New Mexico beckons with family fun, with downhill skiing at Ski Apache, ice skating, cross-country skiing and tubing in Cloudcroft, picnicking and "sledding" the dunes at White Sands National Monument, and camping, fishing, and hiking in the Lincoln National Forest. Other highlights include Smokey Bear Historical Park in Capitan and Alamogordo's Kid's Kingdom with the Toy Train Depot and the Southwest's first zoo, as well as the comprehensive New Mexico Museum of Space History. Warm-weather bat flights out of Carlsbad Caverns are another family favorite.

The forested Mescalero Apache Reservation, home of the elegant yet comfortable Inn of the Mountain Gods, with its Las Vegas–style casino, champion golf course, upscale dining and terrific buffet, is but a fraction of the land formerly occupied by this nomadic tribe of hunters and warriors. Today, efforts are under way to preserve, record, and teach the Apache language and cultures.

For those intrigued by the phenomenon of UFOs, Roswell is the capital of speculation about extraterrestrial life, and Fourth of July weekend is the great gathering of thousands intrigued by UFOs, many in costume.

As the area is large, when navigating or planning your tour, it may be best to think of it in three separate, broadly defined areas: Billy's Stomping Grounds, Cavern Country, and Oil Patch Country. Descriptions of each follow.

The *Green Space* listing is found near the end of the chapter, before the *Special Events* calendar.

Whether or not you believe in UFOs, and whether or not you believe Sheriff Pat Garrett really shot and killed Billy the Kid in cold blood one night in 1881 at Pete Maxwell's ranch, and that Billy actually is the individual interred in Fort Sumner, one thing is sure: in southeast New Mexico you will encounter both the grand beauty and great legends of the American West.

# BILLY'S STOMPING GROUNDS

## CAPITAN, FORT SUMNER, LINCOLN, CARRIZOZO, TULAROSA, ALAMOGORDO, RUIDOSO, ROSWELL, CLOUDCROFT, CLOVIS

Where else can you time-travel between the eras of Billy the Kid and the Roswell crash of 1947? Only here. There is a relaxed pace and lots of space between attractions, which you will need as there are so many interesting sights, and so much information, to absorb. It is hot and dry year-round, with few exceptions, such as the historic district known as the "49 blocks" of Tularosa. The mountains of Mescalero, Ruidoso, and Cloudcroft also provide a refreshing break from the desert. Rich in history and natural marvels, this part of New Mexico is an essential tour for the dedicated roadmeister.

**GUIDANCE Alamogordo Chamber of Commerce** (575-437-6120; www.alamogordo.com), 1301 N. White Sands Blvd., Alamogordo.

**Capitan Chamber of Commerce** (575-354-2748; www.villageofcapitan.com; www.smokeybearpark.com), 118 Smokey Bear Blvd., Capitan.

**Carrizozo Chamber of Commerce** (575-648-2732; www.townofcarrizozo.org), P.O. Box 567, 401 Eighth St., Carrizozo 88301.

**Cloudcroft Chamber of Commerce** (575-682-2733; www.cloudcroft.net), 1001 James Canyon Hwy., Cloudcroft.

**Clovis/Curry County Chamber of Commerce** (575-763-3435; www.clovis nm.org), 105 E. Grand, St., Clovis.

**Fort Sumner/DeBaca County Chamber of Commerce** (575-355-7705; www.ftsumnerchamber.com), 707 N. Fourth St., Fort Sumner.

**Roswell Chamber of Commerce** (575-623-5695; www.roswellnm.com), 131 W. Second St., Roswell.

**Roswell Visitor Bureau** (575-624-6863), 912 N. Main, Roswell.

**Ruidoso Valley Chamber of Commerce/Visitor Center** (575-257-7395; www.ruidosonow.com), 720 Sudderth Dr., Ruidoso.

**GETTING THERE** To get to southeast New Mexico, take US 380 east off I-25 at San Antonio, 13 miles south of Socorro. Continue east on US 380 through Carrizozo to Capitan and Lincoln and on to the Hondo Valley to Roswell; or south on US 54/70 past Three Rivers into Tularosa, Alamogordo, and White Sands. From Tularosa, follow US 70 north to Mescalero, Ruidoso, and San Patricio, then east to Roswell. From Roswell, go south on US 285 through Artesia to Carlsbad.

**MEDICAL EMERGENCY De Baca Family Practice Clinic** (575-355-2414), 546 N. 10th St., Fort Sumner.

**Eastern New Mexico Medical Center** (575-622-8170), 405 W. Country Club Rd., Roswell.

**Gerald Champion Regional Medical Center** (575-439-6100), 2669 N. Scenic Dr., Alamogordo.

**Lincoln County Medical Center** (575-257-8200), 211 Sudderth Dr., Ruidoso.

**Plains Regional Medical Center** (575-769-2141), 2100 Martin Luther King Jr. Blvd., Clovis.

**Presbyterian Healthcare Services Carrizozo Healthcare Center** (575-648-2317), 710 Ave. E, Carrizozo.

**Presbyterian Healthcare Services Capitan Healthcare Clinic** (575-354-0057), 330 Smokey Bear Blvd., Capitan.

**Sacramento Mountain Medical Center** (Presbyterian Medical Services) (575-682-2542), 74 James Canyon Hwy., Cloudcroft.

## To See

**TOWNS Alamogordo** lies at the junction of US 54/70 and US 82. The home of Holloman Air Force Base and one of the region's larger towns, with a variety of restaurants, chain motels, and a shopping mall, Alamogordo makes a good overnight stop or a base for exploring White Sands. Here find New Mexico International Space Museum, IMAX Theater, and children's activities, as well as the Flickinger Center for the Performing Arts.

**Capitan**, where US 380 meets NM 246 and NM 48, makes an attractive lunch stop where kids will love the Smokey Bear Restaurant, and grown-ups can dine splendidly in the Greenhouse across the street, either before or after a tour of the Smokey Bear Historical Park.

**Carrizozo**, at the junction of US 380 and US 54, at the gateway to the Valley of Fires State Park, has a homegrown art scene and cafés worth checking out. A drive around the streets surrounding downtown reveals a growing number of updated homes. The "Burro Trail" reveals colorful sculptures perched on rooftops and peering around corners.

**Cloudcroft.** Twenty-six miles east of Alamogordo on US 82, is high in the Sacramento Mountains at 9,100 feet. Originally founded as a railroad town, early on it became a cool vacation escape for El Pasoans. With its superb Lodge at Cloudcroft, unique shops, and galleries on Burro St., a plethora of B&Bs and other

PLAY "FIND THE BURRO" IN THE CROSSROADS TOWN OF CARRIZOZO, WHICH HAS SPROUTED A FEW INTERESTING GALLERIES AND CAFÉS.

accommodations, tiny Cloudcroft is a the perfect base for hiking the Lincoln National Forest and enjoying winter snow sports or a cool getaway in the summer.

**Clovis**, 67 miles east of Fort Sumner on US 60, named for the French king who converted to Christianity, has roots deep in railroading and agriculture. It is today a superb place for antiquing and for appreciating Pueblo Deco architecture and rock-and-roll history. Joe's Boots is a well-stocked warehouse of discounted cowboy boots, hats, western regalia, and décor. The home of Cannon Air Force Base, Clovis has ample modern amenities, shopping malls, and motels.

**Fort Sumner**, 41 miles southeast of Santa Rosa on US 84, holds the legendary gravesite of Billy the Kid. The pleasant little town, which feels as if it has stepped back in time, also has museums and shopping opportunities for Kid souvenirs and memorabilia. Fort Sumner State Monument, where Navajo and Apache people were confined during the 1860s, with the Bosque Redondo Memorial to that epoch is sited here.

**Lincoln**, 46 miles southeast of Carrizozo on US 380, is the now-quiet, well-preserved site of the Lincoln County War, essentially a rivalry between mercantile factions that indelibly marked New Mexico and western history. Step into that history here at the Lincoln County Courthouse, where Billy the Kid slipped through handcuffs to make his daring escape, and learn the entire story, which is well documented at the Lincoln State Monument museum.

**Roswell**, at the crossroads of US 285, US 70, and US 380, a major stop on the Goodnight-Loving and Chisum cattle trails of the Old West, has reinvented itself several times. After losing Walker Air Force Base in 1967, the town diversified into a thriving hub of business, education, and tourism. Dairies replaced many cattle operations, and the old downtown is filled with UFO museums and shops marketing UFO-themed curiosities and trinkets. Best of all, the Roswell Museum exhibits a must-see collection of Southwestern artists, in particular Roswell native Peter Hurd and his wife, Henriette Wyeth, whose landscapes and portraits of their Hondo Valley neighbors are seldom seen elsewhere.

**Ruidoso**, 32 miles northeast of Tularosa on US 70, famous for Ruidoso Downs, home of the country's richest Quarter horse race, and a bustling community filled with shops, restaurants, and condominiums. In addition to tourists, the town, whose name translates to "noisy water," for the stream, which runs through town, attracts retirees and vacation homeowners. There's plenty to do here, with abundant golfing, arts activities, hiking, shopping, horseback riding, and fishing opportunities.

IF ONLY THE FORTIFIED WALLS OF LINCOLN'S TORREON COULD SPEAK.

**Tularosa**, at the junction of US 54 and US 70, is as charming an oasis as exists in New Mexico. Giant pomegranates, poplars, and sycamores sink deep roots into the ditch banks that run throughout the historic district. This district, known as "the 49," was the original town site established by 19th-century pioneers who moved here from Mesilla after their farmlands were flooded. Following the Civil War, Union soldiers of the California Column settled here, married local women, and built homes, many of which have been restored. The variety of vernacular architecture is well worth a stroll. Tularosa has a variety of eateries but lacks lodgings.

**GHOST TOWNS White Oaks.** Three miles north of Carrizozo on US 54, 9 miles east on NM 349. A full-fledged ghost town, the quiet remains of an 1880s gold mining boomtown has a historic cemetery, the School House Museum and Miners Museum that are catch as catch can for being open, and the No Scum

Allowed Saloon, the place most likely to be open, with a shuttle that runs to Carrizozo. The town has been for some time experiencing a slow-motion revival, with artists occupying the old houses.

### HISTORIC LANDMARKS, PLACES, AND SITES ✍ **Alameda Park Zoo**

(575-439-4290), 1321 N. White Sands Blvd., Alamogordo. Open Wed.–Sun. noon–5. Closed Christmas and New Year's Day. Established in 1898, this is the oldest zoo in the Southwest, with 300 animals of 90 species. $2.20 adults and children over age 12, $1.10 seniors, children under age 12, under age 3 free.

**Blackdom** (no phone), 18 miles south of Roswell, 8 miles west of Dexter. This all-black homesteading town founded in 1911 by 20 families was led by Francis Marion Boyer, who walked from Georgia to New Mexico, hoping to establish a self-sustaining community. Blackdom was abandoned in the 1920s. Very little remains on the site. Free.

**Bosque Redondo Memorial at Fort Sumner State Monument** (575-355-2573), 3 miles east of Fort Sumner, NM 60/84, 3.5 miles south on Billy the Kid Rd. Open daily 8:30–4:30. Closed Tues. and major holidays. This moving memorial commemorates and honors Navajo and Apache forced from their homelands in 1864. Cultural and historic programs are presented throughout the year. A new museum designed by Navajo architect David Sloan and an interpretive trail cast light on this tragic period in U.S. history. $3 adults, children age 16 and under free, Sun. free to New Mexico residents with ID, Wed. free to New Mexico seniors with ID.

THE MONUMENT AT BOSQUE REDONDO COMMEMORATES THE LONG WALK OF THE NAVAJO PEOPLE.

**Fort Stanton State Monument** (no phone; info@fortstanton.org; www
.museumofnewmexico.org). 104 Kit Carson Rd., Fort Stanton. East on US 380
from Capitan, right on NM 220. Check for hours. Established in 1855, abandoned during the Civil War, and reoccupied after the Civil War by Kit Carson,
this was the base of the Buffalo Soldiers of the Ninth Cavalry. After it was
decommissioned in 1896, it served as a TB hospital, later on, it was an intern-
ment camp for WWII German POWs and Japanese. A Merchant Marine cemetery is on the site. Living history programs during the summer months. $5.

**Goodnight Loving Trail** (no phone). Originally spanning 2,000 miles between
Texas and Wyoming, this cattle trail was blazed in 1866 by Charles Goodnight
and Oliver Loving. The New Mexico portion follows the Pecos River to Fort
Sumner.

♪ **Smokey Bear Historical Park** (575-354-2748), 118 Smokey Bear Blvd.,
Capitan. Open daily 9–5. Closed Thanksgiving, Christmas, and New Year's Day.
Opened in 1979 in honor of the bear cub found with burned paws after a disas-
trous 1950 forest fire in the Capitan Mountains, which became the symbol of
forest fire prevention. After living at the National Zoo in Washington, DC,
Smokey was returned to his home and buried here. Presentations and exhibits
on ecology, forest health, and fire prevention, plus a playground, picnic area, and
the original Capitan train depot highlight the park. Smokey Bear Days are held
the first weekend in May. $2 adults $1 children, under age 6 free.

**Three Rivers Petroglyph National Recreation Site** (575-585-3457), 28 miles
south of Carrizozo off US 54. East 5 miles from US 54 at Three Rivers on
County Road B30. Open daily April–Oct. 8–7, Oct.–Apr. 8–5. Closed Christmas.
The mystery of this place is best perceived during the fall, when you are most
likely to have it to yourself. The half-mile gently inclining trail contains outstanding examples of 21,000 petroglyphs, or rock carvings, carved by the vanished
Mogollon people 1,000 years ago. Another short trail leads to a partially excavated prehistoric village. Caution: Stay
on the path as rattlesnakes really do
live here—beware. $5 per vehicle.

ROCK ART IS EVERYWHERE AT THE THREE
RIVERS PETROGLYPH SITE.

♪ **Toy Train Depot** (575-437-2855),
1991 N. White Sands Blvd., Alamogordo. Open Wed.–Sun. noon–4:30.
Closed Christmas and New Year's
Day. Ride the toy train 2.5 miles
around Alameda Park (departures
every 30 minutes) and visit the
century-old depot with a gift and
model train shop. More than 1,200
miles of model train track and toy
trains on display, plus historic railroad
artifacts to intrigue train buffs. Adjacent Kid's Kingdom Park is a great
place for children to play and let off

LITTLE ONES LOVE THE TOY TRAIN DEPOT AND TRAINRIDE IN ALAMOGORDO.

steam. Admission $4; train rides $4. Bargain rate is $6 for both museum and train ride. Age 3 and under free.

**Trinity Site** (575-678-1134)**,** 12 miles east of San Antonio on US 380, 5 miles south through Stallion Range Center. Open the first Sat. in Apr. and Oct. only, 8–2. At the north end of White Sands Missile Range is ground zero, where the first atomic bomb was detonated on July 16, 1945. Free.

THE SITE OF THE FIRST ATOM BOMB DETONATION IS OPEN TO THE PUBLIC TWICE A YEAR.

**Tularosa Basin Historical Museum** (575-434-4438), 1301 N. White Sands Blvd., Alamogordo. The joys of the local on display here, right next to the visitors center, plus research center and photo archive. Mon.–Fri. 10–4 Sat. 10–3, Sun.1–4. Free.

**MUSEUMS** ⚘ **Billy the Kid Museum** (575-355-2380), 1435 E. Sumner Ave., Fort Sumner. Open May 15–Sept. daily 8:30–5, Oct.–May 15 Mon.–Sat. 8:30–5, closed Sun. Learn about the Old West, including a variety of Billy the Kid memorabilia. $5 adults, $4 seniors age 62+, $3 children ages 7–15, under age 6 free.

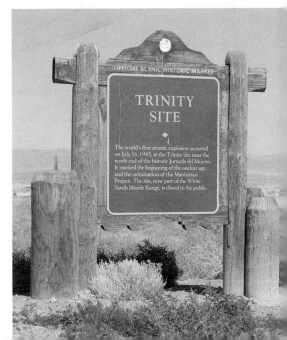

**Carrizozo Heritage Museum** (575-648-1105), 103 12th St., Carrizozo. Open Thurs.–Sat. 10–2. March–Dec. Closed Sun.–Wed., major holidays. Emphasis here is on the town's railroad history and local ranching. Free.

⚓ **Clovis Depot Model Train Museum** (575-762-0066), 221 W. First St., Clovis. Open Wed.–Sun. noon–5. Closed major holidays and February and September. Set in restored Clovis Santa Fe Passenger Depot, with nine working model train layouts and displays of U.S. and British toy trains, this is a great place to share fun between the generations. From the second floor, you have a bird's-eye view of the working Burlington Northern train yard below. $4 adults, $2 seniors, $3 children.

⚓ **Hubbard Museum of the American West** (575-378-4142; www.hubbard museum.org), 26301 Hwy. 70 W. Ruidoso Downs. Open daily 9–4:30. Closed Thanksgiving and Christmas. An affiliate of the Smithsonian Institution. Collection of over 10,000 western items. Exhibits of western and cowboy artifacts, saddles, wagons, Pony Express rig, Kid's Corral, and the Anne C. Stradling collection of antiques, horse equipment, and memorabilia. Includes the Racehorse Hall of Fame, with exhibits dedicated to Triple Crown Champions, All American Futurity winners, women in racing, as well as memorabilia from world champions. $6 adults, $5 seniors and military, $2 children ages 6–16, under age 6 free.

⚓ **International UFO Museum & Research Center** (800-822-3545), 114 N. Main St., Roswell. Open daily 9–5. Closed Thanksgiving, Christmas, and New Year's Day. Expanded hours during Roswell UFO Festival, first week of July. Find in this vast warehouselike space the Roswell Incident Timeline, eyewitness testimonies, photographs, maps, and newspaper and radio reports that endeavor to give a complete account of the purported UFO incident that occurred here in July 1947. This center also contains the largest and most comprehensive collection of UFO-related information in the world, as well as records of those who have experienced sightings, abductions, or contact. $5 adults, $3 military and seniors, $2 children ages 5–15, age 4 and under free.

**Lincoln State Monument** (575-653-4372), 12 miles east of Capitan on US 380, Lincoln. Open daily 8:30–4:30. Old Lincoln Town's main street—actually, its only street—is lined with 11 buildings of stone and adobe that make up this National Historic Landmark. Here history seems very close at hand, because this site looks as it did during the heyday of Billy the Kid and Pat Garrett, and just as it did when the Lincoln County War raged during 1878–1881. The Old Lincoln County Courthouse Museum gives the context of the era, with information on Hispanic settlers, Buffalo soldiers, major players in the Lincoln County War, and the politics of the time. $5 ticket includes four museums open Nov.–Mar. and six museums open Apr.–Oct., under age 16 free. Sun. free to New Mexico residents, Wed. free to New Mexico seniors.

⚓ **New Mexico Museum of Space History** (575-437-2840). 3198 NM 2001, Alamogordo. Open daily 9–5. Closed Thanksgiving and Christmas. Five stories of space history include artifacts, models, and exhibits celebrating space voyage. The Stapp Air and Space Park displays actual rockets; the International Space Hall of Fame and the Tombaugh IMAX Dome Theater (closed Mon.) and

THE FIGURE OF SUSAN MCSWEEN RECALLS THE LINCOLN COUNTY WAR.

Planetarium create a total immersion experience intriguing to children and adults. $6 adults, $5 seniors and military, $4 children ages 4–12, under age 4 free.

✐ **Old Fort Sumner Museum** (575-355-2942), adjacent to Billy the Kid's grave, Billy the Kid Drive, 7 miles southeast of Fort Sumner on NM 272. Historical items from the 1880s give depth to the Billy the Kid era. Open daily 8:30–5, Wed.–Thurs. 9–5. $3.50 adults, $2.50 children, under age 7 free.

**Roswell Museum and Art Center** (575-624-6744), 100 W. 11th St., Roswell. Open Mon.–Sat. 9–5; Sun., holidays 1–5. Closed Thanksgiving, Christmas, New Year's Day. The term "regional" in no way diminishes the fine exhibits of contemporary and classic artists of the West shown here. Permanent exhibits of native Peter Hurd and wife Henriette Wyeth are staggering, while works of such renowned artists as Fritz Scholder

AIRCRAFT AND SPACE EXPLORATION ENTHUSIASTS WILL RAVE OVER THE ALAMOGORDO NEW MEXICO MUSEUM OF SPACE HISTORY DEDICATED TO THEIR PASSION.

and Georgia O'Keeffe appear regularly. The Goddard Rocket Museum is included. Free.

**Robert H. Goddard Planetarium** (575-624-6744), 912 N. Main, Roswell, has science exhibits, including Goddard's rockets. Open Tues.–Sat. 1:30–5, Fri. until 7:30. Free. Planetarium and laser light shows extra.

**NATURAL WONDERS Sierra Blanca.** At just under 12,000 feet, this imposing mountain is a snow-capped beacon throughout most of southeast New Mexico.

**White Sands National Monument** (575-479-6124 www.nps.gov/whsa), 19955 US 70, 15 miles west of Alamogordo on US 70. Closed Christmas Day. Open daily Memorial Day–Sept. 2, 7 AM–9 PM; winter hours 7–sunset. Dunes Drive is 17 paved miles of the 300 miles of pure white gypsum dunes. This place's vastness and beauty make it seem like a moonscape here on Earth. You can get out of the car, hike, and play in the dunes. Reservations required for monthly Full Moon Nights and accompanying programs. The gift shop is vast, and the bookstore has a grand selection of Southwest and nature reading. $3 per person over age 15; under age 15 free. Ticket good for seven days.

WHITE SANDS, A MAGICAL PLACE ANY TIME OF YEAR.

WORLD'S LARGEST PISTACHIO, AT MCGINN'S PISTACHIO RANCH IN ALAMO-GORDO, IS ONE FANTASTIC PHOTO OP.

**SCENIC DRIVES Billy the Kid National Scenic Byway** (575-378-5318; www.billybyway.com). Follows NM 48; NM 220; US 70/380 for 84.2 miles. The Billy the Kid National Scenic Byway Visitors Center, next to the Hubbard Museum of the American West in Ruidoso Downs, is the best place to orient the trip and make the most of it with maps and brochures. The byway links Ruidoso, Lincoln, Fort Stanton, and the pleasant green Hondo Valley. The entire area was Billy's stomping ground.

**Sunspot Scenic Byway** (800-733-6396, ext. 24371), http://byways.org/explore/byways/2093. Eighteen miles on NM 6563 that wind through the tall pines of the Lincoln National Forest along the front rim of the Sacramento Mountains, south of Cloudcroft, leading to the National Solar Observatory on Sacramento Peak. From here view the Tularosa Basin and White Sands National Monument, as well as the space shuttle spaceport.

**WINERIES Arena Blanca Winery** (575-437-0602), 7320 U.S. 54 Expressway, Alamogordo, 6 miles north of Alamogordo on US 54. In combination with McGinn's Country Store at the Pistachio Tree Ranch, Arena Blanca offers free wine tastings plus free pistachio samples. Located on a 111-acre pistachio orchard.

**Tularosa Vineyards** (575-585-2260), 2 miles north of Tularosa on US 54 at 23 Coyote Canyon Rd. Open Mon.–Sat. 9–5, Sun. 12–5. Taste award-winning wines made from grapes specially acclimated to New Mexico. This winery specializes in premium reds and highly drinkable whites and blushes. Tours by appointment. Please call ahead if you plan to visit.

## To Do

**BICYCLING AND WALKING Spring River Hike & Bike Trail** (575-624-6720), Spring River Park, 1101 W. Fourth St., Roswell, offers 5.5 miles of paved, gentle, and scenic hiking and biking.

**BIRDING** See the state parks under *Green Space*.

**BOATING** See the state parks under *Green Space*.

**FISHING Bonito Lake.** Take a left off NM 48 onto NM 37, 1.5 miles to "Y," then left to Bonito Dam to a man-made lake. Well stocked during fishing season, with easy to moderate hiking trails and camping areas. Free.

**Lake Van** is 15 miles southeast of Roswell on NM 256/NM 2, in the hamlet of Dexter. Cool, pleasant Lake Van has lazy fishing, some camping, and swimming, or just picnicking. Free.

**Rio Peñasco** (505-687-3352), 37 miles east of Cloudcroft on US 82 is the south-ernmost spring creek in United States.

**GOLF Clovis Municipal Golf Course** (575-769-7871), 1200 N. Norris St., Clovis. nine-hole public course. Very affordable.

**Desert Lakes Golf Course** (575-437-0290), south end of Alamogordo on US 54. Open year-round. This is an attractive suburban municipal course in the Sacramento foothills with elevated greens and water hazards. Very affordable.

**Inn of the Mountain Gods** (800-446-2963), Carrizo Canyon Rd., Mescalero. Elegant 18-hole public course. $40–55.

**The Links at Sierra Blanca** (575-258-5330), 105 Sierra Blanca Dr., Ruidoso Downs. Open year-round, weather permitting. This challenging, highly rated 18-hole spikeless Scottish-style course was designed by PGA Seniors Tour player Jim Colbert. $35–80.

**The Lodge at Cloudcroft** (575-682-2089), 1 Corona Pl., Cloudcroft. Open Mar.–Oct. High-altitude, mountain bluegrass fairways and Scottish rules of play make a memorable nine holes. $14–30.

**HIKING Dog Canyon National Recreational Trail** (575-437-8284), Oliver Lee Memorial State Park. A 5.5-mile strenuous hike, with panoramic views of Tularosa Basin, Lincoln National Forest, and White Sands, was an ancient Native American Trail. The trail rises about 3,100 feet. $6.

**Sacramento Rim National Recreation Trail**, south of Cloudcroft. Follows rim of Sacramento Mountains 14 miles. Moderate hike. Sprawling views of Tularosa Basin 5,000 feet below.

**Trestle Area Loop Trails (Cloud-Climbing Rail Trail)** (575-434-7200). The Rails-to-Trails Association has created all levels of hiking paths out of the overgrown railroad beds out of use since trains toted logs out of the Sacramento Mountains last, in 1947.

**HORSE RACING Ruidoso Downs Race Track and Casino** (575-378-4431), 2 miles north of Ruidoso on US 70. Open Memorial Day–Labor Day. This track has the reputation as top Quarter horse racetrack in United States, and the richest Quarter horse race, the All American Futurity, where instant millionaires are made, runs Labor Day Weekend.

**HORSEBACK RIDING Chippeway Riding Stables** (800-471-2384 or 575-682-2565), 602 Cox Canyon Hwy., Cloudcroft. Call for prices and hours.

THE LODGE AT CLOUDCROFT IS A FAVORITE SMALL INN, WITH AN EXCELLENT RESTAU-
RANT AND GOLF COURSE.

**ICE SKATING James Sewell Ice Rink** (575-682-4585), Zenith Park, downtown Cloudcroft. Open daily during the season, weather permitting. Skate rentals, and later on warm up with hot cocoa by the inside fireplace.

**MOUNTAIN BIKING Rim Trail** (575-682-1229), Cloudcroft. Access this
steep, difficult 13.5-mile trail, T105, which parallels Sunspot Scenic Byway part
of the way for views of the Tularosa Basin. Visit Altitudes, the local mountain
bike shop, for detailed trail maps and to explore the possibilities.

**SNOW SPORTS Ski Apache** (575-336-4356 or 575-464-3600), 6 miles north
of Ruidoso on NM 48. Left on Ski Run Rd. Owned and operated by the Mescalero Apache Tribe on the Lincoln National Forest; the stated goal is to
"provide the best ski experience for all ages and abilities." Both skiers and snowboarders of all levels find terrain variety on 55 trails served by 11 lifts. Lines are
rare; elevations between 9,600 and 11,500 feet provide abundant snow that
makes for a 180-inch annual average. Free lift ticket for a first-timer with a lesson purchase; children's programs, rentals, and lessons. Moderate.

*✂* **Ski Cloudcroft** (575-682-2333), 1 Corona Pl., Cloudcroft. With 21 trails at all
levels, three lifts, tubing, snowboarding, and a ski school on 68 acres at 9,000
feet, this tiny area could be just right for the whole family. $17–35.

*✂* **Triple M Snowplay Area** (575-682-2205), south of Cloudcroft on Sunspot
Scenic Byway, NM 6563. Snowmobile rentals, tubing with a lift.

## Lodging

### BED & BREAKFASTS, INNS, AND MOTELS

&. **Casa de Patrón B&B Inn** (575-653-4676), US 380, Midtown Lincoln. The original home of Juan Patrón, a legend in the New Mexico territory in the late 1800s. The inn is made up of four separate buildings. The traditional adobe-style main historic house, built around 1860, includes three rooms with an extensive collection of antique washboards. The Old Trail House has two bedrooms rooms plus a conference room, where the full, delicious breakfast is served daily. Two casitas are available and are especially comfortable for families. $82–112.

♂ &. **Ellis Store Country Inn** (575-653-4609), 1435 Calle La Placita, US 380 at Mile Marker 98, Lincoln. To become enveloped in the charm of the past, Ellis Store Country Inn, where Billy the Kid was held captive for two weeks during the Lincoln County War in the late 1800s, cannot be beat. This inn is reputedly the oldest building in Old Lincoln Town. It is located in the Rio Bonito Valley and has been in operation since the mid-1800s. The adobe Main House, built in the 1850s, and the Mill House, built in the 1880s, hold eight guest rooms, filled with antiques, wood-burning stoves, and handmade quilts. The Ellis Store restaurant, Isaac's Table, features an extensive wine list and serves dinner by prearrangement. Innkeepers are David and Jinny Vigil, one of New Mexico's finest chefs. $89–129. Weddings!

**Fite Ranch B&B** (575-838-0958; www.fiteranchbedandbreakfast.com), 7.5 miles east of San Antonio exit off I-25 on US 380. The Fite Ranch B&B is located on a working ranch that has been in existence since the 1930s. In 2002, ranchers Dewey and Linda Brown purchased it from original owner Evelyn Fite and the place is now run with love and care by their family. A home-cooked full and filling breakfast is served every day. The B&B is furnished with antique western décor with a touch of the Southwest. Each of the five lodgings includes at least one bedroom, a kitchen, a personal living area, and a private bath. The ranch borders the Bosque del Apache National Wildlife Refuge and is a favorite of birders. Weekly and monthly rates available. Two-night minimum. $110.

&. **Smokey Bear Motel** (575-354-2253), 316 Smokey Bear Blvd., Capitan. The convenient Smokey Bear Motel has been operating here for 40 years in this, the final resting place of the original Smokey Bear. The clean, comfortable ersatz-rustic motel has some rooms that include refrigerator and microwave. The Smokey Bear Restaurant, with vintage photos of Smokey, on the premises serves hearty breakfast, lunch, and dinner, with such specials as chicken-fried steak and beef stew seven days a week. The motel is located 13 miles from Ski Apache. RV parking, too. No pets, unfortunately. $60

**Wortley Hotel** (575-653-4300), 585 Calle La Placita, Lincoln. So much fun! "No Guests Gunned Down in Over 100 Years" is the motto here in this 1874 creaky adobe building formerly owned by Sheriff Pat Garrett. Western rusticity and a total immersion in the Wild West that was Lincoln County. History comes alive and lives on here. Complimentary breakfast included. $94. (If you can't stay the night, at least try to sit down for a meal. Breakfast, lunch Wed.–Sun. Breakfast served all day Sun.

**LODGES AND RANCHES Burnt Well Guest Ranch** (575-347-2668; www.burntwellguestranch.com), 399 Chesser Rd., Roswell. Thirty-five miles southwest of Roswell. Call for exact directions. If you're looking for a "ranch vacation," this may be the place. This hacienda-style inn with Old West rustic décor has only two rooms. Three generations of the Chesser family live on the property and run a working cattle and sheep ranch. The hacienda includes an inviting covered porch, and a great room with a checkerboard table, hobbyhorse, and piano. Guests have access to a kitchenette and laundry facilities. Capacity is 10 people with some bunk beds. Guests are invited to join in the daily workings of the ranch, including cattle drives. Dutch oven suppers fixed from ranch-raised meats, old-time storytelling, and riding the range to your heart's content are all part of the deal. $250 adults, $189 children; three-night minimum Mar.–Apr. and Sept.–Oct.

**Hurd–La Rinconada Gallery and Guest Homes** (575-653-4331), 105 La Rinconada Ln., San Patricio. Twenty miles east of Ruidoso on US 70 at Mile Marker 281. The exquisite gallery and five guest homes are located on the historic and splendid Sentinel Ranch, home of the first family of American art, the Hurd-Wyeth family. Stay in the Helenita, for example, named for family friend Helen Hayes. Located among quiet rolling hills near the Rio Ruidoso River, the original ranch-hand quarters on Sentinel Ranch have become utterly romantic guest houses with modern conveniences. They are filled with antiques and designer furnishings and art created by the Hurd-Wyeth family. Each of the houses has a private patio. On the southeast corner of the family polo field is an impressive gallery of original works by members of the Hurd-Wyeth family. Rates are based on the number of people in your party, ranging from $145 for two to $355 for six; two-night minimum. Additional fees for single-night stay. Weddings!

&. **Inn of the Mountain Gods Resort and Casino** (800-545-9011 or 575-464-7777), 287 Carrizo Canyon

THE HURD FAMILY RANCH IN SAN PATRICIO IS NOW A LOVELY GUEST RANCH.

Rd., Mescalero. Four miles south of Ruidoso on NM 48. The 273-room stunning, exciting Inn of the Mountain Gods Resort and Casino is set in the picturesque Sacramento Mountains next to shimmering Lake Mescalero. Recreational activities include the Inn of the Mountain Gods Resort Championship Golf Course, a fully equipped workout facility, indoor pool, fishing, horseback riding, and sport clay shooting. Ski Apache is approximately 45 miles away. Las Vegas–style casino gaming at the resort offers everything from penny slots to high roller games. Dining options include steak-and-seafood fine dining at Wendell's, casual barbecue meals including breakfast at Apache Summit BBQ Co., the superior Gathering of Nations Buffet, and burgers, sandwiches, and beer at the casual Big Game Sports Bar and Grill. No need to leave the resort, once you

check in. Some great deals to be had here folks. For example, during Dec. 2012, $160 gets you a deluxe room plus $50 dining credit at Wendell's, Sun.–Thurs. The rooms are gorgeous, spacious and light. Rates vary dramatically, depending on weeknight versus weekend and time of year. $79–389.

**Lodge at Sierra Blanca** (373-258-5500), 107 Sierra Blanca Dr., Ruidoso. Comfortable, well-kept lodgings with a quality breakfast buffet included, kitchenettes, spacious rooms, superlative views. A top choice. $115.

⚭ **The Lodge Resort at Cloudcroft** (800-395-6343), 601 Corona Pl., Cloudcroft. The Lodge Resort & Spa is located in Cloudcroft at 9,000 feet elevation in the Sacramento Mountains, surrounded by the Lincoln National Forest. The resort offers 59 rooms and suites. The original resort

THE MESCALERO APACHE–OWNED INN OF THE MOUNTAIN GODS IS THE LAST WORD IN LAS VEGAS–STYLE LODGING.

was destroyed by fire, and the current property is said to be haunted by characters from its past, in particular a wronged maid named Rebecca. Every New Mexico governor has slept in the elegant Governor's Suite. Amenities include a heated outdoor pool, year-round sauna and outdoor hot tub, fitness room, nine-hole traditional Scottish format golf course, and hiking trails. A variety of treatments are available at the Spirit of the Mountain Spa. Rebecca's, named after the resident ghost, serves breakfast, lunch, and dinner, plus an elaborate Sunday brunch. Rebecca's Lounge, which was once owned by Al Capone, serves drinks throughout the day as well as light lunch fare. The Lodge has had several famous guests: Judy Garland, Clark Gable, and Pancho Villa. If you climb to the top of the bell tower, you can see where Clark Gable inscribed his name. In the 1930s, the resort was managed by Conrad Hilton, who was born and raised in San Antonio, New Mexico. According to reports, Hilton was familiar with The Lodge and wanted to be closer to his family while his hotel chain took off. Words cannot do this delightful and beautifully well-managed place justice. It is simply divine, one of my favorite New Mexico escapes, where you can truly make the world go away. Sit by the fire and you'll agree. My highest recommendation, whether for romance, celebration, or relaxation. It is especially lovely at Christmastime and Valentine's Day. Murder Mystery weekends are a hoot. Great deals Wed.–Sun. $117–350. Average $164.

**CABINS AND CAMPING** For camping, see the state parks listed under *Green Space*.

**Cabins at Cloudcroft** (800 248-7967 or 575-682-2396), 1000 Coyote Ave., Cloudcroft. The 16 delightful cabins at Cloudcroft are open year-round in the aspens and pines, yet still within village limits. Cabins include full kitchens, baths, and firewood, and a coin-operated laundry is on the premises. Guests may choose between a wood-burning stove or a fireplace. Propane grills and picnic areas are available during the summer months. Two night minimum; one-night stay negotiable. Small pets allowed. $75–315.

**Story Book Cabins** (888-257-2115 or 575-257-2115), 410 Main Rd., Ruidoso. Located amid the tall pines of Ruidoso's Upper Canyon along the "noisy" Ruidoso River, these "upscale rustic" cabins feature hot tubs, Jacuzzis, fully equipped kitchens, fireplaces, grills, private porches, and patios, as well as cable TV and DVD. The knotty-pine cabins have between one and six bedrooms. Secluded, yet close to in-town dining, galleries, and shops. $119–189.

## Where to Eat

**DINING OUT Can't Stop Smokin' BBQ** (575-630-0000), 418 Mechem Dr., Ruidoso. Open Tues.–Sun. 10–7. Lunch, dinner, delivery. Wow! Head over here when the big BBQ craving hits. The slow-smoked brisket, ribs, and chicken are fall-off-the-fork tender, and the place can be a tad rowdy and a lot of fun. The "secret spice" mixture is MSG- and preservative-free. Inexpensive.

**❦ Gathering of Nations Buffet** (575-464-7777), Inn of the Mountain Gods Resort and Casino, Mescalero. Open daily. Breakfast 7–10; lunch 11–3:30; dinner Sat.

4:30–10, Sun.–Thurs. 4:30–9. This is quite possibly the best, biggest, tastiest, freshest of the casino buffets. Watch out for holiday specialties, T-bone Tuesdays, and Seafood Extravaganza Wednesdays. The food, plus the warmly lit atmosphere, make it a favorite. Prices keep going up, but watch for bargain nights. Moderate.

**Martin's Capitol Cafe** (575-624-2111), 110 W. Fourth St., Roswell. Mon.–Sat. 6 AM–8:30 PM. Breakfast, lunch, dinner. Martin's has been downtown so long, it must be doing something right—and it is! Absolutely authentic, tasty New Mexican red and green chile, just hot enough to be serious, served in a warm, Mexican-style dining room. Martin's has been discovered so is usually busy. Try for the off-hours. Inexpensive.

**Memories Fine Dining** (575-437-0077), 1223 New York Ave., Alamogordo. Lunch and dinner. Mon.–Sat. 11–9. Closed Sun. Within this two-story 1906 Victorian-style, antiques-filled home may be found delectable food served in style in what must be the area's most popular, well-established "evening out" restaurant. Think pork loin in port wine sauce, fresh tuna grilled to perfection, homemade creamy mushroom soup, and house-baked rolls. Beer and wine, too. Moderate.

**Old Road Restaurant** (575-644-4674), 692 Old Road, Mescalero. Open daily. Hours may vary. Guaranteed some of the most delicious New Mexican food you will ever put in your mouth. Go for the red combination, or just the red enchiladas. Chef-owner Henry Prelo Jr. makes his chiles rellenos fresh every morning. A comfortable log cabin atmosphere with local art and stellar service. A favorite with the motorcycle set. Inexpensive.

**Rebecca's** (800-395-6343 or 575-682-2566), The Lodge, 1 Corona Pl., Cloudcroft. Serves breakfast, lunch, or a very special dinner. Classic fine dining. Try the châteaubriand for two. Famous for its deluxe Sunday brunch buffet and panoramic view of the Tularosa Valley. The finest restaurant in the area. Moderate–Expensive.

**Rockin' BZ Burgers** (575-434-2375), 3005 N. White Sands Blvd., Alamogordo. Lunch, dinner Mon.–Sun. Only one reason—and it's a swell one—to come to this formica-sterile café near the mall: the State Fair Championship–winning green chile cheeseburgers served here. They're stuffed with grilled onions, topped with Hatch green chile and Wisconsin Cheddar—delish! Inexpensive.

**Smokey Bear Restaurant** (575-354-2253), 310 Smokey Bear Blvd., Capitan. See Smokey Bear Motel listing. Inexpensive.

**Tinnie Mercantile Store & Deli** (575-622-2031), 412 W. Second St., Roswell. Church ladies and business-folk alike come to dine on the awesome fresh salads and sandwiches. No better lunch spot in town, and if you have to wait, the shop stocks many lovely gifties, from stationary to jewelry. Inexpensive.

**Tinnie Silver Dollar Restaurant & Saloon** (575-653-4177), 28842 US 70, Hondo. Twenty-eight miles east of Ruidoso on US 70. Dinner Tues.–Sat., champagne brunch Sun. 10–3. If you like elegant atmosphere, history, and ghosts with your steak, or a margarita served up at a 100-year-old bar, head for Tinnie. Classic fare, steaks, rack of lamb, roast chicken, prawns and lobster, fresh oysters, filet Oscar, beautifully served. Wine flights are a reasonable way to sample the wine list. Suites and a general store are also on the premises. Worth the drive, and the cost. Moderate–Expensive.

🍴 **Village Buttery** (575-257-9251), 2701 Sudderth Dr., Ruidoso. Voted Lincoln County's "Best Lunch" many times. Yes, there are plenty of ladies dining here, but the food goes way beyond "ladies lunch" fare. If you have only one lunch to eat in Ruidoso, you'd be wise to head here. Three house-made soups every day, delicious overstuffed sandwiches, daily comfort food specials like pot roast, roast turkey, sour cream enchiladas (priced under $10), plus a display case of luscious desserts. Dine outside on the deck in sunny weather. Inexpensive.

**Wendell's Steak & Seafood Restaurant** (575-464-7777), Inn of the Mountain Gods Casino & Resort, Mescalero. Open dinner only Mon.–Thurs. 5–9; breakfast, lunch, Fri.–Sat. 8–2, dinner 5–9; Sun. brunch 11–2, dinner 5–9. Steaks galore, with a $66 Kobe-style filet mignon in truffle sauce headlining the menu, plus pan-seared fresh halibut, New Mexico elk tenderloin in apple brandy reduction, and other delights. Expensive. The café adjacent Wendell's Lounge serves soup, burgers, sandwiches, and salads daily 11–10. Inexpensive.

**Yum Yum Donut Shop** (575-585-2529), 460 Central Ave., Tularosa. It is worth going out of your way to stop at this tiny, modest-looking café that is so much more than a doughnut shop. Although you won't want to pass up a fresh daily "wildcat paw" or maple doughnut, do not, repeat, do not miss the brisket burrito with green chile. Mrs. Abeyta, who has lunch here every day, says the brisket

is so tender she can "take her teeth out to eat it." Erratic hours, so call first. Inexpensive.

## Entertainment

**Flickinger Center for the Performing Arts** (575-437-2202), 1110 New York Ave., Alamogordo. "The Flick" is a remodeled venue for a lively season of music, theater, and dance entertainment the family can enjoy together.

**Le Cave at Le Bistro** (575-257-0132), 2800 Sudderth Dr., Ruidoso. This is a special place for a glass of wine of an evening.

**Ruidoso Downs Race Track and Casino** (575-378-4431), 1461 US 70; 2 miles north of Ruidoso on US 70. Open Memorial Day–Labor Day. Summer country music stars.

**Sacred Grounds Coffee** (575-257-2273; www.sacredgroundscoffee.net), 2825 Sudderth Dr., Ruidoso. Sun. night movie; Fri. night open mic. Breakfast, lunch Sun.–Thurs.; breakfast, lunch and dinner, Fri.–Sat. Freshly baked goodies, quiche, wraps, light meals.

**Spencer Theater for the Performing Arts** (575-336-4800), 108 Spencer Rd., Alto. Presenting a full season of outstanding theater, dance, and music Sept.–May. Headliners have included Moscow Festival Ballet, violinist Natalie MacMaster, and Mel Tormé. The theater itself, with Dale Chihuly glass décor, is worth seeing.

## Selective Shopping

**Burro Street**, Cloudcroft. Find here a worthwhile row of local craft shops, boutiques, antiques stores, galleries. You can stuff a teddy bear or get a

JOE'S BOOT SHOP IN CLOVIS STOCKS 16,000 PAIRS OF COWBOY AND COWGIRL BOOTS.

gelato, have a beer in an Old West bar or find yoga attire.

**Eagle Ranch Pistachio Groves** (575-437-3792), 7288 US 54 Expressway, Alamogordo. Open Mon.–Sat.

GET YOU A COWBOY HAT IN RUIDOSO.

8–6, Sun. 9–6. Hop on a free tour of these family-run pistachio groves, munch red and green chile–flavored nuts, shop for New Mexico gifts, and splurge on homemade pistachio ice cream.

🐾 **Joe's Boot Shop** (575-763-3764), 2600 Mabry Dr., Clovis. With 16,000 pairs of boots and 10,000 hats to choose from, why shop for western wear anyplace but Joe's? My closet is full of deeply discounted Luccheses I could not afford but for Joe's. This is one of the grandest shopping experiences you will ever know, and it is completely worth the drive to Clovis!

**Sudderth Street**, Ruidoso's premier shopping street. The place to find stylish household décor, western wear, women's clothing—at Rebekah's and Michelle's—and lunch and a cold one. (A favorite gallery and hat shop.)

# CAVERN COUNTRY

## CARLSBAD, WHITE'S CITY

What's great here are the caverns. That's the reason to come. Carlsbad Caverns are one of three World Heritage Sites in New Mexico, the others being Taos Pueblo and Chaco Canyon. You can easily spend days exploring the underground formations, sure to instill a sense of wonder in anyone who views them. It can be very hot in the summer, but it's always cool in the caverns. Bat flights and the water slide at White's City make this an excellent family vacation spot.

GUIDANCE **Carlsbad Chamber of Commerce/Convention and Visitors Bureau** (575-887-6516; www.carlsbadchamber.com), 302 S. Canal, Carlsbad.

**White's City** (575-785-2291; www.whitescity.com), 6 Carlsbad Caverns Hwy., White's City.

MEDICAL EMERGENCY **Carlsbad Medical Center** (575-887-4100), 2430 W. Pierce St., Carlsbad.

**Lea Regional Medical Center** (575-492-5000), 5419 N. Lovington Hwy., Hobbs.

## To See

TOWNS **Carlsbad**, at the junction of US 285 and US 62/180, while known for its underground caverns, has made the most of its location on the Pecos River with its annual "Christmas on the Pecos" boat rides to see the lights along the banks. Make time for a visit to the Living Desert Zoological and Botanical State Park north of the city off US 285, a showcase of flora and fauna native to the Chihuahuan Desert. Also along the Pecos, stroll 2.5 miles of winding pathways. Boating, fishing, swimming, and waterskiing are all available here.

**White's City**, 13 miles south of Carlsbad on US 62/180, White's City is at the entrance to Carlsbad Caverns National Park. Named for Jim White, the discoverer of Carlsbad Caverns, White's City also has the Million Dollar Museum, which displays antique dollhouses and such oddities as a two-headed rattlesnake.

Numerous motels, RV park, dining, water park just outside Carlsbad Caverns National Park.

**HISTORIC LANDMARKS, PLACES, AND SITES** ✍ **Living Desert Zoo and Gardens State Park** (575-885-4476; www.nmparks.com), 1504 Miehls Dr., Carlsbad, northwest end of town, off US 285. Open daily summer 8–8, winter 9–5. Closed Christmas. This marvelous indoor/outdoor attraction highlights native plants and animals of the Chihuahuan Desert. An easy 1.3-mile trail leads through desert habitat. A chief attraction is Maggie, the painting black bear. Yes, she really paints. Another is the greenhouse packed with succulents and cacti. Over 40 species of critters, including mountain lion, endangered Mexican gray wolf, bobcat, javelina, and bear, call this zoo home. $6 per vehicle.

**MUSEUMS Million Dollar Museum** (575-785-2291), 25 Carlsbad Canyon Hwy., White's City. Sixteen rooms of antique dollhouses and dolls, Victoriana, western Americana to browse and get lost in. $3 adults, $2.50 seniors, $2 children ages 6–12, under age 6 free.

**NATURAL WONDERS Carlsbad Caverns National Park** (575-785-2232), 727 Carlsbad Cavern Hwy., Carlsbad. Memorial Day weekend–Labor Day weekend daily 8–7, last entry into cave 3:30. Cave tours begin 8:30. Labor Day–Memorial Day weekend 8–5, last entry into cave 2. Cave tours begin 8:30. The "Eighth Wonder of the World." Year-round temperature of 56 degrees Fahrenheit is constant throughout this phenomenal underground display of stalactites and stalagmites that were formed drop by drop over millions of years. Over 100 limestone caves predate the dinosaurs. An elevator is available for those who prefer to ride the 750-foot descent. Ranger-guided tours available for the Hall of the White Giant, Spider Cave, and others for $8.50–20. Pet kennels are available, and portions are wheelchair accessible. The park also has over 50 miles of primitive backcountry hiking, with trailheads located along park roads. $6 adults, $3 children, under age 15 free. Entrance fee is good for three days.

**SCENIC BYWAYS Guadalupe Back Country Scenic Byway** (575-887-6544). NM 137/US 285, 30 miles. Twelve miles north of Carlsbad or 23 miles south of Artesia, enter at junction of NM 137 and US 285 near Brantley Lake State Park. Travel 30 miles to the southwest for dramatic views of the East Guadalupe Escarpment along a winding road with waterfalls, rugged limestone hills, and canyons. There are many possibilities for discovery here, with jeep trails and opportunities for hiking, caving, and mountain biking. Driving south on the byway, you encounter a sign that directs you to Sitting Bull Falls Recreation Area (open year-round, 8:30 AM to sunset, $5 per vehicle). The road descends 8 miles through winding canyons on the way to the falls. The recreation area is for day use only; stone picnic shelters with grills are available. A paved path leads from the picnic shelters to the falls; a dirt path leads up to the top of the mesa. Two hundred million years ago, in the Permian period, this area was an inland sea. Sitting Bull Falls is a small remnant of the water from this ancient time. The falls are the result of water flowing from a spring located in the canyon above. From the observation point at the end of the paved path, a 200-foot-high wall of tufa looms in front of you. It extends up the canyon for three-quarters of a mile. The creation of this lightweight, porous rock from calcium carbonate precipitating out of the water has taken hundreds of thousands of years. When plants die and fall into the water, a chemical reaction occurs and fossils are formed. This process is still ongoing at the bottom of the falls.

# OIL PATCH COUNTRY
## ARTESIA, HOBBS, LOVINGTON, PORTALES

T his is the land that oil built. Aside from ranching, the fossil fuel business is what keeps folks in beans here. Artesia displays a strong sense of itself as a community with civic roots and pride.

**GUIDANCE** **Artesia Chamber of Commerce** (575-746-2744; www.artesia chamber.com), 107 N. First St., Artesia.

**Hobbs Chamber of Commerce** (575-397-3202; www.hobbschamber.org), 400 N. Marland Blvd., Hobbs.

**Portales/Roosevelt County Chamber of Commerce** (575-356-8541; www .portales.com), 100 S. Ave. A, Portales.

**MEDICAL EMERGENCY** **Artesia General Hospital** (575-748-3333), 702 N. 13th St., Artesia.

## To See

**TOWNS** **Artesia** is located on US 285, midway between Roswell and Carlsbad. This little town built on oil refining has a restored railroad station and an excellent small museum featuring local history.

**Hobbs**, 63 miles northeast of Carlsbad on US 62/180, lies just across the Texas state line. Plenty of parks and swimming pools; fishing in Maddox Lake and Green Meadows Lake; and RV hookups, camping, and fishing in Harry McAdams Park make this friendly town a convenient stop.

**Lovington**, 44 miles east of Artesia on US 82, is the site of the Western Heritage Museum and Lea County Cowboy Hall of Fame, housed in a historic hotel building. With homesteading roots, the town boomed from oil and remains a center of an agricultural and ranching economy. Chaparral Park offers lake fishing.

**Portales**, 18 miles south of Clovis on US 70, is famous for its peanut industry. It is also the site of Eastern New Mexico University, and north of town on US 70 is the Blackwater Draw Museum, where artifacts representing the oldest habitations in North America are displayed. Also nearby is the Blackwater Draw site, where the Clovis points were unearthed in 1928, along with remains of ancient bison and mammoth.

**MUSEUMS Artesia Historical Museum & Art Center** (575-865-6262), 505 W. Richardson Ave., Artesia. Open Tues.–Fri. 9–noon and 1–5, Sat. 1–5. Closed Sun., Mon., major holidays. Exhibits of regional material culture and social history in a 1920's cobblestone-façade home. Free.

✎ **Blackwater Draw Archaeological Site & Museum** (museum 575-562-2202; site 575-356-5235; www.enmu.edu/services/museums/blackwater-draw). 42987 Hwy. 70, Portales. Museum open daily Memorial Day–Labor Day Mon.–Sat. 10–5, Sun. noon–5. Closed Mon. remainder of year. Site open Memorial Day—Labor Day 9–5 daily; Apr.–May, Sept.–October 9–5 weekends only. May be closed major holidays. Museum is 5 miles east of Portales on US 70. Site is 5 miles north of Portales on NM 467. This museum displays and explains the finds made at Blackwater Draw, recognized since 1929 as one of the most significant archaeological sites in North America due to 13,000-year-old remains of Clovis Man's era. In addition to the finely carved "fluted" stone points of Clovis Man, other weapons and tools, as well as the remains of ancient bison, mammoth, and other creatures of the Late Pleistocene era, were found preserved here. $3 adults, $2 seniors $1 children ages 6–13 and students with ID, age 5 and under free.

✎ **Western Heritage Museum & Lea County Cowboy Hall of Fame** (575-392-6730; www.nmjc.edu), 5317 Lovington Hwy., Hobbs. Closed major holidays. Open Tues.–Sat. 10–5. Located on the campus of New Mexico Junior College, this museum features exhibits of ranchers and rodeo performers while sharing history from the perspective of Indians, homesteaders, buffalo hunters, and soldiers. $3 adults, $2 seniors and students, children ages 6–18; under age 5 free.

## To Do

**BICYCLING AND WALKING Pecos River Walk** (575-887-6516; www.cityofcarlsbadnm.com/parksrecreation), Carlsbad. Six and a half miles of paved bike trails and walkways along the Pecos River are a pleasant way to explore the area.

**HIKING Rattlesnake Canyon**, Carlsbad Caverns National Park. Features a 670-foot descent into the canyon on an easy 2.2-mile hike. Trailhead #9 on Desert Loop Dr.

**MOUNTAIN BIKING Cueva Escarpment Mountain Bike Trail** (575-887-6516), Carlsbad. Fifteen miles of single-track riding at all levels of challenge await.

## Green Space

**RIVERS AND LAKES Bottomless Lakes State Park** (575-624-6058), 16 miles southeast of Roswell via US 30 and NM 409. Open year-round. Hang out among eight small lakes bordered by high red bluffs with walking trails, plus pleasant swimming, fishing, and rental paddleboats. $4 per vehicle day use; $10–18 camping.

**Brantley Lake** (575-457-2384), 16.5 miles northeast of Carlsbad via US 285 and County Road 30. Find here boating, waterskiing, and fishing, with lakeside camping on 3,800-acre Brantley Lake. $6 per vehicle day use; $18 camping.

**Oasis State Park** (575-356-5331), 6.5 miles north of Portales via NM 467. Truly an oasis in the high plains, with tall cottonwoods and a fishing pond stocked with catfish and trout. Plenty of wildlife and over 80 species of birds to spot. There's camping, easy hiking, and a playground. $6 per vehicle day use; $18 camping.

**Sumner Lake State Park** (575-355-2541). Calling all water sports lovers: powerboats, canoes, sailboats, and windsurfers abound here. This park makes a great camping base to explore nearby Billy the Kid sites, with sites for large RVs to simple tenting alongside the lake. Gently rolling juniper-covered hillsides frame the rocky shoreline. $6 per vehicle day use; $10–18 camping.

### UNIQUE ADVENTURES

**Bat Flights, Carlsbad Caverns National Park** (575-785-3012), sundown, late May–mid-Oct. Witness an awesome living swarm of thousands of bats as they leave the caverns. Amphitheater seating is available. Free.

**Dalley Windmill Collection** (800-635-8036 or 505-356-6263), 1506 S. Kilgore, Portales. Call for hours. Begun in 1981 when Bill Dalley obtained a Standard-brand windmill, this collection numbers 85 restored, working windmills from around the world, creaking and spinning on 20 acres.

**Norman and Vi Petty Rock and Roll Museum** (575-763-3435; www.petty museum.com/ 105 E. Grand Ave. Open daily Mon.–Sat. Closed 12–1 and Sun. $5. Also, check out the Norman Petty Studio. Tours by appointment. See the original 1950s recording studio where Petty produced the "Clovis sound" back in the day that made stars of Buddy Holly, Roy Orbison, and the Fireballs. It is unchanged from those days, and the studio is in perfect condition. $7.

**Sunspot Astronomy & Visitor's Center** (575-434-7190), National Solar Observatory, Sacramento Peak, Sunspot, 16 miles from Cloudcroft on NM 30, then NM 6563. Open daily Apr.–Dec. 10–6. Guided tours daily 2 during summer months. Self-guided tours sunrise–sunset the rest of the year. Fascinating interactive exhibits on the work of this telescope that tracks solar activity in the visitors center. $2.

✍ **White's City Water Park** (575-785-2294), at Carlsbad Caverns National Park. Open seasonally. This is the only resort water park in the state, with two ample pools, two spas, and two 150-foot water slides. Free to resort guests.

**MOUNTAINS AND DESERTS Lincoln National Forest** (575-434-7200), 1101 New York Ave., Alamogordo. A million acres of hiking, backpacking, trail riding, camping. A 20-mile drive goes through terrain from desert, hills, and valleys filled with orchards to high mountain meadows and peaks covered in tall evergreens. A haven for alpine sports in winter, with good cross-country skiing through the Sacramento Mountains near Cloudcroft. Many camping facilities are

---

### WILDER PLACES

**Hondo Iris Farm and Gallery** (575-653-4062), US 70 and Mile Marker 284, Hondo. Open Tues.–Fri. 10–5. Closed Sun., Mon. Perhaps not exactly wilder, but definitely off the beaten path, this exquisite display of hundreds of varieties of iris, a botanical garden of sorts, is at its height during mid–late May. Exquisite picnic site, outstanding gallery of imported clothing and home fashions, and Alice Seely's affordable, fine original silver jewelry. Free. Weddings

**Lake Lucero** (575-679-2599; www.nps.gov/whsa/planyourvisit/lake-lucero -tours.htm), White Sands National Monument. Monthly three-hour guided tour of the dry lake that is the source of the White Sands. Drive 18 miles and hike 0.75 mile to Lake Lucero. $3.

**Mescalero Apache Reservation** (575-464-4494), 16 miles east of Tularosa on US 70. A magnificent forested place in the Sierra Blanca mountains, recognized in 1874 as the Mescalero homeland, it is now home to 3,100 Native Americans. Famed for its fierce warriors, the tribe is now known for its tradition of the Apache Maidens' Puberty Rites, with dances of the Mountain Gods, celebrated in annual July 4 festivities at Inn of the Mountain Gods, Ski Apache, and St. Joseph Mission. You can find fishing in Eagle Creek Lakes, which also offer camping, and Mescalero Lake, as well as horseback riding, and the fabulous Inn of the Mountain Gods Resort, with Las Vegas–style gambling.

**Slaughter Canyon Cave** (800-967-CAVE or 800-967-2283; www.nps.gov/cave /planyourvisit/slaughter_canyon_cave_tour.htm), Carlsbad Caverns National Park, Carlsbad. Summer tours Fri.–Sun. 8:30 AM, winter tours Sat. and Sun. 8:30 AM. Strictly for the adventurous, this challenging six-hour tour explores an undeveloped cave 23 miles from the visitors center. Meet at the Visitor Center. 15 adults, 7.50 children. Children under age 6 not allowed.

located within a 4-mile radius of Cloudcroft, accessible by Highways 82, 130, 244, and 6563 in the **Sacramento Ranger District.** Contact listed number or drop by the office for maps and permits. Near Carlsbad, the **Guadalupe Ranger District** of the forest includes 285,000 acres and Sitting Bull Falls Recreation Area, open Oct.–Mar. 8–5 and Apr.–Sept. 8–6, with a 150-foot waterfall. $5 per vehicle.

**Oliver Lee Memorial State Park** (575-437-8284), 12 miles south of Alamogordo via US 54 at the western base of the Sacramento Mountains. Open year-round. Tour Oliver Lee's restored ranch headquarters and picnic, plus camping at one of 44 developed sites. $6 per vehicle day use; $18 camping.

**Valley of Fires State Park** (575-648-2241), 5 miles west of Carrizozo on US 380. The park is 426 acres, with picnic and camping areas and a playground. The nature trail has a 0.75-mile wheelchair-accessible portion. The entire Malpais, or badlands, of the lava flow covers 125 square miles. Here are archetypal, dramatic landscapes photographers will love. $6 per vehicle; $18 camping.

**WILDLIFE REFUGES** **Bitter Lake National Wildlife Refuge** (575-623-5695), Roswell. North on US 285, east on Pine Lodge Rd., 9 miles to headquarters. Open daily year-round, dawn to dusk. This Pecos River wetlands is home to over 100 species of dragonflies and damselflies, and 357 bird species visit or live here, plus some endangered species. Several short, easy hikes feature native plants and butterflies. Bike riding is available on the 8-mile gravel drive of the paved 4-mile round-trip trail. Tours available with reservations. The best viewing is available one-half hour before sunrise to one-half hour after sunset. One of my very favorite New Mexico places. Free.

## Lodging and Dining

**No Whiner Diner** (575-234-2815), 1801 S. Canal St., Carlsbad. Old-fashioned American home cooking in small-town diner style—generous portions of real food—meat loaf, chicken-fried steak—prepared and served very nicely. Inexpensive–Moderate.

**Trinity Hotel** (575-234-9891), 201 S. Canal St., Carlsbad. Skillfully renovated downtown1892 bank building with seven rooms provides an interesting alternative to chain motel lodging. In a word: class. However, a bit pricey, for Carlsbad, and the rate does not include breakfast. $149.

Chain motels are your best bet out here.

## Special Events

*April:* **Trinity Site Tour** (575-437-6120).

*May:* ♂ **Smokey Bear Days** (575-354-2748), Smokey Bear Historical Park, Capitan, first weekend, with parade, crafts marketplace, chainsaw carving, music. **Lincoln Fiber Festival** www.museumsoflincoln.com /lincoln1.html), Lincoln State Monument, Lincoln, midmonth. Textile artists, sheep-shearers, basket makers, spinners, and more.

*June:* **White Oaks Miners Day** (no phone), White Oaks, first Sat. **Mountain Blues Festival** (575-257-9535),

Ruidoso, early June. **Mountain Park Cherry Festival** (575-652-3445), High Rolls, midmonth. **Art in the Pines** (575-257-7395), Ruidoso, midmonth. Tour area artists' studios. **Old Fort Days** (575-355-2573), Fort Sumner, midmonth. Storytelling and book signing featuring Navajo literature.

*July:* **Roswell UFO Festival** (575-623-5695), Roswell, first week in July. **Art Festival**, Ruidoso. **Fourth of July Celebration** (575-464-4473), Mescalero; Apache Maidens Puberty Rites, powwow, rodeo. **Smokey Bear Stampede** (575-354-2748), Capitan, Fourth of July week; more contestants than any other U.S. amateur rodeo. **Art Loop Tour** (575-378-8273; www .artloop.org), Lincoln County, first weekend. Tour of diverse artists' studios for some of the most original jewelry, pottery, fiber art, and fine art to be seen anywhere. **Bluegrass Festival** (575-746-9619), Weed.

*August:* **Lincoln County Fair** (575-648-2311), Smokey Bear Historical Park, Capitan, second week. **Old Lincoln Days**, **Billy the Kid Pageant** (575-653-4372), Lincoln Pony Express Race, Capitan Gap to White Oaks. **Lea County Fair and Rodeo** (575-396-4554), largest county fair in state. ✐ **Bat Flight Breakfast**

(575-785-2232), Carlsbad Caverns, second Thurs. in Aug.

*September:* **Chile and Cheese Festival** (575-623-5695), Roswell. **All American Futurity** (575-378-4431), Ruidoso Downs, the world's richest quarter-horse race. **White Sands Star Party** (575-679-3599), White Sands. **Clovis Music Festival** (575-763-3435), Clovis. Rock and roll like back in the day.

*October:* **Lincoln County Cowboy Symposium** (575-378-4431), Glencoe. Second weekend in Oct. Chuckwagon cook-off, cowboy poetry, swing dancing, western art, crafts, cowboy gear, rodeo, roping for kids, country music concert.

*November:* **Trinity Site Tour** (575-437-6120). **Christmas on the Pecos** www.christmasonthepecos.com, Nov. 23–Dec. 31. Closed Christmas Eve. Twelve departures nightly view; over 100 homes decorated with holiday lights along the banks of the Pecos River.

*December:* **Christmas Eve Luminarias** (575-653-4372), Historic Lincoln. **Santa Land** (575-682-2733), Zenith Park, Cloudcroft. Santa and Mrs. Claus arrive with candy and cookies, hot cider, and holiday music.

# Northeast New Mexico: Santa Fe Trail Country

## 8

**SANTA FE TRAIL REGION**
Capulin, Cimarron, Clayton, Des
Moines, Eagle Nest, Folsom, Raton, Roy,
Springer, Wagon Mound

**LAND GRANT COUNTRY**
Las Vegas, Maxwell, Mora, Ocate, Pecos

**ROUTE 66 COUNTRY**
Santa Rosa, Tucumcari

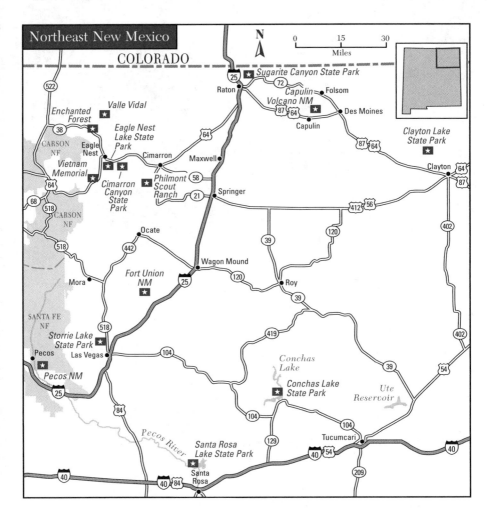

Northeast New Mexico

N

0    15    30
Miles

COLORADO

Sugarite Canyon State Park

Raton

Capulin
Volcano NM

Folsom

Des Moines

Enchanted
Forest

Valle Vidal

Capulin

Clayton Lake
State Park

Eagle Nest
Lake State
Park

CARSON
NF

Eagle
Nest

Cimarron

Maxwell

Clayton

Vietnam
Memorial

Philmont
Scout
Ranch

Cimarron
Canyon
State
Park

Springer

CARSON
NF

Ocate

Fort Union
NM

Wagon Mound

Mora

Roy

SANTA FE
NF

Storrie Lake
State Park

Conchas
Lake

Pecos

Las Vegas

Conchas Lake
State Park

Ute
Reservoir

Pecos NM

Pecos River

Santa Rosa
Lake State Park

Tucumcari

Santa
Rosa

# INTRODUCTION

Northeast New Mexico is an explorer's delight as much as for what it lacks as what it offers. If you like clear turquoise skies and 360-degree views; back roads beckoning onward to the horizon; miles of fields and meadows with few people, billboards, or sign of human habitation save an occasional tumbledown, abandoned cabin; wildflowers galore . . . a place so big it can make you feel small, this could become your new favorite place. Encounters with antelope, elk, deer, wild turkey, and, occasionally, bear and bobcat are part of the journey, and at night, spangled ink-black skies unfurl to dazzle the stargazer. Best of all, the outdoors is easily accessible, right up the road, just about any road.

Still, the visitor is not without familiar diversions. In Clayton you can see a movie in the 1916 Luna Theater, where the same person sells you your ticket, makes the popcorn, and screens the film. You may feel as if you've found the best "last picture show." You can see first-rate theater at the Shuler Theater in Raton and hear the very best live classical music at Music from Angel Fire.

In the great northeast, you can also be the only person hiking a trail for miles; fish for trout in transparent mountain streams, with enough quiet to really hear that stream babbling; and experience a wonderland of butterflies, wildflowers, and birds at Sugared Canyon State Park; or stop the car for a herd of elk crossing the road in Cimarron Canyon.

This place will take you in and wrap you up in its natural warmth and lack of pretension.

Here you can follow the heart line of western history—the Santa Fe Trail, where wagon ruts still trace the path westward, and the place is changed so little it is easy to imagine the sights and sounds of the pioneer experience.

And if you enjoy odd, funky little out-of-the-way museums where history has not yet been gift-wrapped, and where the volunteer at the front desk knows everyone in town, you will be in heaven.

Still, despite the similarities of people, customs, and economies, the place is just so big and diverse, it's best to think of it by breaking it into three main geographic areas: the Santa Fe Trail Region of the northeast corner, where the small towns of northeast New Mexico—Clayton, Raton, Cimarron, and Springer still run on the western mainstays of ranching, railroading, and mining (though coal mining has given way to oil and gas exploration); Land Grant Country, with Las

Vegas as the central and largest town; and Route 66 Country veering off I-40 to the east.

The population of northeast New Mexico is a mixture of descendants who immigrated here to work the mines—from Italy, the Slavic countries, Greece, and Mexico; the descendants of homesteaders; ranchers and ranching families; those who count as their ancestors the original Spanish settlers; and those who somehow found their way here by way of an escape from the bigger cities.

Increasingly, those who grew up here are returning, fixing up the old family house, or building a new one, or fixing up another old one, and joining the retirees from colder and more urban climates who feel like the peace and quiet, the recreational opportunities right out the front door, and the clean air and water are just what their hearts desire. The unspoiled beauty of the place draws artists and celebrations of the arts as well.

The simple, authentic delights of the small town abound here: the ease with which you can get around; the smiles, waves, and hellos you can count on when you go to the post office or the grocery store; the genuine sense of community, a community that still knows and cares about its neighbors; and the joyous, simple American traditions of high school football, the annual lighting of the Christmas tree, Fourth of July fireworks, the county fair, and the rodeo. And if you enjoy the flavor of historic hotels, with the resident ghost or two, northeast New Mexico can charm you with its legendary lodgings.

As much as the world has changed during recent decades, as computer-savvy as we have become, and as susceptible to anxiety and danger, there remains a pervading sense of something else more enduring—a sense of values, of old-fashioned courtesy and respect, of bonds, of deals still done on a handshake, of shared memories and the assumed importance of community. Somehow, this part of the world still seems to have escaped, or been protected from, the stresses, prejudices, angers, and shocking violence seen on the evening news.

Yet these small towns are not immune. Many of the current social problems—domestic violence, drugs, degraded quality of schools, health care, lack of jobs, gangs, and welfare dependence—also exist here. And there is not much to do at night. But for all that, it is possible to live comfortably outside of the compulsion for conspicuous consumption, and thus to have a very relaxed visit. You will be judged on the reliability of your word, not on the model of your vehicle, and you will be respected according to your generosity to friends and the community, not according to the size of your house or the designer labels on your clothes.

Consequently, time takes on a different quality here. There is time to drop in and visit with a friend, to take a neighbor to the doctor, and the lake is close enough to take a child fishing. Hard work is valued, and there is a holdover from blue-collar days when people worked with their hands. It is a good place to kick back, whether for a weekend, a week, or who knows?

Much of this land, including Colfax County, Union County, and San Miguel County—once the hunting grounds and dwelling place of Ute, Apache, and Comanche—has seen mountain men, such as Kit Carson, and giants, such as Lucien Maxwell, whose Maxwell Land Grant, at 1.7 million acres, stood as the largest land holding in the hemisphere. It has seen the wagons of the military and merchants cross the Santa Fe Trail via both the Mountain Route, over difficult Raton Pass, and the more dangerous Cimarron Cutoff—wagon traffic so heavy and frequent that the ruts those wagons left on the landscape are visible to this day. This route of commerce, over which merchants transported goods between Missouri and New Mexico, was used between 1821 and 1880 and died out with the coming of the railroad.

Approximately 19 miles north of Clayton, off NM 406, a portion of the Cimarron Route crosses the Kiowa National Grassland. It is a 2-mile section of trail, with an interpretive site. It has seen those who built the railroads and those who worked a living out of the land with every bit of their strength and ingenuity, and who built the towns and ranches that many of their families still inhabit, three and four generations down the line. The Grassland was planted following the Dustbowl, which took such a heavy toll in this area.

And it has seen the Colfax County War of the 1870s. There is much history to be learned here, and here it can be seen and felt and touched, because it is still remembered. The war pitted the settlers on the Maxwell Land Grant against the big company that claimed the land. And it tore the region apart.

At the Dawson Cemetery, the results of tragic early-20th-century coal mining accidents are visible in the hundreds of crosses marked with the same dates of death, plain crosses standing over the graves of dozens of nationalities.

From the mile Rim Walk around Capulin Volcano, it is still possible to see four states—New Mexico, Colorado, Texas, and Oklahoma. And in Las Vegas, you can visit the Montefiore Cemetery, where the German Jewish merchants of the 1800s lie.

This is where the Great Plains meets the Rockies. Beginning with the Homestead Act of 1862, settlers began to pour in. By the end of the 1870s, the Plains Indian tribes had lost their historic use of the lands. Cattle and sheep replaced the bison, and following their path came soldiers, prospectors, and railroad builders.

Las Vegas, New Mexico, has over 900 buildings listed on the National Register of Historic Places, as well as nine historic districts, each worthy of a walking tour. Brochures are available at the visitors center.

By way of contrast, you can scuba dive in Santa Rosa's 67-foot-deep artesian Blue Hole as well as pet and feed the prize alpacas at the Victory Ranch outside Mora.

Colfax County has over 200 farms and ranches. A wonderful place to experience this culture is at the annual Colfax County Fair, held the second weekend in August at the Springer Armory. Pie sale, junior livestock sale, steer show—all the treasured customs of rural Americana can be experienced here, and the annual cakewalk.

At the annual Fourth of July Santa Fe Trail Balloon Rally, dozens of brilliant hot-air balloons fly aloft over Raton.

So, if you like having the trail to yourself during an early-morning hike, the peace of a glass-smooth alpine lake with trout jumping a foot in the air, going eyeball to eyeball with deer and antelope, poking around and antiquing in little towns without stoplights, and historic hotels loaded with legend and lore aplenty, plus a few hardy ghosts—have we got the place for you!

# SANTA FE TRAIL REGION

## CAPULIN, CIMARRON, CLAYTON, DES MOINES, EAGLE NEST, FOLSOM, RATON, ROY, SPRINGER, WAGON MOUND

The Old West is alive and well out here, where the code of the West still rules and the economy traditionally ran on ranching, railroading, and mining. It's pretty quiet, quiet enough to hear a meadowlark warbling. This is an excellent area to take your own wildlife photo safari. Springtime is windy, so you'll likely be dodging tumbleweeds, and there's a good chance you may get snowed in during winter. Not to worry, it can melt off pretty quick when the sun comes out. If you are sincere, and down to earth, Colfax County folk will befriend you; if you're not, don't expect them to be real sociable. Some of the oldest ranches in the country are located here, and many run by the third and fourth, and even the fifth generation. The Santa Fe Trail winds through the country, and the ruts inscribed on the landscape by Conestoga wagons are still visible. Memories are long with history, and there's probably a cowboy with a good story sitting next to you at the St. James Hotel bar.

**GETTING THERE** *By car:* Private automobile is the only realistic way to travel and see the sights up here. From Albuquerque, drive north on I-25 for 123 miles to Las Vegas. Continue north on I-25 another 102 miles to Raton. Cimarron is 41 miles from Raton via I-25 south to US 64. Clayton is 90 miles east of Raton on US 64. Or, at Springer, exit I-25 and travel US 53 to Gladstone, then on to Clayton.

*By train:* Amtrak stops once daily, both north and southbound, in Raton and Las Vegas.

**GUIDANCE** Please be aware that in small towns, chambers of commerce are often staffed by volunteers and may be closed during posted hours of operation, which may also be irregular. Patience and some advance planning will help cut down on frustration. In general, they are open during the week—generally 10–2 is the safest times to find the staff in—and tend to be closed weekends in the smaller towns (or at best, open a half-day on Saturday). Some do not have a physical location, and others may just ask you to call back.

**Cimarron Chamber of Commerce** (575-376-2417), 104 N. Lincoln Ave., Cimarron. A tiny wooden office in the town's central park off US 64 beside a statue of Lucien B. Maxwell is the place to find out about local happenings.

**Clayton/Union County Chamber of Commerce** (800-390-7858 or 575-374-9253), 1103 S. First St., Clayton, is professional and will return phone calls in a timely manner. It's good to make contact here for specific directions and drive time to more remote locations.

**Eagle Nest Chamber of Commerce** (575-377-2420), 54 Therma Dr., Eagle Nest. Hours are catch as catch can.

**Raton Chamber & Economic Development Council Inc.** (575-445-3689), 100 Clayton Rd., Raton.

**Raton Visitor Information Center** (575-445-2761), 100 Clayton Rd., Raton, is a spacious, comfortable place offering an abundance of regional literature, weather information, and free WiFi.

**MEDICAL EMERGENCY** Miners' Colfax Medical Center (575-445-3661), 203 Hospital Dr., Raton.

**Union County General Hospital** (575-374-2585), 301 Harding St., Clayton.

## ✷ To See

**SANTA FE TRAIL COUNTRY TOWNS** **Capulin.** A place name frequently encountered in New Mexico, the word is Spanish for "chokecherry," or "wild cherry." Here it refers to the hamlet 28 miles southeast of Raton on US 64/87 near the border of Colfax and Union counties. The main attraction is the dormant volcano that is the centerpiece of Mount Capulin National Monument. It was originally a settlement of Hispanic farmers founded sometime after the Civil War.

**Cimarron.** Four miles southwest of Raton. South on I-25 to exit 419, then US 64 west. Cimarron is located at the junction of US 64 and NM 58 and 21. While the exact meaning of this word is not certain, as it may refer either to wild Rocky Mountain bighorn sheep or the wild plum or wild rose that once grew here abundantly; the word *wild* is applied with accuracy to the town, which still exudes a Wild West flavor. Founded in 1841 as the headquarters for the Maxwell Land Grant and home of land baron *Lucien* Bonaparte Maxwell, it became known as a hideout for desperados as well as a gathering spot for traders, miners, and travelers on the Santa Fe Trail. The *Las Vegas Optic* once reported, "It was a quiet week in Cimarron. Only three shootings took place." Nearby are the Philmont Scout Ranch and the home of Kit Carson. Cimarron is a pleasant stop for exploring Santa Fe Trail history, browsing the unpretentious shops and galleries, and absorbing the energy of a place still inhabited largely by cowboys, ranchers, old-timers, and artists. The saloon of the recently updated St. James Hotel, with 27 bullet holes in the ceiling, is a good place to meet up with as many characters as you deserve to.

**Clayton.** Ninety miles east of Raton on US 64/87. Dating to 1888, Clayton was born with the arrival of the railroad, when it became a major cattle-shipping point. It remains to this day a center of ranching activity that pioneer descendants still call home. Among its historic treasures are WPA murals of the New Deal, the 1916 Luna Theater, the Herzstein Memorial Museum, and the recently restored 125-year-old Eklund Hotel. Nearby are Clayton Lake State Park and the Dinosaur Trackway, the second-largest preserved field of dinosaur tracks in the western hemisphere. The town was named for Sen. Stephen Dorsey's son, Clayton. Dorsey was a crony of Albert Fall, of Teapot Dome notoriety. Originally home to Indians, then a resting point for Santa Fe Trail settlers, Clayton grew from a campground for cattle drovers. The railroad came through in 1888, and the town subsequently became a prosperous shipping and supply station, as well as a target for Black Jack Ketchum, a notorious train robber. Clayton High School has a WPA museum, but appointments must be made in advance to see it. Check with the chamber of commerce.

**Des Moines.** Thirty-eight miles southeast of Raton on US 64/87 at the junction of US 64/87 and NM 325. Originally a village of homesteaders founded in 1887 when the railroad came through, Des Moines is named for the town of the same name in Iowa and pronounced with an audible *s* at the end of *Moines*. It supposedly got its name when two cowboys, wondering what to call the place, noticed a railroad car and saw the words *Des Moines* painted on the side. Today it remains a proud, small community of ranching folk and, if you are an artist or photographer, a gold mine of opportunities for making images of weathered barns, windmills, and tumbledown houses.

WINDMILLS ADORN WINTER LANDSCAPES.

**Eagle Nest.** Sixty-four miles southwest of Raton, at the junction of US 64/87 and NM 38. The hamlet, in the shadow of 13,161-foot-high Wheeler Peak, the state's highest, is the gateway to Cimarron Canyon. Originally called Therma, for the daughter of the postal inspector, Eagle Nest is a lovely mountain village on the shore of Eagle Nest Lake State Park, a haven for fishermen, ice fishermen, and RV campers. Back in the day, Eagle Nest was known as a wide-open gambling town patronized by politicians traveling across the state. Now it is a quiet, restful place to kick back and enjoy the clear mountain air and excellent fly-fishing. Fourth of July is celebrated with a mighty fireworks display over Eagle Nest Lake; New Year's Day is celebrated with the Polar Bear Plunge.

**Folsom.** Across scenic Johnson Mesa, which may be closed in winter on account of snow, 38 miles east of Raton off NM 72, lies sleepy Folsom. When President Grover Cleveland's wife, Frances Folsom, came through on the train in 1888, the little railroad settlement known as Ragtown changed its name in her honor. Today the tiny town is known as the place where George McJunkin, the observant African American foreman for the Crowfoot Ranch, in 1926 made a remarkable discovery. He found large bones in an arroyo containing ancient Pleistocene bison skeletons and 19 chipped stone spear points that revised how long man had inhabited this area—at least 10,000 and as much as 15,000 years. The originals are housed in the Denver Museum of Natural History, and the Folsom site is designated a National Historic Landmark. Folsom was proclaimed a State Monument in 1951. It is also the site of Folsom Falls, a spring-fed waterfall on the Dry Cimarron River, 4 miles northeast of Folsom on NM 456. But beware of rattlesnakes if you go there! Folsom Museum is housed in the historic 1896 Doherty Building. The Folsom Hotel was built in 1888 and was originally the Drew & Phillips General Mercantile Store.

**Raton** is 225 miles north of Albuquerque on I-25. Originally called Willow Springs, this town on the edge of Raton Pass into Colorado was a watering stop for military and Santa Fe Trail travelers coming over the Mountain Route. The town came to life in 1880 as a support stop for the Santa Fe Railway roundhouse and shops. Yet earlier, following the Civil War, the government mail stage carrying passengers descended challenging Raton Pass and stopped at the Clifton House Stage Station below Red River Peak for dinner, then galloped into Cimarron on the way to Fort Union. Raton has plenty of motels and eateries left over from the era of La Mesa Racetrack, a well-preserved historic walking district alongside the railroad tracks, and a museum packed with coal mining history, and it makes a good base for exploring the area.

**Roy.** Nine miles east of the Canadian River, Roy was originally a homesteading community that found its reason for existence when the railroad came through. Founded by Frank Roy and three brothers from Canada, it became a ranching center that was then decimated by the Dust Bowl. Today it is a sleepy village in the middle of Harding County, the biggest county in New Mexico by area, but with only 900 inhabitants.

**Springer** is 131 miles north of Santa Fe on I-25, at the junction of US 56. Formerly the capital of Colfax County, today Springer is the site of the Colfax

County Fair and Rodeo held in early August, and the Santa Fe Trail Interpretive Center and Museum.

**Wagon Mound.** Twenty-five miles southwest of Springer on I-25, and a stop of the Santa Fe Trail, the town is named after the butte on its eastern edge that resembles a covered wagon, a Santa Fe Trail landmark. Its previous name was Santa Clara.

**HISTORIC LANDMARKS, PLACES, AND SITES Black Jack Ketchum's Grave** (575-374-9253), Clayton Cemetery, Princeton Ave., Clayton. This is the final resting place of the notorious train robber who was hanged in 1901 at Union County Courthouse. His last words were reputedly, "I had breakfast in Clayton, but I'll have dinner in hell!" Free.

**Dawson** is a ghost town 5 miles northwest of Colfax, formerly a prosperous Phelps-Dodge mining town. In its heyday it was one of the liveliest towns in northeast New Mexico, known for its many winning teams, particularly baseball. Here miners from all over the world, of various ethnic backgrounds, and their families lived, worked, and played together. While the town has been dismantled, the Dawson Cemetery, where hundreds of miners killed in tragic accidents in 1913 and 1923 are buried beneath simple white crosses, remains a moving sight and an important, if often overlooked, chapter in the history of the West. Free.

**Historic First St.**, Raton. Paralleling the railroad tracks, this four-block historic district includes the Old Pass Gallery, occupying a former Wells Fargo freight

DESERTED CALIFORNIA MISSION–STYLE RAILROAD STATIONS PUNCTUATE US 60.

office; the classic California Mission Atchison; Topeka & Santa Fe Railway station, antiques shops; and well-preserved late-19th- to early-20th-century buildings.

**Mandala Center** (575-278-3002), 35 miles east of Raton on US 64/87, Des Moines. An ecumenical spiritual retreat center open to all, the Mandala Center on Sierra Grande Mountain offers workshops year-round, as well as opportunities for private retreats and workshops for leadership, spiritual development, writing skills, and health and wholeness, as well as personal renewal. Based on Christian religious principles, it is indeed welcoming to people of all faiths. And the food is wonderful!

AT THE MANDALA CENTER, TIBETAN MONKS CREATE SAND PAINTINGS THEY WILL BEGIN TO DESTROY AS SOON AS THEY ARE FINISHED.

Santa Fe Trail (SFT) sites: **Point of Rocks** (no phone), 23 miles east of Springer on US 56, north on County Road 52. Seven miles from rest area, 2 miles east, then 1 mile north, look for SFT sign-in box at ranch house, which is on the Santa Fe National Historic Trail. Wagon ruts, graves, Indian campsites. **McNees Crossing** (575-374-9653), 25 miles north of Clayton on NM 402. Santa Fe Trail site named for trader killed there in 1828. Nearby are trail ruts.

**Philmont Scout Ranch** (575-376-2281), 137,000 acres 10 miles southwest of Cimarron on NM 21, Rayado. Oklahoma oilman Waite Phillips donated this lush property to the Boy Scouts of America. Each summer, it is used by scouts from all over the world for backcountry camping.

**Shuler Theater** (575-445-4746), 131 N. Second St., Raton. Completed in 1915, this European Rococo jewel box of a theater, with WPA murals depicting the history of the area, continues to host a variety of outstanding theater and music productions year-round, from ballroom dance to mariachi, Neil Simon to Brazilian dance. Tours available by appointment.

**MUSEUMS Aztec Mill Museum** (575-376-2417), 220 W. 17th St., Cimarron. In May and Sept., open weekends: Sat. 9–5, Sun. 1–5. In summer (Memorial Day–Labor Day), open Sun. 1–5, Mon.–Sat. 9–5, closed Thurs. Originally known as the Aztec Mill, it was built by land baron Lucien Maxwell in 1864 to grind wheat and corn flour for nearby Apache and Ute, as well as Fort Union, with whom he had contracts to supply provisions. You can easily spend half a day wandering the three floors that tell the history of the Maxwell Land Grant, Native Americans, ranchers of the area, and scouting. $3 suggested donation.

**Folsom Museum** (575-278-2122), junction NM 325 and NM 456, Folsom. Open daily 10–5 Memorial Day–Labor Day, weekends only May and Sept. 10–5, winter by appointment only. Displays of Folsom Man, whose points (arrows) were first found in this area by African American cowboy George McJunkin. It has been a long time since this museum was updated, and the crowded walls recall a bygone, nostalgic perspective on the world. $1.50 adults, $.50 children ages 6–12, age 5 and under free.

**Frank Brownell Museum of the Southwest** (575-445-3615), NRA Whittington Center, 10 miles south of Raton on US 64. Open Daily. There's much to learn about the region and the wars of the 20th century here. $20 range fee, dawn to dusk.

**Herzstein Memorial Museum** (575-374-2977), corner Second and Walnut St., Clayton. Open Tues.–Sat. 10–5. The museum, donated by the pioneer Herzstein family, is home of the Union County Historical Society, which lovingly tends the collections housed in a former 1919 church. Collections include a wealth of homesteader artifacts, memorabilia, furniture, and art, and the museum makes for a surprisingly refreshing experience. Free.

**Kit Carson Museum** (575-376-2281), Philmont Scout Ranch, Rayado. Eleven miles south of Cimarron on NM 21. Open June–Aug. daily 8–5; Sept. and May Mon.–Fri. 8–5. This hacienda, and home of Indian scout and mountain man Kit Carson, was actually the original Fort Union, protecting the frontier from Indian raids, built before the fort now bearing that name was constructed. As historically accurate as it can possibly be, down to the flour sacks in the storehouse, this living museum is an excellent way to get a true feel of the Santa Fe Trail day, the fur trade, and the early settlement of New Mexico. A really special experience is the Wed. 7 PM candlelight and storytelling tour, June–Aug., $3. Reservations necessary. Free.

**Raton Arts Gallery** (575-445-2052), 145 S. First St., Raton. Open Tues.–Sat. 10–4. Closed major holidays. Here you will find exhibitions of local watercolorists and photographers, as well as art of regional interest and a renovated Wells Fargo freight office. Free.

**Raton Museum** (575-445-8979), 108 S. Second St., Raton. Open Wed.–Sat. 10–4. A collection of mining, railroad, Santa Fe Trail, and ranching artifacts that provides a history lesson for all

THE KIT CARSON MUSEUM IN RAYADO IS RESTORED TO HISTORIC ACCURACY.

who want to understand this place. Upstairs are changing exhibits of contemporary artists. Free.

**Santa Fe Trail Interpretive Center and Museum** (575-483-5554), 606 Maxwell Ave, Springer. Open Memorial Day–Labor Day 9–5; hours otherwise variable. This collection is housed in the 1882 former Colfax County Courthouse. Here you will find a tangled trove of Santa Fe Trail exhibits, historic photos, artifacts, old letters and maps, and information on the New Mexico Territorial period and pioneer life in northeast New Mexico. Free.

**Villa Philmonte** (575-376-2281), Philmont Scout Ranch, Rayado. Ten miles south of Cimarron on NM 21. Guided tours offered in spring and summer. Please call for times and dates. This grand, elegant Mediterranean summer home of oilman Waite Phillips and his wife, Genevieve, is now the property of the Philmont Scout Ranch, of which Phillips is the benefactor. Built 1926–27; all art and furnishings remain intact, as does the splendid original tile work. $4.

**NATURAL WONDERS Capulin Volcano National Monument** (575-278-2201), Capulin. North of Capulin 5.5 miles on NM 456. Closed major holidays. Open Memorial Day–Labor Day 7:30–6:30, Labor Day–Memorial Day 8–4. This natural cone of a relatively young volcano, only 7,000 years old, is one of the few places in the world where you can hike inside a cinder cone. Visitors may walk 2 miles round-trip into the 415-foot-deep crater and hike along the 1-mile rim trail overlooking much of the Raton-Clayton volcanic fields. From the rim trail, you can see four states, and to the west, view the snowcapped Sangre de Cristo Mountains. $5 per vehicle.

**Sierra Grande.** Ten miles southeast of Folsom, off US 64/85, is the largest single mountain in the United States, measuring 40 miles around the base, covering 50 square miles, at an altitude of 8,720 feet.

**Tooth of Time** is a prominent, toothlike rock formation visible from Cimarron that was significant to Santa Fe Trail travelers. When trail pioneers saw the Tooth of Time, they knew they only had seven more days to reach Santa Fe.

**SCENIC DRIVES** For information on New Mexico's Scenic Byways, visit www. newmexicoscenicbyways.org or call 800-733-6396, ext. 24371.

**Dry Cimarron Scenic Byway** NM 406 north to NM 456, it extends 40 miles north of Clayton. The Dry Cimarron River ran mainly underground but would surface occasionally. This mostly deserted scenic road runs through Union and Colfax counties, and it has served as an alternate route between Clayton and Raton. There is much history in the way of Santa Fe Trail wagon ruts, old mining camps, and many landmark features. The drive brings the traveler through high prairie, national grasslands, nature preserves, volcanoes, mesas, and colorful geologic formations.

**Johnson Mesa** is 41 miles from Raton to Folsom along NM 72. Spectacular views of the Sangre de Cristo Mountains are yours here above Raton, and there is no better place for stargazing in the entire state. Settlers believed this was a paradise of rich grasslands. Many of the early settlers worked in the coal mines. When winter came, survival became difficult. The little stone church on the mesa is always open. This is truly a scenic byway, but it's not passable for much

SIGHTING THE TOOTH OF TIME MEANT ONLY SEVEN MORE DAYS TO SANTA FE FOR THE PIONEERS.

of the winter. Summertime, the mesa is covered with white flowers and herds of antelope gallop, while the land serves as summer pasture for local ranchers. Homesteader cabins and dugouts are visible still, and a few hardy souls continue to live up here.

**Santa Fe Trail Scenic Byway** (www.newmexico.com/tours/santafe_trail.htm). Follow the actual path of the Santa Fe Trail wagons and see wagons and abandoned forts in the rugged landscape of mountain canyons. The byway extends 480 miles altogether. If you are following the route, you can go to Santa Fe via Clayton, Raton, Cimarron, and Springer, to Las Vegas. In New Mexico, highlights include Fort Union National Monument in Watrous, Kiowa National Grasslands in Clayton, Pecos National Historical Park, Pecos, and the Santa Fe National Forest.

## ✳ To Do

**FISHING Charette Lakes** (no phone), 35 miles southwest of Springer. I-25 exit 404 and west on NM 569. Boating and fishing as well as primitive camping are yours on the shores of this deep natural volcanic lake, which can be windy in the evening.

**Cimarron Canyon State Park** (575-377-6271), US 64 east of Eagle Nest. One of the state's prime German brown trout fisheries, with 9 miles of fly-casting along the Cimarron River. $6 day use; $10–18 camping.

**Eagle Nest Lake State Park** (575-377-1594), 42 Marina Way. NM 64 north of Eagle Nest. Boating, fishing, and ice fishing are popular on this 2,400-acre lake that yields some of the finest trout and Konkani salmon fishing in the state. The patient wildlife watcher will see elk, deer, bears, and eagles. This is a beloved lakeside summer picnic area. $6 per vehicle.

**Springer Lake** (no phone), 4 miles northwest of Springer on CR 17. Picnicking, camping, and fishing for northern pike and catfish make this small lake a favorite with locals. Free.

**GOLFING Raton Country Club and Municipal Golf Course** (505-445-8113), 510 Country Club Rd., Raton. Voted "Best Nine Hole Course in New Mexico," this lovely 6,500-foot-high course, with plenty of hazards, was built in 1922 by a coal baron. Greens fee for nine holes around $20.

**MOUNTAIN BIKING** *See* **Sugarite Canyon State Park** under *Green Space, Route 66 Country.* You can just about choose your own level of terrain here, with this uncrowded, premium area that is pretty much an insider's secret. Here are challenging up-and-down trails and sweet flats packed with greenery, wildflowers, meadows, forests, and lake views. It's a fairly easy ride through ride former coal camp, around Lake Maloya, to the Colorado border. The visitors center provides trail maps. $6.

**SNOW SPORTS Enchanted Forest Cross-Country Ski Area** (575-754-6112). At the summit of Bobcat Pass, just north of Red River, the Enchanted

Forest is the state's premier cross-country and snowshoeing venue, offering everything you could want or need, including rentals, yurt rentals, and lessons. There are almost 20 miles of groomed Nordic ski trails for varied skill levels, and close to 10 miles of snowshoe trails, plus designated dog trails, though you may use the trails if you are pet-free. Under $20.

## ✳ Lodging

**BED & BREAKFASTS, INNS, AND MOTELS** 🐾 ♿ **Best Western Kokopelli Lodge** (575-374-2589), 702 S. First St., Clayton. Clean, light, spacious rooms with Southwest décor and all conveniences make this a most pleasant stop. A café serving a better-than-average complimentary hot buffet breakfast, swimming pool, and a swell gift shop are on the premises. $99.

🐾 **Budget Host Melody Lane** (575-445-3655), 136 Canyon Dr., Raton. My out-of-town guests rave about the in-room steam baths. Continental breakfast, pet-friendly (to small pets), friendly service, too. Although affiliated with a chain, this 26-room lodging retains its local ambience. $60.

♿ **Casa de Gavilan** (575-376-2246), 10 miles south of Cimarron at 570 NM 21. Still very much the gracious home it was, originally built with 18-inch-thick walls and stout wooden vigas (ceiling beams) for Jack and Gertrude Nairn, this 1910 Pueblo Revival white adobe villa perched directly below the Santa Fe Trail landmark known as the Tooth of Time retains the essence of traditional New Mexico. Remingtons and Russells adorn the patio, and comfortable sitting rooms furnished with plump, cushy sofas call you to curl up with a book or enjoy a relaxing conversation. The inn is located beside the Philmont Scout Ranch. Stargazing is superb, as is the wildlife viewing on the 225 acres of pine forests. There's more cowboy than chichi in the hearty, wholesome breakfasts that provide the fuel you'll need to spend the morning exploring. $104–134.

**Heart's Desire** (575-445-1000), 301 S. Third St., Raton. This sweet three-story, 1885 Victorian home in comfortable walking distance of downtown, the historic district, and train station happens to be run by an antiques lover. This bed & breakfast reflects the charm and cozy clutter of her love. Plus, if you feel like doing a little shopping, many of the collectibles are for sale. You will feel cared for and catered to here, with evening snacks, chocolates, and egg puffs for breakfast. The third-floor Hunting and Fishing Room, with its views of nearby mountains, is truly a getaway, and the Blue Willow Room will romance the heart of any lady. An evening at this retreat into the past would make a darling Valentine's Day surprise. $88–$120.

🐾 **Econo Lodge** (575-377-6813), 715 Hwy. 64 East, Eagle Nest. With balcony rooms overlooking Eagle Nest Lake, this contemporary lodging can accommodate all size groups with apartments, suites, and rooms, and is conveniently located near Angel Fire, Red River, and Taos. Ski where you like and vacation at bargain rates. $85.

🐾 **Oasis Motel** (575-445-2766), 1445 S. Second St, Raton. With a popular café on the premises, and 14 clean

HEART'S DESIRE B&B IN RATON IS AN ANTIQUE LOVER'S DELIGHT.

and serviceable rooms in classic motel décor, this locally owned and operated motel is a good choice. $75.

**St. James Hotel** (See "Historic Hotels," page 000).

**LODGES AND RANCHES Vermejo Park Ranch** (575-445-3097), 1000 Vermejo Road, Raton. Once part of the Maxwell Land Grant, later the private getaway of Mary Pickford and Douglas Fairbanks, this piece of grand history is today the property of media mogul Ted Turner. Former guests include presidents, industrialists, and celebrity movers and shakers from Hollywood to Washington, DC. An exclusive hunting and fishing lodge for the privileged, it is possible, for a price, to visit and enjoy the Vermejo, with its 21 stocked lakes, legendary trout streams, and abundant herds of elk and bison. Since Turner purchased the property in 1996, the

Vermejo has actively sought to restore the ecology and bring back native animals, including black-footed ferrets and wild wolves. Two-night minimum required, guide services extra. Gourmet meals, served in the clubby dining room overlooking the Sangre de Cristo Mountains, are included. Fishing season is May–Sept. Starts at $550 per guest per night; $275 children. A winter season has recently been added.

**CABINS AND CAMPING**
🐾 ♿ **SummerLand RV Park** (575-445-9536), 1900 Cedar St., Raton. With 42 full hookups, tent camping, cabins, a playground, laundry, store, free WiFi, and even minor RV repairs available, this pet-friendly, handicapped-accessible park has a reputation for friendliness and service. It's at 7,000 feet, so nights can be chilly, but it's a great place for stargazing and wildlife watching. Located

on a frontage road off I-25, it somehow manages to be a quiet spot. $28.50. Pet restrictions.

## ✳ Where to Eat

**DINING OUT** **Dining Room, St. James Hotel** (575-376-2664), 167 S. Collinson, Cimarron. Dinner only. Decent steaks, Mexican food, and salad bar. Warmth emanates from the hearthlike fireplace in the center of this refurbished western saloon, and cowboy photos and memorabilia grace the walls. Originating in 1873 as a saloon operated by Lincoln's chef, Henri Lambert, this fine establishment offers a convivial full bar and café in addition to the dining room. Today it is part of the Express Ranch empire. Moderate.

**Pappas' Sweet Shop Restaurant** (575-445-9811), 1201 S. Second St., Raton. Closed Sun. A place for a nice lunch or dinner out, especially if there is business to be conducted, with decent prime rib, home-cooked stews, homemade soup daily, and dessert created by a respected local chef, plus a sense of itself as a bastion of gentility in a fast-food world. The new ice-cream parlor is pure nostalgia. It's still in the family, generations after the original Mr. Pappas started out selling candy to the coal miners. Wine and beer. Moderate.

**EATING OUT** *✐* **All Seasons Family Restaurant** (575-445-9889), 1616 Cedar St. (just off Clayton Rd.), Raton. It's fun to browse this well-stocked curio emporium, which has joke gifts as well as country preserves and candles. The weekend breakfast buffet is a good deal, and there's always the salad bar and kids' menu, which can solve a lot of problems.

Breakfast is served all day, and daily specials highlight the big variety of American and New Mexican offerings. There's something for everyone, for sure, and it continues to feel delightfully nonfranchise here. Inexpensive.

**The Brown Hotel & Cafe** (575-483-2269), 302 Maxwell Ave., Springer. Imagine homemade cinnamon rolls big as pie plates in granny's parlor, more than respectable huevos rancheros, counter stools that spin, and furniture covered with lace doilies. Homemade pie, too! Time stands refreshingly still at the Brown, a favorite meeting site of the Silver Spur CowBelles and a lunch stop for locals and visitors alike. Inexpensive.

**Colfax Tavern, Cold Beer, New Mexico** (575-376-2229), 11 miles east of Cimarron on US 64. You can see the tall white letters on the red-painted building from a mile out. The only establishment in the ghost town of Colfax, this bar has been here since Prohibition, so they say. Right up there with the best cowboy bars, with live music and lots of locals who'd never let the truth stand in the way of a good story. It's friendly and comfortable, with live music and dancing on weekends in summer on the outdoor dance floor. Monday, and burgers and pizza are served the rest of the time. The highly competitive summer Jeopardy tournament, for real money, held each July, is a social highlight. Mardi Gras is also celebrated in high style. Do wear your boots. The slogan here is: "Where there's not much going on, you'd better be there when it is." Inexpensive.

**Elida's Cafe** (575-483-2985), 801 Railroad Ave., Springer. With plastic tablecloths, fluorescent lighting, and a menu tilted toward south of the border, Elida's couldn't be a more real, down-to-earth stop for homemade, from scratch, every day, sopaipillas, Frito pie, or a torta—a "Mexican sub." Try the *gorditas*, a homey, hard-to-find specialty of fried masa (cornmeal) stuffed with ground beef and served with beans and rice. The service is caring and thorough. A three-item combo will set you back $7.50. Inexpensive.

**Enchanted Grounds** (575-445-2219), 111 Park Ave., Raton. WiFi, fine lattes, pastries, wholesome soups and sandwiches, plus occasional live music and open mic on weekends, served in the lovely old Silver Dollar bar. Read the paper, check your e-mail, and catch up on the local gossip. Patio. Moderate.

**Gladstone Mercantile** (575-485-2467), 4618 US 56, Gladstone. Just when you thought there was nothing out there but the high lonesome sky and the wind, along comes the quintessential stop in the road, where you can find a welcome with fresh hot coffee, hot soup, yummy barbecue brisket sandwiches, gifts to warm the heart of any cowgirl, and books by local authors. The place also doubles as a local grocery store. Inexpensive.

✍ **Minnie's Dairy Delite** (575-483-2813), 42 US 56, Springer. Open summer only. Wash down those cheeseburgers and fries with a chocolate malt or a thick, creamy milk shake at this old-fashioned, down-home favorite roadside stop. You'll have trouble spending more than $7 on lunch or dinner. Inexpensive.

**Mulligan's Restaurant & Bar** (575-445-8501), 473 Clayton Rd., Raton. Soups, salads, pizza, pasta, appetizers, American fare, convivial bar. Since

opening in the remodeled Best Western, spacious, comfortable Mulligan's has become the most popular local hangout in town. Moderate.

**Rabbit Ear Cafe** (575-374-3277), 1201 S. First St., Clayton. The local favorite lunchtime destination in town. Hardly gourmet fare, but the lunch counter menu is filling and tasty. Standard burgers and Mexican fare. Inexpensive.

**St. James Cafe** (575-376-2664), 617 S. Collison Ave., Cimarron. This light and bright, friendly café, located in the historic St. James Hotel, is well worth a stop for lunch or breakfast, as it serves up soups, fresh salads, New Mexican fare, and burgers, all at a fair price. Inexpensive.

## ✳ Selective Shopping

**Cimarron Art Gallery** (800-253-1470), 337 Ninth St., Cimarron. They've got it all! Strong coffee, hand-dipped ice cream treats at the old-fashioned counter, beautiful regional jewelry, hand-carved wooden wares, handmade pottery and fine art. Best of all, the kind of friendly service that will keep you coming back. They even remember your name!

**Heirloom Shop** (575-445-8876), 132 S. First St., Raton. This is just the place to find those missing pieces in your grandmother's china set. Fine quality sold by reliable dealers.

**Jespersen's Cache** (575-843-2349), 403 Maxwell Ave., Springer. Extraordinary hodgepodge warehouse collection of secondhand collectibles, from Depression glass and boxed Barbies to an electrified antique British puppet theater. Be alert, as contemporary items that may appear vintage are mixed in with the rest. It's easy to

IF YOU KNOW WHERE TO LOOK, YOU CAN FIND VINTAGE WEAR THROUGHOUT NORTHEAST NEW MEXICO.

spend a good chunk of an afternoon browsing here, and you have a good chance of making a real find. If it is closed, don't be shy about calling the number on the door. The owner will be right down to let you in.

**The Outfitter** (575-376-9128), 129 E. 12th St., Cimarron. Here find handmade leather goods and Whitney blanket coats, plus a mind-boggling array of vintage boots, hats, quilts, and whatever you need for a rendezvous or western reenactment outfit. But do check it out, even if you are just a wannabe.

**Pack Rat** (575-445-3242), 132 N. First St., Raton. Lively collection of ceramics, regional books, gifts of all sorts, as well as ice cream and cold drinks. A good stop if you're waiting for the train.

**Santa Fe Trail Traders** (575-445-2888), 100 S. Second St., Raton. This is a well-established, reputable place to shop for high-end Indian-made wares, including jewelry, pottery, baskets, storytellers, and sand paintings, with the work of many well-known artists on the shelves.

**Solano's Boot and Western Wear** (888-898-6813), 101 S. Second St., Raton. You'll look like a cowboy if you shop here, where all the most beloved brands are in stock—in your size. Boots and jeans, belts and hats in a wealth of styles and colors. Vintage-look and retro, too. Check out the collection of well-worn hats on the wall. Each has a story to tell. This family business has been around a long, long time, and does quite a bit of business online, too.

# LAND GRANT COUNTRY

## LAS VEGAS, MAXWELL, MORA, OCATE, PECOS

**GUIDANCE** **Las Vegas/San Miguel County Chamber of Commerce** (575-425-8631), 1224 Railroad Ave., Las Vegas, housed in the renovated Santa Fe Railway Depot, is professionally staffed and well stocked with information about local attractions.

**Mora Valley Chamber of Commerce** (575-387-6850 or 575-387-6072), P.O. Box 800, Mora, is the place to learn about the work of local artists and small-town festivals that feel like family gatherings.

**MEDICAL EMERGENCY** **Alta Vista Regional Hospital** (505-426-3500), 104 Legion Dr., Las Vegas.

## ✳ To See

**TOWNS** **Las Vegas.** Sixty-four miles northeast of Santa Fe on I-25. Named "the meadows," part of an original Spanish land grant, Las Vegas has 900 buildings listed on the National Register of Historic Places and a rough-and-tumble past. The historic structures may best be appreciated in individual self-guided walking tours described in chamber of commerce brochures. The "hanging tree" still stands on the Plaza, which is dominated by the 1880s Plaza Hotel, and a revived Bridge Street radiating out from that Plaza is a pleasure to stroll and browse, with bookshops, cafés, and antiques shops. Another interesting area surrounds the restored Santa Fe train depot, which houses the visitors center, next to the old Hotel Casteneda, an original Fred Harvey hotel that stands vacant, except for the questionable bar. A major Santa Fe Trail stop, then railroad town, Las Vegas was once the dominant city in New Mexico. Now home of New Mexico Highlands University and Armand Hammer's College of the American West, the town is an interesting mixture of descendants of old families, college students, and recent retirees. There is much history, including that of the German Jewish merchant pioneers, and much of the outdoors to explore here. West Las Vegas, originally called Nuestra Señora de los Dolores de las Vegas Grandes, was begun in 1835 as a land grant community of Spanish sheepherders. After the Santa Fe Trail days, when it was an important trail destination 650 miles from

ADELE ILFELD AUDITORIUM IS THE PRIDE AND JOY OF THE NEW MEXICO HIGHLANDS CAMPUS.

Missouri, the Plaza area thrived. Later, as a result of the Atchison, Topeka, & Santa Fe Railroad line, Las Vegas split into a whole separate city to the east, and it remained so until the 1970s. Locals referred to these separate towns as Old Town and New Town. Most of the adobe structures, both residential and commercial, are west of the Gallinas River in Old Town. Plentiful lodging and a variety of restaurants make Las Vegas a reasonable travel base.

**Maxwell**, 30 miles south of Raton on I-25, is important chiefly as the site of the Maxwell National Wildlife Refuge, a superb birding locale. It was formerly the shipping center for the Maxwell Land and Irrigation Company, and a significant site for the Maxwell Land Grant.

**Mora.** Thirty-one miles north of Las Vegas on NM 518. A town remaining on the huge Mora Land Grant of 1835, located in the Mora Valley, that was inhabited since ancient times by Pueblo and Plains Indians, as well as the migrating Jicarilla Apache. Subsequently, Mora became rich territory of French Canadian mountain men and beaver trappers. Small farms and ranches populate the delightful valley, which offers excellent camping in lovely mountain campgrounds. Here may be found tiny, well-weathered Hispanic villages, churches, fishing, and wildflowers, and a feeling of the long ago as well as the faraway. The place and its people prefer their old ways and remain more or less isolated and somewhat off the grid. Expect to encounter the old wood carvers, *santeros*, weavers, farmers, and remnants of the Penitente brotherhood. This is not an easy area for an outsider to penetrate. Tread lightly.

**Ocate.** Twenty-three miles northwest of Wagon Mound on NM 120. A largely abandoned, scantly populated village that was home to Hispanic settlers about 150 years ago, and before that, was a hunting ground for Indians. Today, it makes appealing inspiration for photographers and artists.

**Pecos.** The gateway to the Pecos Wilderness, a popular fishing, hiking, and backpacking area, this little town on the Pecos River was once a mining center.

### HISTORIC LANDMARKS, PLACES, AND SITES **Bridge St.** The

restored Plaza Hotel on the Las Vegas Plaza anchors Las Vegas, and this is a neighborhood of interesting cafés, bookstores, restaurants, and shops that appeal to locals and visitors alike. A stroll down the three-block area, with its imposing late-19th-century architecture, suggests the powerful position Las Vegas once enjoyed as a major stop and trading center on the Santa Fe Trail and later on the Atchison, Topeka, & Santa Fe Railway. Free.

**Casteñeda Hotel** (505-425-8631), 524 Railroad Ave., Las Vegas. Falling into increasing disrepair, the once-proud Casteñeda, an original Harvey House railroad hotel built in 1898, is closed. Only the bar, a dark, cramped outpost (worth a visit mainly to say you have been there), remains in operation. Free.

**Fort Union National Monument** (505-425-8025), 3115 Monument Lane, Watrous. Take I-25 for 12 miles north of Las Vegas, exit 366, then 8 miles on NM 161. Open daily Memorial Day–Labor Day 8–6, Labor Day–Memorial Day 8–4. Built in 1851 of adobe near the Mountain and Cimarron branches of the Santa Fe Trail, Fort Union became the largest fort in the Southwest, serving as defense and supply depot. It became a longed-for destination of Santa Fe Trail

FORT UNION, SANTA FE TRAIL DESTINATION.

travelers. When they arrived here safely, they were as good as home. Living history programs, candlelight tours, and cultural demonstrations take place during summer months. An interpretive trail of 1.6 miles takes you through the ruins of the fort, and nearby, 1.1 miles east of the visitors center on Utah State Highway 24, are Native American petroglyphs. $3 adults, age 16 and under free.

**La Cueva National Historic Site** (575-387-2900), 25 miles north of Las Vegas via NM 518, Buena Vista. The mill, built by Vicente Romero, is the centerpiece of this historic site, along with the San Rafael Mission Church, known for its restored French Gothic windows and the mercantile, now the Salman Ranch Store. It is part of the Mora Land Grant of 1835, and Romero is believed to have been an original grantee. Much horse and ox wagon traffic between here and Fort Union took place, as La Cueva was a major shipping center for livestock and agricultural produce. Today, from Labor Day into the fall, depending on weather and harvest, visitors flock to purchase the fresh raspberries and raspberry sundaes sold in season on the **Salman Raspberry Ranch** located here (575-387-2900). Free.

**Montezuma Castle** (505-454-4200), 5 miles northwest of Las Vegas on NM 65, Montezuma. This recently restored 1882 grand hotel is now part of Armand Hammer United World College of the American West. Originally known as the Montezuma Hotel, it was designed for the Atchison, Topeka, & Santa Fe Railroad in Queen Anne style. After a series of fires, in 1886, the final Montezuma Castle opened. In its heyday, it was a popular destination with casino, bowling alley, stage, dance floor, stained glass from Europe, and a staff from the finest hotels in New York, Chicago, and St. Louis. Guests included Theodore Roosevelt, Rutherford B. Hayes, Ulysses S. Grant, and Jesse James. Closed in 1903, it was from 1937 to 1972 a seminary for Mexican priests. In 2001, the landmark underwent a $10.5-million renovation, transforming it into an international center. Call for public tour information. Free.

**Pecos National Historical Park** (505-757-7200), 2 miles south of Pecos on NM 63. Closed Christmas Day. Open daily Memorial Day–Labor Day 8–5, Labor Day–Memorial Day 8–6. This abandoned site of pueblo ruins and 18th-century mission church ruins reveal 12,000 years of history. The ruins are all that remain of the ancient pueblo of Pecos. Additional historic and cultural layering is present in two Spanish colonial churches and plentiful Santa Fe Trail sites, while the museum in the visitors center tells of the history of the Forked Lightning Ranch (previously owned by actress Greer Garson, now the property of Jane Fonda) and the Civil War Battle of Glorieta Pass. A 1.25-mile self-guided trail through Pecos pueblo and mission ruins is the best way to see the park. Guided tours of the ruins and Glorieta Battlefield are available to groups booking in advance. The trails are 80 percent wheelchair-accessible. An essential stop. $3 adults, age 16 and under free.

**MUSEUMS City of Las Vegas Museum/Rough Rider Memorial Collection** (575-426-3205), 727 N. Grand Ave., Las Vegas. Open Tues.–Sat. (in summer, Sun.) 10–4. This museum houses extensive displays of city history,

PECOS NATIONAL HISTORICAL PARK.

particularly around ranching and railroading, and Santa Fe Trail history, with maps, photos, ranching gear, household items, and Native American pottery. The distinctive feature is memorabilia of the Rough Riders who fought in the Spanish-American War, which was fought by the United States and Cuba in 1898, and who held their first reunion, led by Theodore Roosevelt, here. New Mexico contributed over one-quarter of the troops that fought. The Rough Rider Museum began as a private memorial. Between 1899 and 1968, reunions were held in Las Vegas. The museum is housed in a New Deal–era building. Free.

**Cleveland Roller Mill Museum** (575-387-2645), NM 518. Open weekends Memorial Day–Labor Day, 10–3. Two miles south of Mora in Cleveland, the 1901 mill only operates once a year, during the Cleveland Roller Mill Festival, Labor Day weekend. The Mora Valley was once a significant wheat-growing region, hence the need for the mill. This adobe mill was the last to be built in northern New Mexico and was one of the largest mills in the Southwest in its day. Free.

**NATURAL WONDERS Hermit's Peak** is a massive boulderlike butte of pink granite, north of Las Vegas and visible from I-25, that is believed by some local folk to have been the home of a hermit who would care for all who were lost by rescuing them, taking them to his cave, and feeding them bread.

**BIRDING** **Las Vegas National Wildlife Refuge** (575-425-3581), Route 1, Las Vegas. Six miles southeast of Las Vegas off I-25. Providing wintering and migration habitat for ducks and geese of the Central Flyway, plus some 250 migratory bird species. With 14 species of raptors, this is a great place to see eagles. There is an 8-mile auto loop through the heart of the refuge with interpretive panels and observation decks. The Gallinas Nature Trail Walk is a half-mile round-trip into a beautiful canyon, but open only on weekdays. Free.

**Maxwell National Wildlife Area** (575-375-2331), Maxwell, just off I-25. Winter wildlife viewing includes mule deer and much birdlife, with golden and bald eagles, owls, herons, cranes, and Canada geese. Established in 1966 at an altitude of 6,050 feet, the refuge includes over 3,000 acres of rolling prairie and prairie lakes and farmland. This untouristed refuge is capable of providing a truly thrilling birding experience, with numbers that can top 990,000 migratory birds, including snow geese and numerous varieties of ducks. Free.

**FISHING** **Pecos River**, Pecos Wilderness, Santa Fe National Forest (505-425-3534), Pecos. Apr.–late Sept. To escape the crowds and find the native browns and Rio Grande cutthroats, it is necessary to hike into the high country of the wilderness area. If you want to cast your line without the effort required, seek the streams below Cowles.

**HIKING** **El Porvenir Canyon** (no phone), 17 miles northwest of Las Vegas on NM 65, past Montezuma. Take Hot Springs Blvd. northwest out of Las Vegas to where it dead-ends. The Skyline Trail, accessible out of El Porvenir Campground, is a 13-mile moderate hike with altitude that ranges from 7,520 to 11,280 feet. Wildflowers are abundant, particularly wild iris in late May–early June. Once the summer resort of Las Vegas families, this canyon is now a favorite locals' place to hunt and fish. There are two creekside campgrounds close to Hermit's Peak, in the Santa Fe National Forest. $2 hiking permit; $8 camping.

**Pecos Wilderness**, Santa Fe National Forest (505-425-3534), Pecos. While there are dozens of trails through this stunning landscape, Jack's Creek and Baldy and Beatty's Trail among the most traveled, there are not really any easy ones. Most are difficult or moderate to difficult. Be prepared for weather changes and afternoon rains, and remember, altitudes are from 9,000 to 12,000 feet. Tread carefully.

**HORSEBACK RIDING** **Circle S Riding Stables** (505-757-,8440 or 575-520-5775), Pecos Wilderness. Hunting, fishing, trail rides, aspen rides. Call for directions. Closed Nov.–Apr. Take one of their two-hour or overnight trips, or personalize your own journey for a half-day, a day, or longer. $75 two-hour rides.

**Terrero General Store & Riding Stables** (505-757-6193), 14 miles north of Pecos via NM 63, 1911 NM 63, Terrero. Open May 31–Sept. 30. Started in 1940, this remains a family-run business where you can outfit for an overnight camping trip with a wrangler to hoist your gear and make camp at 10,500 feet in the Pecos Wilderness, or just take a leisurely ride into the Santa Fe National

Forest for an hour or two. Reservations a must. $30 per hour; $185 per person overnight.

**HOT SPRINGS** **Montezuma Hot Springs** (no phone), 5 miles west of Las Vegas on Hot Springs Blvd. at NM 65. Here find a very rustic, rather undeveloped hot natural spring in outdoor baths, adjacent to the Montezuma Castle. The setting is not secluded, and you need to bring your own towels. Free.

**GOLFING** **Pendaries Village Golf & Country Club** (800-733-5267), Rociada. Open Apr. 15–Oct. 15. A stunning 18-hole mountain golf course perched at 7,500 feet, with, naturally, mind-blowing mountain views. Greens fees for nine holes under $30.

**SNOW SPORTS** *✍* **Sipapu Ski & Summer Resort** (800-587-2240), 11 miles east of Peñasco on NM 75 and NM 518 or 20 miles southeast of Taos on NM 518. With 33 trails, four chairlifts, snowboarding, a variety of trails, and terrain for all skill levels, with skilled, patient instructors, Sipapu has a well-earned reputation as a moderately priced family-friendly resort. The base elevation is 8,200 feet. It has become over the years a year-round resort, with fly-fishing in a private pond and the rainbow-stocked Rio Pueblo River. Fall is a grand time for mountain biking on the over 300 miles of trails, and bike rentals are provided. Disc golf. You can kick back quite happily here, in the midst of the Carson National Forest. Café on the premises serves popular eats, such as burgers and fries. Tent campsites and RV hookups are also available.

**WINERIES** **Madison Vineyards & Winery** (575-421-8028), 696 NM 3, Villanueva. Twenty-six miles south of Las Vegas on I-25, exit on NM 3. Starting with 80 French hybrid vines in the village of El Barranca on the Pecos River, Bill and Elise Madison have been making wine here since 1980. They have kept their operation small and family-run, crafting only 5,000 gallons per year. Come enjoy a beautiful operation in an exquisite setting. Wines include European-style dry and semisweet. Tasting room open Mon.–Fri. noon–6; Sat. 10–5; Sun. noon–5. Closed Wed. Irregular winter hours; call ahead.

## ✳ Lodging

**BED & BREAKFASTS, INNS, AND MOTELS** **Crow's Nest B&B** (505-425-2623), 524 Columbia St., Las Vegas. Satisfy your appetite for Victoriana here, in this painted lady overlooking the dignified green square of the historic Carnegie Library district. Dream or daydream of bygone days, escape, and enjoy a generous breakfast of frittata, French toast, and another cup of coffee.

Three rooms, one with Jacuzzi. $85–105.

**Wilderness Gateway Bed and Breakfast** (505-757-2801), NM 63 at #1 Tree Farm Rd., Cowles. Luxury in the wilderness of the Santa Fe National Forest; and, walking distance to Pecos River fly-fishing. Private cabin available. Gourmet breakfast, and lunch and dinner may be ordered separately. $135–160.

## RANCHES AND LODGES

✒ 🦞 **Cow Creek Ranch** (505-757-2107), 975 Forest Rd. 92, Pecos. If you choose to visit this well-weathered and well-loved mountain guest ranch in the Santa Fe National Forest, you will have a vacation to remember all year long. Cow Creek is an Orvis-approved historic fly-fishing guest ranch about 40 miles from Santa Fe off I-25 (please see website for driving instructions). Open May 21–Aug. 21. It has 20 guest rooms, each with a kiva fireplace. The ranch bell chimes when it's time to dine. All meals are included, and there are enough outdoor activities to keep you busy all day, including riding, mountain biking, and children's programs, so you can enjoy a deeply restful slumber. Fishing trips offered beyond the full-service season. Minimum three-night stay, $1,260; children over age 4 only, $1,185.

🦞 **Los Pinos Guest Ranch** (505-757-6213), Panchuela Rd., 45 miles from Santa Fe, 20 miles north of Pecos via NM 63, Terrero. Since the 1920s, this small family-run guest ranch on the Pecos River in Cowles, with only 12 aspen log rooms, has been delighting guests with its superb birding, fly-fishing on the Upper Pecos River, hiking from trailheads right on the property, wildflowers, riding, and fine dining on home cooking prepared by dedicated owner Alice McSweeney. Breakfast and dinner are served in the lodge. The rooms have neither phones nor televisions. This is a perfect place to be cared for, and to renew and retreat. Rates include all meals. Open June 1–Sept. 30. $140 per day; children over age 5, $45–75.

**Pendaries Lodge** (800-753-0447), Rociada. Go twelve miles north of Las Vegas on NM 518, then left at Sapello onto NM 94/105 for 12.5 miles. Go left into Pendaries Village and follow the signs. Justifiably well known for its golf course, Pendaries is a secluded, quiet, unpretentious lodge with 18 rooms plus additional accommodations in summer homes. The restaurant serves dinner daily, and breakfast and lunch are available in the Club House. The Moosehead Saloon must be seen to be appreciated and is certainly the place for a drink. Golf packages are available at this challenging high mountain golf course tucked away in the Sangre de Cristo Mountains. $74–94.

## CABINS AND CAMPING **Mark Rents Cabins** (505-988-7517). Open May 1–Oct. 30. Offering nine fully furnished, renovated log cabins overlooking the Pecos River a mile from Tererro, near Pecos, this is a place that can comfortably accommodate families and larger groups. Rustic comfort is the word. There is a three-night minimum, and reservations are required. $110–190.

**Pendaries RV Resort** (505-454-8304), 3 Park Pl., NM 105, Rociada, 22 miles north of Las Vegas, NM 105, Rociada. Open May 1–Nov. 1. With 50 RV units and six comfortable, two-bedroom, two-bath cottages. Jean Pendaries (Pan-da-rey) moved from France to build the Plaza Hotel in Las Vegas, then in 1875 moved to the Rociada area, still a gorgeous, quiet hideaway deep in the northern New Mexico mountains. There he built a sawmill and gristmill, which can still be seen near Pendaries Village. And today those visiting here can enjoy the high mountain golfing as well as serenity you dream about. Cottage $125; RV pad $26.

## ✷ Where to Eat

**DINING OUT El Fidel** (505-425-6659), 510 Douglas Ave., Las Vegas. Emphasis on fresh, seasonal and local ingredients, altogether, a lovely experience.

**EATING OUT Charlie's Bakery & Cafe** (505-426-1921), 713 Douglas Ave. Open daily. Breakfast, lunch, dinner. Excellent green chile, tortillas so fresh you can watch them being made, a showcase of pastry delights, and Starbucks coffee. This is a local hangout for college students, professors, and old-timers, where everyone knows one another by their first name. Service is inconsistent; sometimes quicker than others. It is a clean, pleasant, spacious place that is a sentimental longtime favorite frequently referred to by its former name, the "Spic 'n Span." Charlie's is just about always open. Inexpensive.

**Dick's Restaurant** (505-425-8261), 705 Douglas Ave., Las Vegas. One of the best sandwich shops in the state fronts the funky bar that is a favorite with college students and hard-cores. Order to go for a picnic. Ask about the imaginative daily specials, and anything with avocado, Everything is fresh, homemade, and fabulous. Love the cream of asparagus soup! Inexpensive.

**Frankie's at the Casanova** (505-757-3322), 12 S. Main, Pecos. Closed Mon. Breakfast, lunch, dinner. Housed in the old Casanova Bar dating to the 1920s, Frankie's is an authentic Southwestern grill with a spiffy new outdoor patio bar serving a good selection of beer and wine. Go for the piñon pancakes for Sunday brunch. The chile, red or green, is hot and flavorful, and the fajitas practically sizzle off the plate. Live music Fri., Sat., and Sun. nights. Moderate.

CHARLIE'S SPIC 'N SPAN IN LAS VEGAS IS A MUST-STOP FOR MEXICAN-FOOD LOVERS.

❧ **Kocina de Raphael** (505-454-1667), 610 Legion Dr., Las Vegas. Off the beaten path. A little tricky to find, but if you like humongous portions, worth the search. Packed with generations of families, who know a good deal. All traditional New Mexico fare served here. Inexpensive.

**Teresa's Tamales** (575-387-2754), 3296 NM 518, Cleveland. You might have to search for a parking place between the big pickup trucks if you arrive during lunchtime. Excellent tamales, plus plates of traditional homemade New Mexico food. Consider calling your order in. Teresa makes everything to order in her tiny kitchen. Inexpensive.

## ✳ Selective Shopping

**New Moon Fashions** (505-454-0669), 132 Bridge St., Las Vegas. Whether you're looking for a cut-velvet outfit for a wedding or a linen jacket, this boutique is fun to shop. Colorful, international-style travel clothing purchased here will set you apart at the party and bring compliments. One of my favorite shops. Reasonable.

**Plaza Antiques** (505-454-9447), 1805 Plaza St., Las Vegas. The altar of the old Our Lady of Sorrows church stands as part of the back wall of this superb emporium. The best selection of Fred Harvey–era turquoise and silver bracelets I've seen, and the emporium is filled with alluring treasures from cowboy nostalgia to quilts.

**Rough Rider Antiques** (505-454-8063), 501 Railroad Ave., Las Vegas, across the street from the restored Train Depot and Visitor Center. Walk in and surrender. This spacious, freshly restored historic building holds the premier collection of antiques, sold by assorted consigners, in a town jam-packed with antiques shops. Whatever your interest—vintage postcard collecting, finding that embroidered Mexican felt jacket from the 1950s, a fiesta skirt, or a Fiesta pitcher—your chances of finding it here are quite good. Prices are fair, and fun is guaranteed.

**Tapetes de Lana** (575-387-2247), NM 518 Junction 434, or Main St., Mora. Check out the handmade rugs, table runners, and shawls, in beautiful, natural colors at reasonable prices. This is a wonderful place to find gifts. Tours of the mill are available here during the week. This is a nonprofit organization that is an important local employer.

**Tome on the Range** (505-454-9944), 158 Bridge St., Las Vegas. The only independent bookstore between Santa Fe and Colorado Springs, and one of the best. Excellent selection of regional literature, trendy reads, and delightful kids' section, plus cute gifts and tchotchkes. Supports local authors with frequent events.

# ROUTE 66 COUNTRY

## SANTA ROSA, TUCUMCARI

Getting your kicks is no problem out here. You'll find plenty of vintage neon and a culture that celebrates the Route 66 era. In addition, Santa Rosa and Conchas Dam have swimming and boating and a way to stay cool. It's hundreds of miles of nostalgia.

**GUIDANCE Santa Rosa Visitor Information Center** (575-472-3763), 244 S. Fourth St. Santa Rosa, is a sophisticated stop with all the information and contacts you could want to experience the area fully.

**Tucumcari/Quay County Chamber of Commerce** (575-461-1694), 404 W. Route 66 Blvd. Open Mon.–Sat. 9–5; closed Sun. Tucumcari is a traveler-friendly, professional road stop.

**MEDICAL EMERGENCY Dr. Dan C. Trigg Memorial Hospital** (575-461-7008), 301 E. Miel de Luna, Tucumcari.

**Guadalupe County Hospital** (575-472-3417), 111 Camino de Vida, Santa Rosa.

## ✳ To See

**TOWNS Santa Rosa**, 114 miles east of Albuquerque on I-40. This railroad-era Fourth Street Business District with its Ilfield Warehouse and many old storefronts has been known as a Route 66 stop since 1926, when the Mother Road first came through. Many landmarks are still visible in Santa Rosa, where part of the film *Grapes of Wrath* was shot. Plenty of colorful Route 66 establishments are still going strong in Santa Rosa, and it is, unexpectedly, known for its lakes and water sports, in particular, the Blue Hole of scuba diving fame.

**Tucumcari**, 173 miles east of Albuquerque on I-40. With probably the most and best-preserved vintage Route 66–era neon, including several that have recently been refurbished, Tucumcari is the largest town closest to the eastern border of the state. Nostalgia rules when the Blue Swallow Motel lights up at twilight.

There is good access here to Conchas Lake State Park, Ute Lake State Park, and the Mesalands Scenic Byway, with plenty of wildlife viewing and excellent birding. Tucumcari has, in addition to marvelous Route 66–era architecture, with a restaurant shaped like a sombrero and a curio shop shaped like a teepee, the longest mural devoted to Route 66 in the United States at its convention center. Two museums of note are here—the Mesalands Dinosaur Museum and the Tucumcari Historical Museum. The name of the town is possibly derived from a Comanche term

GOTTA LOVE THE CLASSIC NEON SIGNS OF TUCUMCARI.

meaning "lookout point" or "signal peak." Tucumcari Mountain was, in fact, used as a lookout for Comanche war parties. The town's original name was "Six Shooter Siding."

**MUSEUMS** ✿ **Mesalands Dinosaur Museum** (575-461-3466), 222 E. Laughlin Ave., Tucumcari. Open Labor Day–Feb. Tues.–Fri. 10–5, Sat. noon–5; Mar.–Labor Day 10–6. Who doesn't love a dinosaur? An in-depth collection of dinosaur skeletons, fossils, sculptures, and exhibits are shown at Mesalands College. $6.50 adults, $5.50 seniors age 65+, $4 children and teens, under age 5 free.

**Route 66 Auto Museum and Malt Shop** (575-472-1966), 2436 Will Rogers Dr., Santa Rosa. Open Nov.–Mar. Mon.–Sat. 7:30–6, Sun. 10–5; Apr.–Oct. Mon.–Sat. 8–5, Sun. 10–5. If you love vintage autos, this is the place for you. While dedicated to the preservation of Route 66 custom cars and memorabilia, this museum serves darn fine chocolate malts. $5.

**Tucumcari Historical Museum** (575-461-4201), 416 S. Adams St., Tucumcari. Sept.–May Mon.–Fri. 8–5; June–Aug. Mon.–Sat. 8–5. If you like looking into the way people lived in the past, from their parlors to their kitchens, you will enjoy this sentimental collection of furniture, farm and ranch exhibits, Indian artifacts, and early town memorabilia. Free.

**SCENIC DRIVES** **Mesalands Scenic Byway**, 320 miles total, in Quay and Guadalupe counties. *Mesa*, meaning "table" in Spanish, is the term used to describe high, flat plateaus. This is the country of high lonesome, a dry, dramatic and evocative landscape. On the southern edge of this scenic byway is the El Llano, Estacado, or the Staked Plains, a 32,000-mile mesa. *Estacado* refers to the cap rock, a geologic feature throughout this area. The habitat of pronghorn antelope and sandhill cranes, this byway encompasses Santa Rosa in Guadalupe County and Tucumcari in Quay County.

**BOATING** See the state parks listed under *Green Space.*

**Santa Rosa Park Lake Historic District** (575-472-3763). Will Rogers and
Lake Drive. Open for swimming Memorial Day–mid-Sept. Certified lifeguards
are in attendance, and Park Lake is the Southwest's largest swimming pool featuring a free water slide. Kids and seniors can fish in two stocked ponds. You can
rent a pedal boat for $1 each half-hour. No overnight camping. Free.

**GOLFING** **Tucumcari Municipal Golf Course** (575-461-1849), 4465 Route
66. Five miles west of Tucumcari. Closed Mon. This pleasant, tree-lined nine-
hole golf course with the greens located between high mesas will satisfy your
need to putt while in town. Greens fees for nine holes $10.

## ✳ Green Space

**MOUNTAINS** **Sugarite Canyon State Park** (575-445-5607), northeast of
Raton on NM 72 for 11 miles. Although the area endured the Track Fire during
the summer of 2011, the area is still popular for camping, fishing, and hiking.
During the height of summer, this is a busy place, with coal camp tours, kids'
programs, and occasional evening talks by local historians and naturalists. From
the wild iris of late May to wild rose, bluebell, larkspur, scarlet penstemon, blue
flax, and sunflowers and aster, Sugarite is unbeatable for wildflowers. Butterflies
love it here, too. Find a fine exhibit of coal mine camp. There is year-round trout
fishing on Lake Maloya, one of three alpine jewel lakes surrounded by an
extended cliff of basaltic rock. Hikers and mountain bikers have access to more
than 12 miles of trails. This is the only place in New Mexico where you can
explore the ruins of a coal mining camp. The former camp post office is the colorful visitors center. The first mine in the canyon opened in 1901, with full-scale
mining beginning in 1912 with the building of the Sugarite Coal Camp. In its
prime, 500 people lived, worked, shopped, worshipped, and went to school here.
It was a melting pot of Italians, Slavs, Japanese, Mexican, and British. The coal
camp ended in 1941, when oil replaced coal. $6 day use per vehicle; $8–18 overnight camping.

**Villanueva State Park** (575-421-2957), Villanueva. Take I-25 exit 323, go south
23 miles, then 15 miles south on NM 3. Nestled between 400-foot-high red and
gold sandstone bluffs along the Pecos River near the Spanish colonial village of
Villanueva is a picturesque campground shaded by giant cottonwoods along the
Pecos River. This park is a haven with fishing, hiking trails within views of old
ranching ruins, and one trail that leads to a prehistoric Indian ruin. The 2.5-mile
Canyon Trail loops from the river to the top of the canyon and back. Kayaking
and canoeing are enjoyed when the water level is high enough, from early May–
mid-June, usually. $6 day use; $8–18 overnight camping.

**RIVERS AND LAKES** **Cimarron Canyon State Park** (575-377-6271), 3
miles east of Eagle Nest on US 64. Open year-round. The clear Cimarron River

## UNIQUE ADVENTURES

✑ ♿ **Dinosaur Trackway** (575-374-8808), Clayton Lake State Park. (See **Clayton Lake State Park** under *Green Space*.) More than 100 million years ago, this area was an inland sea extending from the Gulf of Mexico to Canada. The creatures that roamed here left their footprints, and at least eight different kinds have been identified among the 500 dinosaur tracks that have been preserved, including some of the winged pterodactyl. The tracks are located on the dam spillway, at the end of a gentle 0.25-mile trail. The best times to view the tracks, when they are most clearly visible, are in morning and late-afternoon light.

**NRA Whittington Center** (575-445-3615), 10 miles southwest of Raton on US 64. Amid these 30,000 acres are Santa Fe Trail ruts. Shooting ranges and lessons in all sorts of weaponry are offered. Lodging, camping, and RV hookups are available, too. Many of the world's top competitions are played here. A variety of ranges available—skeet, sporting clays, black powder pistol, and more.

**Santa Rosa Blue Hole** (575-472-3370), Will Rogers Hwy., Santa Rosa. A unique geological phenomenon—a natural bell-shaped artesian pool 81 feet deep with a constant water temperature of 62 degrees Fahrenheit year-round and visibility of 80 feet, making it ideal for training. It is in the high desert at 4,600 feet above sea level, making the bottom equivalent to over 100 feet of ocean depth. Winter is actually the busiest season. The Santa Rosa Dive Center is open weekends to rent gear and fill tanks, and midweek

runs through the 8 miles of forested land on both sides of US 64, with abundant elk, deer, turkey, grouse, and bear for the sighting. Two billion years of complex geology are visible here, notably, the 400-foot-high crenellated granite Palisades. But the Cimarron is best known for its excellent fly-fishing for German brown and rainbow in a variety of waters: gravel pits, beaver ponds, and running streams. For peace, wildflower viewing, and getting away from it all, whether for a day or a longer stay, the Cimarron can't be beat. Many campers make long stays; make reservations early. The 96 sites in several campgrounds—Maverick and Tolby are favorites—offer good river access. $5 day use; $10–18 overnight camping.

**Clayton Lake State Park** (575-374-8808; reservations 877-664-7787), 141 Clayton Lake Rd., Clayton. Twelve miles northwest of Clayton on NM 370. Fishing and boating Mar.–Oct.; hiking, camping, Dinosaur Trackway. One-hundred-seventy-acre lake, a blue jewel in the desert. Boats are restricted to by appointment. Go to the visitors center to purchase permits, 8–5 Mon.–Fri. Permits $8 weekly; $25 annually. To dive in the Blue Hole, you must have PADI or NAUI or other certification papers.

✧ **Victory Ranch Alpacas** (575-387-2254), MM 1, 1 mile north of Mora on NM 434, Mora. Open daily 10–4. Closed Jan. 1–Mar. 15. Visit, pet, and feed the alpacas, gentle small cousins of llamas, grown for their wool. The Victory Ranch herd is one of the largest and finest in the United States. A 3,000-square-foot clothing and gift store stocks rugs, jackets, sweaters, toys, yarn, and fiber on this magnificent 1,100-acre ranch. $5 hand feedings.

FEEDING THE ALPACAS IS ENCOURAGED AT VICTORY RANCH.

trolling speeds (no whitewater). During winter, the lake is a migration point for waterfowl. It's an excellent place to spot bald eagles. The Dinosaur Trackway and boardwalk along the gentle half-mile trail provide extensive information. Among rolling grasslands near Santa Fe Trail, the lake is a waterfowl resting area in winter. $6 day; $8–18 overnight camping.

**Conchas Lake State Park** (575-868-2270), New Mexico State Park and Recreation Division, Conchas Dam. Thirty-two miles northeast of Tucumcari on NM 104. This is an outstanding getaway and prime recreation spot for fishing, boating, waterskiing, wind surfing, and swimming, with 60 miles of shoreline and plenty of coves, canyons, and sandy beaches to explore. Both north and south recreation areas have well-developed marinas, stores, cafés, camping, and picnic areas. South Conchas Lodge (505-868-2988) has cozy rooms as well, plus 110 RV units. Completed in 1939 by the Army Corps of Engineers, Conchas Dam rises 200 feet above the Canadian River. The lake covers about 15 square miles,

IT'S FUN TO COOL OFF IN THE CIMARRON RIVER.

extending 4 miles up the Canadian River and 11 miles up the Conchas River. Open year-round for fishing. Abundant walleye, catfish, and largemouth bass swim the waters. Have fun! $6 day use; $8–18 overnight camping.

**Coyote Creek State Park** (575-387-2328), 17 miles north of Mora on NM 434. At 7,700 feet in the eastern foothills of the Sangre de Cristo Mountains, find in this off-the-beaten-path park mountain trout fishing in the most densely stocked fishing area of the state, lovely solitude, camping, picnicking, and a 1.5-mile, easy trail through ponderosa pine. $6 day use; $8–18 overnight camping.

**Santa Rosa Lake State Park** (575-472-3110), Santa Rosa. The lake is actually a high plains Pecos River reservoir 7 miles from Santa Rosa on NM 91, with waterskiing, wind surfing, and excellent fishing. Canoeing, too! Stay a while with 76 developed camping sites and 25 electric sites, restrooms, showers, and a visitors center. The easy to moderate hiking trails offer wildlife viewing through 500 acres of parkland. Here also is one of the state's few designated equestrian trails and all necessary accommodations for horses. There are two short paved wheelchair-accessible trails as well.

**Storrie Lake State Park** (575-425-7278), north of Las Vegas on NM 518. Wind surfing, fishing, boating, waterskiing, picnicking. Camping and RVs. The park is open to all boating, with no horsepower restrictions, so it is geared for wind surfers and water-skiers. Kayaks and canoes are also popular here. There is year-round trout fishing as well. $6 day use; $8–18 overnight camping.

**Ute Lake State Park** (575-487-2284), 30 miles northeast of Tucumcari via US 54, then 3 miles west of Logan via NM 540. This 13-mile-long, narrow lake, producer of many state record fish, is a happy local camping destination with boating, welcome swimming in the summer heat, hiking, wildlife viewing, and fishing for walleye, bass, and catfish. $6 day use; $8–18 overnight camping.

**WILDER PLACES Canadian River Canyon** runs 13 miles through the Kiowa National Grasslands, approximately 10 miles northwest of Roy. The 800-foot canyon is a natural wildlife refuge in the prairie for mountain lion, wild turkey, eagles, and waterfowl. Mills Canyon Campground, offering primitive overnight camping, is located at the bottom of the gorge. A remnant herd of Barbary sheep roams through this stark, remote, and unforgettable place.

**Kiowa and Rita Blanca National Grasslands** (575-374-9652), 15 miles south of Clayton via NM 402 or east via US 87. Rita Blanca is 17 miles east of Clayton via US 64/56. For those who want to put their feet on the trail, here are 2 miles of Santa Fe Trail ruts, plus grasslands. In their entirety, these grasslands stretch through New Mexico, Texas, and Oklahoma. The New Mexico section of the Kiowa National Grassland covers 136,562 acres near Roy and Clayton, with plenty of habitat for wildlife. This land was purchased by the federal government during the Great Depression following the Dust Bowl, removed from farm cultivation, planted, and maintained as grasslands.

**WILDLIFE REFUGES AND AREAS Colin Neblett Wildlife Area** (575-445-2311). These 36,000 acres between Eagle Nest and Cimarron along US 64 include Cimarron Canyon State Park, making it the largest state-run wildlife area for deer, elk, and other forest critters. The Cimarron River, a great German brown fishery, runs through it. Bring binoculars and cameras, and try your luck with a Rio Grande King.

**Elliott S. Barker Wildlife Area** (575-445-2311), 14 miles northwest of Cimarron. Here, in the heart of the northeast, find over 5,000 acres of hiking, hunting, wildlife viewing, and, should you choose, horseback riding. High-clearance vehicles are strongly recommended, as the roads can be rocky and the streams can swell in this pristine and primitive area. There's a good chance you'll spot bear up here. I have.

**Valle Vidal** (575-586-0520), 27 miles north of Cimarron off US 64. The name of this unit of the Carson National Forest means "valley of life." If you've ever longed to see herds of magnificent, noble elk in their natural setting, this is your best bet, particularly at twilight. The Valle Vidal is 100,000 acres of specially managed prime elk habitat, home to a herd of 1,700 elk, in the Carson National Forest. Also, in season, find fishing and backcountry camping. A word of warning: be sure your spare tire is in good working order. Perhaps it is our karma, perhaps it is the loose rocks in the road, but we get a flat every time we come up here. If you drive the entirety, from north of Cimarron across to Costilla, you'll put 64 miles on your vehicle.

## ✳ Lodging

### BED & BREAKFASTS, INNS, AND MOTELS Blue Swallow

**Motel** (575-461-9849), 815 E. Route 66, Tucumcari. Closed Oct.–Mar. Owned and operated by Lillian Redman, a former Harvey Girl, for over 40 years; current owners keep the tradition of this Route 66 beacon alive. With its classic Route 66 neon, the 1939 humble stucco motel, with eight rooms, preserves its comfy, vintage character. $65–75.

### CABINS AND CAMPING Santa

**Rosa Campground** (888-898-1999 or 575-472-3126), 2136 Historic Route 66., Santa Rosa. Open year-round. With the extra added attractions of the Western Bar-B-Q (served each evening 5–8), homemade peach cobbler (in the restaurant with an outdoor patio), beer and wine, plus free WiFi, you can enjoy all manner of camping. There are 70 pull-through RV sites, tent sites, and a cabin where you can get out of the camper and stretch out for a while. There's a gift shop, playground, heated swimming pool, laundry facilities and 50-amp services, groceries, and supplies here as well. $30.

## ✳ Where to Eat

### DINING OUT Lake City Diner

(575-472-5253), 101 S. Fourth St., Santa Rosa. Dinner only. Unexpectedly located in the midst of Route 66 land, this place is one of those small, cozily elegant establishments where each dish is freshly made by hand and served in a lovingly restored tin-ceiling building with white linen tablecloths. Crisp salads, fresh pasta, and steaks will leave you feeling well dined, indeed. A pleasant change from roadside burgers!

### EATING OUT 🍴 Del's Restaurant

**& Gift Shop** (575-461-1740), 1202 E. Route 66, Tucumcari. Closed Sun. If you are actually eating a meal in Tucumcari, Del's is your best bet. This place, a standard roadside family diner that retains its original 1956 flavor (courtesy of the owners, sisters Yvonne and Yvette), serves reliably good homemade American cooking, the kind you long to find on a cross-country drive, as popular with locals as with travelers. The burgers are juicy, and the chicken-fried steak with mashed potatoes and cream gravy is a triumph, as good as the best on the road. Even liver is on the menu! Yummy beef taquitas, too. The salad bar is more than respectable, and two homemade soups are included. Inexpensive–Moderate.

**Joseph's Bar & Grill** (505-472-1234), 865 Will Rogers Dr., Santa Rosa. I usually eat here when I'm in town, and by now I can't tell if it's for the food or the nostalgia. This establishment is the offspring of the original Joseph's, and it does lean a bit on its reputation. You won't go wrong with the enchiladas, and don't pass up the gift shop. Expect a good helping of local friendliness. Inexpensive–Moderate.

**La Cita** (575-461-7866), 812 S. First St., Tucumcari. You'll want to have your picture taken here, for sure, so you can show the world you dined in a sombrero. The Mexican food isn't the greatest, and some think the portions are too small for the price, but it's not bad, either, and you'll have so much fun you probably won't notice. The neon was part of the Route 66 sign restoration project. Inexpensive.

**Pow Wow Restaurant & Lizard Lounge** (575-461-0500), 801 Route 66, Tucumcari. This place is dark and would be smoky, if smoking were allowed. It is, and always has been, the premier town hangout, the place where visiting politicians rub elbows with the locals, the cowboys, the Indian traders, and the Route 66 tourists from Germany. It is also a good place to order a steak. Moderate.

**Silver Moon Cafe** (575-472-3162), 3501 Will Rogers Dr., Santa Rosa. Open daily. Breakfast, lunch, dinner. Serving travelers since 1959, with that cool Route 66 neon lighting up the night and home-cooked meals lighting up smiles. Tasty Mexican and American food served here.

## ✳ Entertainment

Aside from occasional live performance events at the Shuler Theater in Raton, the best we are likely to come up with in the way of nightlife is a drink at the bar of the historic hotel or the chance to catch a movie at a vintage theater, such as the recently reopened El Raton. Mostly, folks go to bed early here, so it's a good place to catch up on your reading or do some stargazing.

## ✳ Selective Shopping

**Tee Pee Curios** (575-471-3773), 924 E. Tucumcari Blvd., Tucumcari. Not only is this a classic Route 66 photo op, with the front of the shop a white concrete teepee painted in bright turquoise lettering, but inside you can find every T-shirt, shot glass, and travel souvenir of your road trip that you could ever imagine. A highly amusing must-do. Its neon was one of the nine restored Route 66 signs.

## ✳ Special Events

*January:* **Ice Fishing Tournament and Chile Dinner** (575-377-2420), Eagle Nest. Look for this event midmonth, all you frozen fish lovers.

TEE PEE CURIOS IN TUCUMCARI IS WHERE TO GET YOUR SOUVENIRS OF THE MOTHER ROAD.

## HISTORIC HOTELS

**Historic El Fidel Hotel** (575-425-6761), 500 Douglas Ave., Las Vegas. Built in 1923 in Spanish Colonial Revival style, this is another place loaded with local color and offers its 18 rooms at bargain prices. The restaurant is getting good notice for its emphasis on local and seasonal ingredients. $45–85.

**Plaza Hotel** (800-328-1882 or 505-425-3591; www.plazahotel-nm.com), on the Old Town Plaza at 230 Plaza, Las Vegas. Built in 1882, when it was known as "The Belle of the Southwest," this is a great Victorian hotel renovated to preserve a clean, not fussy, 19th-century atmosphere. The Landmark Grill restaurant has never been known for its cuisine, but the Old West Byron T's Saloon (named for the resident ghost), high-speed wireless Internet, room service, on-site masseur, and the fun of returning to those glorious days of yesteryear makes this an excellent choice for travelers. You can even stay in one of four suites overlooking the Plaza. Pet-friendly! $69–149.

ENJOYING A SPRINGTIME ICE-CREAM CONE ON OLD TOWN PLAZA.

LOBBY OF HISTORIC ST. JAMES HOTEL IN CIMARRON.

**St. James Hotel** (866-472-5019 or 575-376-2664), 617 S. Collinson, Cimarron. Every outlaw who was any outlaw stayed at the St. James, as did Buffalo Bill Cody, Annie Oakley, Kit Carson, and Wyatt Earp. Photos of desperados and heroes line the downstairs hallway, decked with an antique roulette wheel. Mounted trophy heads adorn the period lobby. The beds are quilt-covered, the curtains draped in lace, and the rooms of the old hotel are not very soundproof. Twenty-seven bullet holes may be seen in the dining room. Fourteen restored rooms with 19th-century furnishings occupy the main hotel; a two-story annex adjacent provides an additional 10 rooms. The St. James is located smack dab on the Old Santa Fe Trail. Begun as a saloon in 1873, established by Lincoln's chef, Henri Lambert, this place became a haven for Santa Fe Trail traders and mountain men. It has been featured on *Unsolved Mysteries* and is reportedly highly haunted. An elegant restaurant serves dinner, with a decent salad bar, and a comfortable café, plus a legendary bar provide venues for all sorts of social gatherings, though "dancing naked on the bar is no longer permitted." $80–120.

*February:* **Moonlight Ski Tours and Headlamp Snowshoe Tours** (575-754-2374), Enchanted Forest XC Ski and Snowshoe Area, Red River.

*May:* **Guided ruins tours and cultural demonstrations, Pecos National Historical Park** (505-757-7200), weekends, Memorial Day–Labor Day.

*June:* **Mule Days** (888-376-2417), Maverick Rodeo Grounds, Cimarron. **Raton Rodeo** (575-445-3689), York Canyon Rodeo Grounds, Raton. **Las Vegas Celebrates the Arts** (575-425-8631), Las Vegas, tours of artist studios. **Fort Union Days** (505-425-8025), Fort Union National Monument, Watrous. **Santa Fe Trail Rendezvous** (575-445-3615), Raton, mountain man gathering, NRA Whittington Center.

*July:* **Maverick Club Parade and Rodeo** (888-376-2417), Fourth of July, Maverick Arena, NM 64, Cimarron. Longest running open rodeo in the West. **Fourth of July Parade and Fireworks** (575-377-2420), Eagle Nest. **Route 66 Celebration** (505-461-1694), Convention Center, 1500 W. Route 66, Tucumcari.

*August:* **Las Vegas Historic Home Tour** (505-425-8803; www.lasvegas nm.org), Las Vegas, first Sat. **Colfax County Fair** (575-445-8071), Springer Armory, Springer. Cakewalk, parade, pie contest, barbecue dinner; second weekend. **Music From Angel Fire** (888-377-3300; www.music fro-mangelfire.org). Outstanding classical music performances throughout northern New Mexico in Raton, Las Vegas, Angel Fire, late Aug.–early Sept.

OLD-TIME RODEO AT THE COLFAX COUNTY FAIR.

*September:* **Cimarron Days Festival** (888-376-2417), Village Park, NM 64, Cimarron, Labor Day weekend. **Raspberry Roundup**, Salman Ranch, Labor Day weekend into Sept., generally the first three weeks of the month. Fresh raspberries and raspberry treats abound in country store at La Cueva Historic District. **Cleveland Roller Mill Festival** (575-387-2645), Cleveland, Labor Day weekend. This is the only weekend of the year when the creaky old mill operates, and it is a true festival of northern New Mexico dance, food, and crafts. **Wagon Mound Bean Days** (575-666-2410), Wagon Mound, celebrates the days when Wagon Mound was the bean capital of the world, with barbecue worth waiting in line for, crafts, parade, and politicians aboard floats. **Nara Visa Cowboy Poetry Gathering** (575-633-2220), Nara Visa, third weekend. As much local color, with music and rhyme, as you can find anywhere. **Annual Route 66 Festival** (575-472-3763).

Come on out and get your kicks here in Santa Rosa. Shortgrass Music Festival, Cimarron.

*October:* **Clayton Arts Festival** (www.claytonnewmexico.net/activities .html), Clayton, first weekend. A long-established, much-anticipated, profuse display of western art. **Artesanos del Valle Tour**, Las Vegas area, first weekend. Diverse and wonderful artists' studio tour.

*November–December:* **City of Bethlehem** (575-445-3689), Raton. Thanksgiving weekend through Christmas holidays, enjoy a nostalgic tour of life-size cartoon characters that guide the way up into Climax Canyon, where the Christmas story is presented high in the rocky hills, accompanied by seasonal music. This free event is an annual family favorite. **Christmas on the Chicorica**—1,500 luminarias.

# INDEX